CITIES, SOCIETY,
AND SOCIAL PERCEPTION

Cities, Society, and Social Perception

A CENTRAL AFRICAN PERSPECTIVE

J. Clyde Mitchell

CLARENDON PRESS · OXFORD
1987

Oxford University Press, Walton Street, Oxford OX2 6DP
Oxford New York Toronto
Delhi Bombay Calcutta Madras Karachi
Petaling Jaya Singapore Hong Kong Tokyo
Nairobi Dar es Salaam Cape Town
Mebourne Auckland
and associated companies in
Beirut Berlin Ibadan Nicosia

Oxford is a trade mark of Oxford University Press

Published in the United States
by Oxford University Press, New York

British Library Cataloguing in Publication Data
Mitchell, J. Clyde
Cities, society, and social perception: a Central African perspective.
1. Urbanization—Africa, Sub-Saharan
I. Title
307.7'6'0967   HT148.S8
ISBN 0-19-823253-5

Library of Congress Cataloging in Publication Data
Mitchell, J. Clyde (James Clyde), 1918-
Cities, society, and social perception.
Bibliography: p.
Includes index.
1. Cities and towns—Africa, Central.   2. Urbanization—Africa, Central.
3. Sociology, Urban—Africa, Central.   I. Title.
HT148.C46M58 1987   307.7'6'0967   86-23912
ISBN 0-19-823253-5

Set by Colset Private Limited, Singapore
Printed in Great Britain
at the University Printing House, Oxford
by David Stanford
Printer to the University

FOREWORD

Clyde Mitchell is the leading figure in the study of African urbanization. Anyone neglecting his path-breaking researches must do so at their peril. This is so not just for the Africa specialist. Mitchell has made his African researches vital towards the study of comparative urban forms and life, whether these be in the Third World or in the dominant metropolitan regions. The contribution by Mitchell to general sociological theory and to the development of research methodology is clearly evident throughout this book.

The hallmark of Mitchell's approach to theory is that it should never be separated from careful empirical work. For Mitchell ethnography is the heart of a sociology or anthropology, but it is meaningless if it is not directed to the criticism or elaboration of abstract theory, as the latter is pointless without its demonstration through ethnographic or some other form of 'grounded' empirical analysis. Theory and data in Mitchell's work are always in dialectical relation, each constituting progressive corrections on the other's necessary but none the less distorted abstractions or selective descriptions. Ethnography and other forms of empirical data are good to think theory with, as vice versa.

In this sense the lived realities of perceiving and acting human beings (always at the forefront of Mitchell's analytical concern) are not mere illustrations of abstract theoretical principle. They should never be so regarded. To do so would be to place the analysts' theoretical preconceptions, prejudices, in a determining relation to lived reality. The actions and perceptions of human subjects are constituted as systems of meaning by the theory. Objection to this tendency in the social sciences, of course, is widespread. It is central to the 'symbolic interactionist' and broader 'interpretive sociology' critique of objectivist, 'scientist', sociologies. Mitchell is in conscious sympathy with this critique, and he expresses affiliation with symbolic interactionist perspectives in this book and in earlier studies. But Mitchell came to this position independently of such approaches. It was already rooted in the anthropological ethno-

graphic tradition of which he is deeply part (that exemplified by
the work of Evans-Pritchard), to which Mitchell has made
distinguished contribution. I note that some of the 'symbolic
interactionists' draw their inspiration from this very same
tradition (for example Glaser and Strauss, *The Discovery of
Grounded Theory*).

The essentially anti-empiricist direction of Mitchell's analytical course must be underlined. In this volume Mitchell
explores the cultural perceptions of Africans towards urban life
in the colonially dominated and regulated cities and towns of
Southern Africa. He examines the way Africans conceive their
realities and to some extent come to organize their action
through such conceptions. In his exploration of this problem
Mitchell does not sacrifice a major objective, which is to conduct
a rigorous and scientific analysis of the structuring of the ideas
and actions of human beings. Such analysis has been far too
easily and non-reflectively dismissed by those eager to throw off
the 'scientistic' claims of functionalist social science. This,
however, was far from the thought of those thinkers at the forefront of anti-positivist critiques, whatever their form: Marxist,
structuralist, phenomenological, for example. Positivism was
attacked precisely because it was unscientific and concealed
common-sense ideas beneath the mask of methodological
rigour. The anti-positivist argument was not that a 'scientific'
approach to the analysis of human thought and action should be
jettisoned. Rather, it was quite the reverse, and the argument
developed concerning the most appropriate way to constitute
such a 'science of society'. This argument continues, and
Mitchell's example may be considered as a major contribution
to the debate.

In this work the reader will discover a serious scholar who is
concerned to penetrate the processes which underlie common-
sense perception and the action which is organized through it.
Mitchell demonstrates how this may be systematically achieved
and how some of the prejudices and common-sense assumptions
(generated through a variety of ideological presuppositions)
which crowd analyses in the school sciences may be avoided.
The core methodological concept for Mitchell is 'situation' or
'situational analysis'. He discusses this concept at length in this
volume, and in many ways it is the organizing method for the

ethnography and other empirical data which Mitchell presents.

The idea of situational analysis was inspired by Max Gluckman, who introduced it in his study of a bridge-opening event in Zululand. Through the 'situation' of this event (the structural forming of social and political relations around the focus of the bridge-opening) Gluckman explored the wider dynamics of African cultural and social life in the conditions of White domination in South Africa. Gluckman did not develop his concept of 'situational analysis'. This fell to his colleagues and students. Mitchell (with Victor Turner and Bill Epstein) was foremost among these. I might add here that Mitchell was a prime-mover, along with Gluckman, in the development of the so-called 'Manchester School' of anthropology. He was the director of the Rhodes–Livingstone Institute, the research arm of Gluckman's department at Manchester, during its most creative and productive years.

For Gluckman, the 'situation' was a descriptive device for exploring wider structural forces, what Mitchell refers to as 'context', or the embracing structural parameters within which the life of the situation is constituted. The concept of 'situation' is far more than a descriptive device in Mitchell's analysis. It is to be distinguished from 'context' (to which Gluckman, in effect, reduces the meaning of situation), and also from 'setting'. The last is the locale in which certain events routinely occur, and may be characterized by an accentuation or relative suspension of more encompassing contextual parameters. Thus work settings, in the context described by Mitchell, engage critical dimensions of wider colonial-controlled capitalist forces. These forces are less determining, though far from irrelevant, in urban leisure settings. As Mitchell argues in *The Kalela Dance* (in many ways the most important forerunner to the present work), it is in leisure settings that Africans in towns have the greatest agency in generating their own perceptions of their world of organizing their action accordingly.

In his development of 'situational analysis' (a development which bears comparison with his use of case material in *The Yao Village*, and with the 'extended-case method' and 'social drama' of Victor Turner), Mitchell argues for the focusing of attention on everyday events and practice. The meaning of events in his situational perspective (and of the perceptions of the world which are engaged in the action of these events) is in their use. Mitchell is not attracted by more abstract semiotic or structuralist approaches to meaning which seem to be far removed from the analysis of actual practices. (Perhaps he would be more in accord with the recent work by Sahlins on Hawaii, which attempts to 'ground' a semiotic analytic approach.) Of course, numerous anthropologists and sociologists have paid lip-service to Wittgenstein by stressing a meaning in use perspective. But what is so significant about Mitchell's development is that he explores a method whereby the meanings in use can be systematically unravelled, their perceptual texture peeled away, and the social processes which generated them examined concretely.

Mitchell's situational method locates the analysis at the level of practice. It is at this level that social actors 'speak', and it is their 'speech' or their interpretations upon their own action and the actions of others that Mitchell subjects to analysis. For Mitchell the situation has a 'logic' of its own. It is both a 'practice of structure' and a 'structure of practice'. Thus it is formed in the structural processes governing a wider political and socio-economic order, yet is not entirely reducible to these processes nor to their underlying principles. Moreover, Mitchell does not engage a deterministic perspective in his analysis of situational processes. The actors have agency in his descriptions and express a creative energy. It is the very factors underlying their agency and creativity, the processes whereby they place constructions on the world of their experience, which form the focus of Mitchell's enquiry.

Here is a significance of Mitchell's concern, so carefully displayed in this book, with the way in which Africans conceive of their realities. He is not just presenting their views or perceptions, as some ethnographers might by presenting edited versions of statements appropriate to the ethnographer's general argument. Ethnographers who use this descriptive technique in my view often impart a false authenticity to their accounts. 'Native' statements are not treated problematically. Mitchell, however, explores the principles whereby human actors construe their realities and mark significances as these relate to their perception of, for example, ethnicity or individual power and social position. The principles he identifies are part of the logic of the situation. Thus the principles underlying perception, as the perceptions themselves, are situationally constitutive, that is they have force in organizing a world of action, channelling the flow of its process, and having social and political consequence.

I note that Mitchell stresses the non-reductionist, non-psychologistic dimensions of his approach to social perception. He examines the social and political conditions which systematically give rise to certain perceptions of reality. Further, he explores the social processes which engage specific perceptions as *shared* perspectives upon the settings of human habitation, of family, of work, and of leisure. Thus he is able to determine the influence such perceptions (variously engaged within and ultimately having force through the structuring of social relationships) have upon forming the realities of experience.

It is with reference to Mitchell's concern with discovering the logic of situations that some of the major significance of his particular methodological developments and innovations should be seen. The reader will see how Mitchell always *argues* through the mathematical and statistical techniques he develops. Thus he shows how certain aspects of mathematical or statistical method fail to penetrate some aspect of the problematic areas of cultural perception or social action as ethnographically encountered. He accordingly elaborates a particular technique, and so the principles which systematically underlie perceptions of urban life, migration, etc., are revealed more clearly before the analytical gaze.

Through his technical advances Mitchell is able to demonstrate the generality of the principles which are constitutive within the logics of situations. Moreover, the benefit to the reader, specialist and student, is twofold. Mitchell clarifies, is able to sort out, to order, the numerous factors which have been engaged in the formation of Central and Southern African cities and which have framed their distinct cultural life. In the course of this he has forged powerful new tools of sociological analysis. Not only does he show their utility. He shows through example how new analytical innovations should be made. This for Mitchell should always be involved directly in the comprehension of human practice and should not be an activity in and for itself.

I have said that Mitchell's concern (and that of the 'Manchester School' in general) with the situation is one which focuses on the ordering of everyday social action as both a structure of practice and practice of structure. The concern, though not necessarily the analytical strategy chosen, bears some comparison with other current anthropological and sociological critiques of over-structuralist, too strongly determinist, analyses of cultural and social worlds. Bourdieu is an example who, in *Towards a Theory of Practice*, critically acknowledges a similarity in the focus upon practice of the Manchester perspective.

Mitchell is the first to acknowledge the effect of wider forces on the urban social practices to which he attends. The locations of the towns he studied were formed in the conditions of a colonial and racially divided order, characterized by the White domination of Blacks. He provides systematic evidence in his discussion of occupational prestige for the inscription of this political order within African perceptions. Thus the perceptions of African supervisors and policemen cogently reveal aspects of broad African political consciousness. Mitchell's general position would accord with many present-day Marxist interpretations of the structural transformations occurring in the contexts of urban growth and evident within town life. He declares a broad agreement with the work of Castells, whose well-known critique of the folk–urban continuum was already explicit in Mitchell's own earlier studies. In these studies (referred to in this volume) Mitchell is highly critical of various functionalist theses which failed to see towns and urban life as comprising modes of cultural and social practice to be comprehended through reference to their contextual and situated constituting processes. These processes are not always consistent with, or directly reducible to, the terms of general structural or moral theories of change or transformation. Assertions by recent theorists of historical change in Southern Africa, such as Parpart and van Onselen, who write of the proletarianization of Africans and that African workers have severed their rural ties, are distorting and glossing the implications of the evidence, evidence which Mitchell provides. Mitchell would suggest some revisions in interpretation and modifications in general theory.

I hasten to add that Mitchell's situational perspective is not of 'the townsman is a townsman' type made famous by Gluckman, with whom Mitchell's position is cognate. The understanding of urban life is not confined to processes located within areas arbitrarily demarcated demographically, administratively, or spatially. The situated practices of urban migrants may take their form through the fact that they embrace relationships conditioned by urban–industrial and tribal political economies. This is the import behind Mitchell's work on migration. While the structure of return migration in Southern Africa is undoubtedly conditioned within the colonial political economy, the form and content of the relationships between migrants and their home areas has major consequence upon their migration experience and even their cultural constitution of a distinctive urban style of life. Reference to the colonial context sets the parameters of explanation but does not reveal some of the other factors which give the migrants agency in the creation of their own worlds. What is urban life is acutely problematic for Mitchell. Such conventional contrasts like urban/rural and modern/traditional (tribal), for example, are far from straightforward. Indeed, as Mitchell so fascinatingly intimates, such contrasts—like those present in Wirth's classic discussion of urbanism—are part of the cognitive, perceptual, cultural world of people living in towns. The conception of rural life as integrated, face to face, and ordered and opposed to a disordered and impersonal urban world is a construction of those living in towns. The contrasts are idealizations, part of the cognitive reality of urbanites and to be explained rather than used in establishing the definitional parameters of the urban phenomenon. They are part of the practice, integral in situational logics, and are constructs which give meaning to urban relationships rather than being objective definitions of them. In the symbolic interactionist terms with which Mitchell's perspective is allied, urban/rural contrasts are cultural objectivations vital in the way individuals in town order their lives.

This is an important aspect of Mitchell's approach to prestige, the symbolism of status, the cultural language of social and economic distinction. Mitchell does not reduce the attitudes towards prestige to class. Industrial class forces inform an understanding of the attitudes which Mitchell records. But he prefers to see them as part of the process of an urban cultural forming of class relations which in some ways are distorting of the objective structuring of class as this may be conceived in Marxist analysis. Mitchell shows how the colonial administrative authorities in the new towns of Central and Southern Arica were actively engaged in constructing urban African symbolic conceptualization of their own internal difference. Such action was influential in creating politically active groups who on certain occasions acted against their own 'real' class interests. They supported White interests, against, in the context of colonialism, their class interests as Africans.

The power of the structuring principles underlying the social and political order of colonial society as a whole is most clearly seen in the symbolism of status and prestige. Indeed, it is because of the fact that Africans in the towns of Central and Southern Africa are engaged in settings governed by the structure of international capitalism that, as Mitchell observes, there is considerable similarity between urban African prestige scores and those recorded for elsewhere.

Perceptions of tribal or ethnic identity are less obviously formed or determined in wider structural processes. Mitchell demonstrates that the typifications of ethnicity are a major dimension of the cultural creative play of Africans in modern urban/industrial contexts, none the less. Through the symbolic categories of ethnicity, of assumed similarity, and difference in identity, migrants in the situated practices of the new towns negotiate the order of their own social relationships.

This argument was first developed in Mitchell's *The Kalela Dance*. It was of central theoretical importance in sociological debates on the character of Third World urbanization and social change. For the first time it was shown that acculturationist, assimilationist types of argument were seriously faulted. The engagement of tribal or ethnic identity in the towns was not part of a process of cultural adaptation whereby traditional ideas resurfaced and through some kind of irrational atavism continued into contexts inappropriate to such tribal or ethnic ideas. Despite Mitchell's powerful yet subtle argument to the contrary, many critics missed the point. Indeed, they attributed to Mitchell the very argument to which he was opposed.

Mitchell answers his own critics in this book better than I could possibly do. I draw attention to his argument on ethnicity, however, because I consider that it has theoretical resonances still to be explored. Issues concerning ethnicity are of crucial modern significance. Concepts of ethnic identity are germane to present-day nationalism not just in the Third World but in Western metropolitan contexts. The emotional and psychological force of ethnicity and ethnic nationalism are regular cause for comment in the sociological literature.

It is Mitchell's vitally important argument, further developed here, that the formation of ethnic identity and ethnic categories (and their use in the organization and definition of social relationships) is an innovative and original phenomenon. The ethnicity discussed by Mitchell is distinct in consciousness. Its 'imagined' ideological style (to borrow a term from Benedict Anderson's *Imagined Communities*, with which aspects of Mitchell's argument has marked analytical affinity) is one which asserts that the members of ethnic 'groups' are united in solidarity and partnership on the basis of the shared individual attributes of language, history, customs, etc. This ethnicity, also characteristic of modern ethnic nationalism, as Anderson and others have recently remarked, recognizes few internal differences. The character of this ethnicity is shaped in the political and economic conditions of the formation of modern national and colonial states. The particular ideological distortions which it may promote are born of such contexts. The distortions have potential force at the individual emotional and psychological level not for any necessary 'natural' intrinsic reason of an essentialist primordial kind. They have consequence because in the contexted situations of their appearance the constructed ideas of ethnicity become the very basis for the formation of social relationships. In this way ethnic identity becomes critical in the formation of a social self in a manner distinctive to the urban/industrial worlds of its creation and relevance.

I stress the significance of the above point, one which follows from Mitchell's analysis. The very argument expressed by persons who form their social relationships through bonds of ethnicity, who emphasize ethnic identity, is that such ties and identities are primordial. It is because people may regard their ethnic identity as primordial, as vital to their very continued existence, that they may be caused to engage in internal acts of national disruption or (when there is an identity between ethnicity and nation) willingly perpetrate acts of international violence. Mitchell exposes the primordiality of ethnic bonds as a construction. This is not in the sense that they are fictive or in some way unreal. Ethnicity is a construction because it takes its form, is constituted as primordial, in a common-sense, taken-for-granted world, in particular structural contexts. Ethnicity in the world which Mitchell explores becomes the *sine qua non* of personhood, of self. It is the force which generates common-sense views of the kind that ethnic identity *is* primordial and 'natural' to the person which contributes to the emotional power of ethnic identity, and creates it as a potent political force in both a positive and negative sense. Mitchell, by exploring the condition under which ethnicity comes to be a powerful factor in everyday life, has not obscured the 'reality' of the contexted situations he explores, as others have charged. These others have sometimes argued that the perceptions of ethnicity which Mitchell studies have created a kind of 'false consciousness'. I think that recent history would expose the ludicrous nature of this charge, and that it demonstrates the important contribution of Mitchell's work to the understanding of a modern pheno-menon of increasing social and political significance.

I have given only a glimpse of the numerous issues central to any modern urban research explored in this work. There is barely an important problem critical to urban studies left critically unexplored by Mitchell. The arguments are presented in the best possible way, through a systematic examination of the variations in urban experience over historical time and in a single overall political and social and economic context. But I stress too that the volume is a model of the comparative method, which, in my view, is critical for a generalizing anthropology and sociology. Thus Mitchell places his findings and arguments into critical relation to North American urban materials and in particular to the formative analyses of the Chicago urban school. The comparison develops, as all systematic comparison should, from the foundation of a detailed knowledge of a single major context of urban formation. In this way superficial parallels leading to false theoretical generalizations which obscure vital areas of difference in urban development and which inaccurately gloss the meaning of situated urban practices are avoided. By focusing on his Central and Southern African materials Mitchell presents data which will be crucial for future scholarship in the region. The reader is also presented with the evidence upon which one of the most important scholars of the modern urban process has developed his analytical and theoretical thought. This is one of the greatest pleasures I have had in reading this book.

Clyde Mitchell is the most outstanding teacher of anthropology or sociology that I have encountered. He is generous with ideas in the extreme and in such a marvellous way. Thus while he generates ideas in others he always seems to impart the impression that these ideas are those of his students or colleagues rather than his own. There is a wonderful sense of this here. The book continually provokes ideas in the mind of the reader as it simultaneously instructs in the methods of ethnographic and empirical description and demonstrates the very best in analytical and theoretical argument.

BRUCE KAPFERER

University College London

PREFACE

This book arises out of a suggestion made to me by one of my colleagues that I should republish in book form a selection of some of my papers relating to urban problems in South Central Africa. The argument was that while in general the essays reflected a common orientation, they were nevertheless published in a wide variety of places and some of them, therefore, were not easily available. I started assembling a set of essays while I was a Fellow at the Center for Advanced Study in the Behavioral Sciences in Palo Alto in 1969/70.

But it soon became clear that the essays would need some rewriting in order, firstly, to make explicit the theoretical orientation lying behind them, and secondly, to provide some rationale linking the different essays to one another. At the same time I was increasingly aware of new developments in quantitative analysis which were then becoming available through the general extension of the use of computers into academic life. It was abundantly clear in the essays that many of the procedures I had used, all of which were conducted without access to modern computing facilities, could be extended considerably.

When I returned to my teaching post at Manchester University I was faced with the onerous task of preparing material processes on punched cards or in manuscript form for use on computers. This took me more than five years to complete because I was also engaged at this time in normal teaching and departmental duties. As the material slowly became machine readable I was able to carry out the additional analyses which had now become available to me. From time to time I was able to publish some of these and have been able to incorporate these results in the material in this book.

I had been appointed to the Rhodes–Livingstone Institute in 1946, and my first assignment was to make a conventional anthropological study of the Yao of Malawi. The Rhodes–Livingstone Institute was then headed by Max Gluckman, and I was greatly influenced by his thinking at that time, as is manifest in this book. At the conclusion of the Yao study I was appointed to initiate some sociological studies on the Copperbelt in what is now Zambia. The original plan was for these sociological studies to begin with a general social survey of the African population of the region. Because of my undergraduate training in quantitative techniques I was to undertake this task. The general social study, however, was to be accompanied by two separate 'observational' studies, to which the social survey would provide some general background. The first of these 'observational' studies was to be directed to the general pattern of social relationships, and A. L. Epstein was appointed to do this. He has published several works deriving from that study, some of which are referred to in this book. The second was to be of family economics, but the person appointed to make this study got married soon after the fieldwork was completed and, as far as I know, has never published any results from it.

After I had been conducting the social survey for about two years and involving myself in as many observational activities as I could manage, Elizabeth Colson (who had been director of the Institute at this time) resigned, and I was appointed in her place. This meant that I had to move from the Copperbelt to Lusaka, from where I had to direct the social surveys then in progress. Merran McCulloch (now Mrs Merran Fraenkel) who was secretary of the Institute when it was in Livingstone, and later when it moved to Lusaka, was able to conduct the survey in Livingstone, and start the survey in Broken Hill (now Kabwe).

Most of the data I had available to me thus were quantitative and not of the 'ethnographic' kind normally available to anthropologists. This was supplemented, of course, by my general knowledge of the ethnography of the region and the experiences of my colleagues in the Rhodes–Livingstone Institute, especially, as is apparent in the material in this book, to A. L. Epstein.

The aim of the book, therefore, is to provide a collection of essays concerning social relationships in the towns of South Central Africa, based on the material I was able to assemble personally at intervals during the twenty-one years I was there. The essays, however, are connected not only because they refer to urban conditions in a particular region but also because they are all based upon the theoretical perspective—situational analysis—which we inherited from Max Gluckman. On the whole the situational perspective has remained implicit rather than explicit in the writings of those of us influenced by this approach. I have tried, therefore, in this book to provide some formulation of what I take the approach to imply and to make its implicit assumptions explicit.

I am indebted to many agencies and people over the years who have provided me with help of various kinds. The British Social Science Research Council and the Rockefeller Foundation provided me with help to convert my material into machine readable form. I am grateful to Messrs S. Katilungu, G. Mukonoweshuro, E. Tikili, D. Chansa, K. Mubuyaeta, M. B. Lukhero, P. Manda, A. Nyirenda, P. Changala, L. Bweupe, and H. Ng'wane, who were the research assistants who were the interviewers in the social survey. I am particularly indebted to Mr M. B. Lukhero, who helped with the collection of data in Harare. Bruce Kapferer, Kingsley Garbett, Ulf Hannerz, and Elinor Kelly have all read the manuscript at various stages of completion, though I confess that I have not always been able to comply with their suggestions. Lastly I am grateful to the secretarial staff of Nuffield College who have put the manuscript on to a word processor and patiently made the changes that I have far too frequently required.

J. C. MITCHELL

Oxford

CONTENTS

LIST OF TABLES

LIST OF FIGURES

LIST OF MAPS

1

THE SITUATIONAL PERSPECTIVE

One of the dramatic consequences of the impact of Western capitalism on those countries to which it has turned for raw materials and markets for its products has been the spectacular growth of cities. Typical rates of growth of towns in South-East Asia, Africa, and in Latin and Middle America have been in the order of 10 per cent per annum, implying a doubling of the city populations approximately every seven years. Rates of this size far exceed the rates of natural population increase, so that a considerable part of the growth of these towns is made up of the inflow of migrants from rural areas. These migrants, attracted as they are by the apparent—but often unreal—wage-earning opportunities in the cities, originate in economies of a much simpler kind than that which underlies the expanding cities. They are forced, therefore, to adjust their behaviour to a mode of production and its supporting administrative, legal, and political institutions which has had its origin not in the societies out of which they have come but in an alien country pursuing its economic ends by means which are part and parcel of its own style of existence and quite at variance from those of the migrants. Even those domains of private living which on the surface appear to be relatively independent are inexorably affected by urban circumstances. The Western industrial and commercial types of production, and the private and public bureaucracies associated with them, penetrate into almost all aspects of the lives of those involved in them.

The social and theoretical difficulties raised by this combined process of what may be loosely termed 'urbanization' and 'Westernization' have constituted a key problem in the urban sociology of developing countries, in the sociology of development, and in urban anthropology. As such the process has been subjected to a wide variety of theoretical approaches about which there is little consensus. I have argued earlier (Mitchell 1966a) that there is no a priori reason why the problems should be cast in terms of acculturation or historical change: many of the 'changes' are merely situational adaptations to constraints imposed by urban conditions. But part of the intractability of the study of the process of urban growth or the characteristics of urban living arises from the fact that they are both part and parcel of a much more pervasive and general societal process. Cities and city life are always parts of larger wholes and some of the difficulty with which the analyst is faced is that of separating for analytical purposes the part from its integral whole.

The geographical region with which I am here concerned—today known as Zambia and Zimbabwe—in South Central Africa has provided a textbook case of this problem. Both countries were established as colonial societies at the peak of British imperial expansion at the end of the nineteenth century. They served in due course as markets for British products, outlets for British capital investment, and sources of scarce raw materials produced through the exploitation of cheap indigenous labour. For the purposes of theoretical argument about the social processes involved, however, this region has a very strong advantage: the consequences of the growth of towns and the impact of economic expansion have been the topics of both social and sociological enquiries for nearly fifty years.[1]

An appreciable part of this research was carried out as part of

[1] The literature is quite extensive and cannot be fully documented here. It started in Northern Rhodesia in the 1930s, largely out of concern about the social consequences of industrialization on labour migrants to the mines, e.g. Coulter (1933), Robinson (1933), Moore (1948). Among the anthropologists of the time Richards (1939, 1940) and Read (1942) were particularly sensitive to the impact of economic changes on rural life. Theoretical concern with urban problems started with Wilson's work in Broken Hill (1941-2). The Rhodes–Livingstone Institute's series of studies on the Copperbelt started in 1950, and results from those studies are still appearing. Some relevant examples are Epstein 1953, 1958, 1978, 1981, Mitchell 1954b, 1956a, McCulloch 1956, Bettison 1959, Boswell 1969, 1975, Harries-Jones 1975, Kapferer 1966, 1972, and van Velsen 1975, and it still continues with van Binsbergen (1979). Powdermaker (1962) was attached to the Institute but drew from a different anthropological tradition. A rare study of the attitudes of the White population was carried out independently of the Institute by Holleman and Biesheuvel (1973). In Zimbabwe the coverage of urban studies has not been so extensive but is nevertheless appreciable. Gray (1960) has dealt effectively with the historical background to urban problems. A concern for social conditions arising from industrialization was aired in Ibbotson 1943. Serious sociological work started with Gussman (1952), and has been continued by Schwab 1959 and Kileff (1975). Other aspects have been dealt with by Mitchell (1964b, 1969d).

the programme of the Rhodes–Livingstone Institute (now the Institute of African Studies of the University of Zambia), and this book continues in that tradition. In the earlier phases of that research a particular theoretical orientation stemming from the earlier work of Max Gluckman was developed. Epstein and I in particular adopted this perspective, though since then we have developed it in different ways.[2] In this book I attempt to set out the basis and assumptions of this approach in more formal terms than I have done before and to apply it particularly to an aspect of urban life in South Central Africa which—even in Africa as a whole—has not attracted much interest: the social perception town-dwellers have of significant aspects of city life as reflected in attitude-type studies. In so doing I hope to show how this approach may be used to resolve some apparent inconsistencies in research findings and to give some leads to the difficult problem of what the appropriate unit of analysis should be.

Cities and Society

The fact that cities are always embedded in some wider economic, social, and political order, whether in antiquity or in modern times, has led some sociologists and anthropologists to argue that the proper field of study ought to be the wider system rather than the city itself. This point of view has been propounded by Abrams (1978), who argues forcibly for looking at social phenomena in towns as reflecting with particular clarity the characteristics of the wider social system of which the towns are part. He argues that the problems which are treated as 'urban' are merely aspects of the wider social system, that is of the 'setting' as I shall later call it, which are manifested in particularly visible form. He argues that 'the town is a social form in which the essential properties of larger systems of social relations are grossly concentrated and intensified—to a point where residential size, density and heterogeneity, the formal characteristics of the town, appear to be in themselves constituent properties of a distinct social order' (1978: 10). In fact he argues

[2] Recently this tradition of analysis has been appraised by Hannerz (1980: chaps. 4 and 5), an outsider who has followed the development of this work very closely. Epstein, however, in his recent book (1981) seems to have moved more to words examining cultural responses without specifying the context and situation as clearly as before.

that 'in an important sense the city is not a social entity; that we have been victims of the fallacy of misplaced concreteness [sic] in treating it as such; and that one object of urban history and urban sociology now might be to get rid of the concept of the town' (1978: 10).

Those who advocate a Marxist orientation to the study of urban phenomena are similarly constrained by their theoretical framework to concentrate on molar features of the social system in which the towns are located rather than on the day to day behaviour of people living in those towns. Marx himself made reference to towns in only the most general way (see Harvey 1973: 302 ff., Castells 1977: 3, 1983: 296) and was not concerned directly with the impact of industrial conditions on the behaviour of those living in towns. It fell to Engels (1950) to deal with urban conditions *per se*. Those who adopt a historical materialist orientation towards the study of urban problems must, because of the conceptual framework underlying their analyses, concentrate on the general class structure of the entire social order in which these urban conditions occur. The issue is essentially that of the circumstances under which entrepreneurs are able to increase their share of the surplus product in urban circumstances.

The attention of writers operating within this framework must therefore be focused primarily on the general structure parameters in which the operations of issues of this sort are located, the control over the means of production, and the relations of production that flow from it. These are the characteristics of total societies. For Harvey, therefore, 'urbanism has to be regarded as a set of social relationships which reflects the relationships established throughout society as a whole' (1973: 304). For him, 'in certain important and crucial respects industrial society and the structures that comprise it continue to dominate urbanism' (1973: 311). This is a natural consequence, Harvey argues, of the ontology and epistemology underlying Marxism, whereby the social reality is seen as an 'emergent' totality that has an existence independent of the parts it contains. Explanation in 'this . . . case has to focus on the laws governing the behaviour of the totality and can proceed without reference to its parts' (1973: 288). Variations such as urban behaviour within social reality may be understood as transformations of the totality in towns of specified rules dictated by the theoretical precepts assumed to underlie the totality. The weight of the analysis, therefore, must be in the wider system of which the urban phenomena are merely a part.

A similar perspective suffuses the earlier writings of the foremost modern exponent of a Marxist approach to urban problems. In an influential essay Castells (1976) has argued that urban sociology at the time of his writing had, as he put it, no theoretical object, that is the topics studied by urban sociologists were part and parcel of, say, industrial sociology, the sociology of education, etc. The writings of Castells (1976a, 1976b, 1977, 1983), which have been very influential in forwarding Marxist orientations in urban studies, reflect a similar concentration on the wider societal factors bearing on urban life as against a concern with the detailed analysis of the day to day activities of town dwellers. Castells' earlier writings (1967, 1968, published in English as 1976a and 1976b) were primarily a critique of current sociology, in place of which he advocated a Marxist reformulation of the problems. His objection to the urban sociology with which he was familiar was that since the problems tackled by current sociology were theoretically disparate its only unity was its ideological underpinning. His later work (1977) was an English translation of an influential work published in French in 1972, *La Question Urbaine*. However, Castells took the opportunity in a postscript to review his attitude towards urban sociology at that time. Castells looks upon the book on urban sociology not as empirical findings relating to urban problems so much as a prolegomenon for empirical research in which the approach of locating the urban phenomena in the wider set of class relations constituted the main feature. He writes: 'The translation of urban problems into terms of the reproduction of labour power and their formalization by means of the urban system is useful only so far as it is a step towards expressing the forms of articulation between classes, production, consumption, the state and the urban' (1977: 439). The focus of interest is clearly in the analysis of the social context in which the towns are located rather than in the *de facto* events in the towns.

Subsequently Castells pursued one of his particular interests, the study of urban social movements, and published an account of ten instances of urban protest movements from different parts of the world. His experience in trying to interpret the detailed ethnographic data he had assembled about these movements had forced him to modify his attitude towards the formal historical materialist approach which he had been advocating in his earlier writings. Summarizing the orientation to emerge from his research, Castells writes:

although class relationships and class struggle are fundamental in understanding urban conflict, they are not, by any means, the only primary source of urban social change. The autonomous role of the state, the gender relationships, the ethnic and national movements and movements that define themselves as citizen, are among other alternative sources of urban social change. (1983: 291.)

My own view, which is developed below, is that structural analyses, whether Marxist or not, deal by definition with the general *forms* of social relationships and must therefore be abstract. The analysis of social action, however—of which incidents of class struggle would be an example—is located in complex reality in which circumstances other than class relationships may be involved. These other circumstances, as Castells points out, may in fact dominate the social action from the point of view of the actors themselves and from the point of view of outside observers so much that the analyst is forced to acknowledge them in any account of the events.

Considerations of this sort seem to underlie the objections that Marxist writers such as Magubane (1969, 1971, 1976: 188–9) have levelled against the analyses of my colleague A. L. Epstein and myself. He argued that the interpretations of the phenomena we were examining, in particular of ethnicity and social status, were inadequate because our analyses failed to give due weight to the class structure of the colonial society in which these phenomena were taking place. In effect Magubane was saying that instead of trying to interpret the interactional data relating to ethnicity or social status as located as they are in urban conditions constituted by the wider colonial order (which we took as given in our analyses), we ought really to have been conducting a Marxist analysis of the colonial social system itself. The issue is essentially that raised earlier: what is the appropriate unit of analysis? This question must be resolved to clarify further discussion.

The Situational Perspective[3]

The analytical strategy I have adopted is broadly that of 'situational analysis', by which I mean the intellectual isolation of a set of events from the wider context in which they occur in order to facilitate a logically coherent analysis of the events. My inspiration for this strategy came from Gluckman's analysis of the official opening of a bridge in Zululand in 1936 (Gluckman 1958), in which the behaviour of a number of participants in the proceedings could be made intelligible by relating it to the structural position they occupied in an over-arching system of Black–White relationships in South Africa at that time. I adopted the same procedure in my analysis of the *Kalela* dance that I was able to observe in Luanshya in the early 1950s (Mitchell 1956*a*). In that publication I described the procedure as follows:

I start with a description of the *Kalela* dance and then relate the dominant features of the dance to the system of relationships among Africans on the Copperbelt. In order to do this I must take into account to some extent the general system of Black–White relationships in Northern Rhodesia. By working outwards from a specific social situation on the Copperbelt the whole social fabric of the Territory is therefore taken in. It is only when the process has been followed to a conclusion that we can return to the dance and fully appreciate its significance. (1956*a*: 1.)

Subsequently I outlined the basic approach in a discussion of theoretical orientations towards the study of urban life (Mitchell 1966*a*), but at that time I had not distinguished sufficiently clearly two different aspects of the situation which I have subsequently realized should be kept separate. These are the distinctions between, on the one hand a situation as defined by the actors, and on the other a setting as defined by the analyst as a heuristic construct to facilitate analysis. This is a distinction which G. Kingsley Garbett (1970: 215 ff.) has appreciated and discussed incisively.

---

[3] My approach has much in common with that set out in van Velsen 1967 and Garbett 1970, though van Velsen refers more specifically to the analysis of a series of connected events. In so far as the application to urban life is concerned, the approach has been discussed by myself (Mitchell 1966*a*), by Eames and Goode (1977: 276), by Kileff and Pendleton (1975: 13), and in some detail by Hannerz (1980).

The starting-point in situational analysis is the assumption that social behaviour exists as a vastly complex set of human activities and interactions about which any one observer can appreciate only a limited part. In order to make these activities and interactions intelligible the analyst must fit them into explanatory frameworks. These explanatory frameworks are arrangements of concepts relating to social behaviour such that a logical nexus linking them may be communicated to those who share the same general domain of discourse.

It should be clear from this point of view that the objective nature of social behaviour is assumed to be problematic. We have access only to the interpretations that observers (and the actors themselves!) have made of such aspects of social behaviour to which they had access. Analytical objectivity therefore is dependent on the extent to which these interpretations are communicable to others who are operating within the same universe of discourse. Another analyst perceiving the same events but using the perceptual apparatus of a different explanatory framework will by definition present a somewhat different account of those events.

The analysis of social situations consists then of selecting from the vast set of current activities and interactions (or social phenomena in general) a limited set of events which the analyst has reason to assume may be linked together in some way and be capable of being interpreted logically in terms of general understanding of the way in which social actions take place. These general understandings might be thought of as 'theory', and there could be, of course, many different kinds of general understanding. My own predilections are for those formulations which relate to personal interactional rather than to large-scale structural phenomena. In other words I am personally more interested in social behaviour in interpersonal situations (including, of course, the meanings actors attribute to their actions) than in more abstract aspects of social structure, but this does not deny the validity of other kinds of analysis. Clearly studies are needed of large-scale structural phenomena as well as small-scale interactional events; one does not preclude the other. But what is essential is that studies of one genus should be so phrased as simultaneously to admit of the possibility of the other.

The general perspective then is that the behaviour of social actors may be interpreted as the resultant of the actors' shared understandings of the situation in which they find themselves and of the constraints imposed upon these actors by the wider social order in which they are enmeshed. Both components of the situation—the shared understandings and the notion of a wider social order—are in fact constructs erected by the analyst as a means of interpreting the social situation as a whole.

Cognitive Specifications of the Context: Situations

There are, therefore, several epistemologically distinct components of the social structure which the analyst must take into account.

1. There are the particular sets of events, activities, behaviour, or other social phenomena which, in the analyst's opinion, constitute a challenge to interpretation—a theoretical conundrum of some sort. These phenomena will have been assembled by whatever techniques of data collection were available to the analyst. The way in which inferences are drawn from the data so generated is a subsequent problem and is not a specific part of the social situation.

2. There are the meanings which the actors attribute to the activities, events, behaviour, and other social phenomena with which the analyst is concerned. Here again the observer may use any of a number of different techniques to adduce these meanings, but at this stage this is taken for granted. It is possible that, as in the abstract study of symbolism, the actors' meanings may themselves be the prime focus of the analyst's interest, in which case the first and second components overlap to a high degree. But they need not.

3. The third component consists of the wider social framework or setting within which the first two components are located. Once again the analyst may use a variety of techniques to assemble data to support the specification of the setting. The basis of inference from the data, as before, is a separate problem. In fieldwork at the interactional level, data relating to the wider context and its interpretation will typically be based on studies conducted by other analysts, frequently analysts working within

other disciplines. Even if this is not so, there will be generally less attention to detail and sophistication of analysis devoted to this component than to the first or the second. The intellectual justification for this lack of detail will be presented later in this chapter.

The implication of this orientation is that there are in fact quite different 'definitions of the situation' involved. The more familiar notion is that deriving from W. I. Thomas's classic formulation in *The Unadjusted Girl* (1923), which is characterized in his words by 'a stage of examination and deliberation' prior to a self-determined act of behaviour. Thomas was aware of the latent opposition between an arbitrary definition by an individual of a situation and a societal definition of the same situation. He wrote of a rivalry between the spontaneous definition of the situation made by a member of an organized society and the definition society has provided for that member. The analytical utility of the idea, however, derives from the extent to which the rationale of otherwise puzzling behaviour becomes intelligible when the observer is able to appreciate the meanings the actors are attributing to the cues and symbols being presented in that situation.

But the opposition of individual and society in this formulation assumes prior normative consensus. In fact, of course, circumstances under urban conditions vary all the way from highly explicit and formal definitions of situations, as in traffic rules, court-room procedures, or other public ceremonial performances, to extremely vague and inchoate situations, such as those in public places where the cues and signs which index the meaning to which actors may respond are not at all explicit, even to the regular participants in these situations. In these circumstances the definitions of the situations must be negotiated among the participants. It is by no means certain at the beginning of an interactional sequence which of several alternative interpretations of the meanings will be attributed to the actions of the participants. I described an example of the negotiation of the definition of a situation of this sort in *The Kalela Dance*, in which a man took sexual liberties with a woman in a public place and tried, unsuccessfully, to define the situation as one of ethnic joking in which such liberties would have been acceptable.

In these terms this type of definition of the situation is basically cognitive, in that the meaning which actors recognize in the cues and signs in the situation provide the basis for coherent social behaviour for as long as the participants accept that the situation persists. As such it is an organization of experience or a perceptual phenomenon. But the sociological analysis of such behaviour turns on the extent to which the behaviour of the protagonists in the situation is directed towards others, that is, has a 'social' orientation. It is possible to conceive of a series of social interactions proceeding on the basis of a disparate set of different, even opposed, individual definitions of a situation without the latent contradictions becoming explicit and leading to a breakdown in communications. But this seems counter-intuitive, and the basic assumption in using the notion of the cognitive definition of the situation must be that there is at least some modicum of meanings shared among the actors.

The sharing of meanings among actors, whether these meanings are imposed upon them by a formal and publicly recognized occasion or by a process of negotiation in an unstructured situation, defines the perception involved as *social* as against *individual* perception, and the notion is used here to connote the identification and organization of meanings achieved and shared by actors in some social situation.

In so far as social behaviour is concerned, however, the achievement of an agreed set of meanings in some situation implies that the meanings carry with them explicit or implicit rules about the appropriate behaviour related to those meanings. In essence it implies that the public recognition of norms will prevail as long as the situation persists. In the example relating to ethnic joking the man is question had fondled the breast of a woman in a public place, behaviour which could only be accepted as 'normal' if in fact the two could be taken to be identified with appropriate ethnic groups between which such behaviour is an accepted characteristic of institutionalized joking behaviour. The dispute arose not because the woman rejected the whole notion of ethnic joking or of the practices defined as appropriate within the behaviour, but because she disputed that the relationship in fact existed between the group to which she claimed identity and the group to which the man claimed identity.

The extent to which meanings attributed to cues, signs, and behaviour in public (and private) situations may be shared turns upon the extent to which there is general recognition of these meanings. The term 'culture' is normally given to the stock of shared meanings, but in so far as culture is an anthropological or sociological concept is carries with it connotations which go beyond what I feel is the basic minimum needed for an appreciation of social perception. Constituted as an analytical concept, culture implies some patterning and structuring of the meaning into categories germane to the understanding of the cognitive life of the people in general. The cultural analysis of myth, symbols, or kinship terms, for example, would consist in demonstrating the logical nexus of discernible parts of these phenomena to one another in some patterned way.

In the analysis of urban phenomena by some anthropologists (e.g. Parkin 1978 and to a lesser extent Epstein 1981), assumptions of this sort are much more central than they are in the sort of analysis with which I am here concerned. Parkin (1978: 17–22), for example, expressly discusses the analytical relevance of the logical consistency (from the point of view of the actors) and the logical necessity (from the point of view of the analyst) of institutions and cultures. Epstein, introducing his analysis of forms of domestic behaviour in towns, refers to culture as 'a structure of assumptions and values that serves as a template or grid by which the individual is enabled to define and respond to his situation' (1981: 6).

Conceptualizing culture as a structure constituted largely of mutually consistent beliefs, customs, and institutions flows almost certainly from its hypostatization as an analytical construct of central interest. Parkin's interest in his analysis of the domestic behaviour of Luo migrants to Nairobi is to show how those migrants are able to cope with the economic and political situation in Nairobi by appealing to their traditional way of life, even if some aspects such as polygyny and philoprogenitiveness appear at first sight to be at variance with the values underlying Western urban economies of which Nairobi is a part. Parkin recognizes quite explicitly that inconsistencies and contradictions occur in the behaviour of townspeople but that the people with whom he was concerned, the Luo, consistently appealed to ideas and notions drawn from their traditional stock of concepts in order to appraise this behaviour.

In order to appreciate the processes of urban social perception in the colonial towns with which I am concerned, however, a sophisticated formulation of the 'culture' of the actors is not strictly necessary. All that needs to be assumed is that 'culture' exists as extensive storehouses of meanings which people have built up over time and to which they are constantly adding or from which they are constantly dropping elements. Meanings may coexist in these storehouses in a way that implies that interpretations may be made of the same cues, signs, and phenomena in ways which are quite opposed to one another. The contradictions among different coexistent meanings do not become explicit unless they are mobilized simultaneously in the same social situation. If this should happen the actor must determine which is to prevail in that particular situation. This is the basis, of course, of Evans-Pritchard's 'situational selection', by which he was able to show how the contradictions inherent in witch beliefs among the Azande were accommodated. The protagonists were able to define effectively the situation in which they were placed by appealing to contradictory meanings which could be construed as appropriate to those situations.[4]

From this point of view social perception at the negotiated, as opposed to the structural end of the spectrum has the quality of Necker boxes and other perceptually ambiguous drawings popular with *Gestalt* psychologists. I mean by this that just as a change in visual perceptual organization may transform a Necker box from one with its open top to top right to one with its open top to top left, so a renegotiated definition of a social situation may completely transform the meaning to be attributed to the actions of individuals involved, even when exactly the same behaviour has up to that point constituted the perceptual stimuli. An example of this occurred once more in relation to ethnic joking, where a potentially tense situation

---

[4] He writes: 'I have tried to show . . . the plasticity of beliefs as functions of situations. They are not indivisible, ideational structures but are loose associations of notions. When a writer brings them together in a book and presents them as a conceptual system then insufficiencies and contradictions are at once apparent. In real life they do not function as a whole but in bits. A man in one situation utilizes what in the beliefs are convenient to him and pays no attention to other elements which he might use in different situations. Hence a single event may evoke a number of different contradictory beliefs among different persons.' (Evans-Pritchard 1937: 540.)

involving a child's theft of some carrots from a garden was transformed into one of amusement by its sudden redefinition as a
consequence of ethnic joking (Mitchell 1956a: 39).

The regularities that the analyst adduces from social
behaviour by this formulation derive not from the regularities in
the culture, therefore, but rather from the process of definition
either by fiat, as in structured situations, or by negotiation in
unstructured situations, by which the behaviour may be related
to sets of meanings which the actors share.

Structural Specifications of the Context: Settings

The social situation in which the actors are involved, however,
may be defined in a totally different way. The situation may be
defined as the structural context within which the interactions
are located. This specification of the *setting*—a term I use to
distinguish it from the situation as specified by the actor's cognitive definition—is based on the analyst's formulation of the
more general circumstances which impinge on the actors and
need not depend at all on the meanings the actors attribute to the
events in the situation. The distinction here is parallel with
Schutz's (1967: 3–47) distinction between the observer's model
and the actor's model as different constructions of reality, and is
similar to the familiar anthropological distinction between emic
and etic analyses (Harris 1969, 1976).

Gluckman adopted a structural definition of the situation in
his description of the opening of the bridge in Zululand, when he
recounted the historical background of the conquest of the Zulu
by the Boer Trekkers and the establishment of an administrative
system in which White administrators controlled the activities of
Black subjects. Part of the specification of this setting involved a
description of the urban industrial mode of production in which
Black workers participated as labour migrants, thus affecting
their relationships with their rural kinsfolk. Part of the specification, also, was the role of the White missionaries, whose relationships with their Black parishioners were very different from
those of the administrators, although they were none the less
affected by the colour bar. This specification of the context
provides an interpretation of the behaviour of the various actors
in the day's proceedings through which the rationality of the

otherwise opaque manifestations of behaviour can be made apparent. In effect, the abstract system of general Black–White relationships in this form of analysis was given concrete manifestation.[5]

This notion of the structural specification of the context was implied by my previous notion of 'the external determinants' of the urban context (Mitchell 1966a). These I outlined as follows:

1. The density of residential accommodation and the demands upon public places.
2. The geographical mobility of the population between town and country, between towns, and between parts of the same town.
3. The ethnic and regional heterogeneity of urban populations.
4. The selected demographic characteristics of the urban populations, particularly age and sex.
5. The economic differentiation and mode of production upon which the towns were based.
6. The political and administrative system in which the towns were located.

These were termed 'external' in the sense that in analysing any set of social interactions the analyst could take them as given. They could be looked upon as features which, in the sense that Garbett has described (1975: 124 ff.) as a heuristic procedure, the analyst construes as constraints impinging upon the behaviour of actors enmeshed in personal relationships within them. In interpreting the behaviour of the *Kalela* dancers and their audience, for example, we need to appreciate the colonial setting, which determined where in the town Africans could live and where the dance could take place. The setting meant that most of the dancers occupied low-status unskilled positions in enterprises owned and controlled by Whites, that they were drawn from a wide variety of regional backgrounds with differing ethnic origins, that most were recent migrants to the town with fairly recent rural experience, that they were young, as

---

[5] It is interesting that in the course of his account of events Gluckman provides a neat example of the Necker-box type of switch in the cognitive definition of the situation, when the Zulu chief with whom Gluckman was travelling addressed a Black policeman first as a representative of an oppressive White Government and then as a upholder of law and order through his apprehension of a sheep thief (1958: 2–3).

were their audience, and mostly male since in this population women of commensurate age were heavily outnumbered by men, and that the type of housing provided in the area where the dance took place was so densely packed that the beat of the drums could announce to a sizeable population that a dance was about to begin. It is when all these characteristics were described as part of the colonial setting that the significance of the dress of the dancers, the songs they sang, and the appreciation of their audience could be properly understood.

The phrase 'external determinants' was not the happiest choice. First the word 'determinant' seems to imply a somewhat rigid relationship between the social conditions and the behaviour: this was not implied. Secondly the term 'external' is confusing: external to what? I had originally intended it to imply that the conditions designated as external were not themselves the prime topics of analysis but nevertheless had an influence on the action being analysed. Pendleton (1975: 18) has also objected to the term and has suggested that externality resides in the fact that the determinants are 'factors which influence urban dwellers' lives which lie beyond their [the actors'] immediate influence'. This, indeed, captures part of what is implied by the notion, but the real distinction is, I think, that for purposes of the analysis of behaviour at the interpersonal level we are operating with data which are not immediately part and parcel of the directly observable situation under examination. It is partly for this reason that I subsequently suggested the procedure as establishing the *contextual parameters* of the action (Mitchell 1970*b*), implying by this that the specification of the context in which the behaviour took place was based on data of a rather different order from that upon which the analysis of the behaviour itself was based. Usually the contextual parameters of an urban situation must be specified by reference to the work of political scientists, economists, demographers, macro-sociologists, geographers, and other specialists whose work would normally be conducted in terms of a somewhat different conceptual vocabulary from that used by an anthropologist or micro-sociologist.

But an additional reason for preferring a more general terminology was that the notion of external determinants, as I presented it in 1966, seemed to imply a discrete set of circumstances—that, for example, the age and sex structure and the mode of production were separate from one another, and that both were separate from the political and administrative system in which the towns were located. In fact they were of course all to a greater or lesser extent manifestations of a single general condition, the structure of colonial society. The contextual parameters of the towns at the time when I was collecting my data were those of a colonial system, and setting the parameters entailed specifying those aspects of the colonial system which could be construed as having some bearing on the behaviour being examined.

The setting and the situation, therefore, stand in a reflexive relationship to one another. I mean by this that an analyst wishing to interpret a specified type of behaviour in a town needs to work with two different referents simultaneously. The first of these is an appreciation of the set of circumstances in which the actors are placed and which determine the arena within which the analyst postulates the behaviour must take place. The second is an appreciation of the set of meanings the actors themselves attribute to the behaviour. The analysis then consists of an interpretation in general theoretical terms of the behaviour as articulated both with the setting and with the actor's cognitive definition of the situation. An analysis of kinship in towns, for example, would entail a specification of the administrative, economic, and demographic parameters of the town within which the kinship relationships must operate, a specification of the rights and obligations both excepted (that is the meanings attributed to the behaviour) and enacted (that is the behaviour) among the actors defined as standing in particular kinship relationships to one another, and analytically a statement of the general logical nexus among all three components.

It follows from this that there can be no universal set of contextual parameters in terms of which all analyses of situations and events may be conducted. The contextual parameters must be set, or at least partially respecified, for each particular piece of analysis, even in the same town, since the structural features of the town will impose different constraints or provide different avenues for various kinds of activities. An essential part of the analysis of social situations is a specification of the way in which the structural features constitute the setting within which the behaviour is located.

The Urban Context

It is clear, nevertheless, that although I have differentiated between the cognitive definition of the situation and the context or setting as established by the analyst, it may in fact often be advantageous for the analyst to distinguish different levels of specificity in the overall context. To provide an illustration, it will be convenient to locate the material with which I shall be concerned in two nested contexts. For the most part I am dealing with a colonial-type society, and this immediately implies a general set of social relationships, the relevant aspects of which I shall need to identify in connection with the data I shall be examining. But I am also dealing with *urban* contexts. These urban contexts, in turn, are themselves embedded in the wider colonial social system, so that we must take cognizance of the extent to which the pattern of social relationships in which the specific phenomena we shall be examining occur is itself affected by both the colonial context and by general urban conditions. For particular analytical purposes it may be fruitful to distinguish even finer contexts in the city as a whole, such as, for example, middle class as against working class residential areas.

The issue is to specify what is particularly *urban* about the activities of town dwellers as against the activities of, say, rural inhabitants in the same national group. The attempt to provide a universal definition of the city (or town) has been part of urban sociology and urban anthropology for a long time, and there would be little point in recounting the history of these attempts. The basic dilemma is that in order that the definition should be universal it must be based on primitive or rudimentary characteristics. These characteristics are generally demographic or geographic, such as, for example, Wirth's classic 1938 definition of a city (1964a: 66) as 'a relatively large, dense permanent settlement of socially heterogeneous individuals' (1960: 33), whether elaborated by Sjoberg's insistence on a system of writing or not, and are deceptively simple. There is almost always some town or city which is undoubtedly a town or city but which lacks one or more of these characteristics. Much misplaced scholarship has been spent on trying either to adjust the definition to make it fit the phenomenon the scholar takes to be a city, or to respecify the characteristics of the given city to make it fit the definition. The dilemma arises simply from the fact that the criteria evoked in the definition relate to quite disparate conceptual frameworks. In the definition quoted there is a demographic criterion—the size of the body of population involved; a geographical criterion—the density of settlement; and an economic one—the sort of subsistence in which the population is involved.

The size of the population which is taken to represent a 'town' or 'city' is usually set at a conventional limit. It has long been conventional, for example, to define towns and cities in terms of certain population sizes. Those set in 1967 by the United Nations,[6] for example, were as follows:

(a) Town   = 20,000 or more inhabitants.
(b) City   = 100,000 or more inhabitants.
(c) Big city = 500,000 or more inhabitants.

These are standards established to make feasible some degree of comparability of urban incidence across nations, but the fundamental, arbitrary basis of the division is apparent. From the point of view of the consequence of size on the social behaviour of the inhabitants, these size ranges probably have little meaning.

The fact that this population must be concentrated in a relatively small area in order that the settlement should be accepted as a city is also arbitrary. Some suburbs of cities may in fact be relatively sparsely populated, whereas there are agricultural regions which are very densely populated. Nevertheless the density of the population in cities usually greatly exceeds that in agricultural regions. Density, however, is not in itself sufficient to define a city or a town: the size of the population concerned and the nature of the basis of subsistence must also be taken into consideration.

The non-agricultural basis of urban life is widely accepted as

[6] Recommendation of the Ad Hoc Committee of Experts on the Programme of Demographic Aspects of Urbanization, Sydney, 29 Aug.–2 Sept. 1967 (E/CN. 9/ZC 7/L.9). Quoted by the United Nations Economic Commission for Africa, 'Size and Growth of Urban Populations in Africa' in Breese (ed.) 1969: 130.

essential to distinguish towns from densely populated rural regions. Yet there are difficulties with accepting this criterion as a *sine qua non* for the definition of towns and cities. There have been in the past, and there are no doubt at present, a number of population agglomerations of considerable size and density which are dependent directly on agricultural activities for their existence. A striking example is the Yoruba city described by Bascom (1955, 1959, 1962, 1963), Lloyd (1953, 1959), and Krapf-Askari (1969), which appears to consist of agglomerations of farmers who cultivate the land surrounding densely settled concentrated communities in the centre of agricultural land (cf. Krapf-Askari 1969: 25–6). Even here, as Lloyd points out, craftsmen begin to emerge and trade begins to become the mainstay of existence for a considerable proportion of the citizens.

The characteristics upon which a universal definition of the city can be based must be very general: population size, density of settlement, type of economic activities, etc. The town or the city as a phenomenon is in fact a *common-sense* construct, or alternatively a 'real' phenomenon. (See also Abrams 1978: 10.) The same city or town is likely to be conceptualized by anthropologists, political scientists, economists, social geographers, and other specialists in different ways, since each will select from the total set of diacritical features of the city those which are theoretically pertinent for analysis in terms of a specific discipline. The 'city' must therefore be reformulated in terms of the concepts of some analytical schema in order to make it amendable for analysis. Castells makes essentially the same point in different words. He writes: 'It is interesting that the two best recent urban sociology readers published in the United States . . . are characterized by an interdisciplinary approach and the emphasis they give to political analyses' (1976*b*: 64 n. 14). He makes the point in connection with the production of data in response to the demands for solutions to practical problems, but the point is also germane to the description of the city as a common-sense phenomenon: this is only possible in terms of a combination of different perspectives.

From this point of view I would argue that any attempt to establish a sociologically or anthropologically universal definition of a town or description of urban social behaviour is misplaced. The most we can do is to establish types of cities with similar basic demographic, geographic, and economic characteristics, such as Southall started to do in 1961 or as Fox (1977) has done, and then specify the urban contexts implied by these characteristics. Having specified the context, the task of interactional urban sociology is to state explicitly the assumptions about the way in which these characteristics are likely to bear upon the social behaviour of the inhabitants of these towns. When this is done we may then try to verify and elaborate these assumptions by analysing social behaviour in specific situations. From this perspective we may take Wirth's universal definition of the city as a statement of some essential features of the context of urban behaviour, but not in itself as a definition of the city. His exposition of the effect of these circumstances on urban life may also be looked upon as an attempt at the specification of the context. His essay then becomes a prolegomenon for urban sociological research rather than a statement of empirical findings. Equally, the attempts to falsify Wirth's findings by using data from cities located in entirely different contexts and without ensuring that the nexus between the context and behaviour has been replicated do not, in my opinion, constitute a valid test of Wirth's ideas.[7] An essential part of any comparative analysis is specifying the context.

The problem of defining the specifically urban has been expressed as establishing the 'city-as-context' in anthropological writing, and has been addressed in general terms by Jack Rollwagen (1975, 1975), Kenneth Moore (1975), and M. Estellie Smith (1975). The problem has been phrased as the difference between studies of behaviour or culture which happens to be located *in* the city as against studies of behaviour or culture which is characteristic *of* the city: the 'locus' as against the

---

[7] I am referring to such studies as Bascom 1955 and Sjoberg 1960, who use Yoruba towns to criticize Wirth's generalizations. I would accept Krapf-Askari's criticism of my earlier (1966a) formulation of 'urban' as strictly commercial and industrial towns (1969: 161). My position now would be that the commercial and industrial are merely one specific kind of setting in which interpersonal social relationships are constrained. The problem of Yoruba-type towns becomes that of describing in theoretical terms how social relationships in these large, dense settlements are structured, given that the lineage framework provides a basis for relating to defined others, that the sheer size of the population implies that there must be ways of handling relationships with strangers, and that the mode of production constrains the degree of social differentiation.

'focus' of the city (Smith 1976: 254–5, Hannerz 1980: 3). Philip Mayer had expressed the same polarity earlier in terms that may be paraphrased as 'in the city' as against 'of the city' (1963: 1). The point of view taken here is that it is precisely by the process of specifying the context that the urban references of the city for the behaviour of the town dwellers are established. While there is much in common in the approaches of Rollwagen, Moore, and Smith with that set out here, the major distinction is the way in which the contextual parameters are fixed at the city level. The process of establishing the contextual parameters encompassing the form of behaviour being examined demands an explicit specification of which features of city circumstances are relevant to the problem under review and a statement in general terms of the way in which these features constitute constraints and opportunities for people living within them. But the setting of the contextual parameters, as I shall argue later in this chapter, need be conducted at only a fairly general level. The detailed examination of the necessary connections among phenomena is part of the analysis of the situation.

But the city context is itself located in a wider economic and political system. The identification of what is specifically urban turns on separating out features of the phenomenon under examination from those of the wider society of which it is only a constituent part. In fact all cities, even the Greek city-states, can exist only in relation to some hinterland with which the city is in economic, political, and social relationship. One of the pioneers of comparative urbanism, Gideon Sjöberg, clearly recognized the problem. He postulated the existence of a feudal order in which cities arose, and then examined the patterns of social relationships which emerged in these cities. He found that he could not isolate the pattern of social relationships which emerged in these cities from those of the wider embracing social order. He wrote:

Throughout recognition has been given to the theoretical distinction between a city and a society. But empirically these fuse—our efforts to analyse one force us to treat the other. In practice, the city is our starting point, but we have branched outward from it to encompass the total feudal order. This work is, in the end, a survey of the pre-industrialized civilized society with special emphasis upon the city, the hub of all major activities. (1960: 332.)

The city may well be the hub of all activities in pre-industrial civilized society, but in so far as specifically urban behaviour exists in pre-industrial society it will be identifiable with the specific geographic, demographic, economic, political, and social circumstances in feudal towns that mould the behaviour of their inhabitants as against those living under, say, rural circumstances, but nevertheless within the same social order.

Richard G. Fox (1972: 218–28) has sharply criticized my earlier presentation of this approach (1966a) and similar approaches adopted by Epstein (1958, 1967) and Plotnicov (1967). In short, Fox argues for a macroscopic and holistic anthropology of cities in which the institutional and historical features of cities become the focus of study. He objects on four specific grounds:

1. That treating the city as a research locale other than the object of investigation has given urban anthropology a limited theoretical perspective. By this he seems to mean that situational analyses do not concern themselves with the specific characteristics of cities as against 'non-cities'. It should be clear from what I have argued, however, that I view the notion of 'the city' as a common-sense construct. For theoretical analysis, therefore, those aspects of city existence which can be shown to bear upon the type of behaviour in the towns being described need to be specified. There are as many definitions of the city as there are theoretical perspectives, and Fox's holistic perspective is only one of them.

2. That the assumed but rarely analysed vision of urbanism which appears in the accounts to which Fox objects is only the Western city (1972: 223). He argues that the familiarity of the Western or capitalist anthropologists with cities of this sort may explain why the notion of the city remains, in his view, unanalysed. The fact of the matter is, of course, that Western capitalistic cities are so extensive and so much urban anthropology has been conducted by Western anthropologists that research experience so far has largely been limited to them. Certainly my own research experience has been limited to colonial cities and my observations must inevitably be limited to cities of that type. Comparative urbanism, as I observe later in this chapter, entails particular problems precisely because of the

difficulty of separating the cities from the wider societies of which they are an integral part. My own excursion into comparative urbanism is limited for theoretical reasons to cities of the Western industrial type (see chap. 7 below).

3. That 'by choosing urbanization and ghetto men . . . anthropologists only confirm their inadequacies in the description of urban life' (1972: 224). What Fox is objecting to here is that 'recently detribalized peoples or newly arrived peasants', in his opinion, 'participate only minimally in urban life', so that urbanism from this perspective would not allow as complete a study of 'the city and larger society' as, for example, a study of 'middle-class Americans or European elites in Africa' would. This objection turns on what the appropriate object of study should be: behaviour in urban circumstances as against the general nature of urbanism. To this question there cannot, of course, be a definitive answer. Both types of study are valid and necessary and neither negates the other. In the best of all worlds they would obviously complement one another.

4. That urban anthropologists have deliberately chosen to study what Fox has called 'the romantic and the foreign' (1972: 226), where the word 'romantic' refers to the definition of the word 'romance' in *Webster's Dictionary*, 'a [prose tale] dealing with the remote in time or place, the heroic, the adventurous and often the mysterious'. Fox argues that 'by embracing the exotica of poverty populations, slum environments and native locations, much urban anthropology falls into an inappropriate ahistoricism, accepts the absence of a holistic viewpoint, denies the city as a goal of research . . . and thus factors out what cities can say about the nature of man and his societies' (1972: 227).

Much turns of course on how the notion of heroic, adventurous, or mysterious is construed. The situational analyses with which I am familiar, however, have dealt precisely with concerns of mundane everyday social and political import, as for example Epstein's study of the struggle for power between African leaders and the colonial government and the mining companies (1958), or my own study of *Kalela* (1956a), in which the 'exotic' is merely the vehicle for an examination of race relations, ethnicity, and social status as reflected in behaviour which could be understood only in the

context of the urban circumstances in which it took place.
But what Fox does not seem to appreciate fully is that the process of setting the contextual parameters, as I have formulated it, takes the holistic macrosociological approach which he advocates merely as the starting-point. As with his description of the different settings which he developed from historical antecedents in the towns of Charlestown (South Carolina) and Newport (Rhode Island) (1977: 149–57), it is based primarily upon secondary sources, except that when construed as a *setting* this analysis must be sufficiently sophisticated to provide a plausible background to the interpretations not only of street behaviour, which in the end may turn out to be the msot urban form of urban behaviour, but also of trade union, political, *and* domestic behaviour.

Warranted Naïvety

A field of enquiry must therefore be specified before we can proceed with analysis. Having elected to describe and interpret characteristics of interpersonal behaviour in cities with which I am concerned, and having decided not to shift the centre of gravity or the main focus of discussion to the wider context of setting which constrains this behaviour, in how much detail need the context itself be described in order to provide sufficient appreciation of the effects of the context on the pattern of behaviour of the actors?

This problem is one which is germane to much sociological analysis, and concerns the difficult question of the degree to which we are entitled for analytical purposes to 'seal off' some part of what is in reality an extensively interconnected series of events and activities and to treat it 'as if' it constitutes a set of interconnected events and activities in itself. The matter is raised explicitly by Epstein in an essay in which he discusses the extent to which he needs to take account of events which are beyond his immediate observation in order to understand the political behaviour of Africans in a copper-mining town (1964). The logical and philosophical problems involved are discussed extensively by Gluckman and Devons in an essay in the same collection. They argue that any scholar must, for analytical purposes, limit the extent of study. Since social activities of all sorts constitute an endless web of interconnected events, if a student of social relationships were not to impose some restriction on the field of study it would mean in the extreme case that the student would be called upon to study with equal diligence all actions through all times at all places. Devons and Gluckman then set out to identify related procedures by means of which analysts may achieve this limitation. The analysts may decide in terms of the analytical context they are using and the techniques of observation open to them to delimit some set of activities as constituting the realm of their enquiry, as, for example, 'the operation of the Bank of England', or 'family life in an English city suburb'. Having done this they may accept as facts without further analysis information that impinges on their topic of study but which they define as being external to it. This information may be derived either from common-sense observation, or from analytical studies using different frameworks of analysis. They may thus work with simplified notions of the relations of the elements in their analysis they take to be germane to external features and concentrate instead on an analysis among these elements. In other words, a degree of warranted naïvety is not only desirable but is essential if the analysis of social phenomena is to achieve any depth. Devons and Gluckman refer to this as 'incorporation' (1964: 163).

Devons and Gluckman call the isolation of a feasible unit of analysis the process of circumscription. They describe it thus:

Every anthropologist uses this procedure to isolate a manageable amount of interconnected data, as when he studies social relations in a tribe or in a factory over a certain period. The delimitation may also be of what Fortes calls a 'domain' of activities, such as domestic relations, or political relations or the interpersonal linkages between kinsfolk, or the relations between legal or religious activities and social relationships . . . When an anthropologist circumscribes his field he cuts off a manageable field of reality from the total flow of events, by putting boundaries round it both in terms of what is relevant to his problems and in terms of how and where he can apply his techniques of observation and analysis. (pp. 162–3.)

The example of circumscription most relevant to comparative studies is that used by Epstein in the same set of essays. Using social anthropological procedures he wanted to explain the

course of the development of trade unions and political organization among Africans in Luanshya. This selection of the
topic or problem of study is in fact the first act of circumscription. The African town-dwellers in Luanshya were
obviously involved in a whole set of other activities, religious,
domestic, economic, recreational, and so on, which Epstein felt
were marginal to his main interest and could therefore be set
aside. In a more detailed analysis he may have found it profitable to include some of these other fields, but at the level of
analysis that he set himself he decided—justifiably, in my
opinion—that he could treat these events as having no substantial bearing on his major interest. The criterion of relevance
here, presumably, is the plausibility, in terms of what we know
about human behaviour as a whole, of the essential connections
between apparently disparate sets of social activities.

Epstein explains the weak organization of trade unions in the
municipal housing areas, in contrast to the mining housing
areas, as being due to the fragmented structure of institutional
arrangements in the former as against the unitary structure
of institutional arrangements under the 'monolithic' mine
'company' organization. Nevertheless, we are entitled to ask,
what is the relationship between the circumscribed part of the
flow of events and that part of the flow which is excluded from
analysis? This is a problem which Epstein specifically raises, for
he initially contrasts studies of 'tribal' communities with
anthropological studies of urban communities. He concludes:
'The town cannot be handled in the same way as the tribe . . .
they belong to different orders of social organization. The tribal
community is, in general terms, an isolable unit, culturally self-
sufficient; it exists in its own right. But in contrast the modern
urban community has no independent existence.' This is
because 'major decisions which affect most intimately the life or
the community are taken in remote centres; the institutions
which flourish in the town, and most deeply influenced
behaviour, frequently have a national or regional, not a local
referent' (p. 84).

In these terms the unit of study is a set of relationships and
activities which the analyst is able to treat as interconnected in
some way. Some of these relationships and activities take place
within the town and some of them outside. The problem of

circumscription here is to decide how many of the external relationships we need to take account of to provide a plausible explanation of the activities in the town, the assumption being that the interconnections are not all synchronous. But later in the same essay Epstein criticizes the study of urbanization as 'the movement from the ordered way of tribal life to the anarchy of the urban jungle.' He argues:

In fact, of course the town is not a jungle; it has its own specific and highly complex form of organization into which the African who comes to town has to fit himself. In a word we have to view the town as a single field of social relationships in which the different and sometimes opposed sections of the urban population are also closely linked by ties of interdependency. (p. 99.)

If this is true then a second type of circumscription is necessary. Since all the activities going on in the town and all the sections of the population cannot be studied at the same depth, some isolation of the sections or sets of activities within the town would seem also to be necessary. But this requirement may be more a consequence of the assumptions involved than a substantive issue, for the question is what is meant by the word 'town' when Epstein writes: 'There is very little novel in affirming that the modern towns of Africa form part of a national and colonial structure' (p. 85). Does it refer to an agglomeration of population, to a layout of streets, buildings, and industrial plant, or to sets of activities of the people living in the town considered as a totality? Clearly, when one is operating within an anthropological or sociological framework the reference is to activities and relationships, but the assumption is that there is in fact some identifiable part which, in so far as comparative urbanism is concerned, can be treated as a unit of study in its own right. Epstein meets this criticism by arguing that for certain purposes it may be convenient to regard a town as having its own internal structure; but that in other contexts it is essential to bear in mind that a town represents the point of intersection of a number of different activity systems (p. 101). My own feeling is that there is little point in trying to conceptualize the town or the city as a single sociological unit: the only feasible approach is to examine what Epstein calls 'activity systems' in the circumstances which are created by the size, density, heterogeneity, and division of labour of the town.

But there are, of course, new problems created by examining parts of activity systems as they operate within different urban environments, since the criteria of circumscription will almost certainly have to be expanded in comparative studies. Epstein notes, for example, that he could have pursued his study of trade unions and political organization comparatively, that is by examining its forms in other mining towns in Northern Rhodesia, in non-mining towns in Northern Rhodesia, in mining towns in neighbouring territories such as the Congo (now Zaire) or Rhodesia (now Zimbabwe), and eventually also in cities in other parts of the world. Here Epstein appreciates that his range of circumscription, adequate for his study of Luanshya, might then prove to be inadequate, for he comments:

One might well have to take into account and analyse many of the factors and variables which in Luanshya I was able to accept as given or exclude as irrelevant—such as the attitudes and policies of colonial powers, the view of social governments on urban stabilization and agricultural development, the cultural background and personalities of those making up the population of the new town and so on. (p. 102.)

Devons and Gluckman recognize that new problems of analysis are introduced when what they call 'historical and comparative studies' are embarked upon. They write:

But in dealing with complex comparative and historical problems, a different kind of judgement and evaluation is required. In our present state of knowledge at any rate, we are likely to have many apparently conflicting but equally convincing interpretations, and there is no clearly agreed way by which one can decide which is the 'right' answer. This is not to deny that studies of this kind can be made in a highly 'disciplined' way: but the issues raised are very complex and difficult . . . (p. 201.)

Devons and Gluckman, therefore, see the problem of comparative studies as rooted in the complexity and difficulty of the issues involved. My own interpretation would be that regularities in social action and relationships can be demonstrated only when the logical nexus between aspects of the social actions and the relationships is sufficiently clear to enable us to trace the effects of different circumstances. Since real historical events are always, in this primitive sense, unique, they cannot be directly comparable. In order to conduct comparative studies, therefore, sociologists and anthropologists must of necessity abstract from their data those relationships whose patterning in different circumstances or settings they wish to compare: they compare models not realities. The task of comparison is simpler if the effect of contrasting contexts is reduced, such as by comparing relationships in cities located, say, in the same phase of capitalist expansion,[8] or those located in a simple urban–rural exchange economy. But the object of comparative analysis may be subverted by this procedure: it may well be more instructive to compare relationships in cities in different settings, provided that the linkage between the setting and the patterning of relationships can be clearly stated.

From the point of view presented here, then, the difficulties in any form of comparative urbanism are obvious. The cities, to start with, are in no sense separable and isolable entities which can be 'sealed off' and treated as a 'system' for analytical purposes. Instead they are, minimally, collocations of populations geographically concentrated in order to facilitate the performance of certain tasks and provision of certain services which are necessitated by the larger social orders of which the cities are merely a part. Several activity systems, as Epstein calls them, may in fact intersect in the city, but the unit of analysis must be the activity system itself and not just the people living in the city[9] (1964: 107). Even if we designate the activity system itself as the domain of a study, for example, the organization of protest through political and trade union activities which Epstein describes, we must still confine our field to those parts of the system for which we have data adequate for our analysis. Thus Epstein finds he is able to deal with the organization of protest in Luanshya, where he is able to make direct observations and collect the information he needs in terms of the framework of his analytical schema.

    [8] I have attempted some preliminary and rather elementary comparisons of this sort in chap. 7.
    [9] The synechdochical use of 'town' and 'city', or even 'city population' to stand for sets of social relationships and activities among a population in a city or a town may at times be confusing. When Devons and Gluckman write, for example: '[Epstein] feels able justifiably to circumscribe as his field the African population of Luanshya', they are presumably using the word 'population' as a shorthand term to stand for 'the political organization of the population' and not the population in a demographic sense.

Comparison, Case Studies and Generalization

The strategy which Epstein adopted, that of choosing to analyse in depth a limited aspect of urban life in one particular town instead of comparing the manifestations of some ostensibly common phenomenon in different towns influenced by different political, administrative, legal, economic, and general social circumstances, would seem to preclude the possibility of making general statements. But there is a danger in our becoming too beguiled by trying to reproduce in comparative studies the positivistic assumptions underlying experimental procedures. The issue raised here is the question of the basis upon which we proceed to draw general conclusions from our analysis, having chosen to examine some sequence of events located in a particular city in a particular country at a particular time.

The formal basis of drawing inferences and hence of making generalizations from limited sets of data is usually expressed in terms of ensuring that the examples being examined are in some way 'representative' of the general universe from which they have been drawn. Recourse may then be had to sampling theory to estimate the range of error that any generalization from the same may have in extrapolating the findings in the sample to the parent population.

This type of inference was equated with enumerative induction by Florian Znaniecki as early as 1934 (pp. 221 ff.). He was reacting to the assumption widely made then, as now, that this was the *only* way of making generalizations from a limited set of data. Accordingly, he drew attention to an alternative procedure resting on somewhat different epistemological foundations but nevertheless still valid. This he referred to as 'analytical induction', so called because the induction was based on the validity of the analysis, not upon the representativeness of the data. The argument is that an analysis in depth of a limited set of data will enable the observer to adduce the necessary linkages among the theoretically significant features in the data and so make generalizations about the relationships among those features which are independent of their appearance in those particular data. The generality of the conclusions therefore depends not upon the 'typicality' of the data but rather upon the extent to which the analyst is able to demonstrate theoretically defensible regularities in the data at hand. (See Mitchell 1983.)

The same logic may be extended to situational analysis of the sort that Epstein conducted, where the analyst has isolated a particular sequence of events and has located them within a wider social context whose general effects the analyst specifies. If it is relevant, the actor's definition of the situation is ascertained, and the analyst then shows how the behaviour of the actors in the particular set of circumstances may be interpreted, given an understanding in theoretical terms of behaviour as constrained by both the setting and the social situation. From this point of view the selection of the situation to be analysed, as with case studies, should be made in terms of its strategic value in deepening our understanding of the theoretical relationships between the elements on the situation, rather than according to some notion of 'representativeness'.

This perspective, I think, throws light on the basis of comparative studies of urbanism. The formal experimental procedure of comparative analysis in which cases for comparison are selected by matching instances on all but a few strategic variables and comparing on those that differ is hardly applicable. It assumes that it is a *conglomeration* of disparate variables rather than a *configuration* of interconnected features which is characteristic of social situations.

With a sufficient degree of technical theoretical sophistication there need in principle be no constraint upon the extent to which the features of two towns in a comparative analysis differ. In fact, however, the task is considerably simplified in our present crude understanding of the urban social processes if at least the contextual parameters can be approximately equated.

This position, of course, is more a prolegomenon for the study of the nature of social relationships in towns and cities in general than a plan for what follows in this book. It represents a statement of the basic epistemological orientation I have adopted in trying to make sense of the data I have been able to assemble about social perception and social relationships among Africans in colonial towns. What follows is less a systematic expositions of these procedures than a number of probes into some aspects of the problem as a whole. In chapters 2 and 3 I present a statement of some of the contextual parameters which operate as constraints on the sets of social relationships which African inhabitants of Central African towns were able to built up around themselves in the colonial period. In chapters 4, 5, and 6 I handle some of the parameters operating in the social perception of the African town-dwellers at this time: the moral and ethical evaluation of town as against country life, social status as reflected in occupational prestige, and ethnicity as reflected in social distance. In chapters 7 and 8 I make some general comparisons between North American towns in the late nineteenth century and early twentieth century and South Central African towns in the 1950s, on the assumption that these towns are the product of an expansive capitalist phase. Finally I conclude with some observations about the different perspectives which some analysts have adopted in the study of towns of this sort.

2

CITIES IN A DIVIDED SOCIETY

The strategy I adopt in this study of urban social relationships, therefore, demands that the 'setting' or 'context' in which the relationships are located should first be specified, since the setting defines the framework within which these relationships must operate.

The data discussed here, mainly in chaps. 4, 5, and 6, were all located in towns which were part of a colonial social, economic, and political order. This is undoubtedly the main feature of the social context of the behaviour of people in these towns. The particular characteristic of the colonial context have been discussed in some detail by those interested in world social systems (e.g. Wallerstein 1974, 1981). These general characteristics may be conveniently adumbrated in terms of the relationships of the periphery (the colonial territories) to the core (the metropolitan countries). The basic tenets of this formulation are that the colonial territories are involved directly in asymmetrical economic, political, and social relationships with the metropolitan societies to which they are attached. The asymmetry arises out of the exploitative relationships between the metropolitan country and its peripheral satellites in terms of which the peripheral country provides a convenient market for the industrial and other products of the metropolitan country while the raw materials from the periphery are acquired by the core country at advantageous terms.

At the time when the data reported here were being collected (1950–6) the territories and the towns in them were typically peripheral in the sense that the economic activities related to cash transactions (as against subsistence activities) were directly related to the international market. The political and administrative systems and the associated pattern of social relationships were directly linked to the peripheral status of the territories concerned. In the most general sense the peripheral and colonial status of Northern and Southern Rhodesia constituted the setting in which urban behaviour of Africans living in towns had to be related.

Castells (1977: chap. 3) characterizes the setting of urban living of the type here considered as 'dependent' urbanization, in the sense that the cities were dependent as part and parcel of the social structure whose articulation 'at the economic, political and ideological level, expresses asymmetric relations with another formation that occupies, in relation to the first, a situation of power'. He goes on to define power as the situation where 'the organization of class relations in the dependent society expresses the form of social supremacy adopted by the class in power in the dominant society'. (1977: 44). Cities, in these circumstances, Castells argues, will be characterized by a growth rate in excess of the natural rate of population growth, given that the natural rate of growth in dependent countries will be high because of the relatively young age structure. The flow of migrants to the towns is a direct consequence of the penetration of the economic system of the core country, since the traditional exchange economy cannot coexist with direct exchange which is a feature of the market economy. In these circumstances, Castells argues, 'with the exception of geographically and culturally isolated regions, the whole of the productive system is reorganized according to the interests of the dominant society'. This leads to a deterioration of living conditions in rural areas and hence to migration to the cities (1977: 47).

Secondly, dependent urbanization leads to a concentration of population in a few urban areas and a consequent estrangement between these urban areas and the rest of the country. This estrangement is derived from the close link between the first urban centres and the mother country. The result is a lack of balance between rural and urban economies leading to migration to the towns which is reflected, as Castells puts it, 'in an attempt to find a viable life in a more diversified milieu, rather than unbalanced nature of urban migration in colonial societies'. (1977: 48.)

These features of the migratory flow led to a third characteristic of colonial towns, which I feel applied only partially to those in South Central Africa at the time when the observations reported here were made. This is that the towns have juxtaposed with the primary urban population an increasing mass of unemployed who have no precise function in urban society, but who have broken their links with rural society. Since the migration towards the towns is the product of the breakdown of the rural structures, it is normal that it should not be absorbed by the productive urban system and that consequently the migrants are integrated only very partially into the social system (1977: 48).

These very general formulations of the wider settings of colonial towns provide a background against which the specific features of South Central African towns may be considered.

They were set up in the first instance by European colonists as centres of economic and imperial expansion. Balandier quotes Dresch, who characterized the situation as: 'They are towns built by Whites and occupied by Blacks' (Balandier 1956: 497). From the very first establishment of the towns, therefore, a pattern was imposed on their inhabitants by their colonial founders. The level of technological and economic development of the people of Central Africa to the end of the nineteenth century did not call for large concentrations of population. We have no exact demographic information concerning the size of settlements up to that time: Travellers occasionally commented on the size of large villages, especially those which were the capitals of chiefs and rulers, but the evidence seems to be that these were seldom more than three or four thousand strong, if they were even of that size. Furthermore, they were based essentially on a near subsistence type of economy, in the sense that while there was undoubtedly a considerable cadre of court officials and dignitaries who did not produce their own food, the majority of the population was directly concerned with producing the items they consumed.

Large towns and cities arose essentially as a result of colonial enterprise. The details of how the centres that exist today came into being need not concern us at present. What is relevant to the discussion of the relationship between the larger social system and the cities that form part of it is the fact that the early European administrators, traders, and miners established urban centres from which they were able to conduct their activities. These Europeans were themselves members of an industrial and commercial urban society based on an economic and administrative system which was in effect centred in Great Britain and South Africa. The towns and villages they set up in the middle of Central Africa at the end of the nineteenth century were merely outliers of this alien political and economic system.

The African populations, on the other hand, were still effectively involved in the local political and social system, which had probably been in existence for centuries before the arrival of the white intruders. The economy was essentially a subsistence one based largely on agriculture finely attuned to the climatic and environmental circumstances. Requirements in weapons, implements, clothing, housing, medicine, and all the other services which are necessary for day to day existence were produced locally or at most obtained by barter from neighbouring peoples.

Sooner or later, however, the African population became involved in the urban economy as well. The process by which this took place has no direct bearing on the argument. There is some evidence that Ndebele men were migrating as far south as the diamond fields in the Cape and the gold-mines on the Witwatersrand several years before the first European settlements were established in Central Africa. There is also evidence that the enterprises the Europeans wished to establish depended directly on cheap African labour, and pressures of various kinds, some subtle, some not so subtle, were put on African men to take up wage-earning employment (Gann 1958: 76 ff.). Most of this labour in the first instance, and indeed until fairly recent times, was used by European farmers and not in the towns. But the implication of the economic diversification, given the market economy in which the European farmers were involved, was that there would be towns and urban centres which could provide the legal, medical and administrative as well as the financial and commercial services upon which their activities relied. So the employment of Africans in the rural areas implied the employment of yet other Africans in the towns.

This was less characteristic of economies based on mining, such as in Zambia. Here the converse was more nearly true. The demand for primary consumer goods stimulated market-orientated agriculture in the rural areas. This type of farming, significantly, was prosecuted particularly by European farmers using paid African labour rather than by Africans themselves. So the growth of considerable populations in mining areas stimulated the growth of rural wage-employment on food producing farms rather than economic development in African occupied rural areas.

But the fact that the market-orientated farming which developed in response to the demands created by the towns was developed by Europeans is of crucial importance to the question of the relationship of towns to the larger society in which they were located. As Barber put it,

With but a few qualifications, the present urban areas may be regarded as the spearheads of the monetized exchange economy introduced and organized by the Europeans. In the 'dual structure' of economic life in this part of the continent—in which a monetized and highly organized set of economic institutions co-exist with traditional indigenous forms of economic organization—urban concentrations have always played a strategic role. They have provided the channel through which commercial contacts with the outside world have been maintained as well as the facilities required for the conduct of monetized exchange and of orderly administration at home. (1967: 96.)

The sociological equivalent of this state of affairs is expressed in the notion of the divided society, in which identifiable segments of the national community pursue their lives with a minimum of interaction or mutual accommodation. In the colonial Central African situation this implied that Europeans (and Indians and persons of mixed racial parentage as well) pursued their daily lives almost oblivious of the existence of Africans, except when they impinged directly upon their lives, as for example, servants, customers, or commercial rivals. This, of course, is a familiar situation in social systems which are organized primarily on the basis of racial differentiation. The implication of this type of organization in Central African societies is that the towns themselves reflected this disparity. Both Africans and Europeans came to look upon towns primarily as 'European' creations drawing their form and organization from an alien source and expressing the eidos and ethos of a social system which had its roots in the metropolitan country of origin of the European colonists.

There is, however, a danger in pushing this argument too far. In saying that both Europeans and Africans in Central Africa came to look upon the towns primarily as 'European' creations we are referring to the perceptions, or, more accurately from a sociological point of view, the collective representations of particular categories of persons. These collective representations were part of the value framework of the people involved and the values served to structure, to some degree at least, the expectations of behaviour of people as townsmen. But in reality, as I have argued, there are several different levels of analysis which we can apply to the study of behaviour in towns of which the perceptual is only one. The social institutions in terms of which Europeans ordered their lives in towns in Central Africa derived to a large extent from the social systems out of which they had come and which, with some modifications, they had brought with them to Central Africa. These social systems, deriving in the main from Great Britain and South Africa, subsumed towns in the sense that categories of appropriate behaviour for townsmen and the institutional structure relating to this behaviour had grown up and developed within them. For Africans, the towns represented alien creations, and the social institutions to which they had been accustomed in the rural areas had little salience for the cultural and physical circumstances in the towns. Instead, the set of economic, administrative, physical and demographic circumstances created in the towns set the framework within which social actions among Africans and between Africans and other racial categories had to take place. Under these conditions customary procedures for some purposes continued relatively unaffected by alien social circumstances, such as, for example, the intimate relationships of husband and wife, or behaviour related to mystical beliefs. Other customary procedures were adapted and adjusted so that they could operate in the towns, while other procedures, unprecedented in the traditional life of the Africans, came into being to meet the peculiar circumstances in towns. The disparity between rural and urban life therefore, was not absolute. Instead, the social behaviour in towns represented reactions to the specified framework set by the administrative, economic, physical, and demographic circumstances. Some of these reactions bore close similarities to rural procedures, some appeared to be urban transformations of rural procedures, and some appeared to be unrepresented in rural areas.

The Extent of Urbanization in South Central Africa

A reasonable starting point in the analysis of social relationships in towns is the extent to which the population of a country or region as a whole is in fact living in towns. Conventionally this is

Table 2.1 *Racial Composition of Settlements in South Central Africa*

Type settlement	Africans	Europeans	Asians	Others	Total
Malawi (September 1966)					
Blantyre	101,711	3,297	4,398	389	109,795
Zomba	18,013	939	640	24	19,616
Lilogwe	18,011	361	746	58	19,176
Other centres	176,713	2,272	4,732	302	184,019
Rural areas	3,708,745	177	364	520	3,709,806
Totals	4,023,193	7,046	10,880	1,293	4,042,412
Southern Rhodesia (May 1962)					
Salisbury	215,819	92,266	2,690	3,426	314,192
Bulawayo	154,830	51,218	2,288	3,608	211,944
Umtali	32,770	8,319	537	293	41,919
Gwelo	29,270	8,981	287	335	38,873
Wankie	18,140	2,123	1	2	20,266
Other centres	202,140	28,787	1,239	1,102	233,268
Rural areas	2,963,610	34,450	488	2,418	3,000,966
Totals	3,616,570	226,144	7,530	11,184	3,861,428
Northern Rhodesia (June 1963)					
Lusaka	100,260	12,684	1,964	421	115,329
Kitwe	101,570	13,481	64	97	115,212
Ndola	76,800	9,961	1,980	756	89,497
Mufulira	69,310	7,105	188	—	76,603
Luanshya	66,160	5,014	684	—	71,858
Chingola	50,690	5,869	120	32	56,711
Broken Hill	40,570	5,150	612	72	46,404
Livingstone	28,840	3,811	668	95	33,414
Bancroft	27,770	2,608	—	—	30,378
Other centres	105,570	5,387	1,982	208	113,147
Rural areas	2,741,000	6,910	678	622	2,749,210
Totals	3,408,540	77,980	8,940	2,303	3,497,763

The totals for Europeans, Asians, and other races in S. Rhodesia and N. Rhodesia for the settlements listed in this table have been extrapolated from the 1961 census figures on the trend shown between 1956 and 1961. Proportional estimation was used to allocate populations into rural areas and other settlements where these were not separately enumerated in 1956 in Rhodesia. The figures of 64 and 188 Asians estimated to be in Kitwe and Mufulira respectively are twice the numbers enumerated in 1961. There were no Asians enumerated in these towns in 1956. Because the trend for each type of settlement was extrapolated separately, the population totals for S. Rhodesia and N. Rhodesia differ slightly from that estimated by the statistical services in these two territories.

Table 2.2 *Degree of Urbanization: South Central African Territories in comparison with other African Countries*

	Per cent in towns 100,000 or more	Per cent in towns 20,000 or more
Northern Rhodesia	—	19.0
Southern Rhodesia	11.5	16.3
Nyasaland	—	2.6
South Africa	26.5	44.9
Tanganyika	1.6	4.7
Uganda	2.0	3.8
Kenya	5.3	7.4
Mozambique	2.7	3.6
Angola	4.7	8.2
Ghana	12.2	23.1
Nigeria	5.3	16.7

Source: Davis (1969 Table C).

measured by the proportions of persons enumerated in towns above a certain size, the size of the towns for this purpose being arbitrary. Table 2.1 sets out the composition by races of the estimated populations of towns in 1962–6, that is shortly after the observations reported here were made.

Table 2.2 sets out the comparison of the degree of urbanization, as measured by the proportion of the population in cities of 100,000 or more or in towns of 20,000 or more in Central Africa with some other African countries in 1960.

In comparison with many other countries in the world Zambia, Malawi, and Zimbabwe were not very highly urbanized, but in comparison with sub-Saharan territories it is clear that apart from South Africa they have a relatively large proportion of the population living in sizeable towns.

There are difficulties, however, in construing these proportions as they stand as representing the 'degree of urbanization', because of the way in which the word 'urbanization' is commonly used. Some of these points, which are substantial issues in the discussion of urbanization and urbanism in an African context will be discussed later. At this point the primary consideration is to discuss the relationship between the degree of urbanization in general and the level of economic activity as a whole. This has formed the topic of extensive study, particularly by Kingsley Davis and his colleagues, who have explored the unexpectedly complex relationship between the proportion of persons living in towns of a given size and the proportion of persons gainfully employed in non-agricultural activities. Since non-agricultural activities tend as a rule to be concentrated in towns and cities, the relationship at first sight would seem to be trivial. But Davis and his associates show that the relationship is not in fact linear and that the increase in the proportion of persons living in towns tends to vary at different phases of its history. Initially, when the first towns are established, the proportion of the population living in those towns tends to rise only slowly. It then tends to increase more rapidly as urbanization proceeds. Later, when the proportion living in towns becomes substantial, the rate of growth tends to decrease again. Thus, when the rural pool from which the towns are able to recruit population for any growth which is larger than that provided by the natural increase of their own populations, becomes small in relation to the population needed to maintain the rate of increase, the rate of expansion of the urban population diminishes (Davis and Golden 1957). Trends in the rate of growth of towns, however, depend on more than simply a numerical rule: the economic basis of the expansion of the towns and the exchange relationship of the towns with their rural hinterland obviously plays a vital role. Australia, for example, could maintain in 1960 a proportion of 81 per cent of its population in settlements of over 20,000 largely because of a highly efficient mechanized agricultural technology. Britain, on the other hand, could in the same year maintain 78.3 per cent of its population in settlements of 20,000 and over largely because it was a manufacturing country and relied on trading relationships with other countries to supply the majority of its foodstuffs.

In South Central Africa towns were established from the very first settlement of the Europeans mainly because the sort of commercial and administrative system which the Europeans introduced relied upon a close integration of activities at urban nodes of transaction. Present-day Blantyre in Malawi was established as an administrative, missionary, and trading centre in 1878 and grew slowly to accommodate the increase in activities following an expansion of economic activities and administration. Zomba in Malawi was established as an administrative centre and grew rather more slowly. Limbe was established within a few miles of Blantyre mainly as a commercial centre

and was amalgamated with Blantyre into a single city administration in 1962. Salisbury in Rhodesia was established as the
headquarters of the Pioneers in 1890 primarily as a fortified
centre. It became, willy-nilly, an administrative and trading
centre. Bulawayo in Rhodesia was established on the site of the
vanquished Ndebele king's court in 1898, and as the junction for
traffic flowing from South Africa into both Rhodesia and
Zambia became the main commercial and industrial centre.
Bulawayo was a larger urban centre than Salisbury until the
later 1930s, when the administrative importance of Salisbury
began to overtake that of Bulawayo. Ndola in Northern
Rhodesia was established mainly as an administrative centre in
1902 but started to grow primarily as a result of the expansion of
trading activities following the mining of copper at Bwana
Mukubwa near Ndola in the early part of the twentieth century.
Broken Hill (now Kabwe) in Northern Rhodesia had been established as a mining centre in the years before the First World
War, but grew substantially when the railway line reached it in
1906. Livingstone was established near the site of the Victoria
falls at a port of entry to Zambia in 1904, and continued to
develop in the earlier years of the century. Later, when the
economic and administrative centre of gravity moved further
northwards, it declined in relative significance. The most rapid
centres of growth have been the Northern Rhodesian copper-
mining towns of Kitwe, Luanshya, Mufulura, Chingola, and
Bancroft. The large sulphide ore deposits were discovered in the
early twenties, but exploitation of them commenced only in
1927. The growth of these urban settlements to their size of
today has taken place within the relatively short period of forty
years. Similarly, Lusaka was established as a Village Management Board on the railway in 1913, but remained a small siding
until it was chosen by an administrative decision in 1935 as the
site for the new capital of the country (Kay 1967: 109–18) The
growth to its present size has taken place within thirty-five years.
Unfortunately, because of the incomplete censuses of African
populations in the past it is not possible to gauge the growth of
towns in Central Africa over the last forty years. Estimates have
been made from time to time though these are usually unreliable. Counts have been made of the number of African male and
female adults and juveniles, who were employed by Europeans

or Asians in towns in Southern Rhodesia since 1931 and in Northern Rhodesia since 1946. Table 2.3 sets out the data for Southern Rhodesia between 1911 and 1961. The rate of growth of employment in the towns understates rather than overstates the growth of the total populations of the towns. This is because in the earlier history of the territories Africans did not as a rule bring their wives and families with them to the towns, while older men and women tended to return to their rural homes more readily than they do now. The number of dependants per adult working man, therefore, has probably been increasing in the recent years. This can be demonstrated from surveys which have been done at successive intervals in particular towns. In Lusaka, for instance, social surveys were conducted in 1954 and 1957. There was also a demographic survey of Lusaka in 1959 and a full census enumeration in 1963. The ratio of total African population to African males aged 15–50, that is effectively the employed adult male population discounting the small proportion of unemployed, was 2.35 in 1954; in 1957 it was 2.72, in 1960 3.11, and in 1963 it was 3.51.

Thus by applying these ratios to the number of African adult males enumerated as employed in the line-of-rail towns in Zambia in 1951, 1956, and 1961, we may conclude that the African population of these towns was growing at a geometric rate, 3.31 per cent per annum between 1956 and 1961. In the period 1956 to 1961 the number of African adult males actually fell from an estimated 132,500 to 124,750, but the rise in the number of dependants means that the total population nevertheless increased during that period.[1] However these figures may be interpreted, the fact is that the town population must presumably have been growing at a rate which was faster than the increase in employment of males.

This growth has in the main been due to the economic expansion of colonial countries following the Second World War. In Zambia this turned on the rise in the price of copper and to a

[1] The rate of growth changes fairly rapidly in response to economic conditions. For example, the boom period of urban growth between 1945 and 1962/3 was between 1950 and 1955. When economic insecurities accompanied the political changes just prior to and succeeding the breakup of the Federation, the rate dropped considerably. From impressions it has regained its rate of growth in Zambia, is continuing slowly but steadily in Malawi, but it is not possible to say what has been happening in Rhodesia since the declaration of independence.

Table 2.3 *European, Asian, and Eurafrican population and Number of Africans in Employment in Salisbury, Bulawayo, Umtali, Gwelo, and Que Que 1911–61*

	1911	1921	1926	1931	1936	1941	1946	1951	1956	1961
Europeans	10,409	15,046	17,790	25,613	28,210	40,746	44,769	85,182	117,985	159,607
Asians	n.a.	n.a.	n.a.	1,184	1,600	1,937	2,268	3,499	4,161	5,804
Eurafricans	n.a.	n.a.	n.a.	1,154	1,683	2,199	2,237	3,422	4,895	7,419
African males in employment	n.a.	n.a.	n.a.	38,684	43,305	65,206	94,929	153,232	191,232	202,157
Estimated maximum African population[a]	n.a.	n.a.	n.a.	79,000	93,000	137,000	196,000	320,000	388,000	447,000
Per cent of population										
Europeans	44.1	44.8	45.5	51.3	50.9	59.1	54.3	62.8	66.6	72.1
Asians	n.a.	n.a.	n.a.	69.7	73.4	76.1	77.9	81.5	81.2	80.0
Eurafricans	n.a.	n.a.	n.a.	48.0	52.8	55.3	49.1	58.4	60.6	70.3
Africans	n.a.	n.a.	n.a.	7.0	7.0	9.3	10.5	13.8	12.2	11.9

[a] Obtained by raising number of persons per 100 African males employed in each category of worker according to place of origin as derived in the 1962 Census of Africans. The ratios per 100 males employed were Southern Rhodesia, 273; Northern Rhodesia, 163; Nyasaland, 132; Mozambique, 134; others, 179.

Source: census reports for years mentioned.

lesser extent lead and zinc, leading to an increased investment of capital in the mining enterprises on the Copperbelt and at Broken Hill. The buoyancy in the economy which accompanied this expansion led to developments in services and in trading in general, leading to secondary urban growth, particularly at Ndola, which has remained to some extent the commercial and administrative centre of the Copperbelt, and at Lusaka, where the seat of government was placed. In Southern Rhodesia the economy was more diversified but the main source of prosperity was tobacco, so that the major expansion in employment was not in the towns but in the rural areas in European farming areas. Mining was scattered in several centres, the largest and most important being the coal-mining centre at Wankie. As a consequence of the general buoyancy of the economy in the middle fifties several manufacturing enterprises were established, so that in Bulawayo and Salisbury in particular, but also to a lesser extent in Umtali and Gwelo, employment opportunities for Africans increased in this sector.[2] In Malawi the economic basis of the growth appears to have been the plantation economy of tea and tobacco.

In a simple way, then, economic conditions seem to set the basic conditions for the growth of the towns.[3] But people react to economic incentives in different ways. A sociological analysis seeks regularities in the way in which people perceive the relative advantages to them of different alternatives and react according to the position they occupy in the overall set of social relationships. One of the points that emerges immediately from the South Central African data is that there is really very little point in observing that a certain percentage of the total population was living in towns of a specified size at a certain census date. If we are interested primarily in the behaviour of categories of persons

[2] A brief outline of the growth of African employment in Southern Rhodesia is to be found in Mitchell 1961.

[3] This is not always directly true. Towns in Latin America, for example, appear to be growing very fast though there does not seem to be a very strong incentive for their growth from the economic point of view. Migrants to the towns appear to be fleeing from rural poverty rather than chasing employment opportunities in towns. It could be argued that the basic causes are still economic but this circumstance seems different from that in Central Africa where the rural homes thus far seem to have provided a reservoir into and out of which labour could flow in response to demand in the towns, mining areas, or European farming areas.

Table 2.4 *Proportions of Persons of Different Races Resident in Settlements of 20,000 or more 1961*

	Africans	Europeans	Asians	Others	Whole population
Nyasaland	3.4	65.2	53.2	36.4	3.7
Southern Rhodesia	12.5	72.0	77.1	68.5	16.2
Northern Rhodesia	16.5	84.2	70.2	64.0	18.2

Calculated from Table 2.1.

this general statement obscures most of the salient divisions in the population relevant to town residence. This could not be more clearly demonstrated than by considering the proportions of persons of different racial origin living in Central African towns. Conventionally the census has distinguished Europeans, Africans, Indians, and others as racial categories sufficiently significant socially to be separately enumerated. By reason of the different involvement of these racial groups in the social, political, and economic system as a whole we would anticipate that there might be differences in the extent to which they lived in towns or rural areas. Table 2.4 sets out the proportion of persons of the different races resident in towns of 20,000 or more around 1961. The striking difference in the concentration of non-Africans in cities and towns as against African populations is clearly shown by this table. The overall level of urbanization is influenced heavily by the number of Africans living in towns, since they are the largest racial category in the population. In Zambia no less than 84.2 per cent of the Europeans lived in towns of more than 20,000, with 72.0 per cent in Rhodesia and 65.2 per cent in Malawi. These figures reflect the particular spheres of economic involvement of the Europeans. In Zambia they were concentrated in the mining towns or in the commercial and administrative centres such as Ndola or Lusaka. The economic activities in which they were engaged were centred particularly on the urban-based economy, which was linked to international trade. Many of them would have been recruited particularly to perform those tasks for which suitably trained Africans were either not available or from which by convention they had in the past been excluded. These were the managerial and skilled tasks linked very closely with the economic and administrative activities usually concentrated in the towns.

Asians were very heavily concentrated in commerce. Forty-nine per cent of those enumerated in the 1961 census in Rhodesia were classified as 'salesworkers', but an additional 18 per cent were classified as administrative, executive, and managerial workers. These, however, were very strongly concentrated in the wholesale and retail trade, and the clerical workers were very likely to be employed in the business of other Asians. A smaller proportion were classified as craftsmen, as motor repairmen, building workers, welders, etc. These occupations were heavily tied to economic activities which took place in towns and partly explain the urban concentration of Asians in Rhodesia and Zambia.

The 'other races' separately enumerated in the censuses were predominantly Eurafricans, that is, persons of mixed racial parentage. They found employment largely in skilled occupations such as motor mechanics or similar occupations. No less than 61 per cent in Rhodesia and 70 per cent in Zambia were returned in the 1961 census as 'craftsmen, production-process workers and labourers not elsewhere classified', large concentrations being motor repairmen, operators of earth-moving equipment, bricklayers, plasterers and other building workers. A high proportion were also returned as drivers. As with the occupations followed by Asians, these occupations are linked particularly to urban economic enterprises, and similarly this fact partly explains the concentration of Eurafricans in towns rather than in rural areas.

The relationship of racial origin to concentration in urban areas in Central Africa may be examined in more detail by considering the proportions in settlements of different sizes. Table 2.5, which sets out the proportion of numbers of different races in settlements of different sizes of the population that would be expected in those settlements if the population were distributed throughout the territories entirely at random, makes some of the finer points apparent. It is designed to bring out the differences in the concentration of people of different races in settlements of different kinds.

In all three territories the trend of concentration of Africans in the rural areas against the towns is clearly shown, which is another way of saying that non-Africans were concentrated particularly in the non-rural areas. The numerical size of the

Table 2.5 *Index of Representation for Races in Settlements in South Central Africa 1961*

	African	European	Asian	Other
Nyasaland				
Cities	93.1	1722.8	1488.3	1107.7
Towns	93.3	1922.7	1327.5	660.9
Other centres	96.5	708.3	955.4	513.1
Rural areas	100.5	2.7	3.7	43.8
Southern Rhodesia				
Cities	75.2	465.7	485.2	461.6
Towns	84.7	328.2	418.6	215.2
Other centres	92.5	210.7	272.4	163.1
Rural areas	105.4	19.6	8.3	27.8
Northern Rhodesia				
Cities	89.8	509.1	344.2	341.3
Towns	91.3	437.8	411.1	358.3
Other centres	95.8	213.6	685.4	279.2
Rural areas	102.3	11.3	9.7	34.6

The index of representation compares the actual number of persons of a given race in a type of settlement with the number one would expect in that town if the races were distributed in the different settlements purely at random. An index of 100 indicated that the number observed is the same as to be expected on a random distribution, an index of less than 100 that there are fewer than may have been expected on a random distribution and an index of over 100 that there are more than would have been expected on random distribution.

Cities are here defined as settlements with 100,000 population or more, towns as settlements with populations of between 20,000 and 10,000, and other settlements as settlements of less than 20,000 but not farms or villages in African rural areas. In the case of Malawi the two towns Zomba and Lilongwe, though technically too small to qualify as towns by this definition, have nevertheless been counted as towns for the purposes of this table.

index is affected considerably by the relative size of the populations concerned, so that in Malawi, where there are 4.7 non-Africans per 1,000 Africans, the difference between the index for cities against rural areas is small while the corresponding differences for the non-Africans is large. In Zambia, where there were 26.2 non-Africans for every 1,000 Africans, the trend in the index for Africans is steeper and for the non-Africans less so. In Rhodesia, where there were 67.7 non-Africans per 1,000 Africans, the trend between rural areas and cities was steepest for Africans and that for non-Africans least so. In general the trend for the index for settlements of different sizes is regular: non-Africans on the whole tend to live in towns and the larger the town the greater the concentration of non-Africans in it as against the rural areas and smaller settlements.

There are some interesting reversals of this trend, the explanation of which lends support to the interpretation of the concentration of the races in towns and rural areas in terms of their involvements in the larger social order. The index of representation for Europeans in towns in Malawi (i.e. settlements of 20–100,000) is higher than in cities (i.e. settlements of more than 100,000), which contradicts the trend for Europeans in the other two territories. The explanation is that Zomba is the administrative centre of Malawi and has concentrated in it a large number of European civil servants. The index of representation for Europeans in Zomba is thus 2746.3 as against 1080.1 for Lilongwe. Were it not that Zomba is a special case the trend for the concentration of Europeans in the towns of different sizes would be maintained in Malawi as well as Rhodesia and Zambia.

The other striking reversal of this generality was the distribution of Asians in the towns of various sizes in Zambia. In contrast to the situation in Malawi and Rhodesia, the Asians in Zambia appear to have been concentrated more in the smaller towns and rural centres than in the larger towns. Special circumstances operated here as well. For many years Kitwe, Mufulira, and Chingola were 'closed' to Asians, in that by regulation they were not allowed to set up businesses in these towns. This meant that Asians were concentrated particularly in Lusaka, Ndola, Livingstone, and Broken Hill, or alternatively in the small rural centres where they set up as retailers. This is reflected in the indexes of representation for Asians in Ndola of 865.6, Livingstone 782.2, Lusaka 666.3, Broken Hill 516.0, and Luanshya of 372.4. On the other hand, Chingola has an index of 82.8 while Kitwe and Mufulira have only had Asians in the towns since 1956 and Bancroft still did not have any in 1961.

These rudimentary demographic data reflect in a striking way the different involvements that persons of different races had in economic activities and their general social alignment in the territories concerned. In general the Europeans established the administrative, commercial, and industrial framework of which the towns were a part. Not surprisingly the occupations related to the pursuit of these activities were concentrated largely in the towns, and accordingly the Europeans lived in the towns. Asians involved in mainly trading activities were also concentrated in the towns, and where they were not traders they were employed as skilled and semi-skilled or service workers within the industrial and commercial complexes of the towns. Persons of mixed racial descent, where they were enumerated as such, were likely to be skilled workers and sometimes clerical workers, as before, tied to the town-based industrial and commercial concerns that employed them. In sharp contrast the Africans were mainly subsistence cultivators, the largest proportion subsisting upon the products of their own agricultural efforts in the rural areas. Only a small proportion had migrated to the towns in search of employment and some of those who had done so, had left their immediate dependants behind them in the rural areas out of which they had moved. Their involvement in the life of the towns was qualitatively different from that of the Europeans, Asians, and other races, so that blanket figures of proportions of population living in the towns tend to obscure important sociological facts with which we should be concerned.

In summary, then, the different distributions of Africans, Europeans, Asians, and Eurafricans in the cities, towns, and rural areas of these territories indicated the fundamentally dissimilar involvements of each in the overall social, economic, and political life of the territories. The cities and towns were derivatives of a specific type of social, administrative, and economic order which in turn incorporated the racial groups within it in different ways. The differential distribution of the racial groups between town and country, therefore, was merely an aspect of this order reflected perhaps more sharply in the administrative arrangements in terms of which city affairs were managed.

The Administrative Context

Towns were established, as we have noted earlier, in the first instance as small enclaves of Whites who were providing the basic services required to establish a rudimentary administrative and commercial system in countries where the vast majority of the inhabitants were formerly involved in social relationships connected with autonomous political systems and self-sufficient economic production. The Whites tended in the main to be people who had originated or at least had experience in South

Africa before moving up to South Central Africa. This was less true of Malawi than of Rhodesia or Zambia, but even there, while the upper-level officials may have been British, the lower-level officials were frequently of South African origin. Those who were of British origin were in any case operating within the framework of an imperialistic ideology which in its translation into action did not differ substantially from that of the South Africans (Gann 1958: 169).

From the earliest establishment of settlements which were later to become towns, therefore, the Whites set down laws and regulations which had as their object, among other things, control over the residence of Africans in these areas. Many of these, like the Municipal Regulations of 1897 in Rhodesia, were based directly upon South African models. They were intended to provide for the control of health and hygiene in the settlements and through this housing. In Northern Rhodesia regulations were passed in 1914 to control residence and the sale of beer in towns, specifically Livingstone, which was in fact one of the first townships to be established there (Gann 1958: 161). The consequence of this was that the right of Africans to residence in the towns became dependent upon their status as employees in those towns. The basic philosophy underlying these regulations seems to have been that the permanent and real home of the Africans was in the rural areas from which they had come and that their stay in the town was temporary. Gray (1960: 107) describes the situation during the middle thirties in Rhodesia thus:

The 1930 Land Appointment Act deprived Africans of the chance of obtaining permanent rights in the European areas, and thereafter it was taken as axiomatic that the towns should be regarded as white areas . . . The African was permitted to visit the towns only under stringent control and his temporary residence was made conditional on his being in full-time employment.

But as the number of African employees increased two separate trends in housing developed. On the one hand the employers of substantial numbers of African workers themselves undertook to provide housing for their workers. This was the pattern particularly for the mining companies, the railways, and some large industrial concerns. But the majority of the employers, many of them private individuals, small shopkeepers, or commercial concerns employing only a handful of workers could not afford to undertake this responsibility. Municipal councils therefore undertook the responsibility for them, as it were by proxy. The municipalities invested considerable capital in building large numbers of standard houses which were in effect rented to employers for their African workers. Right up until the Second World War the control and administration of African housing areas was placed under the Medical Officer of Health, reflecting the origin of the procedure. But the matter had become such a large undertaking by the end of the 1930s that separate departments were established in the municipalities to handle the many matters that arose out of the residence of African workers in municipal areas. This was in the main, of course, rent collecting, allocation to the control of residents in the various types of accommodation, and the provision of basic services such as sanitation, water supplies, and garbage disposal. Later the municipalities began to supply beer-hall facilities, recreation facilities, welfare and health services, and procedures for the settlement of disputes. In Salisbury, in Rhodesia, the central government also entered the field of urban administration when it undertook to supply accommodation on the outskirts of Salisbury for a large number of African workers in housing which they would rent on a long-term lease. For this purpose the Department of Native Affairs set up a section for the administration of Highfields Township which duplicated almost entirely the services which the municipality was supplying in its own townships. In Bulawayo similar facilities were provided within the administrative structure of the municipality.

Developments within housing provided by industrial employees took a parallel course. Here the pattern of the South African 'Compound Manager' system was reproduced. The Compound Manager was an official of the industrial company who was charged with responsibility for all matters arising in connection with African employees except for specific on-the-job problems. He was concerned, therefore, with housing, health, welfare, recreation, and usually with recruitment as well. In time, when many thousands of employees were housed on company property, as soon became the case, a considerable administrative structure was set up to handle these matters.

Housing and other facilities were provided in cities by the municipalities or by industrial concerns for Africans primarily in their status as employees. The security of tenure of accommodation for an African in any of these townships therefore depended directly upon their security of employment. It is true that in time some leeway was allowed for those who lost their jobs, so that provided the rent was paid they could stay for a limited period. Others could be registered as self-employed, mainly as hawkers, and traders or petty craftsmen such as tailors or shoe-repairers were allowed to occupy housing in their own right. But these were small in number: the vast majority were entitled to housing by virtue of their employee status only.[4]

The administrative and political control of the towns, therefore, was firmly vested in the hands of the White residents. The mining towns of Zambia were legally constituted as local authorities separate from the commercial towns already there, so that the control over affairs in both African and White residential areas rested with the company management, which until recently was overwhelmingly White. In those townships, which were not located on private property as were the mine townships, elective town councils constituted the local authorities.[5] Municipal voting rights, however, which turned on the ownership or rental of property for which rates were payable, because of the operation of laws controlling African ownership of property in towns usually precluded Africans from registering on the municipal voters' roll. The interests of African residents in towns were thus represented to town councils primarily through a variety of advisory boards and committees chaired by

---

[4] Several schemes for a more permanent type of housing in urban areas were introduced from time to time. In Broken Hill a scheme was initiated in the late 1930s which allowed Africans to rent five acres of land near the town and to put their own houses on them. On the Copperbelt a series of 'townships' on the peripheries of the mining towns and Ndola were established which were intended for Africans who wished to acquire their own property in an urban area. In Southern Rhodesia schemes were initiated in Salisbury and Bulawayo for thirty-three year leases which would allow Africans to purchase houses in urban areas.

[5] The structure of city government differed in detail in the three territories. In Northern Rhodesia and Nyasaland before independence, the Urban District Commissioner ex-officio had a seat on the town councils. In Southern Rhodesia central government was not involved so directly with local government. These details, however, do not affect the main point of the present argument, that is that Africans had no effective voice in determining their conditions of living in the cities.

a municipal official. The essentially advisory character of these boards meant that they evoked little enthusiasm from the African residents. The major political movements among Africans have usually arisen in towns, probably because they could be organized in the densely populated townships much more effectively than in the rural areas. But in addition the clear-cut separation between the richer, socially separate, and politically dominant Whites and the impoverished and politically emasculated Africans was much more blatant, and in the towns there were concentrated the educated and more articulate workers who not only felt the separation acutely but possessed the requisite skills for organizing and directing political movements (Epstein 1958, van Velsen 1964).

The role of central government in the cities, apart from the general supervision of local government through the control of finance, was confined in the main to the maintenance of law and order and to the administration of justice.[6] The settlement of disputes in towns has presented knotty problems to city administrators in this part of Africa. In Northern Rhodesia a large number of domestic and personal cases were handled by informal courts presided over by Tribal Elders who had quasi-official standing in local authorities and mining administration. There was, however, no equivalent in Southern Rhodesia. In addition, in Northern Rhodesia a unique dual system of courts developed. The official magistrates' court controlled and administered by the central government concerned itself with statutory and criminal cases involving Africans and dealt with cases brought to it through the police force. Parallel with this court an Urban Court presided over by a bench composed of Court Assessors versed in 'customary law' handled the civil and domestic cases that arose in the day to day social relationships in town and which could not be settled informally by Tribal Elders.[7] In Southern Rhodesia, however, where there was no equivalent to the Urban Courts, cases of this sort which ran to ligitation had to be handled in the Native Commissioner's court, which was in fact a magistrate's court. A certain proportion of

---

[6] In Southern Rhodesia the central government took an active role in the provision of housing: see earlier in this chapter.

[7] Epstein (1953, 1954) discusses the constitution and operation of these courts in detail.

domestic and civil cases were handled informally by the Location Superintendents or the officials of the Department of African Administration of the Municipalities.

Africans' relationships with their employers were also mediated through central government agencies. In Northern Rhodesia, Labour Officers were officially charged with the responsibility of overseeing the organization of trade unions, of administering the laws relating to labour conditions, and in general handling complaints of African employees about wages and labour conditions and mediating between African employees and their employers. In Southern Rhodesia these duties devolved upon the staff of the Native Commissioner and no specialist labour officers were employed.

The responsibility for physical living conditions in general rested with the local authorities, whether they were mining companies or city councils. This responsibility was imposed upon the local authorities by legislation of different kinds in the three territories. In Southern Rhodesia it arose essentially out of the Land Apportionment Act of 1926, in which ownership of property by Africans in what was designated as 'European' land was strictly controlled. No suburb of African-owned residences could thus arise. Accommodation for African workers was instead the responsibility of their employers. While the number of African employees was small and their expectations about standard of living low, *ad hoc* arrangements in squalid temporary shelters were common. With the increase in the urban populations however, additional measures were needed. Arrangements for large-scale housing of Africans thus became responsibility of the local authorities.

When large industrial concerns or municipal councils set about establishing townships to house African employees they followed the pattern which was current in South Africa. Here Africans were residentially segregated in 'locations' or 'compounds' while Europeans, Asians, and Eurafricans lived in suburbs—usually separate suburbs for each racial group—in other parts of the town. The ecological layout of the towns in Central Africa, therefore, was overwhelmingly determined by legislation or at least by racial separation. Africans lived in specific areas provided by local authorities or large-scale employers for the purpose. Within these areas houses were allocated by administrative procedures, ostensibly on impartial criteria such as the number of children in the family or the social standing of the applicant. The opportunity for an individual to select where he wanted to live, therefore, was limited to one or two specific circumstances. One of these was that if the African worker was in town without a wife or family he could live in 'single quarters'. This frequently meant that four, five, or as many as twelve men could live in a single room. Here there seems to have been an opportunity for men to choose which room they went to, for it was usual in the mining townships in the fifties, for example, for most of the men in a room to come from one ethnic group and sometimes even from the same district of origin.[8] Another circumstance where the freedom of choice of residence was open to Africans in some of the townships was where 'unauthorized' settlements had come into being. The striking example of this was in Lusaka, where several plots of land owned by Europeans had become the sites of self-built houses by African tenants. The tenants paid a ground rent of a few shillings a month, which entitled them to the plinth area on which the house they built stood but to no other rights. In 1963 some 11,410 of the total population of 100,260 in Lusaka were enumerated as living in 'unauthorized compounds'. From the survey conducted in 1954 and in 1957 and analysed by Bettison (1959), it is clear that there is some self-selection of populations into these areas in terms of age, ethnic group, employment, degree of town residence, and conjugal status, but not in terms of income. This refers to social characteristics: the pattern of social relationships which existed among those living in these areas may well have been quite different from that of people living in other townships, but we have no information on that topic.

In general we are presented with a situation where an administrative system had been established in which Africans were allocated minimal privileges by reason of their employee status in the towns. The direction and running of the administrative structure which controlled their day to day lives was in the hands of whites, although executive officers dealing directly

---

[8] Some examination of the extent of this self-selection is presented in Mitchell 1974*b* and in chap. 6 below.

with the Africans were usually African clerks. The Africans themselves had no say in the decisions which directly affected their lives in the townships. Instead the structure and organization of the township were foreign and alien to them and they had no part and no involvement in them.

If from the administrative point of view the presence of an African male in the town was justified by his function as a worker, the presence of African women was anomalous. African women have not, in the main, entered the labour market in Central Africa.[9] Their presence in the towns has therefore been mainly in the capacity of wives of the employees. But the proportion of men who have their wives with them in town varies considerably from territory to territory. In Zambia, from the social survey conducted between 1950 and 1955 it emerged that 24.8 per cent of the men who were married had left their wives in the rural areas. The proportion of adult men who were not attached conjugally, that is who were widowers, divorcees or who had never married was 29.8 per cent. No comparable figures are available for Rhodesia, but a survey conducted by the Census Department showed that less than 19 percent of the African wage earners in Salisbury were accompanied by their dependants, and approximately 31 per cent in Bulawayo (Mitchell 1961: 238). The proportion of men who brought their families with them to town was partly determined, of course, by the amount of family accommodation available in town. On the other hand it could be argued that municipal authorities would provide housing according to the demand for it. In fact several surveys have shown that accommodation intended for single men had rapidly been filled by men with their wives and families. (For example see evidence quoted by Gray (1960: 259) for Southern Rhodesia.)

The reluctance and the failure of local authorities to provide adequate housing in the past would seem at least in part due to

---

[9] According to the 1961 Census of Africans in Employment 3.9 per cent of the labour force in Rhodesia was made up of women, 1.1 per cent in Zambia, and 3.4 per cent in Malawi. In Rhodesia most (89.5 per cent) were in domestic service, 12.0 per cent in manufacturing, and 10.8 per cent in other services (nursing, teaching etc.). In Zambia 46.0 per cent were in domestic service and 38.3 per cent in other services: in Malawi 34.1 per cent were in manufacturing, 24.7 in domestic service, and 17.3 per cent in other services. *Report of the Census of Africans in Employment taken on 8th May 1956*, Salisbury Central Statistical Office (1957), Table 5.

an implicit assumption, as the commission appointed by the Southern Rhodesian Government to investigate African affairs in the cities phrased it, that the African was 'essentially a member of a rural society with his urban activities regarded as a temporary deviation from the norm' (Plewman Report, para. 133).

Basic social and political attitudes of legislators and administrators had both direct and indirect effects on the social relationships of Africans in towns, in that they eventually became the stimulus for the organization of African political opposition movements which were, initially at any rate, urban based. The social and political attitudes of legislators and administrators, through their influence on material conditions such as housing and other amenities in town, indirectly influenced African social relationships through the restraint and restrictions they imposed on African town-dwellers, restrictions which made normal family life difficult, and traditional ritual and religious and customary practices infeasible; they imposed a social order regulated by the clock, the traffic light, and the whole structure of municipal regulation.

The Economic Factors in Urban Selection

It could be argued, of course, that provision of housing and other urban amenities for urban Africans on a scale comparable with those in towns in Western countries would have involved costs which the slender economies of the colonial countries could not have borne. This is incontrovertible. But at the same time the striking disparity in the access of Whites to urban amenities as against that of Africans points to a more fundamental social and political issue underlying the different absorptions of Africans and Whites into urban life. Towns in Central Africa were set up in the first instance, as I have pointed out, to serve as the bases from which White incomers could direct their administrative and commercial activities. The commercial activities which were introduced by the Whites were part of the larger set of activities rooted in the metropolitan countries from which the Whites had come. Commercial activities even in South Central Africa called for a set of bureaucratic procedures which were an extension of the commercial processes of which the Central

African manifestation was but an element. In other words trading institutions needed stock sheets, account books, correspondence files, managerial records, and the like. At the same time there were a number of tasks that needed doing which, though still essential to the operation of the enterprise, required skills of a differing type: unskilled labouring duties, manual tasks, and the like. Much the same point could be made about administrative activities, and about the various commercial and other services which were a necessary part of a money-based economy such as the banks, the legal profession, conveyancing, surveying, and so on. In the mining industry there was probably much more need for unskilled manual labour than in commercial concerns but the same division of activities existed: there were some posts requiring clerical and managerial skills which involved a minimum level of education, and there were others which required in the main a strong body rather than a trained mind.

Posts requiring education and skills involving prior training were allocated to whites while posts which required little training were allocated to Africans. From the earliest days of economic enterprise in Central Africa, therefore, the familiar division of labour between White managerial and skilled workers and Black unskilled manual workers was established. Some sixty years after the initial establishment of economic enterprises based on the money economy the effect is still seen in the occupational structure of the territories. For example, in the 1958–9 survey of African budgets in urban areas in Rhodesia only 2.72 per cent of Africans in the labour force were employed in white-collar posts, 1.44 per cent in skilled occupations such as carpenters, painters etc., 5.44 per cent in semi-skilled occupations such as drivers of motor vehicles or tailors, 2.06 per cent were in police or guards of various sorts, 46.83 in general unskilled labouring tasks, and 34.33 in domestic and personal services. There were 7.17 per cent in occupations which were described inadequately for classification. A similar survey in Zambia in 1960 showed that 5.78 per cent of Africans in the labour force were in white-collar occupations, 9.98 per cent were skilled workers, 1.22 were supervisors, 5.47 were drivers and tailors, 46.04 per cent were unskilled manual workers, 20.27 per cent were domestic workers, 2.62 were self-employed hawkers, and 4.98 per cent were unclassified. In other words, approximately 82 per cent of Africans in the labour force in Rhodesia were employed in manual and unskilled occupations, and 66 per cent were similarly employed in Zambia.[10] Clearly, more than mere availability of requisite skills is involved here, as the struggle over African advancement on the Copperbelt after 1956 demonstrated. Direct pressure on the part of Whites to exclude Africans from certain types of occupations played a significant part in determining the distribution of occupations between the two racial groups. This indeed constitutes part of the set of circumstances in which the social behaviour of Africans in towns must be located. The wages of Africans were always a good deal lower than those of Europeans or for that matter Asians and Eurafricans. The position is described by an economist in the following terms:

The terms on which towns have been organized have also had an important influence on the distribution of income generated within them. As far as personal incomes are concerned, these communities have been structured on the premise of a sharp discontinuity in the distribution between the races. In the initial stages, this outcome could not easily have been avoided. African labour was unskilled, unreliable, and not very productive, whereas Europeans—who expected higher real incomes than would be available to them elsewhere if they were to remain in these pioneering outposts had to be rewarded at higher rates than their skills could command in other environments. Over the course of time, this pattern has tended to be self-perpetuating. Employers lacked incentive to invest in 'skilling' an African labour force which they could expect to be only migrant and transient. Nor did African employees, given prevailing wages and the terms of living generally, have either incentive or opportunity to commit themselves to urban occupations. The interlocking of these factors in turn, imposed a low ceiling on the position in the economy to which Africans could aspire—a ceiling made more rigid by restrictions in the labour market, backed by custom if not by statute. Though the colour bar in employment has been dented in the recent past, it remains the case that most African employees in the urban economy have yet to rise above the lowest rungs on the skill ladder, where they continue to receive low wages.

The persistence of this pattern is strikingly brought out in the findings of the 1958–9 round of demographic surveys of the urban

[10] Comparable details for Malawi do not exist.

African work force in Southern Rhodesia's four main towns. When the occupational distribution is arrayed by skill grouping, it appears that less than 3 per cent of urban African wage earners can be classified as 'skilled'. Even when interpreted with latitude, the 'semi-skilled' category can account for less than another 10 per cent. The overwhelming mass of the urban labour force has acquired little or no skill and is engaged in ordinary labour or in domestic service. For most of these employers, money wages were less than £7 per month, with lodging but not rations, provided by the employer.

The significance of these findings emerges more sharply when they are compared with the incomes of European urban families. If the results of the October 1960 sample survey of European family budgets are representative, the average monthly income of European families was then nearly £163 in Salisbury and more than £148 in Bulawayo. Not all these receipts were attributable to the employment of the main breadwinner. The earnings of the wife and 'other income' (including property rentals, interest and dividends) accounted for about £30 of the family's total receipts in Salisbury and for £24 in Bulawayo. These findings indicate that cash earnings of the average European head of family in these towns would be in the order of eight times greater than those of the 'skilled' upper 3 per cent of the African labour force and sixteen times greater than the cash wage of the average African urban employee. (Barber 1967: 103–6.)[11]

The economic opportunities open to Africans in towns in South Central Africa, the degree to which they were able to participate in local and central Government, and the amount of contact with Whites on a basis of equality were all aspects of a fundamental disparity in the distribution of political power between the races. With political power resting firmly in the hands of the Whites either as settlers or as colonial civil servants, managerial and higher executive positions in industry and commerce were reserved for Whites. Africans, even if they had the basic education, were excluded from positions where they might exercise control over Whites. This political division of power coincided with an absence of close social contacts so that by and large Whites met with Whites in ordinary social intercourse and Africans with Africans. The contexts in which

---

[11] Baldwin produces evidence to show that in the Northern Rhodesian copper-mining industry in 1940 the ratio of European to African *real* wages was in the order of 20 to 1. Some twenty years later it was still in the region of 11 to 1. See Table 3.4 in Baldwin 1966.

Whites met with Africans were limited to those which involved commercial transactions, employer–employee relationships, or administrator–public, teacher–scholar, missionary–congregation relationships. Relationships outside these contacts remained at the categorical level.[12]

Our interest here is, of course, only indirectly in the relationship of Africans to Whites in the towns; it is rather in the pattern of all relationships which Africans built up around themselves in towns. The presence of Whites living in a different part of the town and making their present felt on Africans primarily as businessmen, industrial managers, administrators, the providers of specialist services, and above all as immediately identifiable units in the streets of the shopping centre clearly constitutes a major element in the social context of town life. Equally the presence of other racial groups such as Asians or Eurafricans, whose relationships with Africans were similar and differed only in detail, constituted another such element. The Africans in the colonial towns of South Central Africa occupied a specific social, economic, and political position which was imposed upon them by the colonial system as a whole. This system limited the economic opportunities open to Africans, defined the extent to which they were able to influence the legislation and drafting of regulations which could affect their daily lives, controlled the markets in which they could live, and constrained the sorts of social relationships they could have with non-Africans. It is to be expected then that the way in which Africans in these towns construed events and phenomena which affected them and the sorts of social relationships they built up with one another on the basis of these understandings were inexorably shaped by the circumstances pertaining in the wider society of which the towns were an integral part.

[12] That is, in which individuals are treated not as individuals but merely as exemplars of categories of persons, such as 'Africans' in the main as against 'Europeans' in general.

3

LABOUR CIRCULATION AND
URBAN GROWTH

The colonial towns of South Central Africa were established, I have argued, initially as outliers of the metropolitan power in territories occupied by indigenous peoples living under economic, social, and political orders very different from those of the colonists. The whole character of colonial expansion determined the sorts of social relationships which grew up not only between the indigenous populations and the colonists themselves but also to some extent among the indigenous people and among the colonists themselves. This was particularly true in the towns into which African workers were attracted right from their earliest establishment.

The White colonists needed African labour for the variety of manual and unskilled tasks that were demanded by commercial, industrial and administrative activities for the prosecution of which the towns had been established. For this purpose they recruited Africans who were prepared to perform these tasks for wages. But Africans who undertook wage-earning employment in this way initially looked upon their involvement in these activities as essentially a temporary matter: their real roots lay in the rural societies out of which they had recently come. Thus in the early days of wage employment the period which Africans worked was frequently very short indeed—a matter of three to six months—before they returned to their rural homes. From the point of view of the African migrant, therefore, wage labour was likely from the first to be a temporary expedient, possibly to meet some unusual financial obligation, but more likely to earn a minimum sum of cash which he needed for his expanding wants, for which money was necessary. Certain cash dues such as taxes, school fees for children, the purchase of agricultural equipment, the purchase of clothing, and more recently the payment of traditional dues such as marriage payments of com-

pensation for adultery meant that some source of cash income
was essential.[1]

Labour Circulation

Labour migration, therefore, was circulatory rather than a
simple translocation of workers from an area of supply to one of
demand.[2] The patterns of migration could vary considerably
with the region from which the migration took place, with the
social characteristics of the migrants themselves, and with the
administrative circumstances of the areas in which they sought
work. Some migrants tended to make frequent short-term visits
to wage-earning areas, whether these areas were towns, mining
centres, or plantations. Other seemed to prefer to spend relatively long periods at the wage-earning centres and then withdraw finally in middle age to their rural homes. The patterns of
migration during early manhood, before family obligations in
the rural areas were strongly established, were likely to be short
and frequent. Later, with the obligation on men to provide for
growing families in the rural areas, the tendency might be either
to move their wives and children to the town where they were
working if they were able to secure suitable accommodation
there, or to withdraw from the cash economy and spend their
time in subsistence agriculture. In addition, a number of international agreements in the past—and some still existed in
1964—required migrants from foreign countries to return
within fixed periods, so that their sojourn in labour centres was
limited by law.

Our interest at present is in the relationships of this pattern of
migration to town growth, particularly in respect to how it
affected social behaviour. One way of looking at this problem is

[1] It seems likely that the absolute flow of migrants to cities has been increasing over
time, but it is very difficult to document this. Recent work by economists Young (1971),
Maimbo and Fry (1971), and Fry (1975) on rural–urban terms of trade suggests that the
economic advantage to potential migrants of staying in the rural areas has been
declining, but we lack the data to confirm that this has in fact influenced the volume of
flow to cities.

[2] Labour circulation has been on the subject of many studies in Central Africa: see
Wilson 1941–2, Read 1942, Mitchell 1959, 1969*b*, van Velsen 1960, Garbett 1960,
1975, Barber 1961, and Scott 1954*a*, 1954*b*. More recently less attention has been given
to circulation than to the supply of labour, see for example Arrighi 1967, van Onselen
1980, Parpart 1980.

to consider cohorts of migrants arriving at some labour centre within a given time period. These migrants would be differentiated in terms of their place of origin, their previous experience of wage labour, the possession of skills and education which would enable them to secure rewarding jobs, the obligations and responsibilities they had in the areas they had come from, and so on. Each of these categories and subcategories of person would be subject to a certain probability of returning to his rural home, according to the balance of involvement he had both in the place where his work was and the place from which he had recently come. In addition a series of chance events might operate to influence his movements. An accident at work, for example, may have crippled him, an office to which he had a claim in the rural society may have fallen vacant because of the death of a kinsman, a factory for which he was working may have closed down and he might not have been able to find alternative employment quickly. The probability that any other particular individual would return to his rural home, therefore, would be the joint probability of these chance events as influenced by the more regular effects deriving from the sociological and economic variables we have been discussing.

Empirically, over time, and leaving aside at present the contingency of death, the original cohort would be diminished successively during each year of continued residence in town, resulting in successively smaller and smaller proportions of the original cohort remaining in town.

But other migrants would be moving into town continuously. Furthermore, they would probably be moving in at different rates, both according to the rural agricultural cycle and from year to year. At any particular moment, therefore, the African population of a town in South Central Africa would be made up of the residues of a number of different cohorts of migrants who had been subject to different rates of return to rural areas (or movements to other towns) for differing periods of residence.

The number of people in a town at any particular time under these circumstances would be the result of two rather different processes. The first and most obvious of these would be the extent to which the urban population was being increased by births and incoming migrants and decreased by deaths and outgoing migrants. The second and less obvious factor would be the change in the mean length of stay in town of migrants. If the average duration of stay of migrants to town was being prolonged then the numbers of survivors from each annual cohort of incomers would increase, so that the total population would increase in consequence.

The rate of growth of the urban population at any one point of time under these circumstances would be deceptive, since as the duration of prolonged stay approached the expectancy of life at the age of migration, so the migrants would be likely to die before they returned to their rural homes. At this stage the rate of return to rural areas would be much reduced but the overall death rate would be higher. The rate of growth of the town under these circumstances would be determined by both births and incoming migrants and diminished by the appropriate age-specific rates of mortality. We do not have the detailed statistics to be able to separate out these different components of the rate of growth of urban Central African populations.

Our interest in this formulation of the growth of South Central African towns, however, is simply to isolate aspects of general urban growth which are particularly significant for the purposes of examining social behaviour. While the inflow was obviously significant from the point of view of determining the circumstances that led to the migration in the first instance, since these might well have had a crucial effect on the behaviour of individuals in town, it is clear also that the outflow may be looked upon as the consequence of a decision at which the migrant had arrived after weighing up a number of factors both inside and outside the towns which might have influenced whether he moved out or not. In this sense the outflow reflected the operation of factors influencing the migratory behaviour of individuals and therefore indirectly reflected the set of social relationships in which the migrant was involved.

There has been a long and extensive debate on the necessary relationships between various aspects of town living. While sociologists and anthropologists are interested primarily in urbanism, that is the way of life that people adopt while they live in towns, the demographic fact that some migrants remained longer in towns than others has suggested that there may be some connection between this fact and the pattern of social behaviour in the towns. For some years the word 'urbanization' was used for both processes, that is the process whereby a migrant adoped urban ways of living and the demographic process whereby a migrant extended his stay in town for longer and longer periods. The older use of the word implying simply the proportion of people at present living in towns is also in current use.[3] In order to facilitate discussion, I have suggested that the word 'stabilization' should be used to denote the demographic process whereby people spend longer and longer periods in town before returning to their rural areas. Obviously the use of this word implies a labour circulation system. The word 'urbanization' ought to be kept for use in the sense in which it is most commonly used at present, that is with reference to the proportion of people currently living in towns of specified size. 'Urbanism' would refer simply to the way of life characteristic of towns. Three other related terms may be useful. We might refer to 'involvement' in town life to refer to the extent to which an individual has built up social relationships in town as against in rural areas, and we might refer to 'commitment' to town life as the cognitive aspect of involvement, that is the degree to which the individual perceives himself as being involved in town life. Both of these terms, like the term 'stabilization', imply a system of labour circulation or at least the alternative of some other way of life in which the individual could involve himself. At one time in African urban studies the notion of detribalization was commonly used. This word has fallen out of use largely because of the assumption of a 'normal tribal way of life' which seems to underlie its use.[4]

Terms like 'involvement' and 'commitment' reflect the more fundamental structural process of proletarianization, which refers to the extent to which workers are increasingly dependent upon the sale of their labour for wages as a basis for subsistence, with the consequent implication for the class placement of workers in this position (see for example Arrighi 1967, van Onselen 1980, Parpart 1982). While the notion of proletarianization is conceptually clear enough its determination is by no means empirically simple. It is by no means easy to adduce

---

[3] The confusion arising out of the different uses of these terms is discussed in Mitchell 1969a, Mayer 1961, 1962, Glass 1960.

[4] For criticisms of this sort see Gluckman 1961, Watson 1958, Mitchell 1969a, Mayer (1962: 584 ff.) has defended its use in the special context of cultural change.

the evidence for assertions such as: 'By the late 1950s most miners were fully proletarianized, depending upon wages and pensions for their long term security. Many had lost, or severely loosened, their ties with their rural homelands.' (Parpart 1982: 15–16.) To establish this assertion we would need detailed budget studies showing the extent to which the worker received aid from rural areas and in turn gave aid to rural areas. In so far as the cognitive orientation of 1950–5 is concerned it seems that a fairly large proportion saw themselves as only lightly tied into the urban economy. During the Northern Rhodesia Urban Survey all those interviewed were questioned about the way they saw themselves with regard to urban residence. Following Wilson's (1941–2) lead three categories could be distinguished. In the first could be placed those who saw themselves in town for the specific purpose of earning a certain cash amount, after which they hoped to return to their areas of origin. These were 38.1 per cent of the adult males in the sample of 8,900. A second category consisted of those who saw themselves as staying on in town but eventually returning to their areas of origin, those whom Wallerstein refers to as the semi-proletarianized of adult males. Finally there were those who said that they had no intention of returning to their areas of origin. These represented 15.3 per cent of the adult males. These categories are, of course, not completely coincident with degrees of proletarianization, but they do suggest that as far as the worker's own self-perceptions were concerned the number completely proletarianized was not very high.

Another approach to the same problem might be through the actual proportion of adult life the workers in town at the time of the survey had spent in towns. Of those aged 25 and under 51.6 per cent had spent one third of their time since the age of 15 years in towns, and 20.6 per cent had spent between one and two thirds of the time in town. The proportions of those aged 25 to 45 who had spent less than one third, between one and two thirds, and over two thirds of their life since the age of fifteen in towns were 39.3 per cent, 33.0 per cent, and 27.7 per cent respectively. For those aged 45 and over the proportions were 21.1 per cent, 33.8 per cent, and 45.1 per cent respectively.

These data do not refer directly to the structural circumstances of the social existence of the workers. Later in this chapter I shall produce demographic evidence to support the view that most urban workers leave town when they get older. Social attributes such as being proletarian or not are 'structural' in the sense that the significance of the attribute is derived from its place in a theoretical schema which may in fact not be completely consistent with the empirical facts. From the perspective adopted in this analysis *behaving* as a proletarian is *situational* and not an immutable characteristic of actors. Contradictions between the apparent attributes of being a proletarian and behaviour as a proletarian could quite easily arise out of the particular historical circumstances in which the behaviour is evoked. Shortly after the survey mentioned above was conducted, for example, a strike of miners was called on the Copperbelt, and as described in Epstein's book (1958) the strike was complete whether the people concerned had seen themselves as peripherally involved in the urban labour system or not.

One of the basic problems confronting our analysis of human behaviour in towns is that of spelling out the connection between these conceptually different aspects of urban existence. For a long time writers seemed to assume that the longer a man stayed in town the more likely he was to be involved in town life and the more likely to be dependent only on the sale of his labour for subsistence. The work of Philip Mayer and his associates in the South African town of East London, however, demonstrated that there was at least one category of migrant who, though he was likely to spend considerable periods living in East London or other towns, was minimally involved in town life. The relationship, therefore, is by no means simple. We could argue that when migrants moved into town looking for work they were all subject to the same general constraints arising out of the embracing economic and administration system. We could argue that the degree of involvement of migrants in town-based social relationships was in every case a matter of chance or of the personality of the migrants. To do this, however, would be to postulate that there were no regularities in who did and did not become involved in town life. We know from Mayer's work and from other work that this was not so, that there were categories of migrants more likely to resist involvement in town life than others. In other words, some types of migrants had resources either to exploit the town environment or to resist it which others lacked. Consequently some migrants became heavily involved in town-based social relationships while others held themselves aloof from them. What we lack at present is an appreciation of what causal factors underlie this distinction among migrants. The process of encapsulation of a particular category of migrant, the 'Red' migrants so vividly described by Mayer, applies to some degree to migrants in other parts of Africa.[5] But the explanation that Mayer offers is not sufficiently general to enable us to apply it to other urban contexts.

We are in no position to solve this problem at present. There is simply insufficient analytical material available to enable us to begin to move towards making general statements about the length of residence in towns, the degree of involvement of migrants in town-based relationships, and the extent of their proletarianization. The work of Mayer and his colleagues has been an important step forward in that they had been able to show that the relationship is not a simple linear one and to demonstrate some of the complexity of the problem. But what is fundamentally lacking is a theory of social relationships which can take into account the peculiar circumstances of town life and trace out their effects on the social relationships of people so involved.

Geographical Mobility

The movements of Africans living in towns were not restricted, of course, to those between rural areas and towns. There was considerable movement both between towns and within the towns. The typical labour history of a migrant to a South Central African town, like those described by Reader (1961: 59–60) for East London, is likely to have a fairly standard sequence of contacts with urban areas. Before occupational opportunities had expanded to the extent they had in the 1950s many migrants made their first trips to seek employment outside Northern Rhodesia, in particular to Southern Rhodesia or to South Africa. On second and subsequent trips they were likely to seek employment in one of the local towns. An analysis of the

---

[5] It might have applied to the Nyakysa migrants in the Copperbelt, and also to the Zambrama in Accra: see Little 1965: 25. There is some evidence that much the same conditions applied to Sicilian migrants in New York, see chap. 7.

findings of the social survey in the towns of Northern Rhodesia
in the 1950s shows that among those migrants at present in
towns in Northern Rhodesia who had made their first trip to
seek work more than fifteen years previously, 25.5 per cent went
outside the country to do so. Of those who went between five and
fourteen years previously the figure was 12.3 per cent, and of
those who sought employment in the five years just prior to the
surveys only 3.7 per cent sought work outside the country. In
interpreting these figures it should not be forgotten that this is a
sample of urban residents and may not reflect the true situation
if former migrants now living in the rural areas had had a
different pattern of first migration from those now living in
towns. There seems no a priori reason why this should have been
so but the possibility should be left open. The switch to first
work-experience in Northern Rhodesia is consistent with what
we know about the expansion of demand for labour in that territory in the years leading up to the time the survey was conducted
(see Parpart 1980: 12).

There was a certain amount of movement between towns as
well. Table 3.1 sets out the results from the social survey in the
1950s, and tabulates the number of direct moves between towns
of male and female migrants against the number of years since
they made their first trip to towns.

There is a clear tendency, naturally, for migrants who have
been away from their rural homes longer to have made more
urban shifts. On average the men had had longer contacts with
town life and had had more opportunity to move between towns
than the women. Roughly two-thirds of the men and 80 per cent
of the women who had left their rural homes less than five years
previously had not made any moves between towns. The mean
number of moves for men who had first left their rural homes less
than five years ago was 0.54, and for women 0.22. This average
increased to 1.93 for men who had been away from their rural
homes for 5–15 years (0.78 for women), and to 3.35 for men who
had first left their rural homes more than fifteen years previously
(1.55 for women). These shifts may have arisen from a number
of different circumstances. Many of them, particularly for those
in Government service or for those working as domestic servants
for White Government employees, arose out of transfers.
Others arose out of second and subsequent trips to seek work,

Table 3.1 *Number of Moves between Towns of African Adult Male and Female Town-Dwellers by Length of Absence from Rural Areas: Line-of-Rail Towns of Northern Rhodesia*

Length of absence from rural areas 'years'	Number of inter-town moves										
	0	1	2	3	4	5	6	7	8 & over	Total	
Males											
0–4	63.8	21.9	11.3	2.1	0.7	0.2	0.0	0.0	0.0	100.0	37379
5–15	23.2	18.4	29.6	12.4	9.7	3.1	2.2	0.7	0.8	100.0	34893
15–25	10.2	13.5	25.3	15.3	14.6	6.8	6.6	2.7	5.0	100.0	15203
25 +	3.1	5.7	17.5	17.5	14.3	13.0	9.5	6.0	12.9	100.0	6279
Total	33679	17027	19480	8572	6790	2982	2383	1010	1831	—	93754
Females											
0–4	83.7	11.4	4.1	0.4	0.4	0	0	0	0	100.0	26698
5–14	59.6	16.3	16.3	4.3	2.4	0.8	6.2	0.1	6.8	100.0	18078
15–24	39.1	17.6	23.4	11.4	4.0	2.4	0.7	0.7	0.8	100.0	6979
25 +	27.4	18.1	20.9	14.7	8.5	3.1	3.4	0.8	3.2	100.0	1798
Totals	36336	7534	6045	1945	978	369	144	71	136	100.0	53562

NB   Totals represent population totals estimated from sampling fractions.
Based on interview with 8,873 males and 5,038 females.

Source: Rhodes–Livingstone Institute Social Survey 1950–5.

where migrants returning to town used their knowledge and experience and what they had found out from others during their visits to their home areas about work opportunities in other towns. But there was also a tendency for migrants to move from town to town in response to work opportunities. Thus migrants from the Eastern Province tended to find their job in Lusaka, at which point the buses from Fort Jameson connected with the railway line. There was in fact a high proportion of Eastern Province migrants in Lusaka because of this. Broken Hill, only ninety miles further north of Lusaka, may have presented slightly better opportunities for some of the migrants because of its mine, and the trip could be made fairly easily either by bus or by train. Beyond Broken Hill the complex of Copperbelt towns lying at a distance of from 200 to 350 km. from Broken Hill provided yet further opportunities. Depending on the skills which migrants had to offer the migration may also have taken place in the opposite direction, that is from the Copperbelt to Lusaka.[6]

The Copperbelt towns were all within fairly easy reach of one from the other, and there was considerable movement among these towns both on a short term and a longer term basis. During the weekend buses plied between the towns taking visitors from one to the other, football teams to compete against one another, dancing teams to compete against one another, or people to visit their friends and kinsfolk. But in addition the easy accessibility of the towns one from the other meant that employment opportunities were quickly transmitted by word of mouth, by telephone, or by letter, so that people were able to move around very easily from one town to the other in search of better posts. The good tarmac road system which connected the Copperbelt towns allowed bicycles to be used without too much difficulty.

Finally, within the towns themselves there was considerable mobility of the population from one part of the town to another. This was partly dependent on labour turnover, for, as we have seen, housing was frequently controlled by the employer, so that when a man lost his job this usually meant his moving to another house, particularly if he were not living in one of the municipal

6 See for example Mitchell 1954b, diagrams; Reader 1961: Fig. 4 p. 44.

housing areas. In these it was possible for a man to retain his house while he sought another employer who would be paying his rent in the municipal housing area. But the mining companies or some of the larger industrial employers such as the railways had their own housing areas, so that if a man was employed by them he was offered accommodation in their housing estate, and equally if he left their employment he had to leave the housing estate.

It is not possible at this stage to present a simple measure of mobility which would allow comparison of the mobility of the urban African population in South Central Africa with that in other countries. The impression an observer has is of constant movement, with neighbourhoods forever changing their compositions. Mobility and change of this sort is an existential characteristic of certain types of town and must be allowed for in the daily social interaction of the people involved. Some neighbourhoods in the towns were no doubt more stable residentially than others, and we would expect the different patterns of social relationships to have emerged in these neighbourhoods. The causes of the mobility itself almost certainly lay in the wider social order, which itself directly influenced the pattern of social relationships in the town. As before, we can look upon the mobility of the population as a variable that intervened between the social order and the town which had come into being because of it on the one hand, and the behaviour of individuals in the town on the other hand.

Age and Sex Selection

Part of the context within which social relationships among Africans in towns existed was the general demographic structure of the populations of those towns. The circumstances of the development of towns in South Central Africa meant that the demand for African labour was highly selective. The qualities demanded by employers for the available occupations were primarily muscular skills, which implied that the demand was for young men in particular. The amount of training required for the tasks was not extensive, although in terms of the lack of familiarity of the workers with the implements and techniques of industrial production the investment for them was probably more than employers realised. The general lack of suitable accommodation for families in towns and the discouragement by the administration as a whole of the presence of women in town implied also that male migrants tended to come on their own. This was reinforced by the tendency for women to remain in the rural areas to maintain the system of subsistence production there.

Reliable statistics concerning the age and sex composition of African town populations during the early stages of their development do not exist. In Southern Rhodesia the first estimate is available as a result of the demographic surveys of 1958-9. In Northern Rhodesia surveys conducted in the 1950s provide some information, and there were demographic surveys of 1950 and 1960. Figure 3.1(a-d) set out the age and sex structure of different racial groups in the main towns in Southern Rhodesia as compared with the non-urban population in 1961-2. The striking characteristic of these diagrams is the extent to which the urban and non-urban age and sex characteristics of the African population differ so markedly from the comparable distributions for other racial groups. The non-urban population is seen as a relatively squat triangle indicating the relatively high birth and high death rates. The estimated total birth rate of the Southern Rhodesian populations in 1962 was 48 per 1000 while the death rate was 14, with an expectancy of life at birth for both sexes of 50 years. The comparable figure for Northern Rhodesia in 1963 was 51 per thousand and the death rate 19, with an expectancy of life at birth for both sexes of 40 years. The proportion of persons living in the towns in both areas barely showed in the age and sex structure. The urban populations, however, reflected a shape that was characteristic of many towns where the African population was involved in a migrant labour system. The structure of the population could perhaps be considered as a combination of the age and sex patterns characteristic of the lodging-house hotel area and the area of first immigrant settlement (the ghetto) in Chicago in the 1920s (Newcomb 1957: 382-92). Indeed, the basic social processes underlying these two types of social area were exactly those which underlay the structure of the African urban population.[7] The lodging-house hotel and hobo areas, as described by Newcomb, represent a population of young people, predominantly males, many of whom were migrant workers or otherwise mobile persons. The area of first immigrant settlement, on the other hand, was, as its title suggests, the area into which migrants of a more permanent type gravitated when they first moved to the city, described by Newcomb as 'an area that is somewhat better organized than the slum and contains immigrants who had brought their cultural institutions with them and maintain them in the new world' (1957: 391). It would, of course, be invalid to infer characteristics of the population simply from its age and sex structure. The position is rather that similar social processes led to similar age and sex structures. An explanation of the peculiar age and sex structures of the African towns in these terms would be that a fair proportion of the inhabitants of the town were labour migrants who had come without their families and who would be moving back to their rural homes before long. A sizeable number, however, would have brought their families with them and were likely to stay for longer periods.

But to interpret the age and sex structure of the urban population we require more information than is available from the censuses. The age and sex structure of the urban population of Northern Rhodesia, for example, was heavily influenced by the distribution of the ages of the men in the town.

The largest part of the population was that made up of the households of men aged 25 to 35 who had wives several years younger than themselves and a relatively large number of children. The younger men just starting their families, that is with young children, were a much smaller category, and least significant of all were the older couples and their dependants. The characteristic of the 'lop-sided hour-glass' shape of the age and sex structure of the population of South Central African towns could be seen as being due to two main factors, firstly the heavy predominance of men under the age of 45 with their relatively young families and secondly the large number of males also between the ages of 15 and 45 who were either single or who

---

[7] Data on the movement of people among the towns are available in the social survey material collected in the Rhodes–Livingstone Institute surveys in the 1950s. I hope to present further analyses of this material in due course.

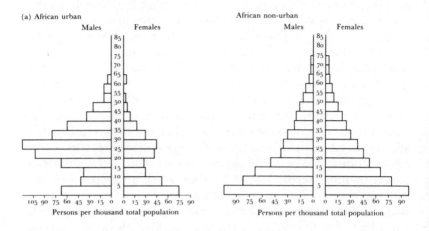

(a) African urban

African non-urban

Persons per thousand total population

Persons per thousand total population

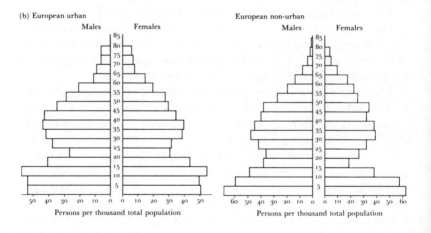

(b) European urban

European non-urban

Persons per thousand total population

Persons per thousand total population

Figure 3.1.(*a–d*) Age and Sex Structures of Urban and Non-urban Populations, Southern Rhodesia 1961

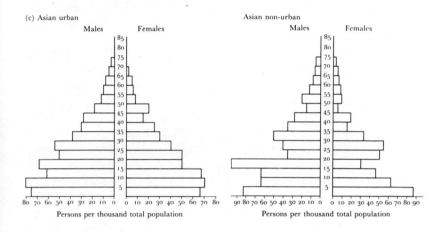

(c) Asian urban

Persons per thousand total population

Asian non-urban

Persons per thousand total population

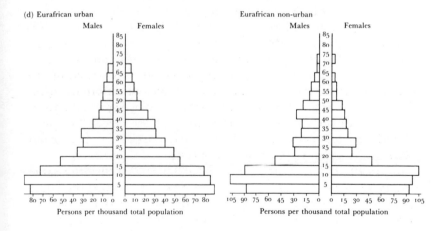

(d) Eurafrican urban

Persons per thousand total population

Eurafrican non-urban

Persons per thousand total population

had left their wives in the rural areas from which they had migrated.

In addition to the population in households of married couples, there were others living in households as single or unattached persons, some of whom may have had children living with them.

This, however, is essentially a static picture of the age and sex composition. To understand the way in which it might have changed we need to appreciate the demographic processes by means of which it was produced. The age and sex structure of the population of the towns at any given point in time is the resultant of three different processes. First there is the process of natural replacement of the urban population. In other words, children are born to town-dwellers and town-dwellers of all ages die. The particular effect of these natural processes will depend upon the overall fertility and mortality levels of the urban populations *per se*. Secondly, there are the processes of ageing, that is the way in which persons in one age category are replaced in due course by another set of persons. This means that the age and sex structure would eventually approximate that of a stable population. Thirdly, there is, of course, the differential effect of in-migration and out-migration. Migrants are constantly moving to towns at different rates according to age and sex. Similarly, they are constantly moving out at different rates.

To study the way in which urban age and sex structure are changing over time we would need studies at different times. Unfortunately not many of there are available. Figures 3.2*a* and 3.2*b* set out the age and sex structures of the larger Northern Rhodesian towns in 1952, which was the approximate median date of the social surveys, and at a census of the urban populations in 1959. This is not a long enough period of time to enable many noticeable changes to occur. Even so, within the short period of approximately eight years the increase in the proportion of children aged 10 to 15 is apparent, as is the correlative reduction of the disproportion in the young adult ages between 20 and 35.

It is, or course, impossible in this material to separate out the changes due to ageing and natural increase from those due to migration. Some estimate of the significance of the migratory process in the structure of towns might be obtained by esti-

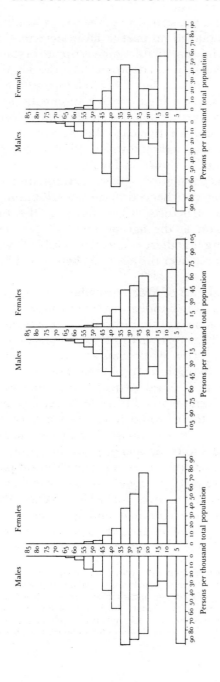

Figure 3.2.(*a–c*) Age and Sex Structures of Line-of-Rail Towns of Northern Rhodesia 1952 and 1959 with Projected Structure at 1960 on Assumption that all Migration had Ceased in 1952

mating what the age and sex structure of the towns would have been if migration had played no part at all in determining it. This can be done if we have available some estimate of the rates of fertility and death. Fertility and death rates for the population in the towns are not available but those relating to the total population are. It is possible using these to compute the age and sex structure of a given starting population after the elapse of a specified number of years.[8] On this basis the expected structure of the population of the Copperbelt towns in 1959, as compared with what it actually was, is shown in Figure 3.2c.

The proportion of the population in the age groups under 15 is accurately predicted by the theoretical age distribution. The theoretical population structure differs most in the higher proportion of population at the age of 45 (9.13 per cent as against 3.00), suggesting that there was a considerable flow back to the rural areas of people over the age of 45 between 1952 and 1960.

Migration was a vital part of urban growth in South Central Africa and what appeared to happen was that urban residence, far from being a phenomenon of simple translocation from rural area to town or from village to town to city, was in fact linked to the life cycle of the majority of Africans at that time. Nearly every adult male then living in a rural area, however remote from the towns in South Central Africa, had at one time or another been to a town and worked there for several years. At any one point in time there would have been a fairly large proportion then working in town who would return sometime in the future. What seemed to be happening was that young men left to go and work in town (or in mining centres or on plantations) when they were 18 or 19 years old. At this stage they were unmarried. They worked in town for several years, during which time they aimed to accumulate enough cash to enable them to make marriage payments and so marry. This they usually did in the rural home from which they came. They might

---

[8] This is based on a standard demographic procedure, in which the birth rate is determined by the age structure of the female population in combination with a known fertility schedule, and the death rate by the age and sex structure of the whole population in combination with a known mortality schedule. In the estimation made here the fertility and mortality rates appropriate to the Coale and Demeny West Level 10 (1966: 11) were used. These seemed to coincide most closely with the observed death and birth rates in Northern Rhodesia in 1952.

then have left for another spell of work while their wives established themselves in their new roles. Later on, if the migratory
career persisted, they brought their young wives and young
families with them to town. There followed a period of more or
less continuous residence in town, during which the wife might
have made frequent visits back to her rural home and during
which children may well have been sent back to the wife's or
husband's parents. Sooner or later, however, the advantages to
the couple of staying on in town as against taking up residence in
the rural areas would have diminished, and at some point, especially after the man had turned 45, he was likely to have left town
for good. Some of his children may have established themselves
in the town by this time, while others would have been too young
to have done so. Some would have been sent back in advance to
their grandparental homes: these children would then have
spent their younger adolescent years in the rural areas until
they were old enough themselves to seek work in the towns.
Thus the age and sex structure of the towns, which was so
much at variance with the general age structure of the population as a whole, may have represented a relatively stable
phenomenon and not, as some have argued, an essentially
temporary phase. The distribution was sustained because
the population spent only a selected part of its life cycle in the
town.[9] The extent to which the age and sex structure of the
towns would have approximated that of the population as
a whole would have depended upon the extent of the circulation between town and country at specific phases of the life
cycle.[10]

A description of the way in which different life phases were
spent in town as against rural areas may have explained the age
structure; the disproportion of the sexes calls for additional
explanation. The number of males per 100 females differs considerably according to age group. Under the age of 20 the sex
ratio in the Northern Rhodesia survey was almost equal (95),
but with increasing age the disproportion increased. Hence in
the age group 20 to 25 it was 111; 25 to 35 it was 209; 35 to 45 it

---

[9] For more extended treatment of this problem see Mitchell 1969*b*, where evidence
from ethnographic studies in rural areas is presented.

[10] This assumes of course that the birth and death rates in town and country become
and remain the same.

Table 3.2 *Number of Adult Males per 100 Adult Females according to Length of Absence from Rural Areas and Distance of Rural Home from Town: Northern Rhodesia*

Distance of rural home from town	Length of absence from rural area			
	Under 5 yrs.	5–14 yrs.	Over 15 yrs.	Total
0–299 km.	106	139	171	129
300–599 km.	129	193	276	175
600–899 km.	130	245	247	185
900 or more km.	272	261	404	285
All distances	139	192	245	175

Based on sample of 8,873 adult males and 5,038 adult females in Rhodes–Livingstone Urban Social Survey 1950–55. Distances measured by shortest road, rail, or waterway route from centre of district of origin to town in question.

was 595. This was almost undoubtedly due to the tendency of older men to have young wives.

The mean age of wives of men whose mean age was 21.9 was 20.4; those of mean age 32.1, 23.2; those of mean age 39.5, 27.4; those of mean age 50, 32.2; and those of mean age 59.5, 36.3. But the accessibility of the town played an important part as well. If we consider the ratio of men to women of people who had come from different areas of origin in the previous ten years, we find that there was a relationship between the distance from town and the masculinity rate. Table 3.2 summarizes the information for persons on the line-of-rail towns of Northern Rhodesia between 1950 and 1955. The trend is regular: the more distance the area of origin was from the town the more likely it was that there would be more men from the area in comparison with the number of women. The same generalization is true for men and women from areas at different distances who had been away from their rural homes for more than five years.[11]

On the basis of common-sense reasoning it is easy to argue that sheer distance must have been an impediment to the transport of wives and families to town. Apart from the discomfort of the journey, the majority of the migrants paid for their own journeys to the towns: they were not recruited, as workers were for the gold mines in South Africa. This means that a considerable outlay was needed for a journey to town if a man's wife and family of young children were to accompany

---

[11] There are of course many factors which influenced the varying accessibility of towns to men and women. I hope to present an analysis of some of these in a future work.

him. The women, in any case, were vital for the subsistence production in the rural areas, and in terms of Barber's interpretation of the economic factors underlying labour circulation their continued residence in the rural area would have implied an increased total income to the family as a whole (Barber 1961). It was important that the women were able to return at fairly frequent intervals to the rural areas to maintain the rural production. Women could afford to come to town, therefore, if they were within a distance from their rural homes which they could traverse fairly easily and cheaply.[12]

Geographical Selection

Distance, and what distance implies from the point of view of ease of migration, was in fact a general factor in the selection of urban population in South Central Africa, though of course not the only one. The effects of distance were also modified by transport facilities.

The major transport facility in South Central Africa, at least until recently, was the railway. A railway connecting Johannesburg to Salisbury was completed in 1901, and one from Beira to Salisbury in 1902. Blantyre in Nyasaland was connected to Chindio on the Zambezi river by 1915. A line from Beira reached Chindio on the Mozambique side of the river in 1922, but it was only in 1955 that a bridge crossing the river was built. The line between Blantyre and Salima on Lake Shire was completed in 1934. There seems little doubt that the urban centres in Northern Rhodesia and, to a lesser extent, in Southern Rhodesia and Nyasaland were sharply influenced by the railway. In Northern Rhodesia, the line of rail was frequently used as a synonym for 'town', and all the larger towns are strung along the line that connects Livingstone and the Copperbelt. In Southern Rhodesia the line was built to connect to Bulawayo and Salisbury and Umtali. But the fact that they were on the line no doubt played an important part in the growth. In Nyasaland, the capital Zomba was not connected to the railway line, and the population centres instead became Blantyre and Limbe, which were. Motor transport did not become common until just before

[12] This argument as related to men is developed in Mitchell 1974a.

the Second World War, and the relatively poor state of the road system was an impediment to the development of large-scale motor transport. After the Second World War, however, roads were improved and a number of bus services, some privately owned by Africans, began to operate. All areas were not served equally with bus services. The bus service to the Fort Roseberry and Kawambwa districts and on to the Northern Province was much better than that to Kasempa, Mwinilunga, Balovale, and Kabompo. Naturally more people used the bus service from those districts better served, and it is hard to tell whether the poorer bus services were because of the lack of demand, or whether the poor use of bus services was due to the poor services available. One of the important elements of a bus service was the existence of efficient feeder services: even if a bus service operated from the local administrative centre into the Copperbelt it may have been difficult for migrants to get to the administrative centre from which the buses operated. It was not much help to a migrant from Kabompo to know that a bus service ran from Mwinilunga. He would have needed to travel some 370 km. before he got to a point where the buses were running, and then he would have been only 195 km. from the Copperbelt. And whether a bus service operated from Kabompo clearly would have depended on the demand that existed for the service. Certainly, where good road networks existed it was correspondingly easy for Africans to get to and from town.[13] Yet a good transport system was not the only determinant of the method of transportation: the ability to pay was obviously an important element as well. According to a survey of methods of getting to the line-of-rail towns of Northern Rhodesia, no less than 15 per cent came all the way on foot. The distances covered were sometimes considerable—the approximate mean distance walked was 352 km. It seems likely that many of these were making their first trip to the Copperbelt and could not afford to pay the bus fare. Subsequent trips might well have been by bus, since they might have been able to save enough to pay for their return trip and perhaps also to pay for their wives and children.

The flow of population into and out of each town would thus

[13] The brief history of transportation and its influence on labour migration is provided by Niddrie (1954).

be influenced considerably by the lines of communication which connected it to its hinterland. From this point of view we could visualize that each town would have had a hinterland from which it drew its population. The extent of this hinterland would have been determined by the probabilities that a migrant would have gone to that town rather than any other. In order to estimate the extent of the hinterlands by this method we need to know the composition of the town's population in terms of its area of origin, and the number of migrants who had left each area of origin. The argument is that if these migrants distributed themselves in labour centres entirely at random—that is without taking the relative attraction of various centres into account—they would have represented different areas of origin in any one centre in the same proportions as the areas were represented in the migrant population as a whole. If, for example, one district provided on average 10 per cent of the migrants, then if no selective factors were operating in respect of the distribution of these migrants in all towns we would expect the proportion of migrants from district X in any town to have been 10 per cent. If there were more than 10 per cent we would conclude that for some reason migrants were choosing to come to that town rather than go elsewhere, and if there were less that they were choosing to go elsewhere. The ratio, then, of the observed proportion of migrants from an area to the proportion expected would provide us with an index of selection. If the index of selection was equal to unity then we could conclude that migrants from this area were just as likely to go elsewhere as to the town we are interested in. The 'watershed' of the hinterland is thus indicated by an index of unity.[14]

Map 3.1 shows these indices, multiplied by 100 for convenience, in respect to migration from within Northern Rhodesia to Lusaka.[15] It is possible to estimate from these indices a contour line for the index of 100 showing the areas from which male migrants, on the evidence available to us, chose to migrate to Lusaka rather than elsewhere. Additional contour lines for the index of 50 indicating a strong preference for

[14] The computation of this index in respect of the population on the Copperbelt is discussed in Mitchell 1974a.

[15] Similar maps relating to the Copperbelt, Broken Hill, and Livingstone are presented at the end of this chapter.

migration to other centres and for the index of 200 indicating a
strong preference for migration to Lusaka are also shown on the
map.[16] This analysis, and similar analyses for other line-of-rail
towns, shows the extent to which the towns drew their populations from contiguous areas. (See end of this chapter for maps
for other towns.)

In calculating the extents of these hinterlands, no account was
taken of the existence or otherwise of communication routes
from the districts of origin to the towns. The contours reflect the
de facto presence of migrants in the towns irrespective of how they
got to these towns. Clearly, however, the shapes and extents of
the hinterlands are affected by communication routes.[17] In Map
3.1, for example, the regions from which migrants were
particularly likely to come to Lusaka mainly straddle the Great
East Road from the Eastern Province. Migrants coming to the
railway line along this road found their first job opportunities at

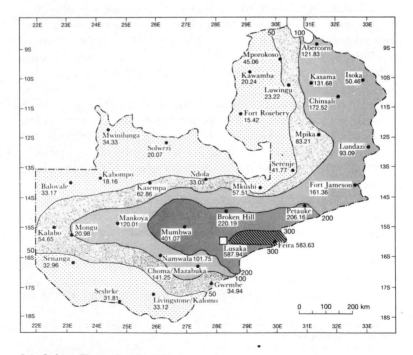

3.1. Labour Flow to Lusaka 1953–4

Lusaka—there were no intervening opportunities for them. Migrants coming down the Great North Road to Kapiri Mposhi had the choice of turning south and going to Broken Hill and then perhaps to Lusaka. There were in fact several intervening opportunities for them before they got to Lusaka. Similarly, those coming in from the west had to make the choice between Livingstone, which was likely to be nearer than Lusaka, or Lusaka itself.

Each town stood, as it were, at the gateway of a flow of migrants into towns in general along specified migration routes. The strategic location of the town at the first point of entry of the migrants to the labour market put that town at a special advantage in so far as migrants from the particular hinterland were concerned. This was most clearly demonstrated by the distribution of foreign migrants in the towns of Southern Rhodesia. The main points of entry along routes of communication were limited to one or two rail centres such as Umtali, Malvernia, Plumtree, Livingstone, etc. If we examine the proportion of migrants in towns at successive points along the main transportation routes, as for example the distribution of migrants from Mozambique in the towns along the line of rail from the border post at Umtali to the most distant at Bulawayo, there is a distinct trend to be seen in the figures. There was a much higher proportion of migrants from Mozambique in Umtali and those towns nearer the Mozambique border than in the more distant towns. A similar observation might be made about migrants from Northern Rhodesia, who were concentrated in the towns in the western region nearest the point of entry. The process may be pictured as a diffusion process along the lines of communication from the town nearest at hand to the towns most distant.[18]

The same sort of selection probably took place when migrants

---

[16] The original maps were produced by SYMAP procedures developed by The Laboratory for Computer Graphics and Spatial Analysis, Graduate School of Design, Harvard University, Cambridge, Massachusetts, in which the contours are derived from overlapping local surfaces fitted over the whole area covered by the map.

[17] There are likely to be different hinterlands for migrants of recent standing, for women as against men, for migrants with different occupational skills, in different industries, and so on. These and other points will the subject of a more detailed analysis in a later publication.

[18] This is discussed in some detail in Mitchell 1954a, 1961.

from local areas moved into town. Presumably they moved into the nearest town and then began to filter along the lines of communication between towns in response to labour opportunities and other personal advantages. The information to test this assumption is not available for the Southern Rhodesian material, but some evidence is available for Northern Rhodesia. An examination of the proportions of migrants from different districts in the Copperbelt towns shows quite distinctly that towns that stood at the point of entry of flows of migrants from particular regions tended to have more of those migrants in their populations. Thus Mufulira, which was the first town on the main transportation route from the Luapula districts to the Copperbelt, tended to have a larger proportion of migrants from these districts than the other towns. Similarly Chingola, which stood at the point of entry of migrants from the districts in the western region to the Copperbelt, had a larger proportion of migrants from this region than other regions. Towns which lay at successive distances from the point of entry tended to have proportionately fewer migrants from the regions which were separated from them by other towns (Mitchell 1954a).

These are, of course, observations on the manifest regularities in the distribution of people of varying regional origin in the towns of South Central Africa at the time of study. We may postulate a 'friction of space' to account for these regularities: that the cost and investment involved for migrants to move beyond the first point at which they were able to enter the wage-earning situation deterred their moving further afield. If so, we might postulate that the 'friction' could be overcome by additional inducements in the form of higher wages, more possibilities of advancement, better housing, or similar inducements further afield. A more detailed analysis of the differences in migrants in terms of the period of residence in the particular towns they were in, and the skills they had to offer in the wage-earning market, might have thrown additional light on this aspect of the migration.

An alternative approach might have been to argue that the first point of entry to the wage-earning market was also the point of easiest access to the region of origin. From this point of view, to remain in the town most conveniently situated to the district of origin would have implied that the migrants were in a better position to keep in contact with that region, either through the constant visiting of kinsmen or others from their home regions or through the possibility of returning if necessary with as little cost and impediment as possible.[19] This hypothesis is also capable of being put to the test by a more detailed analysis, not yet carried out, of the amount of contact migrants had with their home areas when they lived in towns at varying distances from their home regions.

The geographical situation of a town in relation to regions from which migrants come to it is relevant to the analysis of social relationships in urban areas in several different ways. One of the aspects of social relationships in towns in South Central Africa was the operation of regionalism and ethnic identity as categories in social interaction.[20] A common origin, either in terms of ethnic characteristics such as a common culture or a common language, or in terms of having come from the same local area—that is, being a 'home-boy'—served to provide migrants to towns with an identity which enabled them to relate meaningfully to others in their contacts with others in the town.[21] Clearly the position of the town in relation to a particular hinterland would affect to some extent the proportion and pattern of social relationships within it. It is in this way that geographical location was one of the basic parameters influencing social relationships in the towns.

But there is another aspect which has already been touched upon. People living in towns, as elsewhere, maintained personal contacts in the town where they were living, possibly in other towns, and in the rural areas from which they had come. An important factor, though not the only one, which influenced the degree to which contacts could be maintained was the extent to which they were able to communicate and interact with others in their contact sets. One could hypothesize that migrants living in the towns optimally placed for communication with their home

[19] Aspects of a similar approach with regard to distance of migrants from their rural areas are developed in Mitchell 1974a.
[20] This point is developed in Mitchell 1956a and 1970a, and in chapter 6. Recent references to different aspects of the same phenomenon are to be found also in Harries-Jones 1969 and Kapferer 1969.
[21] This point is developed by Wilson and Mafeje (1963) in Langa, and related to the Copperbelt situation by Harries-Jones (1969). Some aspects are discussed in Mitchell 1970a and chapter 6.

areas would be able to maintain the highest investment in links with people in their rural homes. But the ease with which a person could establish contact with someone living elsewhere might modify the relationship he had with that person: it clearly did not determine whether it existed or not. An urban worker had daily contacts with his neighbours and his workmates, but frequently he was most deeply involved personally with kinsmen who were living several hundred kilometres away from the town and whom he seldom saw. His relationships with these kinsmen, for example, would have prevailed over those with his neighbours and workmates should he have been placed in a position where he had to choose between them.

The quality of a person's relationships with people living in his area of origin and the ease with which he was able to maintain contact with them had an important bearing on his involvement in urban institutions in general. It could be argued that the very isolation of migrants in towns from their areas of origin, if these were very distant and difficult to reach, must of necessity have thrown the migrants upon their contacts in the town and led them to become heavily involved in urban activities and institutions. In fact, however, the quality of links with the people in the area of origin appeared to be such that involvement in urban institutions and activities seemed to be dependent upon the extent to which migrants were able to continue to participate in them while maintaining frequent and easy contact with rural compatriots (Mitchell 1974a). There were able in effect to maintain essential contacts with people in the area of origin if it was within easy travelling distance from town without jeopardizing their jobs, membership of employees' unions, church membership, and contacts with friends in town. They were able to make short and frequent visits back home to meet social obligations and maintain investments in the rural system. But migrants from a distant place of origin had to withdraw from their urban involvements for considerable periods if they were to maintain contact with their home area. It is likely, of course, that if the distance of the place of origin was too far from the town of residence, then the time and costs of return might have been too high for the migrants, and they might have had to try to build up permanent relationships and involvements in the town even though the economic and administrative constraints upon their doing so may have been severe. The relationship between distance of place and origin, then, and the involvement of migrants in urban activities and institutions appeared to be a curvilinear one: those from the nearest and most easily reached regions appeared to be able to become involved in urban activities while at the same time maintaining their rural links, those from intermediate distance needed to withdraw periodically from their urban activities and institutional associations to maintain their rural links, and those whose places of origins lay beyond some critical distance were effectively cut off from them.

Contextual Parameters, Social Structure, and Social Perception

A set of circumstances, thus, arising out of the demographic processes which operated within towns and out of their geographical locations in relation to the areas from which their populations flowed into them, provided a set of factors in combination with which the wider political and economic conditions defined the general context within which social relationships had to be negotiated. Our main interest, of course, is not directly in the political, administrative, economic, geographical, or demographic conditions which denoted the context within which the social behaviour had to be negotiated. The need is to provide just enough information and just sufficient analysis to make the processes inherent in these conditions intelligible so that the reader is in a position to appreciate the way in which they constrained or determined specific forms of human behaviour. As sociologists, interested primarily in understanding how social behaviour took the form it did, we can afford to be naïve about these more general processes which did not themselves constitute the focus of our study.

Two connected aspects of social behaviour are involved in this analysis. One is concerned with the regularly recurring patterns of social relationships which the analyst is able to discern in the daily activities of the town dwellers. The analyst seeks to establish these patterns and then to relate them to the social context in which they occur, to trace the necessary connections they have with other patterns which occur simultaneously with or subsequent to them, and to establish the links between these patterns and the norms and values which the actors hold about them. The central concern of studies of this kind is in social morphology, and they are essentially structural in orientation. The emphasis is on the relationships among parts—identifiable social units or cultural patterns—which the analyst is able to present in terms of some logically connected set of concepts.

The second type of study, as yet relatively unexplored, lays emphasis upon the understandings the actors themselves have of the events and the social relationships in which they are involved. These, of course, may differ considerably from those of the analyst. The actor, we presume, organizes the information available to him about socially relevant objects—particularly about the behaviour of other actors—and relates possible future actions in respect of these objects or persons to this cognitive construct. The process of the organization of socially relevant information in this way we have referred to as 'social perception', with the implication that the perceptions are social in so far as they are not purely individual or idiosyncratic but are shared in some way with other actors and form a basis through which actors may address their activities towards one another.

The sociological analyst's task in respect of social perceptions is to try to delineate cognitions which are shared by some category relating to the analyst's area of interest. The actual processes of cognition are properly the field of the psychologist: the sociologist assumes a common-sense stance in respect of cognition as such. Concern rests rather with the consequences of the actor's cognitive constructions for the way in which they address themselves to others. With regard to urbanism, for example, townsfolk of various kinds are presented with a plethora of cues, signs, symbols, and impressions as they go about their daily activities in the town. They organize these sensory stimuli into cognitive constructs which allow them to attribute meanings to the events and phenomena which they perceive.

During the course of my field observations in Northern Rhodesia, I was struck by the extent to which sensitivity to social status and ethnicity influenced the ways in which urban Africans related to each other. It was in order to check these general impressions with systematic data that I undertook two questionnaire studies. The first, with A. L. Epstein, related to occupational prestige, which we knew was closely associated with social status. The second was with Janet Longton and related to ethnic social distance. Some years later, while in Southern Rhodesia, I realized that although there was considerable public interest in and concern with 'problems of urbanization', there was in fact very little empirical material concerning the way in which Africans themselves thought about urban living. This led me to devise a questionnaire study with Mr M. B. Lukhero to probe this field of perception. These three topics were all socially significant issues which were also of general sociological interest. They became the basis of the examination of social perception in the three chapters that follow, which begin with the most general: the perception of urban living.

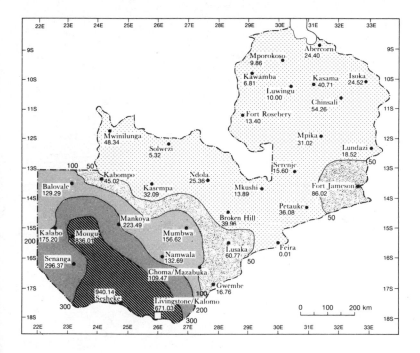

3.2. Labour Flow to Livingstone 1952-3

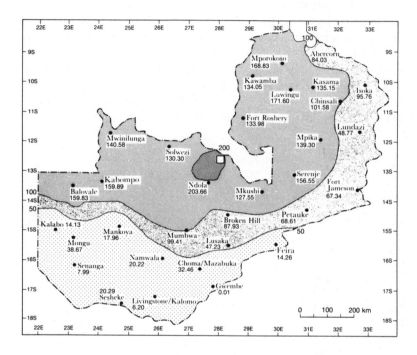

3.3. Labour Flow to the Copperbelt 1950–2

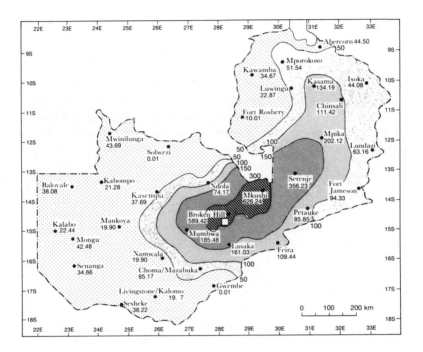

3.4. Labour Flow to Broken Hill 1952-3

4

THE PERCEPTIONS OF CITY LIFE

The analysis of the social context of urbanization implies that the growth of towns in South Central Africa—and presumably in other parts of Africa—has meant for their African inhabitants more than simply a movement from a rurally based set of social relationships to one based on urban institutions. In contrast to Europe or America the political, economic, and social features of the towns were not merely variations of a basic cultural pattern but rather manifestations of a substantially foreign system. Towns in Africa, as Balandier (1956: 497) argued, were especially colonial creations—erected by expatriates on their design to serve their ends.[1]

This is because the political, economic, and social activities of the indigenous small-scale societies were such that they called for no complex set of administrative, commercial, or industrial arrangements requiring a large-scale concentration of populations in towns. Instead the predominantly subsistence type of economy militated against a detailed specialization and division of labour and consequent intensive exchange of goods and services. The processes of trading and government could be conducted without intricate bureaucratic organization, merely with a concentration of functionaries in and around the ruler's capital.

The Europeans who arrived in South Central Africa in the last quarter of the nineteenth century, however, were representatives of a complex but geographically distant social order in which the concentration of population and activities in large urban agglomerations was a necessary concomitant of its political, economic, and social organization. The towns that the settlers established at Blantyre, Salisbury, Bulawayo,

---

[1] The impact of colonialism on city structure is treated at some length in King 1976. He emphasizes in particular how the form and social arrangements in colonial cities served the interests of the colonists.

Livingstone, and Ndola were in fact outliers of the metropolitan overseas society and not a natural outgrowth of the existing social order in Africa. The layout, buildings, streets, traffic, sanitation, and street lighting were all imported fully developed from Europe into South Central Africa, as were the administrative and economic activities which formed the basis of the town's existence. Together with the physical layout and services of the town and the economic and administrative organization, social institutions were imported which allowed the European settlers and colonists to mediate their relationships not only with one another but also with the indigenous peoples.

Africans were absorbed into the towns from the start in rigidly defined roles, predominantly as servants and employees of the European town-dwellers and to a lesser extent as employees of Asian town-dwellers. Their participation in urban activities was highly 'segmental' in the sense that the roles they could adopt were narrowly circumscribed by the Europeans who maintained political, economic, and social control of the towns. Europeans expected their African servants and employees to maintain a substantial involvement in a rural economic and social system and never to become totally immersed in town activities. The 'urbanized' African was in fact viewed as a 'detribalized' person, whose sheet anchor of traditional customs and values had been slipped and who was in consequence a disorganized and dissociated person. Town life on the other hand was considered 'natural' for Europeans in the same way that a traditional 'tribal' way of life was 'natural' for Africans.

Towns, as Sir Godfrey Huggins (later Lord Malvern) as Prime Minister of Southern Rhodesia in 1941 put it, were 'the White Reserves', in the sense that as the natural home of the Africans was in the Native Reserves where special rights were preserved for them, so the natural home of the Whites was in the towns, where equally special rights were there preserved for them (Gray 1960: 276).

It was perhaps inevitable that from the start Africans, living both in rural areas and in towns, should have developed perceptions of the city which were sharply determined by the circumstances in which cities came to be established in Central Africa. As was described earlier, Europeans had brought the towns into being, had created the administrative framework which, in terms of the economic activities in the towns, had decreed the strict residential segregation of the Whites from the Africans in them, had instituted controls of the ingress and egress of African migrants to and from them, and had supplied and controlled the health, housing, and welfare services for the African population. The African image of the town was inevitably going to be coloured by these circumstances.

Yet the overall similarities of African perceptions of city life in general and those of European and American commentators at a stage when there was still a considerable migration of country-men to the towns is striking.[2] In England, Cobbett's famed characterization of London as 'the great wen' reflects the view of a large number of observers who saw in cities nothing but vice and degradation. Derry writes of Cobbett:

To him London was not a glittering metropolis, the gay and splendid centre of the nation's political and commercial life. It was 'the Great Wen', a vile and nauseating sore which was disfiguring the face of the country with its ugliness. More and more Englishmen were going to live in towns, and to Cobbett this implied a deterioration in the national character. As their bodies became tainted with disease, so their minds became perverted and corrupt . . . while honesty withered and died in the anonymity of great towns, fraud and greed flourished.[3]

Likewise in America in the latter half of the nineteenth century, when its towns were growing at an unprecedented rate, the predominantly rural population looked upon the city

as a Babylon, a den of inquiry, the breeding ground of sin and evil and the temptress of the good Christian. It was also the home of the infidel. It was the blood-sucker which strangled the farmer, the stronghold of the heartless, corrupt, immoral industrialists, bankers and politicians who cheated the farmer of his rightful property and drove a wedge between him and the class of town labourers who had always been his brother in arms.[4]

---

[2] This and the following 17 paragraphs follow very closely Mitchell 1969: 1–6.

[3] Derry, J. (ed.) (1968: 15). Asa Briggs reviews English nineteenth century attitudes to towns in this chapter 'City and Society' in Briggs 1963: 57–62. A perceptive analysis of the way in which urban society has been represented in English literature is given by Raymond Williams (1976).

[4] Anselm Strauss (1961: 175). Richard Hofstadter, the historian, has argued that the agrarian myth in the nineteenth century was the sentimental and moral obverse of all that the metropolis at its most wicked stood for. See Hofstadter 1955.

The situation was perhaps most succinctly summarized by a popular nineteenth century religious novelist in America who commented: 'Adam and Eve were created and placed in a garden: cities are the result of the fall.'[5]

No less in present-day developing countries do we find similar points of view being expressed about towns. In South and Central Africa morally and aesthetically evaluative images of town life were common. Here the towns established by European immigrants as centres of economic and administrative enterprise, dating from the seventeenth century in South Africa and the end of the nineteenth and twentieth century in Central Africa, were organized on the basis of a set of industrial and commercial activities which were a part of the wider Western civilization whose outliers the White immigrants in Africa represented. The African migrants to these towns came from small-scale social systems whose basic value orientations were markedly dissimilar from those of the Europeans who had founded the towns. The living conditions and behaviour patterns in the town represented a disjunction from the rural life which was probably more extreme than that experienced when a yokel moved into an industrial town in mid-nineteenth century England or a Polish peasant moved into an American city at the beginning of the twentieth century.

It is not surprising that both Europeans and Africans came to look upon the way of life that Africans adopted in the towns as degraded and disorganized. This was what was implied by the notion of 'detribalization' which has dominated the perceptions of African city life of parliamentarians, administrators, and public-spirited Europeans in Central and South Africa for a long time. The image of the town here is that of a 'non-tribe' in the sense that the departures from tribal norms of behaviour, whether real or imagined, were evaluated in moral terms and given a pejorative connotation. The Africans themselves adopted much the same point of view. Philip Mayer, referring to East London, South Africa, describes how rurally orientated migrants looked upon town and town ways as inherently evil. He writes:

Like other urban populations, especially those at a low standard of

5 J. H. Ingraham quoted by Asa Briggs (1963: 75).

living, the town-dwelling Africans seem to have serious problems in the sphere of morality and social control. From what has been said, it will be realised that these are not just the first shock reactions of a people being newly exposed to the urbanization process. Prima facie the urban locations (i.e. residential quarters to which non-white people are confined, by law as well as by custom) seem to abound in violent crimes, drunkenness, drug addiction, theft, robbery, offences by children out of parental control, and sexual laxity—this last resulting in an extremely high incidence of illegitimate births. There is the dread stereotype of the tsotsi—a figure uniquely associated with urban locations—who is described by Africans as a person without any moral controls at all, 'one who has not got the feelings of a human being'.

Africans themselves often lament the immorality of urban locations, particularly what they see as a lack of respect for parents and seniors. They suggest that town corrupts children as well as women. In the field I know best personally, i.e. East London and the Ciskei, and Transkei, even those parents who are well adjusted to town life themselves may make efforts to send their young children back to the country to be reared by relatives there. Significantly all this moral disapproval is part of the townsmen's stereotypes of themselves, as well as of the country people's stereotype of them. Almost all categories of Africans, in and out of town, seem to agree that the urban locations are immoral places, and that born-and-bred towns people are apt to be the worst in this respect, even if superior to the countryborn in skill and sophistication. There is some realisation that this hangs together with the anonymity of town. The urban location is described as a place where 'nobody knows' or 'nobody cares' as against the rural community where (in a favourite phrase) 'we are all one another's policemen'. (Mayer 1963: 115. See also 1961: 90 ff.)

It would clearly be unjustified, however, to assume that the images of city life were always negative. Derogatory images of town life and townsfolk are usually balanced by contrary images in which cities are perceived as the centres of development and change. In terms of this image the countryman is the ignorant and backward yokel as against the urbane and progressive townsman. The countryman is thus morally upright but unprogressive, the townsman is degenerate but an agent of change and development.

Asa Briggs points to this ambivalence by showing how many commentators saw cities as the sources of strength for change and development:

These men did not argue in the defensive. They persistently carried the attack into the countryside, comparing contemptuously the passive with the active, the idlers with the workers, the landlords with the businessmen, the voluntary initiative of the city with the 'torpor' and 'monotony' of the village, and urban freedom with rustic 'feudalism'. Engels, who wrote incisively about Manchester without being a proud Mancunian, agreed with other Mancunians in this particular indictment. (1963: 65.)

This ambivalence was reflected not only in the voices of different men but also sometimes in the voice of the same man. Raymond Williams (1976: 161, 184–7) traces the changes in William Wordsworth's assessment of the moral qualities of rural and urban life from 'Michael', subtitled 'a pastoral poem', in which he depicts the simple ingenuous life of country men, to *The Preludes*, which contain many sharp comments on the faceless-ness of society in the London he knew, but of which he finally observes:

> . . . that among the multitudes
> Of that huge city, often times was seen
> Affectingly set forth, more than elsewhere
> Is possible, the unity of men,
> One spirit over ignorance and vice
> Predominant, in good and evil hearts
> One sense for moral judgements, as one eye
> For the sun's light.

'The debate about the Victorian city', Briggs concludes, 'was a debate with different voices making themselves heard inside the city itself, with the struggle between the defenders of the city, those who in various ways were proud of it, and its critics, par-ticularly those who were afraid of it, ranging widely and probing deep.' (1963: 68.)

In America there were no less of those who saw in the cities the agents of progress. The nineteenth century moralists had roundly condemned

demon drink and the terrible habits consequent upon sociability in the traverns, the life of the streets with the menace of prostitution, vice and crime, the frivolity of the theatre, and other corrupting forms of recrea-tion, the seduction of men by poverty and riches alike, the loss of identity and morality by submergence in the anonymous crowd . . . But in the curious way negatives often have of turning positive in the

nick of time, the dreaded sides of city life changed from sinful tempta-
tions into challenges of virtue. Impulses to give way to temptation, to
fall from grace, when quashed, could in all good logic only lead to a
strengthening of character. A minor failure could yet be converted to a
moral victory. For a boy armed with a rural upbringing and fortified
with the steadfast practice of Christianity . . . it was possible, and
indeed perhaps a duty, to contribute to the country's welfare by
growing rich in business. (Strauss 1961: 144.)

As Asa Briggs points out:

Walt Whitman on returning to New York in 1870 had praised 'the
splendour, picturesqueness, and oceanic amplitude' of the great
American cities. Another American, Oliver Wendell Holmes, tired of
hearing Cowper's line, 'God made the country and man made the
town', offered his own version—'God made the cavern and man made
the house'. (1963: 75.)

Contrasting images of city life and of townsmen have emerged
in South and Central Africa in exactly the same way as in
England and America. The dichotomy is well captured by the
Swahili terms *kisendji* and *kisungu* with which Congolese Africans
characterized the contrast. *Kisungu* refers to the White man's
way and relates to urbanity, civilisation, and familiarity with the
city ways. *Kisendji* on the other hand refers to village ways and
the traditional way of life, and in an urban context is a pejorative
term (Pons 1956: 64).

Kapferer has indicated that the term *fontini* is used by city
dwellers to refer to the behaviour of those who are unfamiliar
with city ways, while the term *basambashi* would be applied to the
sophisticate who was familiar with town ways and presented an
image of a civilised and urbane man.[6]

The categorization of people into 'villagers', *kamushi*, in
which the diminutive prefix *ka* denotes denigration, and *bena
tauni*, 'townsmen', reflects exactly the same process. Long, who
worked in a rural area, points out that the appellation of *mwina
tauni* relates in fact to the behaviour of the person involved and
not to actual residence, so that a person who has spent a relatively short time in town but behaves like a townsman is still
called *mwina tauni* (1968: 164–6).

---

[6] Kapferer, B., personal communication. Kashoki (1975: 725) translates it as
'ignoramus'.

The images to which I am referring are not merely the personal perceptions of talented individuals. They are, rather, complexes of attitude and perceptions which substantial numbers of people share and hold to be reasonable representations of reality. Where I have quoted the words of poets and literary writers, it is in the belief that they, by virtue of their sensitivity, have been able to present more sharply and more graphically the images to which many of their contemporaries subscribed.

The notion of the image here implies that it represents a perception of a phenomenon such that certain basic characteristics or qualities deemed to be especially characteristic of it are evident. Whether these qualities or characteristics are objectively present or not is irrelevant: the important point is simply that specified sets of persons perceive the phenomenon in terms of these identifiable qualities.

The underlying postulate of what follows is that the perceptions of city and country life will depend to some extent upon the social positions of the observers and that we can understand these images not so much as representatives of reality, but rather as partial reflections of the social positions of those who hold them.

Unfortunately, the evidence of images of the town which we have been able to cull from historical sources can have only circumstantial validity, since it is in the form of the writings of persons who felt strongly about the issue and have for this reason left a record of their feelings behind them. These images are sometimes intelligible in terms of the individual backgrounds of their authors, but we have no ways of testing the extent to which the images were substantially subscribed to by identifiable categories of person. Even in present-day industrialized countries, at a time when public opinion survey techniques have reached a high level of sophistication, there are very few studies which set out to describe the attitudes of people to town and country life in general.[7]

The analytical utility of social perceptions of this sort lies, however, in their dialectical relationship with the structural parameters to which they relate. They represent 'constructions

[7] Fischer (1976: 15-25) reviews recent data relating to 'images of urban life' in 'western culture'.

of reality' which intervene between the abstract structural features of the society in which they occur and the behaviour of people in everyday life. Urban images exist in this respect as reservoirs of meaning from which specific individuals are able to draw interpretations which enable them to order their social actions in a way that is reasonable and rational to them. The difficulty in the analytical use of images, however, is that since they are essentially perceptual and therefore represent ways of organizing cognitive data, they cannot have the general and consistent validity with which structural parameters are invested. At the most detailed level, every individual probably perceives town life in his own way and invests events and actions in it with his or her own meanings. Our interest as analysts, however, is in those meanings which are shared among at least some identifiable set of people and, additionally, in the extent to which there may be regularities in the differences in images with the social positions of people, differences which we are able to appreciate in terms of our general theoretical understanding of social behaviour.

To do this we must go beyond the dramatic and evocative images presented in literature and the popular press to a direct and systematic exploration of aspects of people's perceptions of city life in relation to their social characteristics. It was with this end in mind that in November 1965 I collected some information about African perceptions of town life in Southern Rhodesia (now Zimbabwe), a topic upon which there was a good deal of opinionation but very little systematic information.

The Attitude Study

Having had familiarity over several years with statements and opinions of both Europeans and Africans about the qualities of town life and of the desirability of various social changes, I had become aware of some commonly accepted views on these matters. The object was to see whether the impressions which were obtained from general experience would be reflected in the responses to a formal measuring instrument, and, if so, whether different background factors could be correlated with different perceptions.

Since no previous studies of this sort were known to me, I

had of necessity to develop a set of items for the question *ab initio*. These, with distributions, are set out in the Appendix (pp. 314–16).[8] This was done on the basis of three procedures:

(a) From our general personal and fieldwork experience Mr Lukhero,[9] my research assistant, and I were already familiar with a number of opinions which were frequently expressed about town life or about changing modern conditions in general. We were able, therefore, to write down a number of statements which could be used as items in an attitude questionnaire. Examples are:

6. 'People from rural areas are more honest than those who have grown up in urban areas'

4. 'Town is a place for working in: as soon as a man has earned the money he wants he should go back to his rural area'

(b) Mr Lukhero, who lived in one of the African townships of Salisbury, recorded statements he heard in conversation or in public places which reflected an opinion about or attitude towards some aspect of town life, rural life, or modern or traditional ways of living. Examples are:

9. 'Customs in rural areas are good because young people do not bath together with old people'

23. 'Friendship in the towns is based only on money'

(c) African newspapers and articles were examined for statements which reflected attitudes which could be used in a questionnaire. Not many of these were in fact used. An example is:

27. 'The worst thing that happened to people when they moved from their villages to the big cities was a loss of respect and politeness for one another'

[8] P. J. McEwan (1963) had made a general study in Salisbury earlier but only one question appears to have been devoted to attitudes to town life.

[9] Mr M. B. Lukhero was then a Technical Assistant in the Department of Sociology at the University College of Rhodesia and Nyasaland. He had been a research assistant attached to the Rhodes–Livingstone Institute between 1947 and 1950 and between 1952 and 1957, working in both rural and urban areas. I am grateful to him for his invaluable assistance in framing the items in the questionnaire, administering the questionnaire, and coding the results. I benefited considerably from discussions with my wife Hilary Mitchell concerning the wording and context of the items in the questionnaire. She had had wide experience of research in African towns. I am also grateful to Mr Dennis Masarirambi for punching and verifying the cards and for producing the first set of tabulations, to Mrs Ann Kitchen for the computer analysis, and to Mr David Boswell for help with the historical aspects of this study.

Sometimes the items were phrased rather circuitously and involved some ambiguities. For example, item 29: 'Living in urban areas is bad because it stops good customs, such as worshipping the spirits of dead relatives', contains two aspects, the first relating to 'good' customs in general and the second to worshipping ancestor spirits in particular. A person who disagreed with this could be disagreeing with the notion that it is correct to worship ancestor spirits. But we felt that by specifying ancestor worship we implied that 'good' customs were in fact 'traditional' customs, and it seemed worth risking the ambiguity here. The actual phrasing in English was chosen carefully so that it would be intelligible with as little difficulty as possible to the subjects we wished to use. One statement in particular violated most of the rules of good questionnaire item construction, since it appeared complex and ambiguous (item 32: 'The peaceful quiet of the rural areas is better for people that than the interesting excitement of the towns'), as well as being a leading question. We put the item in the questionnaire more as a general probe than as a substantive item in the questionnaire. In fact it turned out to be a reasonably good indicator of underlying attitudes.

The items were selected to cover the following general fields (see Appendix):

(a) General kinship and family obligations—items 1, 8, 16, 18, 21, 25, 31.
(b) Moral and ethical aspects of behaviour—items 2, 5, 6, 9, 14, 15, 19, 20, 23, 26, 27, 29, 30.
(c) Economic and social amenities in town and country—items 3, 4, 7, 12, 24, 28.
(d) Town and country rootedness—items 10, 11, 13, 17, 22.
(e) General—item 32.

Many of the items covered more than one general topic. Thus some of those that dealt with kinship obligations, for example, could also be construed as relating to town and country rootedness. In fact the subsequent analysis proved that the respondents perceived other aspects than those reflected in this classification.

Thirty-two items were chosen for the questionnaire, a number which we thought would provide enough variation between items to cover the main areas of interest without making the questions too long and too tedious. The thirty-two items were arranged in random order in the schedule, and respondents were asked whether they 'agreed strongly', 'agreed', 'neither agreed nor disagreed', 'disagreed', or 'strongly disagreed' with the statements. The responses were coded in such a way that if the response was strongly in favour of town life or modern conditions it was given a rating of 5 and if it was strongly antagonistic a rating of 1, with appropriate values of 4, 3, and 2 as the intermediate categories. Since the subsequent analysis was based on correlations among the items, a misjudgement in the 'direction' of coding did not materially affect the issue, since the correlation among items coded in the wrong direction would be negative. There were in fact no negative correlations, so our anticipation of the direction of coding was in fact validated.

The background data for each respondent was restricted to a minimum: sex, year of birth, educational level attained, father's occupation, father's educational level, mother's educational level, and length of residence in towns. Each subject was required to check a category in which he rated himself as either a townsman or a countryman along the scale: 'very definitely a townsman', 'mainly a townsman', 'partly a townsman', 'mainly a countryman', and 'very definitely a countryman'. Finally, an open-ended question was provided which enabled the subject to comment in general about town and country life. This has not been analysed here: mostly it was not answered and many of the answers that were made did not add substantially to our insights into their perception of town and country life.

The respondents were 1,392 persons whom I could contact through various educational institutions in Rhodesia. The majority (60.5) were scholars in secondary schools, 29.2 per cent were in teacher training colleges and 6.8 per cent were in adult educational classes. The remainder (4.5 per cent) were members of various professional and conference groups to which I had access. The respondents thus in no way represent a random sample of the African population of Rhodesia. From a statistical point of view the generalizations which emerge from the study are appropriate for this particular set of respondents and for no other, but the plausibility of some of the generalizations suggests that in fact, on other than statistical grounds, we might reasonably assume that the generalizations apply to a wider population.

Table 4.1 (a) to (h) sets out the overall social characteristics of the respondents.

These tables show that the respondents were mainly young, male, scholars, of relatively high education, drawn from varied parental backgrounds, and representing a fairly wide range of contact with both rural and urban conditions.

Response to Selected Items

The following items, measured by the mean response rating, coded here as 'strongly agree' = 1 to 'strongly disagree' = 5, are those with which the respondents agreed most. A low mean indicates agreement, a high mean rating disagreement.

16. A townsman should always help his relatives who live in the rural areas by sending them money and clothes   1.67
20. Parents in towns should sent their children to spend school holidays in rural areas so that they may grow up to respect the older people   1.79
28. Town life is bad because you starve there when you are out of work   1.97
26. Children who have grown up in rural areas are more polite than the children who have grown up in town   2.07
10. It is better for old people to live in rural areas than in towns   2.13

On the other hand the items with which respondents disagreed the most were the following:

14. Customs in rural areas are not good because even the uneducated people expect to be respected there   4.42
 2. Boys who have grown up in rural areas do not know how to behave properly   4.42
21. A man should be expected to look after his wife and children only and not his other relatives   4.32
 1. The relatives of a man who has worked all his life in town should not expect him to go back to the rural areas when he is too old to work   3.99
15. Having a child before marriage is not considered a bad thing by girls and their parents in town   3.93

Table 4.1 Social Characteristics of Respondents

(a) Respondent Category

Secondary schools	Adult education	Teacher training	Professional classes	Others	
841	95	406	16	34	1392

(b) Sex

Female	Male	D/K	
265	1125	2	1392

(c) Age

12–14	15–17	18–20	21–23	24–26	27–30	31–33	34–44	45 +	
23	260	725	260	53	26	19	18	8	1392

(d) Years of Schooling Completed

6	7	8	9	10	11	12	13	14	15	
20	9	7	12	762	144	230	26	1	1	1392

(e) Father's Occupation

Unemployed villager	Farmer	Unskilled labourer	Semi-skilled worker	Skilled worker	Supervisor	Businessman	White-collar	Professional	D/K	
200	312	114	207	114	82	58	292	10	3	1392

(f) Years Schooling Father Completed

0	2	4	6	8	10	12	14	16	D/K	
251	35	115	317	491	121	36	10	13	3	1392

(g) Years Schooling Mother Completed

0	2	4	6	8	10	12	14	16	D/K	
327	50	224	367	346	59	7	6	4	2	1392

(h) Percentage of Adult Life in Town

0–11	12–22	23–33	34–44	35–55	56–66	67–77	78–99	100	D/K	
322	217	165	122	104	115	71	241	20	15	1392

Source: Survey of Attitudes to Town Living.

Items 16 and 21 deal with kinship obligations, and it is interesting that the respondents overwhelmingly supported extended family obligations. Items 20, 26, 14, and 2 refer to the general moral and ethical view of rural life, and once again the respondents seemed, on the whole, to feel that rural values and rural ways of behaviour were desirable. But the response to item 15, dealing with pre-marital pregnancy, shows that general values in this connection took precedence over rural and urban divisions. Items 10 and 1 relate to town rootedness and show that in general the respondents seemed to accept the proposition that people should return to the rural areas eventually. Their reaction to item 28 supports this, since they strongly agreed about the economic disabilities of living in towns while unemployed. These comments refer only to the items in which there was a marked skewing of responses. More powerful techniques of analysis, however, bring out the underlying regularities in the responses to all thirty-two items at once. This analysis is summarized later.

Respondents were most divided (measured by the standard deviation of the rating) in their reactions to the following items (low standard deviations indicate high consensus and high standard deviations low consensus):

5. Girls should always grow up in rural areas because town customs are bad for them   1.55
4. Town is a place for working in: as soon as a man has earned the money he wants he should go back to his rural home 1.45
19. Towns are bad because there women learn to wear short and tight dresses   1.45
11. Fear of witchcraft in rural areas stops those who have finished working from going back to those rural areas   1.44
23. Friendship in the town is based only on money   1.44

Reactions were most concentrated and united in respect of the following items:

14. Customs in rural areas are not good because there even the uneducated people expected to be respected   0.95
16. A townsman should always help his relatives who live in the rural areas by sending them money and clothes   1.02
21. A man should be expected to look after his wife and children only and not his other relatives   1.04

2. Boys who have grown up in rural areas do not know how to behave properly   1.06
28. Town life is bad because you starve there when you are out of work   1.10

The fact that the same items appear in this list as in the extremes of the list concerning the high agreement and disagreement is not, of course, accidental. The standard deviation would be affected by an extreme skewing of the distribution as occurs in these cases. The interest is rather in the items in which there are large standard deviations. The large standard deviations could arise from several different sources. Ambiguity in an item may lead to a wide scatter of responses because the respondents may have been reacting to different and dissimilar interpretations of the item. There may be a wide scatter also because the respondents themselves are divided, so that some agree with it while others disagree with it. For example, in item 19, which refers to the moral censuring of women who wear short and tight dresses, there are likely to be different responses from men and women to this item, as also, for example, between young and old. This particular set of items is sufficiently straightforward to suggest that the real basis of the scatter of responses is in fact the divided opinion among the respondents. Subsequent analyses were directed at trying to isolate some of the social characteristics associated with people who reacted to these items in different ways.

Most uncertainty, as against division of opinion, as measured by the percentage of respondents who did not answer specific items, was expressed in respect of the following items:

3. Because there are no social amenities like cinemas, sports, beer halls, and clubs in rural areas it is better to stay in town where they can be found   1.87
9. Customs in rural areas are good because young people do not bath together with old people   1.29
1. The relatives of a man who has worked all his life in town should not expect him to go back to the rural areas when he is too old to work   1.22
26. Children who have grown up in rural areas are more polite than the children who have grown up in town   1.08

In contrast, the following items were those in which there were fewest 'don't know' responses:

8. Life in the rural areas is good because there are always relatives there who can look after you if you are sick or have lost your job   0.07

11. Fear of witchcraft in rural areas stops those who have finished work from going back to those rural areas   0.22

25. A man should not be expected to help many relatives in these modern times   0.29

20. Parents in town should send their children to spend school holidays in rural areas so that they may grow up to respect the older people   0.29

7. Life in rural areas cannot interest young people   0.29

The scatter of responses did not seem to be related to the confidence or otherwise with which respondents were able to respond to the items. The items in which there were the highest proportion of 'don't know' responses were not those with the largest standard deviations, nor were those with the smallest proportion of 'don't know' responses those with the smallest standard deviations. The standard deviation seemed to relate to a division of opinion rather than to uncertainty of response. It is possible that relatively high proportions of 'don't know' responses arose in some of the items because the majority of respondents were young people and may have felt uncertain about answering these items. For example, item 26, which relates to the politeness of children who have grown up in town, may have been difficult for young people to answer. In other items it is possible that the meaning of the question might have been obscure to the respondents. Item 3, for example, which had the highest proportion of 'don't know' responses, was about 'social amenities', and although we were careful to illustrate what we meant by 'social amenities' it is possible that people were not sure what was intended.

There was a good deal of division of opinion on some topics on which there were relatively few 'don't know' responses. The scatter of responses for some of the items, like that dealing with the influence of witchcraft on persons returning to their rural areas, the item dealing with extended family obligations, or the interest of young persons in rural affairs was high, but

Table 4.2 *Rural–Urban Self-rating*

Very definitely a townsman	131	9.6
Mainly a townsman	152	11.1
Partly a townsman, partly a countryman	767	56.0
Mainly a countryman	210	15.3
Very definitely a countryman	110	8.0
No response	22	
Total	1392	100.0

the respondents apparently had little difficulty in reacting to them.

Rural–Urban Self-rating

A direct indication of the way in which respondents saw themselves is provided by the item in which the respondents were asked to indicate whether they considered themselves to be 'very definitely a townsman', 'mainly a townsman', 'partly a townsman and partly a countryman', and 'very definitely a countryman'. The frequency and proportions in these categories were as in Table 4.2.

The distribution is beautifully regular, with only a slight bias towards the 'countryman' end. Perhaps the most striking feature is the extent to which the majority classify themselves as both townsman and countryman, with only 9.6 per cent classifying themselves 'very definitely a townsman', and 8.0 per cent as 'very definitely a countryman'.

A regression analysis of the influence of social background characteristics on the tendency of respondents to rate themselves either as a townsman or a countryman, which I set out elsewhere (Mitchell 1969d), showed that, holding all other factors constant, the proportion of time the respondents had spent in town had the largest effect: those who had spent most of their life in town not unexpectedly tended to rate themselves as townsmen. Different categories of respondents also differed significantly in their self-rating. Members of adult education classes tended to rate themselves as townsmen more often than other respondents, and students at school more often than students at teacher training colleges. Finally, those respondents whose fathers were in supervisory occupations or white-collar jobs or who were businessmen were more inclined to rate themselves as townsmen than those whose fathers had semi-skilled and skilled occupations, and these more than those in agricultural and unskilled occupations.

In relation to the general population, these respondents, potentially at any rate, were the more 'Westernized' element. In common-sense terms they ought to be the people who were most urban in outlook. The analysis of the relationship of background factors to the self-rating of respondents suggested that this reasoning was not incorrect: what calls for an explanation is rather than such a large proportion of the respondents were not disposed to see themselves as townsmen. Without direct investigation of the problem we can only speculate, but any speculation on this point would need to take into account the whole insecure legal, social, and economic positions of Africans in the towns of Southern Rhodesia. Whatever the skills and orientations of young Africans, in the circumstances prevailing in Southern Rhodesia at the time of the survey keeping one foot in a rural base while taking advantage of economic opportunities in the towns was in many ways the most rational thing for them to do.

The Underlying Dimensions in the Items

Not much is to be gained, however, from examining the responses to items individually, since several items reflect to a greater or lesser extent the same basic attitudes of the respondents. A more efficient analysis may be made if we are able to combine the responses to several items so as to yield scores which reflect the general position along an abstract common dimension which we may reasonably assume underlies these items. Consider for example the responses to these three items:

6. People from rural areas are more honest than those who have grown up in urban areas

26. Children who have grown up in rural areas are more polite than the children who have grown up in the towns

27. One of the worst things that happened to people when they moved from their village into big cities was a loss of respect and politeness for one another

The product–moment correlation coefficient between the scores in item 6 and 26 over all 1,392 respondents was 0.496, between item 6 and item 27 0.319, and between items 26 and 27 0.472. These correlations measure the extent to which respondents scored these items consistently in the same direction. These items seem to reflect a common concern with a perception of town life as militating against honesty and politeness. A common factor, therefore, which underlies these correlations might be so identified, and the location of any respondent along that factor estimated by a weighted sum of scores on the three items. Geometrically, these factors may be seen as axes in the multi-dimensional space which envelopes the items. A principal component analysis, in fact, derives a set of common factors which together account for most of the observed correlations between items, and these may be used to compute scores of respondents on the appropriate factors. In this analysis eight factors were extracted, and they accounted respectively for 16.2, 8.0, 4.6, 3.8, 3.6, 3.5, 3.2, and 3.0 per cent of the variance among the 32 items in the analysis. (See last line of Table 4.3.) The total amount of variance explained by the eight factors was thus 45.9 per cent.

The first axis derived from this analysis is so located among the items that most of the variance is explained by it, the second largest amount of variance by the second axis placed at right angles to the previous axis, and so on. It is sometimes possible, however, to relax the requirement that the first factor explains most variance, the second less, and so on, and to locate the axes at a slightly different position, but still at right angles to one another, so that the interpretation of the dimension is clarified.[10] Thus far we have assumed that the underlying dimensions are uncorrelated, that is that the axes are all at right angles to one another. This is unlikely to be true with the sort of material we are dealing with. Thus we are able to locate each axis independently of the others through clusters of items to maximize their projections on to that axis.[11] In estimating the position of any person along one of the dimensions, however, we need to treat that dimension as independent from the other dimensions. This means that we use the values of the projections of the items on to the dimensions set at right angles to one another as weights in calculating scores. The values of the items on the dimensions

10 The rotation was carried out by the Varimax procedure.
11 The rotation was carried out by the Promax procedure.

Table 4.3 *Correlations of Attitude Items with Underlying Dimensions* (Factor Structure after Promax Rotation)

	Rural–Urban rootedness	General moral and ethical standards	Traditionalism/ modernism	General sexual morality	Social and recreational amenities available	General kinship obligations	Desirability of town or country life	Social and economic investment in rural and urban areas
4. Town is a place for working in: as soon as a man has earned the money he wants he should go back to his rural area	−.556	−.245	.331	.441	−.245	−.308	−.104	.156
24. Tribal life in rural areas is good because there are village headmen there to settle quarrels and troubles according to the customs of the people in the area	−.467	−.291	.557	.138	−.149	−.241	−.267	−.273
20. Parents in towns should send their children to spend school holidays in rural areas so that they may grow up to respect the older people	−.366	−.506	.358	.257	.051	−.0316	−.138	.017
23. Friendship in the towns is based only on money	−.277	−.517	.375	.502	.062	−.151	−.208	−.118
32. The peaceful quiet of the rural areas is better for people than the interesting excitement of the towns	−.370	−.331	.441	.356	−.333	−.025	−.343	.000
13. A man should return to his rural home before he gets too old	−.702	−.316	.228	.224	−.029	−.186	−.170	−.018
27. One of the worst things that happened to people when they moved from their villages into big cities was a loss of respect and politeness for each other	−.305	−.650	.226	.334	.032	−.028	−.218	−.115
26. Children who have grown up in rural areas are more polite than the children who have grown up in town	−.299	−.744	.292	.267	−.044	−.077	−.036	.053
8. Life in the rural areas is good because there are always relatives there who can look after you if you are sick or have lost your job	−.299	−.526	.432	.000	−.143	−.164	−.210	.050
19. Towns are bad because there women learn to wear short and tight dresses	−.308	−.384	.477	.565	−.155	−.120	−.093	.172

5. Girls should always grow up in rural areas because town customs are bad for them	−.223	−.443	.424	.476	−.085	−.173	.134	.349
28. Town life is bad because you starve there when you are out of work	−.244	−.475	.323	.184	.041	−.016	−.397	−.145
6. People from rural areas are more honest than those who have grown up in urban areas	−.188	−.674	.238	.293	−.016	−.014	.137	.103
9. Customs in rural areas are good because young people do not bath together with old people	.333	−.396	.576	.147	−.134	−.237	.015	.086
10. It is better for old people to live in rural areas than in town	−.670	−.322	.267	.191	.027	−.018	.011	.037
14. Customs in rural areas are not good because even the uneducated people expect to be respected there	.155	−.232	−.100	−.172	−.166	−.281	−.393	.150
16. A townsman should always help his relatives who live in the rural areas by sending them money and clothes	−.192	−.234	.148	.169	.142	−.550	−.093	.045
21. A man should not be expected to look after his wife and children only and not his other relatives	−.137	−.081	.165	.009	−.206	−.722	−.099	.063
25. A man should not be expected to help many relatives in these modern times	−0.74	.098	.138	.090	−.321	−.662	−.051	.303
22. People would rather spend all their lives in town if they have enough money to live on after they have stopped working	−.299	.094	.164	.150	−.394	−.225	−.017	.480
3. Because there are no social amenities like cinemas, sports, beer halls, and clubs in rural areas it is better to stay in town where they can be found	−.173	−.010	.069	.024	−.626	−.092	−.390	.085
1. The relatives of a man who has worked all his life in towns should not expect to go back to the rural areas when he is too old to work	−.200	.156	−.036	−.009	−.079	−.155	−.487	−.028

Table 4.3 Continued

	Rural–Urban rootedness	General moral and ethical standards	Traditionalism/ modernism	General sexual morality	Social and recreational amenities available	General kinship obligations	Desirability of town or country life	Social and economic investment in rural and urban areas
29. Living in urban areas is bad because it stops good customs, such as worshipping the spirits of dead relatives	-.084	-.249	.656	.240	.030	-.174	-.183	-.019
17. Most people who work in town would rather buy cattle with their money than a house and land of their own in town	-.194	-.261	.242	.152	.086	-.062	-.182	.534
7. Life in the rural areas cannot interest young people	-.086	.160	.159	-.190	-.606	-.081	-.247	-.024
15. Having a child before marriage is not considered a bad thing by girls and their parents in town	-.173	-.255	.196	.720	.047	-.077	-.025	-.025
18. It is all right for a townsman to marry a woman of his own clan (mutapo)	.135	-.062	.217	-.315	-.142	-.346	-.228	.026
30. Rural customs are better than town customs because only old women attend a woman in child-birth whereas in town nurses who are young women do so	-.235	-.166	.680	-.210	-.131	-.056	.016	.189
31. A townsman should marry a town woman if he wants to have a happy married life	.197	.121	-.076	-.218	-.270	-.222	-.024	.477
11. Fear of witchcraft in rural areas stops those who have finished working from going back to those rural areas	-.231	-.014	.075	.224	.472	.110	-.011	-.225
2. Boys who have grown up in rural areas do not know how to behave properly	.056	-.063	.113	-.008	-.159	-.032	-.526	.093
12. It is better to live in town because the hospitals and clinics there are better than in rural areas	-.012	-.032	.077	-.014	-.634	-.142	.053	.121
Percentage variance explained	3.6	16.2	3.8	3.2	8.0	4.6	3.5	3.0

Source: Survey of Attitudes to Town Living.

under these conditions are set out in Table 4.3.[12] The items and the components in this table have been arranged so as to concentrate the loading simultaneously on both dimensions and items, thus bringing out the relationships of items to the factors.[13] These 'loadings' may be combined with the ratings that respondents give to the various items to derive scores indicating their positions along the various dimensions.

These axes are, of course, features derived mechanically from the data and represent latent regularities in them. The analytical process lies in identifying these axes with abstract sociological qualities. The 'loadings' to which we have referred are correlations of the items with the underlying dimensions, so the interpretation of the axes lies in examining those items which together correlate most highly with an underlying dimension and then using common-sense or theoretical understanding of the items to determine the sociological quality which characterizes the dimension. In terms of this procedure the eight dimensions could be identified as in Table 4.3.

1. Perception of the desirability of rootedness in country or town life.
2. General moral and ethical appreciations.
3. Perception of traditional and modern orientations.
4. Perception of general sexual morality.
5. Perception of social and recreational amenities available.
6. Perception of general kinship obligations.
7. Perception of the general desirability of rural or urban life.
8. Perception of the degree of social and economic involvement in town or country living.

If we locate the axes through the configuration of items in such a way that they are not necessarily at right angles to one another, then we allow some of the dimensions to be aligned to some extent with others, or in other words we allow them to be correlated with one another. The value of the correlations between the various dimensions are set out in Table 4.4.

The eight dimensions that we have distinguished appear to fall into two clusters. In the first traditionalism/modernism,

---

[12] In factor analysis terminology this is the factor structure.

[13] Only the items with the highest loadings were used to deserve the factor scores. The particular items used for each attitude dimension are identified in Table 4.3.

Table 4.4 *Correlations Between Attitude Dimensions*

		(4) Traditionalism/ modernism	(5) Rural–urban rootedness	(1) General moral and ethical standards	(7) Sexual morality	(3) Kinship obligations	(6) Desirability of rural or urban life	(2) Social and recreational amenities	(8) Social and economic investment
Traditionalism/ modernism	(4)	—	.424	.419	.332	.230	.201	.159	– .029
Rural–urban rootedness	(5)		—	.281	.411	.139	.181	.110	.050
General moral and ethical standards	(1)			—	.298	.165	.167	– .014	– .018
Sexual morality	(7)				—	.029	– .007	.021	– .081
Kinship obligations	(3)					—	.170	.222	– .178
Desirability of rural or urban life	(6)						—	.136	.208
Social and recreational amenities	(2)							—	– .244
Social and economic investment	(8)								—

Source: Survey of Attitudes to Town Living.

rural–urban rootedness, sexual morality, and general moral and ethical standards seem to be related to each other, the closest relationship being traditionalism/modernism and rural–urban rootedness, sexual morality being almost as highly correlated with rural–urban rootedness and traditionalism/modernism with general ethical and moral standards. The interconnection is manifested in the way in which some items are associated moderately strongly with two or more dimensions. For example, items 24, 32, and 20 appear both in the dimensions related to attitudes towards rural retirement and town rootedness and in the dimension related to attributes and traditionalism. These items deal in the main with traditional aspects of rural life which by implication are subverted in urban life and presumably contribute to making rural areas more satisfactory for some people to live in. Similarly, six of the items which are associated with attitudes towards general ethical and moral standards are also associated with attitudes towards traditionalism or modernism. These are items 9, 19, 8, 5, 23, and 20. Here the connection is somewhat clearer, since the aspects of urban and rural life which are involved are mainly customs or ways of behaving which relate to the 'modern' atmosphere of urban life and which threaten traditional values. The item which correlates most strongly with the modernism/traditionalism dimension and which is also related to attitudes towards ethical and moral standards is that which states 'Customs in rural areas are good because young people do not bath together with old people.' The relationship between the dimension associated with attitudes to sexual morality on the one hand and attitudes to rural retirement and town rootedness, on the other hand, is not so obvious. Of the items particularly related to town-rootedness, that is 13, 10, 4, and 24, only 4 is moderately correlated with the dimension related to sexual morality, and this item in fact relates to retirement and has nothing directly to do with sexual morality, which is reflected mainly in items 15, 19, 23, and 5. Item 19 is moderately associated with the dimension relating to town rootedness, but this item is about girls growing up in rural areas and is not directly relevant to town rootedness.

The position is rather that respondents who reacted in one direction in relation to a number of items related to town rootedness also reacted in a consistent way to a number of items related to sexual morality. This is shown by the consistent, if low and opposite, correlation of a number of items with both these dimensions. It is probable that this consistency arises out of a deeper-level general attitudinal orientation which relates to all the attitude dimensions in the first cluster of dimensions, traditionalism/modernism, rural/urban rootedness, sexual morality, and general moral and ethical standards. These deal essentially with an evaluative aspect of modern living involving an opposition between the traditional way of life and that associated with modern urban life. Without more detailed data on this, however, it must remain a speculation still to be examined.

The second set of dimensions in Table 4.4 involves attitudes towards kinship obligations, social and economic investment in town and country, and the general desirability or otherwise of town and country life. The extent of the association between these dimensions is not as high as in the cluster of the other four dimensions. The correlations between the axes are around 0.2 as against 0.3 or 0.4. The highest correlation is between the axis relating to social and recreational amenities on the one hand and social and economic investment on the other. The correlation, however, is negative, indicating that those who agreed with the statements which implied superiority of urban conditions because of the availability of amenities there tended to disagree with statements which emphasized the general desirability of rural living conditions. Items which had a strong and positive loading on the one dimension, in other words, were likely to have a negative or small weighting on the other.

In the same way as we regarded the other four dimensions, we may speculate that these four dimensions could be thought of as relating to a pragmatic or utilitarian orientation towards town and country living and modern conditions. The reaction of respondents to items in terms of the hypothetical underlying disposition would be in terms of the recognition of responsibilities towards kin, the availability of medical and recreational and other facilities, the opportunities for investment of funds, and familiar utilitarian considerations. As before, this is an intriguing possibility which arises out of the analysis but one which needs a more directed set of enquiries for it to be established and identified.

The Relationship of Background Factors to Basic Attitudes

On the basis of the identification of the underlying components derived from the way in which respondents reacted to all thirty-two attitude terms we are able to derive 'factor scores' on each of the dimensions so isolated. These factor scores, as described earlier, are derived from the particular rating that respondents gave to each item, weighted by a value which represents the extent to which that item reflects the underlying dimension in which we are interested. Those items which have high loadings on any dimension will contribute more to the score of the individual on the dimension, while items which have only a tenuous relationship with that dimension will make little contribution to the score. For convenience in interpretation, the scores have been modified so that a score of 100 would represent a person who scored each item in the set in a category reflecting the most clearly 'urban' or 'modern' reaction to the item, while a score of zero, commensurately, would occur if the respondent reacted to each item in the most extreme 'rural' or 'traditional' way. These scores have no intrinsic meaning but merely serve to locate respondents somewhere along a continuum for each type of orientation from most extremely 'rural' or 'traditional' in orientation on the one hand to most extremely 'urban' or 'modern'.

The distribution of the scores for each of the different types of attitude identified in the responses are set out in Table 4.5. It is clear from this table that although the distribution of scores in each of the eight identified types of attitude tended to approximate that of a 'normal' distribution curve, the means ranged from between 24.34 at the 'rural' or 'traditional' end, for orientation towards kinship obligations, to 54.94 at the 'urban' or 'modern' end, for orientations to sexual morality. This difference must be appreciated against the context of particular items in the questionnaire which were used to derive the scores. The distribution of responses to the items used to calculate the scores for 'kinship obligations' (that is items 16, 18, 21, and 25 in the Appendix) are in the main slanted towards the 'traditional' end of the continuum, so that the overall mean is skewed towards the zero end of the scale. Similarly, the items used in the construction of the 'sexual morality' score, especially items 15, 19, and 23 (see Appendix), tend to be those to which there is a fairly even division of opinion, so that the mean tends to be located at the middle of the scale. The means, therefore, are heavily dependent upon the general content of the items. For this reason the scores can have no intrinsic meaning. But this does not preclude us from using the internal variability in the scores to assess the effect of background attributes on those scores.

This analysis was achieved by multiple regressions of attitude scores on the background attributes, expressed in dummy variables. Each background attribute was classified into convenient categories: for example, a respondent aged 16 was scored 1 in the first of three age categories and necessarily zero in the other two, a respondent aged between 18 and 20 was scored 1 in the second age category and necessarily zero in the first and third, while a respondent aged 21 or over was scored zero on the first two categories and 1 in the third. The set of eight background attributes of respondent group, gender, own educational level, father's occupation, father's education, mother's

Table 4.5 *Distribution of Scores in Orientations to City Living*

Score	Moral and ethical standards	Social and recreational amenities	Kinship obligations	Traditionalism/ modernism	Rural-urban rootedness	Desirability of rural/ urban life	Sexual morality	Social and economic investments
0	16	2	141	5	33	38	8	18
1–9	117	1	196	24	73	145	27	15
10–19	214	41	304	96	181	342	54	59
20–29	297	99	288	172	271	398	114	158
30–39	279	205	189	247	270	263	140	193
40–49	197	253	131	257	214	121	200	310
50–59	132	279	68	239	147	63	225	230
60–69	72	252	43	200	112	14	248	218
70–79	43	173	21	101	56	3	178	109
80–89	20	63	8	41	25	2	135	59
90–99	3	17	2	7	6	1	54	13
100	2	7	1	3	4		9	10
Total	1392	1392	1392	1392	1392	1392	1392	1392
Mean	33.40	52.59	24.34	45.63	36.53	25.07	54.95	48.23
S.D.	19.08	18.03	18.35	18.82	19.93	14.33	21.86	19.56

Means of known responses were substituted in 'don't know' responses in order to calculate individual scores. Means and standard deviations calculated from scores before tabulation.

Source: Survey of Attitudes to Town Living.

education, and proportion of life spent in town were classified into 26 categories, as in Table 4.6. For computational purposes one category from each attribute had to be excluded. These are indicated by an asterisk in Table 4.6. What the regression analysis produces is a value associated with each category which, when all the other categories are taken into account, indicates the extent to which respondents in that category reflect scores higher or lower than the base level which is attributed to each excluded category. These values, together with the multiple correlation coefficients, are set out in Table 4.6.

The multiple correlation coefficients range from 0.234 to 0.302. These values are not high, indicating that the effect of the particular attributes we have been able to include in the analysis only accounts for between 5.5 and 9.1 per cent of the variance in the scores. Clearly we have not been able in this analysis to capture the most important features influencing attributes towards features of town or country living: they may in fact be purely personal to the respondents.

Given this limitation we may nevertheless ask how the various structural attributes which we felt it feasible to include affected each of the identified cognitive orientations. These were:

1. *Type of respondent* The respondents were classified according to whether they were students in the senior classes of secondary schools, students of teacher training colleges, or people attending adult education courses, trade union courses, or courses run at the local adult education centre organized by certain religious bodies. The general finding, as reflected in the slightly higher scores for secondary school pupils and those on adult education courses, is that those attending teacher training institutions tended on the whole to take up a more 'traditional' or 'rural' orientation to the different kinds of attitude components identified in the study. This was strikingly so in respect of attitudes towards kinship obligations, where respondents at schools and at adult education courses tended on average, holding other attributes constant, to reflect scores of 5.3 and 5.5 points more towards the 'modern' or 'urban' end of the scale than those at the teacher training institutions. With regard to orientations towards the importance of social and recreational amenities in town or country life, respondents at secondary schools were rather more inclined to assess these facilities as

important to town dwellers than those at adult education courses
or those in teacher training colleges. With regard to the other
attitude orientations, the differential between respondents in
secondary schools and adult education courses on the one hand
and those at teacher training colleges at the other was consistently maintained throughout, although the actual difference
were sometimes small. The explanation is probably to be sought
in the character of the particular teacher training institutions
concerned. A sizeable proportion were in fact controlled and
run by missionary bodies located in the rural areas. These
institutions would often draw their students from rural schools
and would represent less urbanized and more traditional
orientations.

2. *Gender* Except for one orientation—attitudes towards
rural or urban rootedness—the female respondents consistently
reflected orientations which were more 'urban' or 'modern'
than the males, other attributes being held constant. The biggest
difference (7.64) was for attitudes towards the effect of social and
economic investment in rural or urban areas. Women were also
more 'urban' or 'modern' in orientation towards attitudes concerning items reflecting traditionalism or modernism (5.34),
towards attitudes regarding kinship obligations (5.11), and
towards sexual morality (4.93). The probable explanation for
these consistent findings is that the women who participated in
these tests (constituting only one-fifth of the sample as a whole)
were almost certainly drawn mainly from that part of the overall
distribution of women reflecting more 'urban' or 'modern'
attitudes.

3. *Age* Overall, the systematic effect of differences in age on
the scores in the eight types of cognitive orientation is small. The
largest effect is just under 5 units of score, from the attitudes
towards the role of the distribution of social and recreational
amenities in town as against in rural areas. The younger respondents tended to appreciate more positively than the older the
provision of hospitals and clinics, cinemas, beer halls, and clubs
in towns as against in rural areas. This is possibly because many
of the older respondents in the sample were rurally based
students taking diplomas in teacher training colleges.

The only attitude orientation in which there was a consistent
trend with age was for the desirability of rural or urban life,

Table 4.6 *Effect of Attributes on Attitude Orientations*

	Moral and ethical standards	Social and recreation amenities	Kinship obligations	Tradition-alism/modernism	Rural-urban rootedness	Desirability of rural/urban life	Sexual morality	Social and economic investment
Test Group								
Scholars	31.02	53.63	19.13	44.49	33.65	24.00	53.15	44.77
Teachers training*	30.19*	47.38*	13.88*	40.20*	29.89*	20.53*	51.81*	41.24*
Adult education	29.01	47.44	19.34	41.34	30.38	25.62	53.04	44.36
Gender								
Male *	30.19	47.38	13.88*	40.20*	29.89*	20.53*	51.81*	41.24*
Female	33.94	49.60	18.99	45.54	28.52	21.25	56.74	48.88
Age								
17 or less	29.56	52.24	14.70	38.85	29.64	24.14	50.26	42.88
18 to 20 *	30.19*	47.38*	13.88*	40.20*	29.89*	20.53*	51.81*	41.24*
21 and over	28.69	49.06	18.49	40.17	30.57	19.65	50.04	43.04
Educational level								
9 years and less	30.74	47.06	14.28	34.20	27.22	25.98	44.21	34.03
10 years *	30.19*	47.38*	13.88*	40.20*	29.89*	20.53*	51.81*	41.24*
11 years and over	32.61	50.65	18.49	42.09	33.67	22.81	56.65	44.41
Father's Occupation								
Agricultural and rural	30.19	47.52	14.14	40.87	33.36	19.97	52.82	41.54
Unskilled and semi-sk. *	30.19*	47.38*	13.88*	40.20*	29.89*	20.53*	51.81*	41.24*
Skilled and supervisors	30.34	47.44	13.43	40.06	32.55	19.40	52.28	41.71
Business and white-collar	33.78	48.40	17.27	43.98	34.20	22.41	55.32	40.65

Table 4.6 *Continued*

	Moral and ethical standards	Social and recreation amenities	Kinship obligations	Tradition-alism/modernism	Rural-urban rootedness	Desirability of rural/urban life	Sexual morality	Social and economic investment
Father's Education								
4 years and less	31.59	46.88	12.32	41.77	32.05	21.07	54.08	42.62
5 or 6 years	30.66	48.02	12.55	40.08	30.74	20.76	53.72	41.97
7 or 8 years *	30.19*	47.38*	13.88*	40.20*	29.89*	20.53*	51.81*	41.24*
9 years and over	32.07	44.44	13.06	41.96	33.84	19.34	54.14	46.13
Mother's Education								
4 years and less	27.65	44.77	15.69	37.60	27.48	19.43	47.49	38.27
5 or 6 years	26.97	43.30	12.32	38.50	25.56	18.29	49.21	38.98
7 or 8 years *	30.19*	47.38*	13.88*	40.20*	29.89*	20.53*	51.81*	41.24*
9 years and over	29.82	44.09	14.28	39.92	27.14	22.03	51.03	39.33
Prop. Life in Town								
22 per cent and less	28.61	46.77	16.15	40.11	29.68	20.04	49.43	43.86
22 to 55 per cent *	30.19*	47.38*	13.88*	40.20*	29.89*	20.53*	51.81*	41.24*
55 per cent and over	38.04	50.53	18.18	45.02	35.05	23.48	57.91	46.00
Multiple R	0.302	0.263	0.254	0.275	0.257	0.278	0.294	0.234

Note: Categories indicated with an asterisk were excluded from the analysis and are attributed an overall value computed from the analysis (i.e. the intercept value). The other categories in each attribute reflect the variation around this value that the presence of that category will have.

where the younger respondents on the whole evinced a more 'urban' orientation than the older.

4. *Educational level* The respondent's educational level had more effect on the scores for various attitudes orientations. In five of the eight orientations there were substantial and regular effects with educational level. Nine years of education would have taken the average respondent to the end of primary education. Ten years of education would have put them into secondary school education, while most of those with eleven years and more would have completed secondary school.

The largest effect, other attributes being held constant, was on the orientation towards sexual morality in rural and urban environments. Those with more education tended to respond more permissively towards items reflecting somewhat puritan orientation towards sexual behaviour in towns. There was a difference of 12.4 units in the expected score of orientation towards sexual morality between the two categories.

A similar trend was found in respect to the role of social and economic investments in rural and urban activities. Those with nine years or less of education had a mean score of 34.0 on this orientation, while those with eleven years or more had a mean score of 44.4, reflecting a considerably more 'urban' orientation. This was also true for attitudes towards modernism or traditionalism, in which those with nine years or less of education had a mean score of 34.2, while those with eleven years or more had a mean score of 42.1.

The expected score for orientations towards rural–urban rootedness was 33.7 for those with eleven years or more of education and 27.2 for those with nine years or less, showing a more 'urban' orientation amongst the more highly educated. The trend in relation to the role of social and recreational amenities in rural or urban areas showed a regular difference in scores with age, but it was much smaller than with the other orientations mentioned.

These findings are consistent with the common-sense appreciation of the effect of Western-type education on orientation towards urban living and the economic and social circumstances surrounding it.

5. *Father's occupation* There were no striking differences in scores relating to orientations towards city life for respondents

drawn from different categories of fathers' occupations. However, there does seem to be a distinction in general in the orientations of those drawn from the homes of businessmen, white-collar workers, and professional men against those whose fathers came from other occupational groups. While in general there was not much difference in scores for respondents whose fathers came from other occupational groups, for most orientations the scores of those with businessmen, white-collar workers, or professionals as fathers was consistently higher. The implication of this finding is that there appears to be a consistent though small effect leading those who have been brought up in these homes to have attitudes more favourable to urban living than rural. Most of these would have been urban and not rurally based occupations.

6. *Parents' education* In general the effects due to level of the respondents' fathers' and mothers' education level were small and revealed little consistent trend when other attributes were held constant.

7. *Proportion of life spent in town* The effect, as a rule, of spending a greater proportion of life in town, not surprisingly, was to skew the scores towards a positive or 'modern' attitude towards town living. The largest effect was upon orientations to moral and ethical standards, where those who had spent 22 per cent or less of their lives in town, holding other attributes constant, were slanted 9.4 points towards the 'rural' end of the scale, as against those who had spent 55 per cent or more of their lives in town. Similarly, those who had spent only 22 per cent of their lives in town were 8.5 units towards the 'traditional' extreme in attitudes towards sexual morality, as against those who had spent 55 per cent or more of their lives in town.

In six of the eight types of attitude orientation the variation in effect was regular in the sense that the effect of the categories increased in accord (but not proportionately) with the change in percentage of life spent in town. On the whole there was little difference in scores between those who had spent 22 per cent or less of their lives in town and those who had spent between 22 and 55 per cent of their lives there. In each of their separate orientations, however, the score for those who had spent more than 55 per cent of their lives in town was appreciably higher than in the other two categories.

In general, therefore, the effect of the proportion of life lived in town on the orientation to city living may be succinctly formulated: a person needs to have spent more than half of his or her life in town for the effect to be registered to an appreciable extent on orientations to city living.

Diffuse and Specific Cognitive Orientations

The attitudes towards city living which emerged from this study, of course, are predetermined by the particular items which were used in the questionnaire. The understanding that Mr Lukhero and I had built up of the way in which townspeople in Southern Rhodesia saw city life had led us to choose those particular items. Since we were unaware of previous studies of attitudes towards urban life in this part of the world we had, as I have stated, no example from which to learn. Clearly another similar study using different items would reflect a different *pattern* of attitudes, though I would not anticipate them to be wildly at variance from those reflected here.

The question naturally arises of what the relationship is between the sort of orientations which have emerged from this study and the actual social perceptions of town dwellers in relation to the characteristics of town life. The general theoretical orientation adopted in this book must lead us to distrust the analytical utility of any notion of 'actual social perception'. The 'reality' of some type of social perception can only be demonstrated in respect of social action of some sort in which the actors' shared beliefs and values, constituting the social perception, serve to provide the common understanding through which these actors are able to order their behaviour to one another. As we have argued earlier, those sets of social perception which are likely to be defined as relevant in any specific social situation will turn firstly on the setting in which the actors are placed, that is on an understanding of the constraints and pressures of the wider social order which impinge upon the actors, and secondly on the definition that the actors themselves accept as appropriate for that situation. The definition of the situation in these terms becomes the process of negotiation through which some particular social perception is going to be accepted by the actors as germane to their social interaction.

It is, of course, obvious that the data used in this chapter were generated within a highly structured and formal test situation. It is unlikely that the orientations towards city life which were evinced in this study would operate in precisely these terms in social interaction—it would be fatuous to expect them to. Later (chap. 6) I shall present evidence relating to a particular type of cognitive orientation—that towards ethnicity and regionalism—to the effect that it would be equally mistaken to assume that there is *no* relation between the findings derived from attitude questions of this sort and social action. The question then is how to construe the findings derived from the material reported here.

The regularities which have emerged from the responses of subjects chosen from such widely divergent groups as were used in this study and the systematic variation of the responses of subjects which emerged from the analysis of the effect of personal attributes on the attitude orientations leads us to surmise, in line with literary references in Western European society, that there are some widely held beliefs and opinions about the qualities of urban life. What role these beliefs and opinions play in everyday life cannot be inferred directly from the data generated in a study of this kind. Shared convictions about the moral and ethical qualities of urban life, for example, might constitute common ground when public issues are raised, but they are unlikely to be the basis of mutual understanding in everyday social situations. The orientations, in other words, are diffuse rather than specific. The generally low multiple-correlation coefficients between scores on the one hand, and a set of personal characteristics on the other which might be thought of as indexing structural positions, support this point of view. The variance in scores appears to be related more to personal than to structural features.

Diffuse cognitive orientations of this kind differ from those which are related to status in the overall social structure. I am referring here to cognitive orientations towards such entities as occupational roles or ethnic identities, where ordinary townsmen would be able to locate holders of a status marked by clearly defined obligations and expectations. It is to the social perception of these types of phenomenon that we now turn.

5

SOCIAL STATUS AND ITS PERCEPTION

We have referred in the previous chapter, to the way in which Africans, whether they lived in towns or not, perceived the quality of social relationships in towns in general. These 'images of the city' referred to very broad cognitive representations of urban living which had moral and emotional connotations for those who held them. Within the city itself 'fields' or 'domains' of social interaction could be distinguished which constituted part of the way in which town dwellers structured their reality. The organization of perception is particularly significant in the study of social interaction in cities, for city dwellers must perforce conduct themselves for at least part of their time in public places in which their individual identities must of necessity must be relatively anonymous. The fleeting, transitory and anonymous character of urban life to which Wirth referred related, as will be argued later, particularly to public places, and it was in these situations that city dwellers had to resort to cues and signs in terms of which they were able to attribute social identities to those with whom they came into contact, however fleeting and transitory that contact might be. These cues and signs are the basis of social perception and as such constitute an important aspect of urban social life.

In so far as South Central African colonial towns were concerned—and I suspect that this possibly applies to all towns—there were two fields of social perception which were particularly important in the study of social interaction. These were social status and ethnicity. These 'fields' or 'domains' of perception existed as cues and signs which actors in urban public places were able to perceive and to which, hence, they were able to attribute meanings. The meanings which they attributed to these cues and signs had social significance in that they could be taken to represent a reasonable prediction of behaviour and so provide the basis of regular interaction in public places.

In this chapter I present some data on a particular but

nevertheless significant aspect of the perception of social status, the way in which people attributed prestige to the titles of occupational roles that townsmen followed. It should be apparent that I am not here concerned with social class in its proper sense, that is in terms of the relationships of the African town-dwellers to the means of production. I take it as axiomatic that in the colonial situation with which I am concerned those who controlled the means of production were essentially Europeans (and to a lesser extent Asians), and that from a strict class perspective all Africans at this point of history occupied a single class position in which as producers of surplus value they stood opposed to the European capitalists and their representatives.[1] I accept Posel's argument that the logical priority of class over race is analytically indeterminate (Posel 1983). From the perspective which I adopt, the overall race/class structure of colonial society constituted the context or setting within which social status was located and which inescapably set constraints and to some extent moulded its expression. By 'social status' I am referring rather to the Weberian notion of social status reflecting life-styles as indexed by occupational roles within the African population itself. Social status in this sense, I assume, refers to the invidious distinctions among persons by which some are expected to take precedence over others in being accorded honour, the exercise of power, and access to consumer resources. Life-styles themselves are indicators of social stratification in that actors may take them to be cues and signs which indicate the deference or precedence that they predicate in respect of those who exhibit these life-styles. Occupational role is an important indicator of life-style, so that it is understandable that occupational studies have long been a simple conventional procedure for assessing how respondents view status stratification.

It is true that it is sometimes not clear whether those using occupational prestige studies as a means of deriving information on status stratification are aware of the distinction between the

---

[1] The 'class' situation in colonial Africa from this perspective has been the topic of some discussion over the last two decades. See, for example, Arrighi 1967, Cohen R. 1972, Burawoy 1972, Kitching 1972, Wolpe 1975, Davies 1979, Perrings 1980, Greenberg 1980, Bozzoli 1981, Innes 1983, and Posel 1983. Some data relating to the general system of stratification in South Central Africa are presented in Mitchell 1970c.

essentially perceptual nature of their data and the structural characteristics of social stratification, particularly when it is treated in terms of such concepts as 'social class'. Perceptual data cannot be assumed to bear a simple one-to-one relationship to structural phenomena. Structural phenomena exist, as I have argued, at a different level of theoretical abstraction from that of perceptual phenomena which must be construed in terms of an analytical framework before they can be related to structural notions. The emphasis here is on the meanings that African respondents attributed to occupations as an aspect of the social prestige through which interaction in public places in towns might be ordered. The assumption underlying this analysis is that the occupations which people followed presented cues and signs to the general public which they in turn interpreted in terms of the social value of these occupations. Occupational roles are overt and as such are amenable to public perception and hence interpretation. In social situations, such as in public places in the city where anonymity was the hallmark of social interaction, external cues such as gender, occupation, or ethnicity were particularly important in ordering social actions. The occupational titles used in the studies reported here, therefore, do not refer to the occupational roles *per se* and their objective functions in production in general. Instead they are assumed to be cognitive constructs to which respondents are able to refer in the abstract and decontextualized situations in which investigations such as the assessment of the prestige of occupational titles operate.

The context in which the data were collected in the studies reported here was in fact a formal questionnaire completion session. Respondents were asked to determine whether a number of occupational titles had high or low 'prestige'. The meaning of the word 'prestige' was deliberately left vague because the interest was primarily in the way in which respondents interpreted the occupational role in terms of *general* social prestige. Since we were interested in social perceptions which were essentially meaningful at the common-sense level of observation, there seemed to be little point in imposing a sophisticated definition of 'prestige' which might not have meant very much to the respondents. That the respondents were likely themselves to be operating with different and perhaps contradictory definitions of prestige must be accepted as a primary datum in the analysis. In fact, part of the analysis must be directed towards trying to recover from the responses what the *structure* of perceptions of occupational roles of those working with different understandings of 'prestige' might be. The object of interest in these analyses is not, therefore, the specific cognitive structure of the perception of occupational roles such as pursued by Coxon and Jones (1978, 1979), but rather the general ordering of occupational roles performed by Africans in a colonial context. The issue is not that of uncovering the cognitive processes through which the occupational roles are assessed but that of representing the overall ordering of occupational roles, which can then be related to the wider-sense social structure within which the social perceptions are located.

The data bearing on occupational prestige from the point of view of Africans in South Central Africa relate to a number of studies which were made over a period between 1954 and 1964. Some of the data refer to Northern Rhodesia (Mitchell and Epstein 1959, Mitchell 1964*a*, Mitchell and Irvine 1965, Hicks 1966 and 1967), and some to Southern Rhodesia (Mitchell 1966*b*). The object of the analysis is to relate the perceptions of prestige in these different studies to the social contexts in which they appeared, both synchronically and at different points in time.

The procedures of data collection were similar in all the studies referred to. The respondents were presented with a selected list of occupational titles and were then asked to check the prestige category, ranging from 'very low prestige' through 'low prestige', 'neither high nor low', 'high prestige', to 'very high prestige', according to how they felt the general public viewed that occupation, or alternatively how they rated the occupation themselves. The distinction between the public view and the view of the respondents is in fact more apparent than real, since subsequent analyses have shown that this variation does not make much difference to the results. The respondents in the studies reported in the Mitchell and Epstein, the 1965 Mitchell and Irvine, the Mitchell, and the 1967 Hicks studies were scholars in the senior forms of secondary schools. The 1966 Hicks study also used railway workers. The respondents in Mitchell and Irvine 1965 included two separate categories of the general public, that is a group of 96 new recruits to the mining industry and 55 employees of the mining industry who had advanced to positions of relative authority. The latter study is of particular interest because criticism is frequently levelled against studies of this kind on the grounds that the respondents are some special category such as schoolchildren or students. The 1966 Mitchell and Irvine study showed that except for a few strategically important occupational titles the general findings for the categories of the general public and those for the school-children were virtually identical. This finding confirms that which Treiman had arrived at after reviewing a large number of occupational prestige studies in different countries. He writes: 'In particular students are no different from other groups in their occupational evaluations, so we can now lay to rest the old bugaboo about student samples producing a Western bias in prestige evaluations' (1977: 78). Two additional points are relevant here. The first is that the scholars in the studies reported here were on the whole somewhat older than would be the case in Europe or North America. Many would be in fact in the young adult age-range. The second is that we are interested here in general social perceptions. If the perceptions are indeed general then they ought to be shared by both scholars and the general public. The results in the Mitchell and Irvine study suggest that this is not an unreasonable assumption.

The sets of occupational titles included in the list were chosen so as to represent as wide a range of occupations as possible. The titles were also chosen so that they would generally be easily recognizable by most respondents. Some roughly equivalent occupations were also included so as to see whether they emerged with substantially the same ranking. Certainly in the earlier studies and perhaps in the later studies, insufficient titles of occupations of the self-employed were included, and this to some extent represents a weakness in the studies. Occupations which referred specifically to rural activities were deliberately omitted since the focus of primary interest in all the studies was the urban context. Most of the occupational titles were related very closely to urban activities, though some of them, of course, like that of school teacher, were more general.

A rudimentary set of social characteristics was collected for the respondents. These were specifically age, sex, level of education reached, religious persuasion, ethnic affiliation, and length of residence in towns. In one of the studies father's and mother's education and father's occupation were also collected. Thus far the analysis of the findings of the studies reported here has been directed to the overall pattern of prestige of occupational titles; the influence of background factors on the perceptions of prestige has not been subjected to much analysis (except for the Rhodesian data (see below)).

In general, patterns in the perception of the prestige of occupations have been adduced from a study of the arithmetic means of the ratings which the respondents gave to the occupational titles. While these procedures produce plausible results, these also make relatively strong measurement assumptions. In essence the basis of the procedure employed in these questionnaires is that prestige is assumed to fall into five ordinal categories from 'very high' to 'very low'. The respondents are required to establish five or fewer equivalence sets of occupational titles so that all the occupations judged as belonging to a particular prestige category are assumed to be indistinguishable from one another as far as prestige is concerned. In the standard procedure of arriving at an ordinal prestige series of occupational titles, however, arithmetic means of the ratings are calculated. Usually the rating categories are given equal interval weights, as for example 1 for very high prestige, 2 for high prestige, and so on down to 5 for very low prestige. The mean ratings of the occupational title may then be calculated using these weights. But the assumption that the distinction between 'very high' and 'high prestige' is the same as say that between 'neither high nor low' and 'low prestige' may be unreal. An attempt to overcome this difficulty was devised by Yaukey (1955), who made the assumption that the distribution of all ratings for the set of occupational titles as a whole would be normally distributed, and on this basis arrived at a weight for each prestige category. The assumption of an overall normal distribution seems equally questionable. In fact the differences between the rank order of occupations derived from equal-interval categories and those derived from weights according to an assumption of a normal distribution were trivial, so that the more complex weighting procedures seemed scarcely worthwhile. Clearly, future analyses of ratings of this sort will need to be made using no other assumption than that of an ordered set of prestige categories. Procedures which extract the underlying regularities in data of this sort are now becoming available but at present we must make do with what we have.

Occupational Ranking and Colonial Society

At a very general level, all the studies in South Central Africa have confirmed the now well-established pattern of occupational prestige hierarchy in which professional and semi-professional occupational titles are ranked higher than white-collar occupational titles, and these higher than supervisory and skilled occupations which were roughly equivalent, and both of these in turn higher than unskilled occupational titles. (See Treiman 1977.) For example, in the studies conducted in Southern Rhodesia and Northern Rhodesia the mean rating of titles classified roughly into the categories above were as in Table 5.1.

While there are some variations of mean rating among the different categories of respondents, such as, for example, the higher rating the Southern Rhodesian sample gave to titles of skilled occupations and the Northern Rhodesia mineworkers gave to the titles of professional and semi-professional and supervisory occupations, these are not marked. Different occupational titles were used in the three studies and this would affect the mean rating slightly. What is significant rather is the rank order of the classes of occupational titles even to the extent that the ratings of supervisory and skilled occupations were substantially equal among all but the sample of mine workers.

Table 5.1 *Ranking of Occupational Categories in four Central African Samples*

Occupational Classification	Northern Rhodesia Samples			Southern Rhodesia Sample
	1954[a] Scholars	1959[b] Scholars	Miners	1958[c] Scholars
Professional and semi-professional	1.30	1.29	1.08	1.20
White-collar	1.64	1.77	1.41	1.58
Supervisory	2.12	2.14	1.76	2.10
Skilled	2.17	2.16	2.04	1.92
Unskilled	2.92	2.77	2.71	2.63

Source: [a] computed from Mitchell and Epstein 1959 Table I.
  [b] computed from Mitchell and Irvine 1965 Table I.
  [c] computed from Mitchell 1966*b* Table I.

The consistency of social perception of the ordering of occupational classes of this kind in nations of vastly differing levels of economic and social development has been the topic of some debate.[2] In the paper in which the problem of the interpretation of the similarities and differences in occupational prestige ranking in different societies was first raised, Inkeles and Rossi (1956) postulated two somewhat different value systems operating in the present-day industrializing societies where they made studies to explain both the similarities and the variations in occupational prestige orderings. One related to industrial society in which a highly organized modern industrial system with its concomitants of highly bureaucratized government institutions and a market-orientated economy imposed a particular value system upon the people involved in it. The evaluation of roles and functions in terms of this value system leads ultimately to the same prestige ordering of occupational titles. It is for this reason that the ordering of occupational titles in terms of their prestige is so similar in all industrialized nations. A second value system characterizes those societies where there are significant variations in the prestige of particular occupations, especially those relating to agricultural pursuits and personal services. There is usually a tradition in which these occupations had especial value which then influenced their prestige ratings in the modern industrial context. Inkeles and Rossi refer to these two interpretations as the 'structural' and 'cultural' interpretations respectively.

Treiman (1977: esp. chaps. 1 and 10) has developed these ideas by assembling occupational prestige rankings from a number of societies including some of the material presented here. The striking similarity of occupational rankings in the societies he examines allows Treiman to reject the hypothesis that the rankings in each society are due simply to the idiosyncratic operation of specific cultural values in each of these societies. He argues that there are three basic hypotheses which may be advanced to explain the similarities in occupational prestige ratings. Two of these hypotheses are basically 'diffusionist' in nature: they argue that the set of evaluations charac-

---

[2] See for example Inkeles and Rossi 1956, Thomas 1962, and Treiman 1977. I have summarized the arguments in relation to the South Central African data in Mitchell 1964a.

teristic of Western industrialized societies has spread to other societies, so that occupations in these societies are evaluated, with minor local variations, in the same way as in all industrialized societies. This is a strictly *cultural diffusionist* interpretation of occupational prestige. By examining data related not only to occupational prestige but also to hierarchies of power and privilege Treiman argues that the evaluation of the prestige of occupations is not simply cultural in origin but structural (103-16). He is thus led to consider the alternative postulate, that the same structure of occupational activities has been taken over by other countries from the industrialized Western countries, so that a similar system of evaluation of the 'social worth' of the occupations is reflected in the ratings of all of these countries. By examining data relating to societies *before* they could be affected by the industrial revolution (either early European, such as Florence, or pre-colonial societies such as ancient Nepal), Treiman shows that occupational differentiation still exists and that these occupations may be arranged in a prestige ranking (116-28).

Treiman is left, therefore, with a structural hypothesis to account for the similarity in occupational prestige rankings in the societies for which he has data. This hypothesis is derived in the first instance from the notion of the division of labour in complex societies in which the level of organization of production and activities associated with production requires the performance of a wide variety of tasks. These tasks, however, necessarily involve the differential control over scarce and valued resources. 'All occupations', writes Treiman, 'by their very nature, entail lesser or greater control over valued resources, and hence greater or lesser power.' (p 13.) These 'valued resources' he describes as (*a*) the knowledge and skills relevant to the performance of socially valued tasks, (*b*) control over economic resources, and (*c*) authority or legitimate control over the activities of others. The power involved in the command over these scarce resources leads in turn to corresponding variations in the public evaluation of these roles. This is effected either through the market position of occupations calling for particular skills or talents or the extent to which incumbents in these positions are able to command special advantages, leading to differences in both income and privileges. The public evaluation of these marks of privilege leads in turn to the prestige of occupations (5–22).

It is difficult to accept Treiman's outright rejection of 'diffusionist' interpretations of occupational prestige in colonial societies as reported here. In South Central Africa the occupations whose titles the respondents rated were part of an industrial, commercial, and industrial system which was established in the first instance by European colonists. The fact that the occupations were rated by African respondents in a way which in effect reproduced the general assessment of occupations by the European colonists who introduced the system is not in itself very surprising. The precise procedure whereby the evaluations of the prestige of the occupations were transmitted to the Africans, however, is not at all clear. Differentiated emoluments to Africans in various occupations, as in the form of wages, housing, and other material advantages of many kinds—Treiman's 'privileges', in fact—were an important component of the perception of occupational prestige. But it would be too simple to assume that this was the whole story. In many subtle ways the European administrators, managers, supervisors, and teachers expressed their own evaluation of the social standing of people who performed different occupational roles by the way they related to people performing these roles. Mass media originating in Europe, such as literature and films, presented the same images, so that the African population soon began to accept the basis of the evaluation of the prestige of occupations.

The perceptions of the African population in a colonial society, however, cannot be separated from their structural position in that society. During the colonial period, as has already been described, economic, political, and social power lay in the hands of the small White minority who were the local representatives of a powerful metropolitan state. An important additional element in the perception of prestige under these circumstances was the extent to which the occupations drew from the cultural resources of the metropolitan country. This was explicitly referred to by many of the respondents who completed an open-ended question about the factors that they saw as contributing to the prestige of occupations. These respondents referred to the extent to which some occupations of

Africans were also the same as those of Europeans, such as that of teacher. Equally, while some Europeans might have held skilled jobs, in general they were managers or supervisors rather than operatives, and practically no European followed an unskilled occupation. There was in fact a coincidence of colour with status in occupations as a whole, and the power and prestige of Europeans in the colonial system was to some extent transferred to the occupations they followed and therefore to the occupational roles themselves.

Intercalary Roles and Occupational Prestige

The African appreciation of the prestige of certain analytically strategic occupations was not simply a reflection of the value system of the metropolitan country: rather, some of the contradictions inherent in colonial society manifested themselves in the way in which certain occupations were viewed. These occupations were particularly those in which, as a result of the growing differentiation of occupational roles in the African population and the need for an effective chain of administrative command, certain Africans came to wield authority on behalf of their European masters over other Africans. This arose in the first instance out of the essentially polyglot composition of the labour strength of large concerns.

South Central Africa lies at the point of juxtaposition of four major divisions of the Bantu peoples. We expected therefore that there would be a wide variation in culture and language in the region. There are in fact over a hundred ethnic groups in the region, and men of all of them were potential labour recruits. Not only these but also men from neighbouring territories were attracted into wage-earning employment. The need for African assistants who could help the European employers to deal with the large variety of people who spoke many different languages and followed diverse customs was thus immediately apparent.

Since the earlier enterprises were essentially small the supervisor was usually one of the labourers who had worked with his employer over a long time and who knew more about the work processes than the others. Since, in the beginning, it was difficult to obtain local labour for employment on the mines and farms, it seems likely that the majority of supervisors in the early stages were Africans drawn from South Africa and Bechuanaland (now Botswana) who had had longer experience in the work in which they were involved. These supervisors soon proved invaluable to the European employers because they could explain the processes involved to the other Africans and could direct the work more easily through their knowledge of the vernaculars. The language used for communication between employer and employee was a hybrid language called variously *Chikabanga*, *Chilapalapa*, or *Fanikalo* using English grammatical structure and Zulu and Afrikaans words. This language evolved to meet the rather restricted needs of communication between employer and employee but could not be used to convey complicated ideas. The supervisors had to translate instructions into the vernacular for the benefit of the labourers who could not understand *Chikabanga*. The supervisor also knew many of the labourers personally and was able to mediate in their personal difficulties and to represent their complaints to the employer. The supervisor therefore emerged as an essential link between the employer and his employees in a situation where the cultural and linguistic divisions between them were wide. He was part foreman, part disciplinarian, and part worker, and was the bridge between the different worlds of the European industrial and indigenous traditional societies.

In many of the small enterprises and on most of the smaller farms this position persisted. But this simple face to face structure of social relationships could hardly survive as the standard practice. As some enterprises such as mines expanded and the work-force increased, the need grew for more specialized personnel to bridge the gap in linguistic and cultural backgrounds between employers and employees. This brought about a specialization in function in which a European officer was appointed specifically to control and to administer matters arising in connection with African labour. These 'Compound Managers', as they were called, were frequently men who could speak one or more of the Bantu languages used by the African workers and who usually knew something of their customs and beliefs. Often they were the sons of farmers who had grown up in close contact with Africans working on their fathers' farms; sometimes they were policemen who had resigned or retired from the police force; as a rule they were men who had spent several years amongst the African peoples before taking up this employment.

With so many different languages and ethnic groups to deal with, the Compound Managers found it necessary to employ a number of Africans to carry out day to day administration. These 'Police Boys' were the employees of the mining companies or industrial concerns and wore special uniforms to distinguish them from the ordinary workers. They were centred in the offices of the Compound Managers and were available to carry out his instructions. Conversely, African employees who wished to see the Compound Manager approached him through the Police Boys. The supervisor continued to operate but now in a strictly industrial capacity: he was the intermediary between a supervisor in charge of a gang of workers engaged in a specific industrial process and the African workers comprising the gang. But in the more complex industrial situation the formerly composite role of the supervisor had been differentiated into that of the Boss Boy within a specific industrial task and that of the Police Boy, whose duties were in the larger field of the overall relationship between White management and Black labour.

The position which these Police Boys came to occupy in the industrial and commercial structure is of particular interest. I have pointed out that the social structure of the enterprise fell into two parts corresponding to the structure of the larger society in which it was placed. By and large Europeans filled the managerial and skilled posts while the Africans performed the unskilled duties. This division of the structure of the enterprise into management and workers coincided in general with the division of the larger social structure into two segments of a divided society.

Partly because of this dissimilarity of culture, particularly of language, between the peoples comprising the divided society, and partly because of the desire of each of the groups to retain its exclusiveness, the relationships between the members of the two groups tended to be superficial and categorical (Allport 1954: 19 ff.; Mitchell 1956a). Thus Europeans tended to see Africans as falling into a single undifferentiated category. Their behaviour towards these Africans was conditioned by stereotypes which they held about them rather than by personal knowledge of the individual Africans. Conversely the Africans saw the

Europeans as one undifferentiated mass and accordingly also reacted towards them holistically. There was, and had been for some time, a formidable barrier to communication between the predominantly White management and predominantly Black labour.

The Compound Manager and his Police Boys arose because of this barrier, but at the same time the social structure imposed a particular strain upon them. This strain was more acute for the Police Boy than for the Compound Manager. The Compound Manager was a member of a socially superior group and could afford to hold aloof from social relationships with Africans. The Police Boy, on the other hand, was in effect a bridge between two opposed groups and was involved in relationships, though of different kinds, on both sides of the cultural barrier. He occupied a position in the industrial society within the framework of the European sector of the divided society, but at the same time was still inextricably involved in social relationships outside the industrial situation with other Africans. Role expectations are naturally part of any network of social relationship and depend upon the value system which supports it. The Police Boy in the early industrial structure was placed at the point of intersection of two effectively separate networks of social relationships: his position was intercalary between two parts of the industrial structure. This implies that he was subject to two different and frequently conflicting role expectations relevant to the position he occupied. The White managers were likely to define his behaviour in terms of his being a representative of the African workers, while at the same time the African workers were likely to see the Police Boy as their representative to the management. Yet these two definitions could be inverted.

Conflict of roles in intercalary positions is a common feature of social systems.[3] The classic example in sociology is the foreman in industry who holds a position intercalary between the management on one hand and the workers on the other. In this position he is subject to different definitions of appropriate behaviour from both management and labour, a fact which places some strain upon him. But the phenomenon is not

---

[3] I have described the intercalary position of African white-collar workers and supervisors more fully in Mitchell 1956b. I have drawn extensively from that paper in what follows.

confined to industry. Gluckman (1955) has pointed out that the prefect in the public school is in a similar position *vis-à-vis* the schoolboys and the masters, and Stouffer (1949) has presented data to show that the non-commissioned officer in the army is in a similar position will regard to the men and the officers. In indigenous social structures the same phenomenon occurs. The village headman, for example, occupies a position intercalary between the domestic system in which he holds a position primarily as kinsman and the political system in which he represents his villagers to the chief (Gluckman, Mitchell, and Barnes 1949). The stress on a person in an intercalary position depends upon the degree of disjunction between the two parts of the social system which he bridges. Therefore a person who links segments of a divided society in which there is a considerable degree of dissociation is likely to be under severe strain. The traditional chief who was incorporated into modern government as in the British system of Indirect Rule was a typical example of a person who occupied an intercalary position of this sort (Colson 1948, Mitchell 1949, Watson 1958). Epstein (1958) has shown that the Tribal Elders on the Copperbelt occupied a similar position *vis-à-vis* the mine management and the African workers. It follows that in an industrial situation in a divided society the opposition between management and labour which is a normal feature of industrial society would be compounded by the disjunction between the component groups of the divided society. Hence the stresses on a person occupying an intercalary position in industry in the societies I am describing are likely to be acute indeed.

Persons in intercalary positions naturally seek to avoid the conflicts in which they are inevitably involved. Indeed, some may be able to exploit their ambiguous status to their own advantages. Normally they achieve this by keeping their contradictory roles separate. The Police Boy, for example, might convey company instructions to the workers and at the same time maintain his personal relationships with his fellows. While there was no disjunction in relationships with the Europeans and the African parts of the enterprise this was possible. When the hostility in industrial relations reached a breaking-point, however, those occupying intercalary positions were subject to acute stress. They were then called upon to declare their position unequivocally, and since they were no longer able to keep their conflicting roles separate their position became untenable. This happened particularly during industrial unrest, as for example on the Copperbelt in 1935 and again in 1940. In 1935 African workers on the Copperbelt withdrew their labour following an announcement of an increase of taxation, and this led to some rioting during which several Africans were shot. The equivocal position of the mine police during this affray emerges very clearly in the statement made by one of the African witnesses at the enquiry which followed the affair. He told the Commissioners that the people thought that the Police Boys should have sided with the people against the Whites and the soldiers and not with the Whites and the soldiers against the Africans (Mitchell 1956a). In this stress situation the Police Boys had to decide on which side of the fence they stood and whatever decision they made put them in the wrong with the opposed group.

The position of the Police Boys as a point of articulation between the disparate parts of the industrial structure was not unique. In fact on the Copperbelt the management soon found that there were some weaknesses in allowing the African workers to approach them through the Police Boys. The Police Boys, they felt, were open to bribes and were likely to push the claims of their own tribesmen and kinsmen before strangers. In other words they were involved in personal relationships with the people they had to represent to management, and this meant that it was difficult for them to separate their industrial role from their private one. The management therefore introduced a system whereby tribesmen elected an 'elder' to represent their interests to the management, and the committee of Tribal Elders became an additional point of articulation between the European management and the African workers. The managements used the committee to convey their decisions to the workers and the workers used the committee to bring their wishes to the attention of the management. But they did not escape the dilemma of the Police Boy, for they were inevitably forced to occupy a similar intercalary position. It is interesting to note that both in 1935 and in 1940 during industrial unrest the body of African workers rejected the Tribal Elders as their representatives to management (Epstein 1958).

The Police Boys and the Tribal Elders, being involved in the

wider and more general field of relationships of African labour
to European management, were inevitably caught up in the
oppositions between these two groups. The Boss Boys involved
in more specific industrial tasks were not so immediately
concerned. Nevertheless, even with them the hostilities spora-
dically rose to the surface. For example, on one occasion a gang
of underground workers rejected their Boss Boy. The workers
were transported down the mine in 'skips' or elevators, and it
was customary for the African workers to be separated from the
Europeans in different compartments. Normally the Boss Boy
rode with the other Africans, but on one occasion, when some
difficulties had arisen, one gang of African workers refused to
have the Boss Boy with them and told him that he should 'travel
with the Europeans with whom he was in league'.

The Police Boys and the Tribal Elders shared a common
characteristic: they were essentially relatively uneducated
tribesmen whose knowledge of the European's language and his
way of life and values, on the whole, was slight. They were thus
incapable, even if the colour bar would have allowed it, of interacting with Europeans except in rigidly defined work situations
where the amount of communication was minimal and the
functions highly specific. But while relationships between White
and Black were being mediated through Police Boys and White
and Tribal Elders another class of employee was already arising.
These were the 'white-collar' workers, the clerks, teachers,
medical orderlies, welfare workers, and other educated workers
who were able to understand sufficient English to read books,
newspapers, journals, and generally, therefore, to share indirectly the White man's culture with him. They were later to
occupy an important position in the industrial structure.

The white-collar workers differed from the other workers
firstly in their education. The missions were the first formal
educational institutions in the territory. The missionaries' first
aim was to spread the Gospel and to bring the Christian way of
life to the heathen. Being able to read the Bible was an essential
part of this process, so the missionaries found that education in
the sense of reading and writing was a necessary prerequisite to
evangelization. Literate Africans were employed very early in
the history of South Central Africa, first as mission teachers and
increasingly later as clerks, medical orderlies, and as other

relatively skilled workers. At the same time other Africans were being employed as drivers, carpenters, bricklayers, and in similar skilled and semi-skilled occupations. This was part of a general process of differentiation of African labour in terms of skills. These new skills were apposite to the industrial society which was developing in South Central Africa, and for someone to invest in a period of education and training to acquire them implied a commitment to a 'Western' way of life. Together with the acquisition of skills went an increasing stay in wage-earning and a corresponding decrease in the intensity of interaction with rural compatriots. This points to additional differentiation of the African population in terms of their different ways of life as well as by skills and education.

Of those thus committed to the 'Western' way of life, the white-collar workers occupied a peculiar position, because, being literate and able to speak English, they were better placed to appreciate the European way of life than most of their workmates. They were thus able to communicate directly with a larger number of White officials, and yet at the same time they were not cut off from other African workers, however unskilled and uneducated they happened to be. The white-collar workers soon fell into the position of having to interpret the way of the Europeans to their less knowledgeable workmates, and at the same time having to interpret the Africans' wishes and views to the White officials. They too were inevitably drawn into a position intercalary between White management and Black labour similar to that occupied by the Police Boys and the Tribal Elders.

But the difference in education between the white-collar workers and the others was crucial, because it lay behind the status stratification of the African community. When they penetrated into South Central Africa the Europeans had brought with them an industrial technology. In addition, their superiority in arms and political organization allowed the Europeans to establish social and political dominance over the Africans. The two major groups in the divided society were thus unequal in political power. In this situation the way of life of the superior group from the point of view of the subjugated African population naturally became invested with prestige: the power of the Europeans became intimately associated with their way of life. The Europeans became an 'élite' or 'standard setting' group for the general African population (Mitchell and Epstein 1959). In other words the Europeans as a whole became a reference group for some sections of the African community: they aspired to the standards set by the Europeans but could not themselves become members of that group (Mitchell 1956b). White-collar workers, in particular the clerks, occupied a position intercalary between the African workers and the European officials, but they also occupied a position of importance within the African community, since they acquired prestige from their approximation to a 'civilized' way of life. Their familiarity with the English language and their understanding of bureaucratic procedures placed the white-collar workers in a significant leadership position within the African community. Not only had they the standards against which they could assess the rationality of their demands, but they also understood the means whereby, and the tactics they could use best, to make them effective. It is no accident that the national independence movement in Northern Rhodesia had its origins in a number of urban welfare societies and cultural clubs founded by white-collar workers. These societies met to discuss their disabilities and their needs and became in fact training schools in which the African élites were beginning to handle the European methods of negotiation and procedure (Epstein 1958). Nor is it surprising that the trade union movement on the Copperbelt was led initially by white-collar workers.

The significance of the white-collar workers in the divided society, however, did not end at this point. Their aspirations to a European level of living in this kind of society were inevitably frustrated, and this provided added motivation to their political leadership. Yet at the same time their leadership in the political field was subjected to the same sort of conflict as in the industrial. Because the white-collar workers were able to associate with Europeans, the illiterate Africans assumed that they were therefore in league with them. Consequently they tended to reject them as their leaders and to turn to others who did not appear to be associated with Europeans. This tendency was shown clearly in an experiment in which respondents were asked to rank the offices of persons who wielded power in urban areas of Northern Rhodesia (Mitchell and Epstein 1957). We found that those who were involved in organizations and institutions which championed the Africans interests in opposition to the European, such as the tribal chiefs, the Congress leader, and the trade union leader, were ranked higher on the scale of power than those who derived their power from institutions which the Europeans had set up. The very familiarity of the white-collar workers with the European way of life thus became both an advantage and a disadvantage to them. The way in which these wider societal features manifested themselves in perceptions of the social rating of an occupation was perhaps nowhere more clearly demonstrated than in the change of the rating of the African policemen in Northern Rhodesia between the years 1954 and 1965. These were the years when African opposition to the constitutional arrangements in Northern Rhodesia was becoming increasingly strident. The Europeans and their way of life, as symbols of the colonial system, became more and more the object of hatred and vilification for the African population. It follows that the perception of those occupations which rested for their prestige upon their association with the colonial rulers must have become ambiguous.

The relationships between Africans and Europeans in Northern Rhodesia inevitably involved a substantial political component. This implies that if Europeans were indeed an 'élite' to Africans, then as political opposition of the Africans to Europeans became more violent, their attitudes towards some occupations must have become ambivalent. Hence perception of the political component became a complicating factor in the prestige of occupations in this sort of social situation. Epstein and I had noted this fact earlier in connection with the large standard deviation observed in the ratings of certain occupations. We noted in particular that this occurred in two occupations which were intercalary between what might be broadly conceived as the European and African sectors of the community. These occupations were those of 'Boss Boy (Mines)', who was the first-line supervisor in the mining industry, and the 'African Police Inspector'. We wrote:

These are the positions which link two different and frequently opposed parts of a social structure. The Boss Boy (Mines) for example, from the point of view of the African workers under him, is seen to be both a representative of Management to them, and their own representative to Management. Clearly the assessment of the prestige of the occupation of Boss Boy must be related to the way in which the respondent sees the situation. We feel that the scatter of response in the case of the Boss Boy and the African Police Inspector may be explained by the ambiguity of the position *vis-à-vis* other Africans. (1959: 27).

The point here is that the occupations might be rated negatively for some respondents against an unfavourable image of, say, the Boss Boys as representing the European-dominated Management, or positively against a favourable image of the Boss Boy being himself a Black worker whose interests were identified with those of the men under him.

The position of the African policeman was a particularly awkward one in a divided society such as this. In terms of intimate social contacts, kinship, and racial alignment the African policeman was strongly linked to the African population. But his duties frequently required him to uphold laws which had been promulgated by a predominately White legislature. As political expression began to take a more violent form, so the policemen had to assume roles in which they wielded the might of the State against their fellow Africans on behalf of White government. As African opposition to the constitutional arrangements increased there were violent demonstrations against the political order and the police were called in to quell many disturbances and to arrest African political leaders. The African image of the policeman must have suffered in consequence.

It is fortunate that we have available the results of three studies of occupational prestige conducted with similar respondents embracing this period. The study in 1954 was conducted with 653 scholars and students of educational institutions near Lusaka. In October 1959 Dr S. H. Irvine, then of the Department of Education in the University College of Rhodesia and Nyasaland, was able to conduct a similar study amongst 147 secondary school students in Ndola, Northern Rhodesia. A comparison between the ratings in the two studies showed that there had been very little change in overall occupation prestige ratings over the five years. The product–moment correlation coefficient between the mean ratings of the two series was 0.9596. Differences in the ratings of occupations were assessed by a regression equation. The only differences at the 5 per cent level of significance (i.e. critical ratio = 1.96 or more) between the ratings in 1954 and those in 1959 were those for the African police inspector and the African police constable. Over the period in question both had lost prestige against the general stability of the ratings of other occupations.[4] It was also a time when the African opposition to colonial government had become much more articulate.

Two subsequent studies of occupational prestige in Zambia conducted by R. E. Hicks in 1965 have lent some support to this interpretation (1966, 1967). In the first he had 85 trainees at the Broken Hill Railways Training School rank twelve occupations according to the prestige they had in terms of a number of characteristics of the occupations such as responsibility on the job, service value of the job, money earned in the job, and so on. In his second study Hicks asked 25 African and 33 European members of the third form of a multi-racial secondary school in Zambia to rate 118 occupations in five prestige categories. In both studies the policeman was one of the occupational titles rated. In the study involving the railway trainees Hicks (1966: 53–5) found that, as against the study involving mining personnel conducted in 1959 (Mitchell and Irvine 1965), the prestige of the police constable had risen dramatically in relation to the seven other occupational titles that had been included in the earlier study. Discussing this, Hicks writes:

At the end of 1963 the former Federation of Northern and Southern Rhodesia and Nyasaland broke up; thus from the beginning of 1964 the Northern Rhodesian area began to prepare for independent rule under a government largely composed of African members; on 24 October 1964 the area became the independent Republic of Zambia. The present investigation was carried out in April 1965 some sixteen months after it had become evident that the Zambian freedom fighters had won their goal. This was sufficient time, perhaps, for the attitude of ambivalence toward the police-constable to undergo change in a

---

[4] This may be peculiar to the position of a policeman in the sort of industrial situation I describe. It is interesting to note that Moser and Hall (1954: 40) also found a relatively wide scatter of ratings for the policeman in England but do not advance a specific explanation for it. Taft (1953: 184) found the same thing in Australia and suggested that this may be due to a discrepancy between the importance of these occupations to the community and the comparatively unpleasant working conditions. D'Souza in India suggested that the explanation is due to the discrepancy between wages and power (1962: 150).

positive direction; since the police-force was now carrying out the law and order of a government no longer alien to the interests of the African majority. In addition, the policy of Zambianization of posts had led to many more opportunities for Africans to reach and hold important posts in the police-force. On Mitchell and Epstein's hypothesis, one would now expect the constable to be regarded more favourably by the members of the public. If this were so, then two things would be expected to occur: the relative position of the police constable in the prestige scale would rise as indicated by a change in rank and in the number of respondents rating the occupation more highly, and the variance would decrease. This in fact has occurred in this study and lends support to political dimension theory. (1966: 54.)

In Hicks' second study, however, where scholars were used, this trend was not so clearly manifested. The rank ordering of the eight occupations (or their nearest equivalent) in the three studies using scholars in 1954, 1959, and 1965 was as in Table 5.2.

Table 5.2 suggests that the prestige of the constable among Hicks' railway trainee sample was abnormally inflated and that except for the steady rise of the garage mechanic and the steady fall of the bricklayer *vis-à-vis* the other occupations between 1954 and 1965 that of the constable and the other occupations seems to have remained steady.

It is possible of course that in the short time after independence until Hicks' studies, in spite of Hicks' assertion to the contrary, the position of the policemen had not yet stabilized. Hicks in fact suggests this in his later paper when he writes: 'It may well be some time before the police constable acquires a firm position within the occupational hierarchy in Zambia, but

Table 5.2 *Comparison of Rankings of eight Occupations featuring in three Zambian Studies between 1959 and 1965*

	Mitchell and Epstein 1954	Mitchell and Irvine 1959	Hicks 1965
Secondary school teacher	1.5	1	1
Garage (motor) mechanic	6	4	2
(African) minister of religion	1.5	2	3
(Senior) clerk	3	3	4
Plumber	7	5	5
(African) constable	5	7	6
Bricklayer	4	6	7
Domestic servant	8	8	8

in political terms he has rather a better chance now that he is no longer supporting an alien government.' (1967: 217.)

Hierarchical Position and the Perception of Status

The perception of the prestige of the African policeman, I argue, would be affected by a secular change in the way in which his role was construed by the general public. Meanings attributed to his duties would be differently interpreted as relationships between the rulers and the ruled became more tense. But social perception may be affected by the structural location of respondents as well as by changes in time. One particular aspect of this has been known for a long time. Davis (1952: 134) pointed out that the same occupations may be appraised differently by people in different positions in the same society. At about the same time North and Hatt (1954: 415) in the best-known early study of occupational prestige, pointed out, according to their data, when a person in the United States rated his own job or one closely related to it his evaluation was almost always considerably higher than the average evaluation of the position. Congalton (1953: 55) in New Zealand found that 'with one exception all the occupations in Classes V and VI were given higher ratings by members of these classes than by members of other classes'. Reiss (1961: 198–237) and Blau (1957) for the United States, Hall and Jones (1950: 42) for Great Britain, and and Taft (1953: 186) for Australia all found that though the evaluations in general favoured the respondent's own occupation the differences were small or non-existent. A study by Gerstl and Cohen (1964) extended these studies to show that engineers rated not only their own occupation higher than the general public did, but also a set of occupations which were connected with engineering, such as, for example, that of company director, accountant, and works manager. They explained this in terms of a sort of egocentrism whereby respondents rated more highly not only their own occupation but also those whose role in relation to their own they clearly appreciated.

These findings, however, are little more than empirical statements of fact. A simple explanation of these facts when they occur might simply be that the respondents' positive self-image influences their perception of the prestige of their own occupations, which is after all an integral part of identity. As such, however, the explanation is little more than a tautology. Brown advances a more subtle interpretation which is more germane to the situation in a colonial society. He observed that Negro respondents rated certain occupations such as public school teacher, social worker, and mortician, categories which Negroes had been able to take up and succeed in, or occupations such as garbage collector, street sweeper, or shoe shiner in which Negroes were numerically preponderant, more highly than did American Whites. Brown suggested that this was because the Negro workers had 'not yet had the opportunity to participate freely in the economic spirit and tradition of urban competitive community life' (1955: 564). This suggests that the perception of prestige is affected not only by the position of the respondents in the society as a whole but also by the meaning that the occupation has to that group as a whole. Thus the Negroes in an underprivileged position in American society with limited opportunities for economic advancement valued highly those occupations in which they perceived opportunities for them to succeed.

The relationship between the structural position of respondents and the way in which they evaluated the prestige of various occupations may perhaps be appreciated most clearly if occupations relate to the same industrial organization and if the position of the respondents in that organization is clearly delineated. This set of circumstances prevailed in a set of occupational prestige ratings obtained by Dr S. H. Irvine in connection with a study of training facilities in a group of copper-mining companies in Zambia in 1959. (See Mitchell and Irvine 1965.)[5] Three sets of respondents were asked to rate forty-two occupations which were at that time open to Africans.

(a) Recruits to the Copper-Mining Industry

Ninety-six respondents who were in the preliminary training school and who were therefore new to the copper-mining industry were in the first category. They were, on the whole, illiterate, and their questionnaires were completed by interviewers. In general they were on the lowest rung of the ladder in

5 The findings that follow, including Table 5.3 and much of the discussion of these findings, are taken from this paper.

the complicated occupational structure of the mine. Most of them were being trained for unskilled jobs both underground and on the surface. Theirs was essentially a worm's eye view of the structure.

(b) *Advancees in the Copper Mining Industry*

Fifty-six respondents were what were then known as Advancees in the copper mining industry. Dating from the Dalgleish Commission Report in 1948, certain jobs previously occupied only by Europeans were filled by selected Africans who had long experience in the industry and who were judged capable of holding down the job satisfactorily. Many had had as much as fifteen years' experience in mining, and at the time of the study occupied the most responsible posts filled by Africans in the industry. They had, as it were, a bird's eye view of the structure.

(c) *Students in a Secondary School*

The third group comprised 147 scholars at a secondary school in a neighbouring town which, while being one of the Copperbelt towns, did not have a copper mine in it. The scholars at this school were drawn from several of the neighbouring towns. Some of them were the children of copper-miners, but they were in the main drawn from all walks of life. For the purposes of comparison the occupational ratings of this group of scholars may be looked upon as representing that of the general public. Some justification in support of this point of view is provided by a comparison with the ratings of a similar group on thirty-one of the occupations which appeared amongst the forty-two in this study (Mitchell and Epstein 1959). The product–moment correlation coefficient between the mean ratings was $+ 0.9506$ with a standard error of 0.0142 (Mitchell 1964a: 86). This indicates a high overall agreement on the ratings of these two sets of respondents drawn from the general public outside the mining industry.

The occupations were rated on a five-point scale. Each category was given an arbitrary score of 1 for very high prestige, 2 for high prestige, 3 for the medial category, 4 for low prestige, and 5 for very low prestige. These scores enabled a mean rating to be computed for every occupation in each of the three categories of respondents. The ratings of the three groups of respondents were compared by means of regression equations.

A regression line was fitted to the mean rating of one category as against the ratings of the other two categories. This enabled an expected mean rating to be computed from the regression equation, and the mean rating expected, on the basis of the association between the two sets of ratings to be compared with the observed mean rating. The mean ratings, expected mean ratings based on the association of ratings between pairs of categories of respondent, and values of the t ratios between mean ratings are set out in Table 5.3.

Personnel officer, senior clerk (mines), trade union branch secretary, social organiser (mines), sub-development cleaner, pipe layer (mines), machine boy, underground instructor, and boss boy (mines) are clearly related to the mining industry. Other occupations such as medical orderly, office messenger, and trench digger could also be considered to be related to mining, but they could be included in industrial and government organizations as well and have therefore been excluded from consideration here.

The average mean ratings of these nine occupations to be expected from the ratings accorded to them by either the Scholars (in relation to the Recruits or Advancees) or by Recruits (in relations to Advancees) when the association between the mean ratings on all forty-two occupational titles was taken into account is set out in the first column in Table 5.4. The average mean ratings actually observed are set out in the second column of Table 5.4 and the differences between the expected and the observed in the third column.

These figures show that both Recruits and Advancees rate the occupational titles in the mining industry higher than do the general public, here represented by the response of the Scholars.[6] This finding supports Gerstl and Cohen's finding that members of an occupational situs[7] tend to overrate all occupations in that situs, though the differences here are small.

[6] The algebraic sum of all differences between the observed and expected ratings is zero. The expected difference or sum of the differences between the observed and expected ratings for any occupation or set of occupations is also zero. A departure from zero value therefore represents an overall higher or lower general rating of the occupation. The sum of differences for the nine occupations is three times the standard error of the estimate.

[7] Benoit-Smullyan (1944: 154) describes a situs by saying: 'Situs distinctions exist whenever a socially accepted classification distinguishes between groups and whenever membership in a group is considered a socially relevant criterion in making distinctions between individuals. To this there may or may not be added distinctions of status.'

Table 5.3 *Differences in Prestige Gradings of Occupations in three Social Categories*

	X	Schools (X) and Recruits (Y)				Schools (X) and Advances (Z)				Recruits (Y) and Advances (Z)				
		Y'	Obs.Y	Diff.	C.R.	Z'	Obs.Z	Diff.	C.R.	Y	Z'	Obs.Z	Diff.	C.R.
African education officer	0.97	0.63	0.76	-0.13	0.56	0.51	0.77	-0.26	1.22	0.76	0.84	0.77	+0.07	0.21
African minister of religion	1.25	0.93	0.96	-0.03	0.13	0.89	0.82	+0.07	0.33	0.96	1.07	0.82	+0.25	0.76
Sec. school teacher	1.10	0.78	1.32	-0.54	2.34	0.69	0.93	-0.24	1.12	1.32	1.47	0.93	+0.54	1.64
Headmaster	1.37	1.06	1.11	-0.05	0.22	1.05	0.96	+0.09	0.42	1.11	1.24	0.96	+0.28	0.85
African welfare officer	1.32	1.01	1.19	-0.18	0.78	0.98	1.00	-0.02	0.09	1.19	1.33	1.00	+0.33	1.00
African personnel officer	1.54	1.24	0.92	+0.32	1.39	1.28	1.26	+0.02	0.09	0.92	1.02	1.26	-0.24	0.73
Shop owner	1.67	1.37	1.39	-0.02	0.09	1.45	1.21	+0.24	1.12	1.39	1.55	1.21	+0.34	1.03
Bus owner	1.63	1.33	1.42	-0.09	0.39	1.40	1.28	+0.12	0.56	1.42	1.58	1.28	+0.30	0.91
Senior clerk (mine)	1.72	1.43	1.13	+0.30	1.30	1.52	1.56	-0.04	0.19	1.13	1.26	1.56	-0.30	0.91
T.U. branch secretary	1.62	1.32	1.43	-0.11	0.48	1.38	1.43	-0.05	0.23	1.43	1.60	1.43	+0.17	0.52
Social organizer (mine)	1.67	1.37	1.41	-0.04	0.17	1.45	1.48	-0.03	0.14	1.41	1.57	1.48	+0.09	0.27
Primary school teacher	1.72	1.43	1.43	-0.00	0.00	1.52	1.45	+0.07	0.33	1.43	1.60	1.45	+0.15	0.45
African police inspector	1.71	1.42	1.55	-0.13	0.56	1.51	1.32	+0.19	0.89	1.55	1.73	1.32	+0.41	1.24
Senior clerk (*Boma*)	1.85	1.56	1.33	+0.23	1.00	1.69	1.41	+0.28	1.32	1.33	1.48	1.41	+0.07	0.21
Medical orderly	1.88	1.59	1.55	+0.04	0.17	1.73	1.68	+0.05	0.23	1.55	1.73	1.68	+0.05	0.15
Underground instructor	2.01	1.73	1.25	+0.48	2.08	1.91	2.06	-0.15	0.70	1.25	1.39	2.06	-0.67	2.03
Boss boy (mine)	2.04	1.76	1.27	+0.49	2.12	1.95	2.04	-0.09	0.42	1.27	1.42	2.04	-0.62	1.88
Garage mechanic	1.95	1.76	1.43	+0.33	1.43	1.83	2.06	-0.23	1.08	1.43	1.60	2.06	-0.46	1.40
Carpenter	2.08	1.80	1.65	+0.15	0.65	2.00	1.94	+0.06	0.28	1.65	1.84	1.94	-0.10	0.30
Typist	2.13	1.86	1.52	+0.34	1.47	2.07	2.11	-0.04	0.19	1.52	1.70	2.11	-0.41	1.24
Sub-development cleaner	2.32	2.06	1.99	+0.07	0.30	2.32	1.76	+0.56	2.63	1.99	2.22	1.76	+0.46	1.40
Bricklayer	2.16	1.89	2.05	-0.16	0.69	2.11	2.10	+0.01	0.05	2.05	2.29	2.10	+0.19	0.58
Pipe layer (mine)	2.40	2.14	2.13	+0.01	0.04	2.43	1.77	+0.66	3.10	2.13	2.38	1.77	+0.61	1.85

Plumber	2.11	1.84	2.05	-0.21	0.91	2.04	2.45	-0.41	1.93	2.05	2.29	2.45	-0.16	0.49
Machine boy	2.30	2.03	2.06	-0.03	0.13	2.30	2.61	-0.31	1.46	2.06	2.30	2.61	-0.31	0.94
Lorry driver	2.38	2.12	2.21	-0.09	0.39	2.41	2.37	+0.04	0.19	2.21	2.47	2.37	+0.10	0.30
Painter-builder	2.33	2.07	2.20	-0.13	0.56	2.34	2.44	-0.10	0.47	2.20	2.46	2.44	-0.02	0.06
Contractor (Capitao)	2.36	2.10	2.23	-0.13	0.56	2.38	2.15	+0.23	1.08	2.23	2.49	2.15	+0.34	1.03
Shoemaker	2.45	2.19	2.23	-0.04	0.17	2.50	2.50	0.00	0.00	2.23	2.49	2.50	-0.01	0.03
Fish seller	2.47	2.21	2.26	-0.05	0.22	2.53	2.63	-0.10	0.47	2.26	2.52	2.63	-0.11	0.33
Boma (Messenger)	2.69	2.44	2.14	+0.30	1.30	2.82	2.50	+0.32	1.50	2.14	2.39	2.50	-0.11	0.33
African constable	2.54	2.29	2.61	-0.32	1.39	2.62	2.48	+0.14	0.66	2.61	2.92	2.48	+0.44	1.34
Petrol pump boy (filling station attendant)	2.69	2.44	2.14	+0.30	1.30	2.82	3.05	-0.23	1.08	2.14	2.39	3.05	-0.66	2.00
Office messenger	2.61	2.36	2.41	-0.05	0.22	2.71	3.04	-0.33	1.55	2.41	2.69	3.04	-0.35	1.06
Station boy	2.79	2.55	2.31	+0.24	1.04	2.96	3.05	-0.09	0.42	2.31	2.58	3.05	-0.47	1.43
Hotel waiter	2.87	2.63	2.44	+0.19	0.82	3.06	2.87	+0.19	0.89	2.44	2.73	2.87	-0.14	0.43
Domestic servant	2.80	2.56	2.44	+0.12	0.52	2.97	3.22	-0.25	1.17	2.44	2.73	3.22	-0.49	1.49
Trench digger	2.83	2.59	2.84	-0.25	1.08	3.01	3.05	-0.04	0.19	2.84	3.17	3.05	+0.12	0.36
Road worker	2.88	2.64	2.79	-0.15	0.65	3.08	3.09	-0.01	0.05	2.79	3.12	3.09	+0.03	0.09
Woodcutter	2.83	2.59	3.08	-0.49	2.12	3.01	3.23	-0.22	1.03	3.08	3.44	3.23	+0.21	0.64
Scavenger	3.10	2.87	3.05	-0.18	0.78	3.37	3.30	-0.01	0.05	3.05	3.41	3.30	+0.11	0.33
Garden boy	3.09	2.86	3.11	-0.25	1.08	3.36	3.52	-0.11	0.52	3.11	3.47	3.52	-0.05	0.15

r = +0.9285 ± 0.0212
Y' = 1.0501 (X) - 0.3789
S.E. of Estimate = 0.2310

r = +0.9595 ± 0.0122
Z' = 1.3428 (X) - 0.7899
S.E. of Estimate = 0.2128

r = +0.9402 ± 0.0282
Z' = 1.1190 (Y) - 0.0051
S.E. of Estimate = 0.3294

Table 5.4 *Overall Differences between Expected and Observed Mean Ratings of nine Occupation Titles related to the Mining Industry*[a]

Difference	Average expected rating	Observed average rating	
Observed mean rating of Recruits and mean rating estimated from mean ratings of Scholars	1.67	1.51	+0.16
Observed mean rating of Advancees and mean rating estimated from ratings by Scholars	1.84	1.77	+0.06[b]
Observed mean rating of Advancees and mean rating estimated from mean rating by Recruits	1.68	1.77	−0.09

[a] The values used in computing those averages were taken from Table 5.3 for the appropriate occupational titles.
[b] The discrepancy is due to rounding errors.

Discrepancies in Respect of Occupations

It is clear that discrepancies also exist between the ratings of respondents occupying different positions within the situs. The Advancees, for example, hold positions in the upper half of the occupational ranking scale and tend to rate the occupations in the mining industry somewhat lower than the Recruits as a whole, but the difference is small.[8]

Additional insight may be gained by examining the way in which individual occupations were graded by the three categories of respondent. In general the agreement in ratings among the three categories was high. The product–moment correlation coefficents and their standard errors were: Scholars with Advancees 0.9595 (0.0122), Scholars with Recruits 0.9285 (0.0212), and Advancees with Recruits 0.9042 (0.0282). The ratings of the Scholars and the Advancees agree most closely, the Scholars and the Recruits next, and the Advancees and the Recruits least. From this emerges the interesting point that although both Recruits and Advancees in the mining industry

[8] Blau (1957: 394) notes that those in the professions are more critical in their ratings and rate all occupations lower than respondents in other occupations.

tended to rank the occupational titles associated with mining slightly more highly than people outside the mining industry did, the ratings of all occupational titles by Recruits and Advancees differed more than the ratings of either Advancees or Recruits as against the Scholars. The prestige structure of the occupations as a whole, in other words differed most from the viewpoints of those who were situated at most widely differing positions in the occupational structure. However, the observed mean ratings of some occupational titles for one set of respondents differed appreciably from the expected ratings computed from the overall relationship of mean ratings of another set of respondents (see Table 5.3). Why the ratings of many of these occupations should have differed in the way they did may be interpreted to some extent in terms of the social position of the respondents concerned, both in respect of the mining industry and of the wider social structure. For example, the Recruits rated the secondary school teacher and the woodcutter lower, and the underground instructor and the boss boy (mines) higher than the Scholars. Both the boss boy and the underground instructor held positions of authority in respect of the Recruits; equally, the Scholars rated the secondary school teacher who exercised authority over them, more highly than the Recruits did.[9] It seems clear that the authority-bearing aspect of the occupations in relation to the two categories of respondents is an important element in the prestige ratings. This finding is of particular interest in terms of Caplow's contention (1954: 55) that the major component in general prestige is the 'behavioural control' element.

It is more difficult to explain the discrepancy in the ratings of the woodcutter. Here the Recruits rated the occupation substantially lower than the Scholars. It is possible that the Scholars confused this occupation with that of carpenter and therefore tended to rank it higher. The Recruits would be aware, however, that it was an occupation requiring only the rudest of skills. This, however, is an *ad hoc* interpretation, and a definitive explanation of the discrepancies is not possible within the limits of the

---

[9] The secondary school teacher carried higher prestige than the headmaster. This is because the headmaster is frequently a person with secondary school qualifications in charge of a primary school, whereas the secondary school teacher is frequently a university graduate with correspondingly much higher prestige.

information we have available to us.

When we turn to the differences between the Scholars and Advancees we find that there were two occupations for which the ratings differ significantly. We find that the Advancees rated the sub-development cleaner and the pipe layer (mines) more highly than did the scholars. The reason for differences in ratings for the two occupations is not difficult to find. The Advancees, far better than the Scholars, appreciated the importance of the job of sub-development cleaner and the pipe layer (mines), however unprepossessing these occupations may sound. Both of these occupations were concerned with underground operations demanding considerable responsibility. They had only recently become available to Africans, having formerly been occupations filled exclusively by Europeans, and were in fact examples of the posts which had become open to Africans under the African Advancement scheme.

When we examine the ratings of the Advancees as against those of the Recruits we see that for only two occupations was the difference appreciable: the Recruits rated one of these, the underground inspector, more highly than did the Advancees. The Recruits also rated the boss boy more highly than the Advancees did and the pipe layer somewhat lower, but not to the same extent as for the underground inspector.

Once again it is not difficult to interpret the difference in ratings of the Recruits and the Advancees with respect to the underground instructor and the boss boy. Many of the Advancees were senior to the underground instructor and the boss boy in the mining occupational hierarchy. From the point of view of the Recruits, however, the underground instructor and the boss boy occupied positions of immediate authority and hence of prestige.

From our understanding of the roles of these occupations in mining and of the positions of the respondents in relation to them we are able to postulate that the way in which the prestige of occupations was appreciated by respondents was influenced by their structural positions, either inside the mining industry or outside it altogether. Furthermore, the differences could be made intelligible by an understanding of the specific occupational roles within the industry and the extent to which the respondents in the positions in which they were situated were able to appreciate those roles.

There were, however, several occupational titles which were not part of the mining industry for which the ratings of the three categories of respondents differed significantly. The difference in the rating of the secondary school teacher by the Scholars and by the Recruits has already been referred to. In addition the Recruits rated the woodcutter significantly lower than the Scholars and the petrol pump boy higher than the Advancees did. The Scholars rated the plumber higher than the Advancees, but the difference was not very large. The context to which these differences in perception of prestige must be related is not the mining industry but the wider economic and industrial structure within which the three categories of respondents must also be located. However, here we are on less firm ground, since our understanding of the articulation of occupational roles in the wider economic system of Northern Rhodesia (and Zambia) at the time when these studies were made is more fragmentary than that for the more specific context of the mining industry. It seems likely that the Recruits to the mining industry might have known that the woodcutters were relatively unskilled lumber-men employed by private contractors to cut trees for use on the mines. As new members of a secure and prestigious industry they might well have contrasted their own position favourably with a class of workers amongst whom they might easily have numbered themselves. The Scholars, somewhat removed from this status threat, would have experienced no pressure to denigrate the prestige of the woodcutter.

In the same way we might postulate that the Recruits rated the petrol pump boy (filling station attendant) more highly than did the Advancees in particular but also more highly than the Scholars because it is a highly visible occupation performed in public and indexed by conspicuous uniforms, an occupation to which many of them (but not the Scholars or Advancees) were potential recruits and which, according to popular belief, was a highly lucrative calling. Without detailed information on how the general African public occupying status positions commensurate with those of the Recruits to the mining industry looked upon the occupation of petrol pump boy, however, our postulates must remain speculation.

General Social Position and the Perception of Status

The argument so far is that the meanings which respondents attributed to cognitive phenomena, in this case their appreciation of occupations as general perceptual constructs, were related to the positions that those respondents occupied in a general social system. We were able to adduce some evidence to support this proposition by examining the different reactions of respondents, whom we knew occupied different positions in an industrial organization, to a set of occupational titles which were connected with that industry.

This contention, however, may also be tested on a general set of respondents if we are able to allocate them to positions in the general social structure. We could then examine the systematic variations in their responses to significant occupations. The data I have used to do this are the responses to a set of occupational titles that Dr S. H. Irvine and I were able to collect in Southern Rhodesia in 1964.[10] The respondents were 1,485 scholars at African secondary schools. Fifty-six occupations, as set out in Table 5.5, were used. As before, the respondents were asked to rate each occupational title on a five-point scale ranging from 'very high prestige' to 'very low prestige'. In this study the questionnaire was printed in both Shona, one of the main African languages, and in English. The respondents were also asked to express their own occupational aspirations and to say what aspects of the occupations they felt led them to accord prestige to them.[11] The respondents were also asked questions relating to their personal attributes. These were date of birth, level of education, ethnic affiliation, religious persuasion, gender, father's occupation, father's education, mother's education, and length of residence in town.

These personal attributes are rudimentary but they were chosen because from what we knew about status groups in the

---

[10] Preliminary findings from this study have already been reported in Mitchell 1966*b*.

[11] This was an open-ended question. The responses were coded (with percentage of respondents mentioning that characteristic) as financial gain (51.6), service to community (25.7), smartness of appearance or cleanliness of job (25.1), working conditions including respect from employers (9.2), responsibility (8.8), manners, behaviour, and deportment in the job (5.0), amount of skill needed (4.2), lack of colour bar (1.6), and miscellaneous others (2.2). The differences in distribution of responses among the three categories of respondents were small.

African population of South Central Africa it was likely that we could use them to allocate respondents to status categories. Latent structure analysis was used to do this. Five of the status-related attributes were used for this purpose, educational status of respondents, father's occupation, father's education, mother's education, and length of residence in town. Since these attributes could not be deemed to be measured along interval scales but at best arranged in ordinal categories, they were dichotomized at roughly the median point of each distribution. Attribute patterns, that is combinations of the presence or absence of each of the five attributes, were established for each respondent. Latent structure analysis makes no assumptions about the underlying distributions of the attributes used in the analysis. It merely assumes that if a suitable set of 'latent classes' can be established to which the respondents can be allocated, then the relationship among the attributes within each latent class will disappear. Appropriate procedures exist to establish latent classes of this sort and to estimate to which of the latent classes any individual with a particular attribute pattern is most likely to belong.[12] In this analysis it was postulated that respondents could be allocated to one of three classes.

These, it transpired, could be typified as follows:

1. 'High socio-economic status respondents of mixed rural or urban residence.' These are respondents whose education status is average but whose fathers were drawn disproportionately from supervisory, business white-collar, or professional occupations; whose parents were more highly educated than the average, and who were just as likely to have lived in towns for more than five years as not. There were 612 respondents in this category.

2. 'Low socio-economic status, of overwhelmingly urban residence.' The educational level of these respondents was slightly better than the average. Their fathers had low socio-economic status occupations and less than average education, as did their mothers. They were, however, essentially urban residents. There were 185 in this category.

3. 'Low socio-economic status, of rural residence.' These

---

[12] A maximum likelihood procedure developed by Clifford C. Clogg was used. See Clogg 1977.

respondents had rather lower than average education; their fathers had low socio-economic occupations, and their parents had less than the average level of education. They had lived in rural areas to a greater extent than the average. There were 482 in this category.

A total of 206 respondents were excluded from the analysis that follows since data were missing on one or more of the attributes in the set.

The index of dissimilarity—that is the percentage of the 1,279 respondents used in this analysis which would be needed to be redistributed to make the theoretical distribution derived from the latent structure analysis coincide exactly with the original distribution—was only 7.0 per cent. In other words, it is reasonable to assume that the categories defined by the analysis reflect a reasonably good classification of the respondents in terms of the attributes used.

The ratings of each set of respondents and of the total set of respondents were analysed separately. The procedure used to do this was to compute the average Euclidean distance of each occupation against every other occupation, using the item weights of 1 to 5 for the categories of 'very high prestige' to 'very low prestige'.[13] Occupations which respondents on the whole tended to rate in the same prestige category under this procedure would have small inter-occupational 'distances', while those which they rated differently would have large 'distances'. The set of $(56 \times 55)/2 = 1,540$ interoccupational distances was analysed by multi-dimensional scaling procedures.[14] The object of this procedure was to try as much as possible to estimate from the basic prestige ratings systematic but different components in rating the occupations.

---

[13] The rating for occupation I was subtracted from the rating for occupation J for each respondent. This difference was squared and summed over the whole set of respondents and then divided by the number of respondents in the set. The square root of this value was taken to represent the distance between occupations I and J. Means of known values were substituted when missing ratings were encountered.

[14] Roskam–Lingoes MINISSA solution incorporated in the Davies P. M. and A. P. M. Coxon 1983 MDS(X) suite of the Edinburgh Program Library Unit was used. A two-dimensional solution proved acceptable. The coefficients of alienation for the 'high status rural/urban' category was 0.058; for the 'low status urban' category it was 0.069, for the 'low status rural' category 0.074, and for the total sample it was 0.062. A coefficient of 0.15 is conventionally accepted as a reasonable fit.

Although our main interest lay in the major dimension along which the occupational titles could be ordered, it is instructive at this point to consider briefly the second, minor dimension. At one extreme of this dimension, at a position far removed from any other occupation, was placed the diviner. At the opposite extreme were placed, in order, The Native Commissioner's messenger, The African constable, the domestic servant, the African police inspector, and the sergeant in the army. Of the occupations listed in Table 5.5 the diviner was the only one which was not part of the general industrial and commercial system introduced by the White colonists. Diviners operated within a set of traditional beliefs and values concerning the causes of illness and misfortune. Some of their practices, such as those based on witchcraft beliefs, were expressly proscribed by the White administration. At the other extreme of this dimension was arrayed a set of occupations, all of which (except the domestic servant) referred to Africans who were exercising authority over other Africans on behalf of the White administration. The domestic servant, while not exercising authority, nevertheless was closely associated with the White sector of a divided society. What emerges from this analysis, therefore, using a completely different sample of respondents and a much more sophisticated mode of analysis, is a striking confirmation of the point made earlier about the African policeman in respect of the Northern Rhodesian sample. It seems certain that the way in which some of the respondents in this study were rating these particular occupations introduced sufficient disturbance in the Euclidean distances for them to emerge as placed along a second dimnsion unassociated with the major dimension. This dimension, arising as it does from respondents located in essentially the same general colonial position as those in Northern Rhodesia, clearly reflects what I referred to above as a 'political component'.

Our main interest, however, is with the major dimension along which the occupational titles were arranged in terms of their general prestige. These are set in Table 5.5 for each of the three latent classes identified and for the sample as a whole.

The overall ordering of these occupational titles reflects the now familiar pattern revealed in the other occupational studies reported here and confirmed by Treiman (1977) for most capita-

Table 5.5 *Ratings of Occupational Titles by Categories of Respondent*[a]

Occupational Title	High status rural urban	Low status urban	Low status rural	Total sample
Lawyer	1.55	1.55	1.53	1.55
School inspector	1.47	1.50	1.44	1.46
Secondary school teacher	1.36	1.34	1.31	1.35
Medical officer	1.28	1.31	1.31	1.30
Priest	1.19	1.22	1.25	1.21
Headmaster	1.26	1.26	1.09	1.20
African minister of religion	1.20	1.16	1.15	1.18
Senior clerk	1.06	1.10	1.00	1.04
Sergeant in the army	0.99	1.03	1.06	1.00
Radio announcer	0.92	0.97	0.87	0.91
Bus owner	0.91	0.88	0.87	0.90
African police inspector	0.91	0.91	0.93	0.90
Newspaper editor	0.90	0.98	0.83	0.89
Radio mechanic	0.84	0.78	0.94	0.89
Medical orderly	0.82	0.67	0.81	0.79
African welfare officer	0.81	0.77	0.71	0.78
Health demonstrator	0.80	0.77	0.76	0.75
Typist	0.74	0.81	0.64	0.73
Primary school teacher	0.75	0.67	0.64	0.70
Trade union branch secretary	0.61	0.67	0.79	0.70
Laboratory assistant	0.73	0.57	0.51	0.65
Garage mechanic	0.60	0.53	0.70	0.62
Preacher	0.67	0.58	0.59	0.62
Carpenter	0.26	0.19	0.43	0.32
Reporter	0.29	0.42	0.12	0.27
African constable	0.23	0.25	0.38	0.26
Storekeeper	0.21	0.10	0.14	0.18
Bus driver	0.10	0.07	0.33	0.17
Taxi driver	0.14	0.07	0.15	0.14
Diviner	−0.04	−0.04	−0.06	−0.03
Foreman	−0.03	0.05	−0.11	−0.04
Painter	−0.18	−0.21	−0.02	−0.13
Lorry driver	−0.22	−0.06	−0.13	−0.15
Plumber	−0.23	−0.31	−0.14	−0.20
Lift operator	−0.29	−0.42	−0.16	−0.29
Office messenger	−0.37	−0.40	−0.31	−0.35
Native commissioner's messenger	−0.40	−0.27	−0.44	−0.37
Shoemaker	−0.47	−0.43	−0.43	−0.45
Station boy (railway)	−0.65	−0.69	−0.61	−0.64
Bus conductor	−0.65	−0.58	−0.64	−0.64
Bricklayer	−0.67	−0.66	−0.62	−0.65
Market seller	−0.79	−0.76	−0.83	−0.81
Domestic servant	−0.80	−0.78	−0.82	−0.81
Petrol pump boy	−0.90	−0.73	−0.89	−0.88
Hotel waiter	−0.95	−0.74	−1.02	−0.94
Cook	−1.12	−1.04	−1.01	−1.07
Pedlar	−1.05	−1.00	−1.19	−1.10
Newspaper boy	−1.20	−1.13	−1.18	−1.19
Tea boy	−1.38	−1.37	−1.29	−1.35
Lorry boy	−1.44	−1.44	−1.45	−1.44
Woodcutter	−1.39	−1.44	−1.51	−1.45
Road repairer	−1.55	−1.60	−1.48	−1.53
Garden boy	−1.63	−1.70	−1.53	−1.61

Table 5.5 *Continued*

Occupational Title	High status rural urban	Low status urban	Low status rural	Total sample
Builder's labourer	-1.64	-1.75	-1.69	-1.67
Sweeper of sanitary lanes	-1.71	-1.71	-1.78	-1.74
Scavenger	-1.86	-1.92	-1.96	-1.92

a The ratings were derived from a two-dimensional MINISSA representation of the average inter-occupational Euclidean distances. The occupational titles were arranged in terms of the ratings for the total sample. The order of apparently tied ratings was determined from third and fourth decimal places not shown here.

list countries. At the top of the scale are the professional occupations, followed by white-collar. There follows a mixed set of skilled and semi-skilled occupations, followed finally by the unskilled workers. Since the ratings in Table 5.5 are derived from a scaling procedure and reflect metric intervals, one might expect that class discontinuities might manifest themselves in the values. The values for the total sample show the biggest discontinuity between the preacher at 0.62 and the carpenter at 0.32. There is a gap of 0.17 scale units between the taxi driver at 0.14 and the diviner at − 0.03, and another gap of 0.19 between the shoemaker at − 0.45 and the station boy (railways) at − 0.64. These might be considered to be breaks between the skilled and semi-skilled and between the semi-skilled and unskilled, but there are also gaps of 0.16 and more within the 'unskilled' range, so that too much credence should not be placed on these divisions. In terms of what we know about the role of education in respect of social status in colonial societies and the role of formal education in those societies the split between the preacher and the carpenter could possibly represent a real discontinuity in the ratings.

Turning now to the difference in the ratings reflected by the different socio-economic categories isolated, the first point to note is that the overall agreement in the ratings of the occupational titles is very high. The product–moment correlations of the 'high status rural/urban' with the 'low status urban' category was 0.9938, with the 'low status rural' category 0.9907, and of the 'low status urban' with the 'low status rural' category 0.9904. This suggests that there was marginally more disagreement between the 'rural' and the rest of the respondents than between the high status and low status. Given that there was substantial coincidence of the ratings among all three categories we can nevertheless ask whether there were specific occupations on which the ratings disagree more than on others. An examination of the ratings for the categories in Table 5.5 will confirm that there were indeed reversals of rank ordering for some occupational titles. The procedure adopted was that of estimating from the rating in one social category what the ratings of an occupational title would be in another category, given the overall agreement of the ratings as a whole. The actual rating as against the expected rating may then be assessed against the standard deviation of all the differences. Using this procedure not many occupational titles reflect a difference between observed and expected ratings of more than 1.96 (that is at the 5 per cent probability) of the standard deviation of differences. However, in assessing the difference between the expected and observed ratings for any two categories we need at the same time to take into account the differences in respect of the third category, since we are seeking an interpretation of the differences in the ratings of occupational titles given the characteristics of the three social status categories we have isolated. In all there were only nine occupational titles for which the difference between observed and expected ratings between two of the three socio-economic categories was greater than 1.96 times the standard deviation of the differences. These were the laboratory assistant (between the 'high status' and 'low status urban' categories and also between the 'high status' and 'low status rural' categories), the medical orderly (between the 'high status' and 'low status urban' categories), the lorry driver (between the 'high status' and 'low status urban' categories), the petrol pump boy (between the 'high status' and 'low status urban' categories), the hotel waiter (between the 'high status' and 'low status urban' categories), the trade union branch secretary (between the 'high status' and 'low status rural' categories), the bus driver (between the 'high status' and 'low status rural' categories and between the 'low status urban' and 'low status rural' categories), the reporter (between the 'low status urban' and 'low status rural' categories), and the carpenter (between the 'low status urban' and 'low status rural' categories).

Where the laboratory assistant is concerned the prime distinction is between the 'high status' respondents on the one hand and the 'low status' on the other. Both the rural and urban 'low status' respondents rated the laboratory assistant considerably lower than the 'high status' respondents. The explanation is almost certainly the particular knowledge and understanding that the respondents from higher educational and social status backgrounds would have of the duties, skills, and responsibilities of the laboratory assistant. The pattern in respect of the medical orderly was quite different in that both the 'high status' and the 'rural low status' respondents rated this occupation considerably higher than the 'low status urban' respondents. A possible explanation is that in rural areas the medical orderly may well have been the sole officer in charge of a clinic, whereas in towns he would almost certainly have served only in a subservient role under the control of a nursing sister or physician.

The hotel waiter and the petrol pump boy were both rated at about the same level by 'low status urban' respondents but considerably lower by 'high status' respondents and 'low status rural' respondents. The distinction seems to be in the rural–urban differentiation rather than in the social status of the respondents. The explanation possibly lies in the quite obvious difference between the international-class hotels demanding highly professional waiter services and the elaborate filling stations in the larger towns as against cafés and filling stations in rural areas.

The 'low status urban' respondents rated the lorry driver higher than the 'low status rural' respondents, and they in turn rated it higher than the 'high status' respondents did. The distinction here seems to be an interaction of status and rural–urban experience. Respondents from 'low status' backgrounds tended to rate the lorry driver higher than respondents from 'high status' backgrounds, but those with urban experience tended to compound this high rating with an assessment deriving from their appreciation of the high status of the long distance lorry drivers, most of whom were based in the larger towns.

Somewhat surprisingly, the 'low status rural' respondents rated the trade union branch secretary considerably higher than either the 'low status urban' or the 'high status' respondents.

The 'low status urban' respondents rated this occupation higher than did the 'high status' respondents. While it is easy to see that the 'high status' respondents, coming as they did from backgrounds in which class interests were different from those of the 'low status' respondents and where a tradition of trade unionism was not strong, might not accord much prestige to the trade union branch secretary, it is difficult to see why the 'rural low status' respondents should have rated that occupation so highly. One could only speculate that since trade unionism was strongest in the towns they probably had an exaggerated sense of the power of trade unionism in a country where this form of organization was frowned upon.

The bus driver was accorded a similar pattern of ratings: the 'rural low status' respondents rated this occupation considerably higher than either the 'high status' or the 'low status urban' respondents. Most bus drivers were based in urban areas and would have been the agents providing an essential service between town and country. While from the countryman's point of view the prestige of the bus driver may have seemed appreciable, from the point of view of urban residents, accustomed as they were to the considerably differentiated range of opportunities open to semi-skilled persons, the bus driver must have appeared considerably less important.

The ratings of the carpenter show a similar differentiation, with the 'rural low status' respondents rating the occupation much more highly than either the 'high status' or the 'low status urban' respondents. Once again it is difficult to explain why there should be this difference, except that the occupation is well known and that in comparison with the opportunities open to skilled people in towns the relative advantage of a carpenter there would be slight as against in the rural areas. This explanation is lent some support by the fact that except for the bricklayer the same pattern of relatively higher rating by the 'low status rural' respondents as against the other two categories holds for all artisan-type occupations.

The pattern for the reporter contrasts with that for the carpenter and other artisan-type occupations. The reporter is most highly rated by the 'low status urban' category, next by the 'high status' category, and lowest of all by the 'low status rural' category. The same pattern emerges for the newspaper editor and the radio announcer, though the differences are much reduced for the latter two occupations. At the time when the study was made the major African newspapers and the only radio station were based in the largest town. It seems likely that the peculiarly urban flavour of these white-collar or semi-professional occupations lent them some prestige in the perception of townsmen.

It appears that several different and sometimes opposed principles underlay the prestige ratings of occupational titles. The overall order of the occupations seems to have been derived from the evaluation, explicit or implicit, which was part of the colonial social system in which the respondents were embedded. This reflects the familiar rating of professional, white-collar, skilled, semi-skilled, and unskilled occupations in that order. But within this overall order there were variations in particular occupations which arose from different processes. First of all, it appears that the occupations remotely placed outside the direct experience of the respondents have been rated in terms of a general response deriving from the overall system of assessment connected with the colonial industrial and commercial system, in which the respondents had no clear appreciation of the specific role and power attributes of the occupations. But particular knowledge of occupations because of the placement of respondents in the social system as a whole may have led to variations. The differential ratings of the sub-development cleaner and the pipe layer (mines) by the mining Advancees and the Scholars is an example. This effect seems almost certainly to explain why the Southern Rhodesian sample 'high status' respondents rated the laboratory assistant more highly than 'low status' respondents.

Secondly, respondents with experience of an employment market characterized by an elaborate division of labour, such as obtains in the complex urban industrial, commercial, and bureaucratic contexts, will have had the opportunity to assess well-known occupations, such as the carpenter, against a vast variety of more lucrative and more responsible posts. By contrast, in a rural economy where the majority of the populace are subsistence cultivators a carpenter would have enjoyed a relatively high income and would carry considerable prestige.

Lastly, it seems likely that as reported in studies in America respondents will accord more prestige to those occupations to which they may reasonably aspire, so that lower status respondents in general were more likely to rate occupations in the lower part of the scale more highly than high status respondents. It should not be forgotten, however, that the respondents designated as 'low status' in the Southern Rhodesian sample were so styled because they had *originated* in low status background. In fact they were all in secondary school and would have had the same aspirations as those respondents from 'high status' backgrounds.

Social Structure, Social Status, and Social Perception

The social perceptions of the respondents in the various studies reported here—in so far as these perceptions are captured by responses to formal questionnaire enquiries—may be construed as reflecting the public evaluation of the status with which certain occupational roles came to be invested in colonial society. This status arose directly out of the colonial society in which the politically, socially, and economically dominant sector—the colonists—had at the time of these studies provided a relevant reference group for the African respondents used in the study. The African respondents appraised the occupations, nearly all of which were part and parcel of the economic order introduced by the colonists, in terms of a set of meanings which reflected the power structure in that society. These perceptions were the substance of a set of collective representations through which behaviour in public places or in general categorical relations could become intelligible to the majority of ordinary actors. Social status in this sense presumably affected such behaviour as appraising candidates for political office, or addressing behaviour towards others in the street, shops, and other public places.

But these perceptions were by no means static and uniform across all parts of the population or over time. The evidence from the study conducted in the mining industry of Northern Rhodesia showed that the perceptions of respondents varied situationally with their location in the industry itself. The data from the Rhodesia study showed that the ratings of occupations also varied with location of respondents in the wider social structure. Finally, the evidence about the changing perception of certain occupations located critically in the overall structure of the system of social relationships—in the intercalary positions—and about the ambivalence towards these occupations lends support to the contention that in everyday behaviour actors construe the prestige of occupations in terms of quite opposed evaluations. Locating the actors within the social setting as a whole and also within the situations as they defined them enables us to effect a resolution of apparent inconsistencies.

6

THE PERCEPTION OF REGIONALISM
AND ETHNICITY

The social standing accorded to people because of the work they do derives its rationale from the division of labour in the social system as a whole and from how this division of labour is supported by the values and beliefs of the people operating within the system. In South Central Africa in the closing stages of colonial rule the prestige which Africans attributed to occupations within the colonial economic order was derived from the organization of power relationships between Blacks and Whites.

The prestige accorded to an occupation was less the prestige of the occupation itself than a recognition of the relative power positions of incumbents in these occupational roles in the struture of colonial society. The occupational roles were patently observable when actors were performing these roles. In the anonymity of urban public places, however, occupational roles were to a large extent invisible except in so far as clothing served as an indirect symbol of a job and hence as an advertisement of the position of the wearer in the economic and political order.

But a separate and to a large extent independent system of public identification operated which was rather more easily perceptible. This was the regional, hence ethnic, origin of towns-folk. The language, deportment, general appearance, and other subtle cues and signs enabled the average townsperson to identify the place of origin of strangers in public places and so structure their behaviour in relation to others. These perceptions, as will emerge in the argument, were the basis of establishing categorical relationships in public places. They were not, and indeed did not need to be, a fine appreciation of ethnographical distinctions, but were part of relationships in the fleeting and transitory situations of urban public places.

A wide range of possible identities existed for an African

townsman to adopt in Northern Rhodesia at the time when these studies were conducted. Within small-scale settings identities derived from traditional cultural values were undoubtedly used, as for example identities based on clanship or kinship categories. Epstein (1969: 100) provides a graphic account of how two townsmen discovered a kin link which they had not previously appreciated, and which served as additional identity bonding them together. But in wider settings where social relationships were more categorical, as indeed most of the transitory interactions tended to be among townspeople, social status and ethnicity, because of their visibility (apart, that is, from gender) provided by far the most significant basis of identity.

Membership of distinctive religious sects, when this membership was apparent, also provided a basis for identity. Jehovah's Witnesses, for example, who militantly advertised their faith by aggressive proselytization, were an example of this sort of identity. Members of some of the separatist sects who wore distinctive dress in the same way displayed a religious identity, as did some Moslems by their distinctive dress. But the important difference was that these identities were essentially minority identities. The majority of townspeople belonged to orthodox Christian congregations which could not provide distinctive identities. Social status and ethnicity, however, were pervasive and in general provided distinct identities in nearly all urban social situations.

Epstein, basing his comments on observational material, confirms this point of view. In respect of social status or prestige, for example, he writes:

In this context [the general urban context] then prestige emerges as a pervasive concept in the sense that it enters into almost every social activity and into every social relationship; or rephrasing it more forcefully, there are very few facets of human behaviour which may not be seized upon in evaluating prestige. This is perhaps what one would expect for the general fluidity of the urban situation, the heterogeneous and differentiated character of the African urban population with its concomitant diversity of norms and standards of behaviour, and the, marked emphasis on achieved as against ascribed status create a set of conditions in which the struggle for prestige becomes a major preoccupation of the new urban-dwellers. (1969: 105.)

Epstein confirms the general pervasiveness of ethnicity when he writes 'Every African in Ndola is a member of a tribe, and the veriest tot will answer without hesitation if asked to what tribe he belongs' (1969: 101–2), and he goes on to specify the way in which dress and custom become diacritical features which allow ethnic identities to be attributed to townsmen.

Ethnicity has been a continuing topic of interest both in sociological studies in America and Europe and in anthropological studies in other parts of the world.[1] Since ethnic and regional identities are so apparent in the polyglot environments of cities, analytical interest in ethnicity has arisen particularly in urban studies (see for example A. Cohen 1974). Some disagreements exist, however, about the place of ethnicity in explaining social behaviour. A good deal of this disagreement, I contend, arises out of the use of the notion of ethnicity at very different analytical levels.[2]

Initially we need to distinguish between ethnicity construed as the way in which a set of actors make use of and display their particular common cultural characteristics in some social situation and ethnicity as the way in which observed or presumed differences in culture become an element in inter-group relationships in some social setting. The former approach, characteristic of most anthropological studies, is essentially 'internal' since it is construed as shaping the behaviour of some specified ethnic group. A good example of this sort of study in an urban setting is Parkin's (1978) detailed study of the way in which the dominant features of Luo culture shape the responses the Luo in Nairobi make to the situations which confront them in town. While Parkin contrasts findings about Luo reactions to urban conditions with the Kikuyu, the overall relationships of ethnic

[1] One of the earliest forays into this field was Barth 1969. In the same year A. Cohen presented an important structural analysis of an example in Nigeria, and R. Cohen and J. Middleton (1970) covered the topic from a structural perspective in respect to nation building. R. Cohen (1978) has provided a useful resumé of anthropological writings. In sociology most of the interest seems to centre on America (Greeley 1974, Glazer and Moynihan 1975), though Hechter 1975 has analysed some data in relation to the United Kingdom. Banton 1983 provides a broad review of current thinking about race and ethnic relations.

[2] The point of view expressed here is similar to that of Eames and Goode, who write: 'One of the difficulties with the urban anthropological literature dealing with ethnic groups is that ethnicity is frequently viewed as both a cultural and a structural phenomenon—without adequately distinguishing between the two' (1977: 172). In relation to Central Africa see Epstein 1958, Mitchell 1956a, 1970a, 1974b.

groups to one another in Nairobi are not central to his analysis. In contrast, a second more general type of study of ethnicity, characteristic perhaps more of sociological studies, concentrates essentially on inter-ethnic relationships in general. Here the cultural differences distinguishing the ethnic groups operate as diacritical features by means of which the ethnic groups are identified. Detailed consideration here of the cultures themselves is not really relevant to subsequent analysis. What is significant rather is the process whereby actors in social situations attribute identities to others. These are categorical identities in the sense that broad classifications based on general ethnic characteristics may serve adequately to allocate some individual to an ethnic category and so provide some rationale for adopting attitudes and adjusting behaviour towards that person. This is the approach that Epstein and I have adopted in looking at inter-ethnic relationships in Northern Rhodesian towns in colonial times. In this approach ethnicity as the attribution of meanings to cultural signs and cues operates as social perception and is part of the process of social cognition. The relevant context of behaviour is interactional. Ethnicity, as the existence of interests shared by groups identified in terms of ethnic or regional criteria, is one of an analyst's structural or morphological interpretations of behaviour and operates at a level entirely different from that of social perception. The major topic of the relationship of ethnicity to social class is similarly a structural problem. But the connection between the cognitive and structural orders of interpretation of social behaviour is by no means clear.

In what follows I start with evidence bearing on the social perception of ethnicity and then proceed to examine the effect of the structural position of respondents on their perceptions from the data I have available. I am then able to compare the manifestation of an ethnic or regional component in actual behaviour with the perceived distance among ethnic groups. This provides the basis for discussion of the situational correlates of cognitive and structural ethnicity.

Cognitive Ethnicity: A Northern Rhodesian Example

I shall be concerned here with the analysis of data which was systematically collected about the perceived social distances relating to ethnic identities in colonial Northern Rhodesia.

One of the striking characteristics of South Central African towns, as emerged in chapter 3, was the extent to which the populations in any specified town were drawn from extensive though fairly clearly defined hinterlands. The ethnographic variation in the populations of the towns was therefore wide.[3] Ethnographically the indigenous population of Northern Rhodesia could be classified into four main types, the rough distribution of which is set out on Map 6.1. The Western Bantu, of whom only the southern division penetrated into Northern Rhodesia, were part of an extensive division of peoples with matrilineal descent who were located mainly in the then Belgian Congo and Angola. The majority of the peoples of Northern Rhodesia were matrilineal peoples subsisting in the main on slash-and-burn cultivation and could be classified as Central Bantu, within which several subclassifications were distinguishable. The southern division of the Central Bantu peoples was made up of the Tonga/Ila/Lenje/Sala/Soli cluster of peoples. The northern division of the same category of people could be divided into an extreme northern group composed of the Bemba, Bisa, and Aushi and a southern section comprised of the Lamba, Swaka, Lima, and Kaonde peoples. In the extreme north of the territory a number of peoples such as the Mambwe, Nyamwanga, and Tambo who were cattle-keeping patrilineal people were part of the great mass of the East African peoples. To the east of these peoples was another branch of the East African peoples, in this case matrilineal peoples in Nyasaland and some of the eastern districts of Northern Rhodesia. These people were the Chewa, Nsenga, Nyanja, and Lakeside Tonga. Several regions were subjected to invasions in the past and therefore contained complexes with mixed ethnographic backgrounds. For example the people of the Luapula valley emerged out of the several invasions of Western peoples overlaying Central Bantu peoples. In Barotseland a basic population of Western and Central Bantu peoples was overrun in the nineteenth century by Sotho invaders from further south. In the eastern province the Eastern matrilineal peoples were overrun by Zulu invaders in the nineteenth century. As a whole the

[3] For an outline of the ethnographic composition of Northern Rhodesia see Mitchell 1960b.

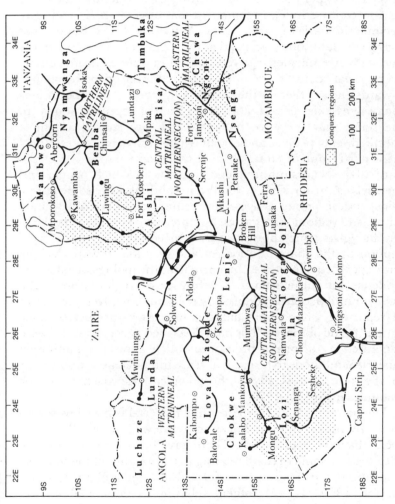

6.1. Distribution of Main Ethnic Groups in Northern Rhodesia

territory presented considerable ethnographic diversity and this diversity manifested itself in the composition of the urban population.

Cultural differences quickly become part and parcel of the everyday experience of town dwellers, whether they are attributed to ethnic, regional, or national origins, and may become the basis of social action. Why this should be so is not easy to explain, but it seems that throughout history and across many diverse peoples, the recognition in others of some ethnic or regional identity provides some expectation of behaviour towards one another for the parties concerned. The expectations themselves exist presumably as 'collective representations' in the sense that they are notions which are shared among a specified set of people, and that these 'collective representations' arise partly out of cultural inheritance and partly out of the particular social situations and contexts in which people find themselves. In addition, no doubt, individuals have some purely idiosyncratic points of view concerning members of specified ethnic and regional categories, but interesting as these may be to psychologists, our interests here are confined to social perception or the shared notions of and attitudes towards people with specified identities. In normal anthropological analysis, evidence for the existence of ethnicity or regionalism in the behaviour of people is adduced by the time-honoured procedure of reporting what actors did and how they interpreted their actions to the observer. The data described here, however, were generated by a formal procedure which allowed quantitative analytical methods to be used, and are intended as a supplement to the more classically anthropological approaches, as for example in Epstein 1978.

The data on which the perceptual material is based were collected by means of a modification of the well-known Bogardus social distance scale (1933). There have been several criticisms of this scale, some of them relating to the validity of the findings from the test in respect of social action (e.g. Hill 1953: 2991; Banton 1960: 171–2), others relating to doubts about the inherent uni-dimensionality of the items on the scale (Kretch and Crutchfield 1948: 223–4; Hill 1953: 221–2; Banton 1960: 174–5). With regard to the question of the relation of the results derived in a formal test situation to social action, I argue that the two are not directly comparable and relate to different universes of discourse, but I describe empirical tests of the overlap later in this chapter. I am using the findings of the formal test here as a way of exploring 'shared understandings' of respondents who have certain common social characteristics. The set of understandings does not predicate social behaviour in a deterministic way: it exists rather as a set of perceptions through which the individual may structure reality and thereby provide indirectly the rationale for social action. In fact the observation of field-workers shows that the findings from the formal test situation, if used in this way, provide a useful background to the understanding of social action (Epstein 1958, 1978; Mitchell 1956a; Harries-Jones 1969: 300 ff.; Boswell 1969: 288 ff.).

If social perceptions of social distances, though shared by some respondents, are nevertheless likely to differ among other respondents, then this implies that the scale is inherently multi-dimensional and not uni-dimensional. At one level of analysis it is possible that the items relating to social distance may be differentially evaluated by respondents. For example Banton (1960: 175) points to Bogardus's finding that a general American sample stated that they were less antagonistic, in contrast to other ethnic categories, to working with Mexicans than they were to accepting them as kinsmen through marriage or neighbours. This was explained by their 'docile manner which excites no antagonism'. The differential ordering of the social distance items in this way can be a fruitful way of revealing less obvious aspects of the shared social perceptions of respondents.[4]

At a different level of analysis, if distance scores of respondents in respect to specified ethnic categories are computed, allowance being made mathematically so that the distance is measured along one dimension only and the score is not contaminated by extraneous dimensions, then these scores themselves may be construed as indicators of the differential ethnic (or regional) perceptions of the respondents. Various techniques

---

[4] Banton (1960: 78) perceived some of the implications of the analysis of this aspect of the social perception of ethnicity. His puzzles about the rank order of relationships of the Northern Matrilineal group in my own material, however, were resolved by the fact that in the edition of *The Kalela Dance* which he was using Table 1 was quite erroneous. The correct table appears in subsequent editions. In fact the ranking of the items for the Northern Matrilineal group was quite regular, but the invasion in rank for 'share a meal' in respect to the Western Matrilineal group shown in his table is correct.

of multi-dimensional analysis may then be used to bring out the regularities in these perceptions.

Both of the approaches explored here, based on the reactions of respondents to 'distance' items in respect of specified 'ethnic' categories, are of course independent of more direct expressions of the respondents' perceptions of the features of ethnicity. These are described below.

The Social and Historical Setting of the Analysis

In South Central Africa at the time when these data were collected the major ethnic categories were undoubtedly those associated with race. The division of the population into the physically visible categories of European, African, Indian, and Coloured (persons of mixed racial descent) provided a fundamental basis of ordering the behaviour between members of these racial groups. The racial categories, however, were not strictly anthropometric. They were rather social categories in which the observable physical features, particularly skin colour but also other physical features, were accorded social and political meanings. A distinctive way of life was associated with manifest racial characteristics, so that an African, an Indian, a European, and even in some ways a Coloured way of life was postulated. These categories once again were not ethnological categories established by formal scientific procedures. They were rather social perceptions on the part of the people concerned, and these perceptions served to provide an understanding and a rationale for the social actions they observed and in which they were involved.

Within these broad folk categories there were subdivisions which were obscure and indistinct to outsiders. By this I mean that among the Europeans, for example, there were ethnic and also status distinctions which were clear to them but which to the Africans would have remained quite indistinct. There were, for example, people of European descent who had been brought up in South Africa and others who had been brought up in Britain and in continental Europe. But it is doubtful whether these differences in origin had much significance for the Africans who interacted with them. Some evidence in this is provided in a survey conducted by P. J. M. McEwan (1963) in which, of a sample of Southern Rhodesian Africans asked the question 'Which kind of Europeans do you prefer, if any, according to where they come from?', no less than 64 per cent of the respondents said that they had no preference, while the remaining 36 per cent distinguished between English, Scottish, American, Rhodesian, South Africans, and others. Similarly, the distinctions between different Indian categories may have been appreciated by some individual Europeans and Africans, but these distinctions would not have constituted shared social categories which for either Europeans or Africans could have been taken to predicate differential behaviour.

By the same token the differences among the various African groups may have been appreciated by some Europeans and Indians and some may have become the basis of stereotypes, as for example the widespread European perception of the Ngoni as superior leaders. In general, however, the distinctions were vague and uncertain: the major perception was of a single undifferentiated category of Africans to whom Europeans attributed a fixed status and a set of rather rigid role expectations.

Africans also made distinctions amongst themselves in the customs and behaviour of categories of persons which they identified with regional and ethnic backgrounds. These distinctions once again would not be the same as those made by a professional ethnologist: they were emic or folk categories through which the behaviour of individuals may be rationalized and ordered. These distinctions have commonly been denoted by the adjective 'tribal' in the past. Subsequently there was a reaction against the use of this term, arising partly out of an ideological position in which the existing differences within the African population as a whole were construed as divisive tendencies in a context where unity in the establishment of a national state had been a matter of crucial importance. Accordingly some anthropologists and political scientists prefer to use the term 'ethnicity' to denote the circumstances when perceived differences in culture become the basis of social interaction, and I shall follow this procedure here.

The degree to which the identity which I refer to was based on ethnic rather than regional considerations is difficult to determine. The question, however valid from the point of view of the scholarly analyst, was probably unreal in the folk categorization which provided the rationale for social behaviour. The original study was conceptualized in terms of ethnic distinction and consequently there is no direct way of testing the extent to which the respondents made the distinction between regional and ethnic aspects of social identities. Nevertheless some evidence emerged during the course of the analysis which provides at least some indication of the way in which regional and ethnic categories were interfused.

The way in which perceptions of ordinary African townsmen appreciated ethnically or regionally identifiable patterns of behaviour in their day to day activities and used these perceptions to relate to others was a commonplace observation of people living in Northern Rhodesia at the time when the studies upon which this analysis is based were made. The ordinary townsmen were aware of this—not, it is true, as an example of the abstract property of ethnicity as such, but as an everyday feature of living in a town. The anthropological field workers who had been working in towns had also observed this (see in particular Epstein 1978), and naturally felt it necessary to try to understand this behaviour as part of the general phenomenon of ethnicity.

Yet it was reasonable to assume that if indeed 'ethnicity' was so clearly a feature of the social life of Africans in Northern Rhodesia at the time, as was apparent from observational material, then it should manifest itself in data assembled by more formal means—by survey techniques in fact. At that time, as director of the Rhodes–Livingstone Institute based in Lusaka, I did not have much opportunity for the direct observational work characteristic of normal anthropological fieldwork. I could, however, devote some time to devising instruments for the collection of data and to the analysis of the results, in which techniques I had had some training as a sociologist. The field data reported here, then, are based entirely on survey data which were adapted to take account of anthropological observations and were designed to check these observations and to amplify them. Epstein's analysis of ethnicity on the Copperbelt (1978: chap. 2), the data for which were collected at about the same time as the data for the studies reported here were collected, provides detailed ethnographic evidence supplementing the formal analyses presented here. The detailed analysis of the survey material had to wait until I had access to computers and to computer programs embodying procedures which were only in the earliest stages of their development when the data were being collected.

The first attempt to supplement standard anthropological observations by formal procedures was addressed to the issue of perceived 'social distance' among ethnic groups. I had suggested it to Janet Longton, who at the time was the Secretary of the Rhodes–Livingstone Institute and who wished to become involved in a limited way in the research activities of the Institute. The model for the enquiry was the Bogardus 1933 study of social distance. The distance categories that Bogardus used in his study, however, were not directly relevant to the relationships between people from different cultural backgrounds in Northern Rhodesia. They were accordingly modified. This was done in discussion with a team of African research assistants who at this time were engaged in interviewing in the social survey which was then being conducted in the line-of-rail towns of Northern Rhodesia. Eventually the form the questions took was as follows:

Would you willingly agree to share a meal with a . . .?
Would you willingly agree to near kinship by marriage with a . . .?
Would you willingly work together with a . . .?
Would you willingly allow . . . to settle in your tribal area?
Would you willingly agree to exclude a . . . from your tribal area?
Would you willingly allow a . . . as a visitor to your tribal area?
Would you willingly allow a . . . to live near you in your village?

The respondents were asked to write in 'yes' or 'no' to the question and to check a box indicating the intensity of their feeling on this issue ranging from 'very strong' on the one hand to 'no special feeling' on the other. Information on the standard of education of the respondent, year of birth, 'tribe', church membership, father's occupation, and the number of years lived in town was asked for. In addition, at the conclusion of the formal part of the schedule the respondent was asked to respond to a question phrased in this way: 'Do you think tribalism is important in the behaviour of Africans to each other? (Give reasons)', and a space of five lines was left on the schedule for this purpose.

The following ethnic stimulus categories were used in the questionnaire: Aushi, Bemba, Bisa, Ila, Tonga of Mazabuka, Lenje, Soli, Lunda of Mwinilunga, Kaonde, Chokwe, Luchaze, Lovale, Lozi, Mambwe, Nyamwanga, Tumbuka, Nsenga, Chewa, Ndebele, Ngoni, and Azande. These categories were selected primarily in order to provide as wide as possible a representation of the main ethnographic types in Northern Rhodesia at the time. Their approximate locations are shown on Map 6.1. Some, such as the Tumbuka, Chewa, and Ngoni, were located mainly in the neighbouring territory of Nyasaland (now Malawi). The Ndebele were a people from Southern Rhodesia (now Zimbabwe), and were in Northern Rhodesia mainly as migrants. The Azande were included in order to provide a people with whom none of the respondents was likely to have come into personal contact: they were in fact a people in the Southern Sudan who had been the subject of a well-known ethnographic study at the time. Some of the respondents may have known about this study.

The respondents were scholars at a local secondary school. The headmaster was kind enough to allow us to use a portion of normal class time during which all the scholars completed the questionnaire. The vast majority of the scholars were between the ages of 15 and 24, 47 per cent being in the age group 15–19 and 48 per cent in the age group 20–24. As a category they were obviously better educated than the African public at large, with an average of 9.8 years of schooling as a whole. Two-thirds claimed allegiance to a Protestant Free Church, 15 per cent to the Roman Catholic faith, and 10 per cent to the Church of England. The majority of the rest were from the Seventh Day Adventists, African Independent Churches, and Watchtower Bible and Tract Society. Three respondents said they were not affiliated to any Christian Church. Twenty-four per cent said that their fathers were unemployed or had no occupation, that is they were villagers, 40 per cent said that their fathers had unskilled occupations of various kinds, 11 per cent skilled occupations or supervisors, and 24 per cent said that their fathers were white-collar workers of various kinds. Thirty-five per cent said that they had lived in towns for 8 years and over, another 35 for between 3 and 7 years, and the remaining 30 per cent had been in town for less than two years. Since this school was in a town there is some bias in these figures. The mean number of years the scholars had spent in secondary school was 2 years and 9 months. These figures probably over-represent to this extent the degree to which the scholars were town-dwellers.

The 325 respondents, in response to a question, classified themselves in the following categories, as in Table 6.1, which for some purpose of analysis later I have aggregated into clusters.[5]

The questionnaires were completed in November 1954, and Janet Longton read a paper on the preliminary results to a staff conference at the Rhodes–Livingstone Institute in March 1955. Subsequently she published a short paper on the results in the magazine of the school where the study was carried out. I reanalysed the material for inclusion in *The Kalela Dance* (Mitchell 1956*a*), and subsequently read a paper incorporating additional results to a conference at the Rhodes–Livingstone Institute in February 1962 (Mitchell 1962). These early analyses, however, did not exhaust the material available in the data, and the purpose of this chapter is to reanalyse the material using more of the information that is available and to apply more powerful techniques of analysis to the material. In particular the data referring to the intensity of the response was not incorporated in any of the previous analyses, and a good deal of interesting material arising from the open-ended question on the perceived role of tribalism has not been published previously.

Unfortunately the original schedules appear to have been destroyed. Three sets of material, however, have survived, which has enabled me to check it for coding and punching errors. One set was a deck of 80-column cards in which the personal detail and the 'yes/no' responses to the 147 items were recorded. Another was a deck of cards in which the personal data were repeated (including an identification number) and the responses to the intensity items were recorded. Finally Janet

---

[5] These clusters differ slightly from those in Mitchell 1956*a*. The material was recoded according to the more detailed ethnographic scheme for this analysis, and this has entailed some reclassification of individuals and categories.

Table 6.1 *Ethnic Categories to which Respondents Allocated themselves*

Central Bantu: Northern Division

Type / Category	N
Aushi type	
Aushi	3
Ng'umbo	3
Total	6
Luapula type	
Lunda (Kasembe)	3
Chishinga	4
Total	7
Bemba type	
Bemba	37
Bisa	5
Tabwa	3
Senga	4
Total	49
Lamba type	
Lala	6
Lamba	9
Luano	1
Swaka	1
Ambo	3
Total	20

Central Bantu: Southern Division

Type / Category	N
Ila type	
Ila	5
Totela	1
Lumbu	1
Total	7
Tonga type	
Tonga	31
Total	31
Lenje type	
Lenje	11
Sala	3
Soli	2
Total	16

Western Bantu: Southern Division

Type / Category	N
Ndembu type	
Lunda	9
Kaonde	10
Total	19
Luena type	
Chokwe	2
Luchaze	3
Lovale	7
Mbunda	1
Total	13
Luyana type	
Lozi	29
Total	29

Eastern Bantu: Eastern Division Central Section

Type / Category	N
Nyakyusa type	
Nyakyusa	1
Total	1
Mambwe type	
Mambwe	11
Lungu	8
Nyamwanga	7
Total	26
Henga type	
Henga	10
Tumbuka	14
Fungwe	2
Total	26
Nyika-Safwa type	
Nyika	2
Total	2

Eastern Bantu: Eastern Division Southern Section

Type / Category	N
Chewa type	
Nsenga	17
Chewa	16
Lakeside	7
Tonga	7
Nyanja	3
Total	43
Yao type	
Yao	2
Total	2

Southern Bantu: Ngoni Conquest State

Type / Category	N
Ngoni type	
Mpezeni	
Ngoni	28
Total	28

Longton had the personal details and the verbatim responses to the open-ended questions separately typed. These details could be linked to the responses through an identification number. This document also allowed me to check the coding and punching of the personal data.

In the succeeding analysis the yes/no responses have been combined with the intensity responses to create a six-point scale of both intensity and direction. Thus a person who said that he would willingly share a meal with a member of a given ethnic group would be coded in the range 1 to 3 according to his intensity response (1 for the highest, 3 for the lowest) and in the scale 4 to 6 if he said 'no' (with 4 in the lowest intensity scale and 6 in the highest). The scale thus extends from 1, which means a positive reaction of the highest intensity, to 6, which indicates a negative response of the highest intensity. Responses 3 and 4 are respectively positive and negative but at the lowest intensity level. 'Don't know' responses were coded zero and category means used for these responses in calculating distance scores subsequently. The responses, together with the personal data and Janet Longton's original coding of the open-ended responses, were transferred to a magnetic tape for analysis on a computer. In the process, however, four of the original cases seem to have been lost. There were 329 cases used in the original analysis but only 325 have survived for the present analysis.

The Ordering of the Items

We originally developed the distance categories on the model represented by Bogardus. As described in *The Kalela Dance* (Mitchell 1956a: 23–4), we had anticipated that the ordering of the categories from closest to most distant would be as follows:

1. Would admit willingly to near kinship by marriage
2. Would willingly share a meal with
3. Would willingly work together with
4. Would willingly allow to live nearby in the village
5. Would willingly allow to settle in the tribal area
6. Would willingly agree to the tribal area as a visitor
7. Would willingly agree to exclude from the tribal area

In fact, when the results were analysed we found that this

postulated order was not in fact the order in which the smallest number of inconsistencies appeared. First of all it appeared that the last item, which was in negative form while the others were in positive form, seems to have caused some difficulties to the respondents. Excluding this and arranging the 6 remaining responses to all 21 stimulus groups of all respondents in scale patterns led us to an order in which the least number of inconsistent responses appeared. This was:

1. Would willingly admit to close kinship by marriage
2. Would willingly allow to settle in tribal area
3. Would willingly allow to live nearby in the village
4. Would willingly share a meal with
5. Would willingly work with
6. Would willingly allow as a visitor

Clearly the significance which the respondents attributed particularly to the notions of settling in a tribal area or living near in a village was different from that which we had attached to them in our initial ordering of the items.

But we are assuming here that the items were ordered in terms of a single dimension. This was in fact the rationale behind the coefficient of reproducibility which, for the adjusted order, varied from .91 to .95 on a test group for 92 respondents for different ethnic groups on the original material. The coefficient of reproducibility for the 325 cases with the revised ordering was .94.

This analysis did not take the intensity measure into account. By combining the intensity measures with the original yes/no responses we have in fact differentiated both the 'yes' and 'no' responses into three ordered categories each, so that as a whole the scale discriminates social distance much more sharply. The Guttman scale analysis techniques, on the other hand, are difficult to use with more than three categories. With this added refinement of the level of measurement we are in a position to explore more fully the relationship among the items used in the test. To do this I made use of an estimate of the 'distance' between the items. We may think of the response/intensity scores themselves as reflecting the distances between items. For example, a person is given a score of 6 if he says that he is not prepared to admit a person of some designated category into close kinship through marriage and that he feels very strongly on this issue. The respondents would be scored 4 if they said that they would not be prepared to allow a person of the same category to settle in their area but that they had no special feeling about the matter. They would be scored 1 if they said they would willingly work with a person of the specified category and that they had a strong feeling about this. The 'distance' between the items could then be taken as proportional to the differences between the response/intensity scores. Thus the distance between not 'allowing into close kinship through marriage' and 'working with' in our hypothetical example would be proportional to $6 - 1 = 5$. The distance between 'close kinship through marriage' and 'settling in the tribal area' would be proportional to $6 - 4$ or 2, and that between 'settling in the tribal area' and 'working with' would be proportional to $4 - 1$ or 3, giving three distances between the three items. There are $325 \times 20 \times (7 \times 6)/2$ or 136,500 distances of this sort relating to the way in which the 325 respondents rated 20 ethnic groups on each of 7 items. From these distances we may now compute the mean distances between these items and represent them in an inter-item distance matrix in which, naturally, the entries in the main diagonal representing the distances of items from themselves would be zeros. To avoid problems arising from the cancellation of negative and positive differences between items we square these differences between summing them. The entries in the distance matrix are therefore sums of the squares of inter-item distances rather than the actual distances themselves. This procedure has certain subsequent advantages should we want to examine the distance between items in a multi-dimensional space.[6]

The technique of analysing the way in which items relate to one another depends on linking together those items which are closest to each other. Respondents could possibly perceive some items as being in some way more closely linked together than others. We may examine this possibility by analysing the distance matrix by means of a hierarchical clustering technique.

[6] The sum of squared distances which were used in the hierarchical clustering analysis would be equivalent to the Euclidean distances between the points in a seven-dimensional space. Techniques for relating the distances to the centroid of the points and of determining the smallest set of dimensions are described in Torgerson 1958.

This technique aims at identifying those elements which are closer to one another than to any other element. It then treats these as a single unit at the next level of linkage to link together other elements (or clusters of elements) which are closer to one another than other elements or clusters. This procedure continues until all the elements have been combined into a single over-arching cluster. There are various ways of deciding what may be taken to be the distance between clusters treated as units. Here the median distance between all the elements in the clusters is taken to be the distance between the clusters as wholes. This is a compromise between the 'minimum' and 'maximum' method as proposed by Johnson (1967).

The result of an analysis of this sort is presented in Figure 6.1. This diagram shows that in general the respondents perceived the items as falling into two general clusters. In one the items relating to item 4 'sharing a meal', item 6 'allow as a visitor', and item 5, 'working with', were perceived as more like one another than the items in the other cluster, i.e. item 2, 'settling in a tribal area' and item 3, 'living nearby in a village' were perceived to be closely linked to each other. The negatively expressed item, item 7, 'would exclude', is perceived to be

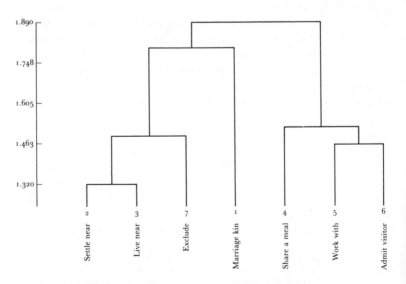

Figure 6.1. Hierarchical Clustering of Social Distance Items

linked relatively closely to item 3, 'living nearby in a village' and item 2, 'settling in a tribal area'; the ratings have been inverted for this item in the analysis. The item relating to item 1, 'close kinship by marriage', was perceived to be more related to these two items than to the items related to item 4, 'sharing a meal', item 6, 'allowing as a visitor', and item 5, 'working with'.

The two major clusters derived from this analysis reflect the different aspects of social life also shown in a principal component analysis. What is interesting is the extent to which item 6, 'allow as a visitor', and item 5, 'working with', are seen as closely linked, presumably reflecting superficial contact, while item 4, 'sharing a meal with', is seen as being only slightly different from these. Equally, item 1, 'close kinship by marriage', while linked more closely to item 3, 'live near in a village', and item 2, 'settle in a tribal area', than to the other items, is nevertheless linked only loosely with these two items. In several of the more detailed analyses in connection with the reactions of respondents of identified ethnic alignment to particular stimulus categories, which are not reported here, the item relating to kinship by marriage stands apart from the other items in the perceptions of the respondents.

This analysis, however, is intrinsically non-dimensional in that it deals only with the gross 'distances' between items. A more sophisticated procedure allows us to postulate different aspects to underlie the items along which they might be ordered. The extent to which all seven items relate consistently to one another, in the sense that pairs of items are scored roughly in the same way, may be measured by correlation coefficients. If a respondent objects strongly to kinship by marriage to a member of a particular ethnic group and is consistent in reactions to the other items, then we would expect that the scores would all be in the same direction, though possibly not so extreme in all of them. In other words we might expect the respondent to agree to accept a member of the ethnic group as a visitor but without too much enthusiasm. Under these circumstances we would expect that the items would all be positively correlated with one another. The items were correlated for each respondent for all twenty stimulus groups, i.e. for $325 \times 20 = 7500$ instances of scores relating to each of seven items. The resulting correlations are reflected in Table 6.2.

Table 6.2 *Correlations among the Social Distance Items*

	Kinship by marriage	Settle in tribal area	Live nearby in village	Share a meal with	Work with	Allow as a visitor	Exclude from tribal area
Kinship by marriage	0.5009	0.5755	0.6189	0.5354	0.4718	0.4546	−0.5290
Settle in tribal area	0.5755	0.6654	0.7550	0.5264	0.5039	0.5204	−0.6804
Live nearby	0.6189	0.7550	0.7184	0.5702	0.5571	0.5395	−0.6475
Share a meal with	0.5354	0.5264	0.5702	0.5256	0.5765	0.5670	−0.4957
Work with	0.4718	0.5039	0.5571	0.5765	0.4743	0.5611	−0.4568
Allow as a visitor	0.4546	0.5204	0.5395	0.5670	0.5611	0.4660	−0.4588
Exclude from tribal area	−0.5290	−0.6804	−0.6475	−0.4957	−0.4568	−0.4588	0.5412

Diagonal entries are communalities used in the factor analysis.

In this table the correlations of 'would exclude from tribal areas' with the other items were, as we would expect, negative. The highest correlations, indicating greatest consistency, were between the three items 'would admit to kinship by marriage', 'would allow to settle in tribal area', and 'would allow to live nearby in village', with a rather high negative correlation with 'would exclude from tribal area'. The other three items, 'would share a meal with', 'would work with', and 'would allow as a visitor', correlate marginally less well with the other four items and with themselves.

We may postulate that the consistency among the items derives from the notion of 'distance' which was built into the framing of the questions. Each item, in a sense, reflects to a varying degree the same underlying common factor. We wish to make use of this postulate to examine the extent to which the items perhaps reflect more aspects than that of 'distance', and to use the correlations of the items with the underlying common factor to derive an overall distance score for each respondent towards each stimulus group.

When a factor analysis of the correlation matrix was made the correlations among the items were consistent with the assumption that the items could all be aligned along a single dimension.[7] The highest correlation with the hypothesized underlying distance dimension, i.e. the item most consistently related to it, was that of the item 'would allow to live nearby in a village' (0.85), followed by 'would allow to settle in tribal area' (0.82), 'would exclude from the tribal area' (– 0.74), 'would share a meal with' (0.72), 'would admit to kinship by marriage' (0.71), 'would work with', (0.69), and lastly 'would allow as a visitor' (0.60).

Social Distance Scores and Perceptions of Inter-ethnic Distances

On the assumption that the reaction of a respondent in a yes/no response together with an indication of the intensity of feeling relating to that item reflects the perception of a general social distance towards other groups, we may now use the set of response/intensity ratings to compute a measure of perceived

[7] The communalities used are set out in the leading diagonal of Table 6.2.

distance from any particular ethnic category. Clearly, a person who says in respect of any particular ethnic category that he or she is prepared willingly to accept a member of that category into all social relationships, and feels strongly about the issue, may be considered to perceive himself or herself to be as close as is possible to that category. Equally, a person who says he or she would not willingly admit a person of a specified ethnic category into any social relation and who also feels strongly on this issue may be considered to be as distant as possible from that category. Those who vary in their responses will be placed somewhere in between. But some of the items, we know, are less consistent in respect to the underlying distance dimensions than others. We ought then to scale down the contribution of scores on those items accordingly. This weight, in accordance with a standard practice, may be computed from the factor loadings of the items and applied to the standardized score of each item (see Harman 1960: chap. 16). A final step in the computation of the social distance score is to modify the score so that it takes a value of zero if the responses indicate a perception as close as is possible, i.e. a 1 on each of the first six items and 6 on the seventh, and a score of 100 if the responses indicate perceptions as distant as possible, i.e. a 6 on each of the first six items and 1 on the seventh.[8] A social distance score for each of the 20 ethnic categories may thus be computed from the responses of each individual. We are now able to use this score to examine in detail some of the aspects of the respondents' perception of social distance in respect of specified categories.

The structure of the perceptions of distances among the 20 stimulus categories may be revealed by hierarchical cluster analysis in the same way as the structure of inter-term relations was examined. The distance matrix here would be the mean squared differences in scores among the 20 stimulus tribes computed over all 325 respondents. Figure 6.2 shows the structure of the perceived distances between the stimulus tribes

---

[8] The general form for the score for individual i is $I_i = w_{ij} z_{ij}$ where w_{ij} is the weight for the item j and z_{ij} is the standardized score for individual i on item j. This is transformed into $I'_i = w'_j s_{ij} + c$, so that the values used are the raw scores of the individuals on each of the items. The expression for the general social distance score for an individual in respect of a specified group k would be: $I'_{ik} = 1.99_{1k} + 3.41_{2k} + 4.51_{3k} + 2.83_{4k} + 2.44_{5k} + 2.63_{6k} - 2.19_{7k} - 4.67$, where s_{ik} are the raw scores for each item for stimulus category k.

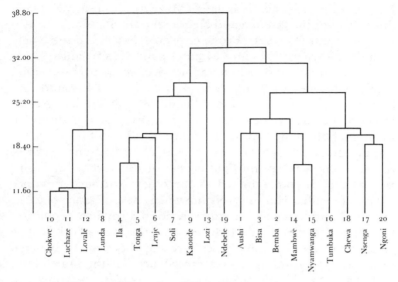

Figure 6.2. Hierarchical Clustering of Ethnic Groups

as determined by the median distances between elements in the clusters. At the first level of linkage five pairs of stimulus tribes are linked, the tightest among them being the Chokwe/Luchaze cluster. The Ila are perceived to be closely linked to the Tonga at a distance of 15.9, and the Mambwe to the Nyamwanga at a distance of 15.7. After this the Nsenga and Ngoni are linked at a perceived distance of 18.8, and the Aushi and Bisa at a distance of 20.4. At this level ethnographic and regional similarities are clearly combining to associate similar peoples, each of the members of these pairs being close to the other member of the pair both in language and custom and in residence. At the next level of linkage, however, variations in the basis of linkage begin to appear. The tightest cluster is still provided by the Lovale linked to the ethnographically similar Luchaze and Chokwe at a distance of 12.2, while the Lenje, similar ethnographically to the Ila and Tonga, are linked to them at a distance of 19.1. But the linguistically and ethnographically somewhat dissimilar Chewa are linked to the Ngoni/Nsenga cluster at a distance of 20.2 and the matrilineal Bemba are linked to the Mambwe/Nyamwanga cluster at a distance of 20.4. The basis of the linkage here appears to be regional association, the Chewa representing an

Eastern Province and Nyasaland (Malawi) people associated in this way with the Nsenga and Ngoni, and the Bemba, a Northern Rhodesian Northern Province people, associated regionally with the Northern Province Mambwe and Nyamwanga.

The regional and ethnographic principles of association continue to operate at higher levels of linkage. The Lunda are linked to the regionally and ethnographically similar North-Western peoples (Chokwe/Lovale/Luchaze) at a distance of 21.0, the Soli to the Central Province members of the so-called Bantu Botatwe people (Ila/Tonga/Lenje) at a distance of 20.4, representing a relatively tight cluster at this level; the Aushi/Bisa cluster becomes linked to the other Northern Province peoples (Bemba/Mambwe/Nyamwanga) at a distance of 22.6, and the Tumbuka to the other Eastern Province peoples of the Ngoni/Nsenga/Chewa cluster at a distance of 21.2. The variation in ethnographic types here suggests that the regional principle is beginning to take precedence. At the fourth level of linkage the Northern and Eastern peoples are combined into a single cluster at a distance of 26.6, while the Kaonde, a people of the North-Western Province, become linked at a distance of 26.1 to the Tonga/Ila/Lenje/Soli cluster. The Chokwe/Lovale/Luchaze/Lunda people remain perceived as a distinct cluster until they are finally linked to all the other stimulus groups. The Lozi, loosely related regionally to the Western Province people, become linked to them at a perceived distance of 28.1. The Ndebele, in fact a people from Southern not Northern Rhodesia, are linked loosely to the Northern and Eastern people at a distance of 31.1, presumably because of their association with the Ngoni, sharing a common origin with them from the Zulu people. Finally the Eastern, Central and Southern, and the Northern Province people are perceived to be linked more closely to one another than to the Chokwe/Lovale/Luchaze/Lunda cluster, to whom they are perceived to be linked finally at the overall distance of 38.8.

It is, of course, difficult to separate the effects of ethnographic similarity from those of regional contiguity since, as I argued earlier (1956a: 22), in Northern Rhodesia the population was dispersed over the territory with no absolute demarcations between the ethnographically distinct categories. Peoples classified as ethnographically distinct fade relatively imperceptibly from one into the other. The hierarchical clustering suggests that the two principles may operate, however, at different levels of perception. At the lowest level, where the finest distinctions between the ethnic groups are being made, ethnographic criteria seem to take precedence. Thus the Chokwe are distinguished from the Luchaze and the Lovale from both of these although all three are seen to be very similar. But at more inclusive levels ethnographic differences become subjugated to regional perceptions, so that the Bemba are associated with the ethnographically dissimilar but geographically adjacent Mambwe and Nyamwanga.

This is consistent with the notion of 'categorical perception' as described in my earlier analysis[9] (1956a: 29). In a general way the levels of linkage could represent levels of categorization—the Mambwe and Bisa, forming members of the same cluster at the third level of linkage, would be seen as equivalent, as are the Chewa and Nsenga at the same level. But the argument should not be pushed too far. Although the respondents may have perceived the Lozi to be closer to the Kaonde than to the Ndebele, it would be difficult to argue that for that reason the Lozi and Kaonde would be treated categorically in social relationships in this way. An essential element in categorization as a social process is that the marginal differences between ethnic categories should be overlooked in terms of their distinction from ethnic categories which are to seen to be quite different. Social perception as gauged from a social distance matrix of this sort is not exactly the same as social categorization which is, in fact, an aspect of social behaviour. The two are related in a way similar to that of social attitudes and social behaviour.

Multi-dimensional Distance Analysis

Our interest so far has been in the ordering of the stimulus categories in terms of the respondents' perceptions. But a difficulty in analysis of this sort is that the respondents may be responding in terms of differing stereotypes of the stimulus groups. This is tantamount to arguing that there are several dimensions to the perceptual framework of the respondents.

[9] I referred to this possibility in discussing the way in which the Ila were ranked by the Central Matrilineal people as against the other groups (Mitchell 1956a: 26).

Our task then becomes that of trying to establish a space of minimum dimensions in which the stimulus groups may be located in such a way that the distances among them are preserved.

It would have been possible to approach this problem by computing the sum of the squared distances among all twenty stimulus categories and by analysing these inter-point distances by the procedure we used in connection with the relationships among the seven distance items in the questionnaire. (See above.) However, a procedure of this sort makes the assumption that the distances among the points are measured on interval scales. While there is some justification for treating the difference between ratings as distances in this sense, there seems to be less justification for doing so when the measures are scores constructed from a combination of these ratings. At most we need assume only that the distances between the stimulus categories reflect the ordinal relationship among them—that is, that stimulus category C is perceived to be nearer to stimulus category B than stimulus category A is to B: the difference in scores between C and B should be smaller than the difference between A and B, the amount of difference being irrelevant.

A set of numerical procedures which is available makes it possible to determine the dimensions of a space in which the points may be represented on the basis only of the ordinal relationships between them.[10] In these programs the relationships of the distances between points are systematically examined in terms of spaces of different dimensions in order to determine one in which the ordinal relationships of the points is maintained while at the same time utilizing as few dimensions as possible. The actual numerical distances between points are not taken into account except in so far as they are taken to reflect the ordinal relationships among the points.

The 190 Euclidean differences in scores among the 20 stimulus categories averaged over the 325 respondents were analysed

---

[10] These are the Guttman–Lingoes smallest-space programs. The general procedure is set out formally in Guttman (1968). The particular program used here is described in Lingoes (1965). The MINISSA program developed by E. E. Roskam and J. C. Lingoes is included in the MDS(X) suite of programs in The Program Library Unit, the University of Edinburgh, Edinburgh, Scotland. This suite was developed by A. P. M. Coxon and his colleagues.

Table 6.3 *Coordinates of Stimulus Groups in Hypothetical three-dimensional Space*

	I	II	III
Aushi	13.25	-34.77	-44.19
Bemba	67.09	-7.07	-29.34
Bisa	41.29	-11.58	-35.56
Ila	-17.73	94.09	-6.10
Tonga	-2.54	100.00	5.41
Lenje	8.66	79.00	-24.67
Soli	-13.15	54.34	-17.70
Lunda	-64.49	-25.02	-1.94
Kaonde	-40.79	33.13	-31.50
Chokwe	-97.10	-44.65	11.51
Luchaze	-97.89	-42.92	9.74
Lovale	-100.00	-41.55	7.61
Lozi	-37.37	33.23	44.04
Mambwe	42.02	-35.14	32.76
Nyamwanga	33.69	-45.67	-55.75
Tumbuka	46.78	-43.82	12.17
Nsenga	57.14	-9.04	10.09
Chewa	44.63	-44.64	39.84
Ndebele	45.17	8.93	100.00
Ngoni	71.34	-16.40	39.10

Derived from a Guttmann–Lingoes SSA.1 analysis.
Semi-strong monotonicity coefficient of alienation = 0.051.

by a Guttmann–Lingoes smallest space program.[11] Table 6.3 sets out the coordinates of the stimulus categories in three dimensions as derived from a smallest space analysis. The coefficient of alienation of 0.051 reflects that the 'degree of fit' of the original relationships among the 20 stimulus categories to those in the hypothesized three-dimensional space is very good (an acceptable measure would be 0.15). The coordinates have been normalized so that the absolute largest coordinate is equated to 100 or – 100 as the case may be. Figure 6.3 brings out the complexities of the relationships among the perceptions more clearly than the hierarchical linkage diagram (Figure 6.2). The four main clusters of stimulus groups isolated by hierarchical cluster analysis are here seen to be four clusters in the three-dimensional space. The clearest is the tight cluster of Chokwe/ Lovale/Luchaze peoples in the (– – +) quadrant of the space.

[11] SSA-1 1969 version. The analysis was initially conducted on the Stanford University IBM 360-70 while I was a Fellow at the Center for Advanced Studies in the Behavioural Sciences. I am grateful to Ann Rice, who arranged for the analysis, and to Dr James C. Lingoes of the University of Michigan, Ann Arbor, for useful discussions of the interpretation of the results. The data were subsequently reanalysed using the Edinburgh Program Library MDS(X).

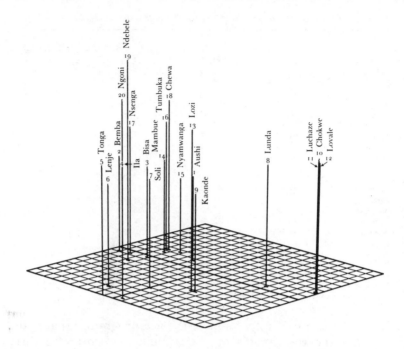

Figure 6.3. Representation of Stimulus Groups in three-dimensional Space

The Ila/Tonga/Lenje/Soli cluster is located in the (+ – +) quadrant of the space. The Bemba/Bisa/Aushi/Mambwe/ Nyamwanga is in the (+ – –) quadrant and the Ngoni/ Nsenga/Chewa/Tumbuka cluster the (+ – +) quadrant. Several of the original twenty stimulus groups do not seem to be unequivocally associated with any particular cluster. These are the Lunda, Kaonde, Lozi, and Ndebele. The placement of the first three stimulus groups in relation to the major clusters is instructive. They are placed in intermediate positions between the Chokwe/Lovale/Luchaze cluster on the one hand and the Ila/Tonga/Lenje/Soli cluster on the other. The Lunda are placed much closer to the Chokwe/Lovale/Luchaze cluster, at a Euclidean distance[12] of 40.0, than to the

[12] The distances were computed from the coordinates in Table 6.3 by taking the square root of the sum of the squares of the differences of coordinates of the stimulus tribe in question and the centroid of the cluster involved. This is the Euclidean distance in terms of the perceived distance space and bears no direct relationship to the original distances scores.

Ila/Tonga/Lenje/Soli cluster (Euclidean distance 122.1). Similarly the Kaonde were placed closer to the Ila/Tonga/Lenje/Soli cluster (Euclidean distance 63.3) than to the Chokwe/Lovale/Luchaze cluster (Euclidean) distance 103.9). The Lozi are placed roughly equidistant from the two clusters and from both the Kaonde and the Lunda, but they are nevertheless displaced in the third dimension, indicating that although they are seen to have resemblances to the two neighbouring clusters of the Chokwe/Lovale/Luchaze and the Ila/Tonga/Lenje/Soli and the Kaonde and Lunda, they are, nevertheless, distinguished from them. The Ndebele are placed nearest to the Ngoni/Nsenga/Chewa/Tumbuka cluster but more distant from any other cluster in the three-dimensional space.

There appear to be some regularities in the ways in which the stimulus group within any cluster is seen in relation to the mean position of any of the other clusters. The ordering of stimulus groups in this way seems to be related to both geographical proximity and to certain outstanding cultural characteristics and reputations. If we consider, for example, the distances between the Bemba/Bisa/Aushi/Mambwe/Nyamwanga cluster as a whole and the component stimulus tribes of the Ngoni/Nsenga/Chewa/Tumbuka cluster, the order, with Euclidean distances in braces, is Tumbuka (54.9), Nsenga (59.1), Chewa (80.0), and Ngoni (87.0). The order in terms of geographical proximity would be Tumbuka, Chewa, and Ngoni and Nsenga placed about equally (see Map 6.1). The Nsenga are seen to be closer to the Bemba/Bisa/Aushi/Mambwe/Nyamwanga than to the Chewa, but this reversal of ordering could possibly be because of the greater similarity of Nsenga culture to that of the Bemba/Bisa/Aushi than to the Chewa. Whereas the ordering of the component units of the Bemba/Bisa/Aushi/Mambwe/Nyamwanga cluster in respect of the Ila/Tonga/Lenje/Soli cluster as a whole is in general according to geographical proximity, i.e. Bisa (107.7), Bemba (116.7), Aushi (122.9), Mambwe (128.4), and Nyamwanga (141.0), the ordering of the component units of the Ngoni/Nsenga/Chewa/Tumbuka cluster reveals a reversal. The order of these units is: Nsenga (112.7), Ngoni (134.7), Tumbuka (138.3), and Chewa (145.4). Here the Nsenga are perceived to be closer to the Ila/Tonga/Lenje/Soli cluster, and they are also closest geographically.

The perceived distances between the Ngoni/Nsenga/Chewa/ Tumbuka cluster as a whole and the constituent units of the Bemba/Bisa/Aushi/Nyamwanga and Ila/Tonga/Lenje/Soli clusters show a similar reversal of the ordering by geographical distances of the units. While the constituent units of the Ila/Tonga/Lenje/Soli cluster are ordered roughly according to geographical proximity (Soli (115.5), Lenje (127.3), Tonga (142.2), Ila (145.9)), the units of the Bemba/Bisa/Aushi/ Mambwe/Nyamwanga cluster are arranged thus: Mambwe (59.5), Bemba (59.9), Bisa (64.6), Aushi (81.3), and Nyamwanga (85.54). The geographical ordering would have been Bisa, Bemba, Nyamwana, Aushi, Mambwe. Apparently the Mambwe are perceived to be much closer socially than we would have predicted from the general geographical ordering. If the social proximity were being judged on the basis of father-right and cattle-keeping, which would be in accord with the culture of Ngoni and Tumbuka respondents, then both the Mambwe and Nyamwanga would have been perceived to be closer to the Ngoni/Nsenga/Chewa/Tumbuka cluster than the Bisa/Bemba and Aushi. But the separation of the Mambwe from the Nyamwanga in the ordering by social distance discounts this explanation. I have not been able to offer any explanation for this reversal other than that it is possible that the Mambwe were categorized with the Bemba and were accorded some of the overall prestige of the Bemba.

The constituents of the Chokwe/Lovale/Luchaze cluster were generally perceived to be so close to one another that there was little differentiation among them by others. The perceived social distances between the Chokwe/Lovale/Luchaze cluster as a whole and the units of the Ila/Tonga/Lenje/Soli cluster were Soli (132.0), Ila (159.8), Lenje (165.9), and Tonga (172.2). This reflects the now familiar patterns of a rough correlation of social distance with geographical distance, except that the Soli are displaced from what would have been the most distant position in the geographical ordering to the closest position in terms of social distance. It appears that, in spite of the general ordering of stimulus groups in terms of geographical distance from the Luchaze cluster, the Soli are seen to be closer to the

Chokwe/Lovale/Luchaze as a whole than we might have expected. A similar reversal of ordering in terms of an expected geographical ordering takes place among the units of the Bemba/Bishi/Aushi/Mambwe/Nyamwanga cluster. The social distances from the Chokwe/Lovale/Luchaze cluster as a whole were Aushi (124.2), Mambwe (146.8), Nyamwanga (147.3), Bisa (150.1), Bemba (173.7). The Aushi were geographically nearest to the Chokwe/Lovale/Luchaze cluster as a whole and were also seen to be the closest socially. On the basis of geographical proximity we would expect the Bisa to be the next closest socially, but in fact they were placed virtually next to the geographically more distant Nyamwanga at a distance of 150.1. The Bemba were seen to be most distant of all the component units in the cluster.

The general perceived social distance seems to be a combination of different components, of which we have thus far been able to identify geographical location or region, the ethnographic characteristics of the people involved, and their reputation from the past. It is naturally of interest to determine whether the dimension which emerged from the smallest space analysis of the perceived distances among stimulus categories could be related in any way to geographical, reputational, or ethnographical variables. If we are able to interpret the dimensions intuitively, then we are able to understand more clearly the basis of the perceptions. In fact, however, the dimensions are arbitrarily placed in order to contain most effectively the twenty points and to reproduce the ordinal distance relationships among them. An interpretation of the dimensions would be a bonus: there is no necessary reason that they should be interpretable. Yet, since we know that the stimulus categories in the clusters in general came from the same region, it is clear that geographical separation, whether it is compounded with ethnographical differentiation or not, was intrinsically involved in the perception.

Since the dimensions of the perceived distance space are arbitrary, the question arises whether a set of geographical coordinates, such as the latitudes and longitudes of the locations of the stimulus categories, and a set of social coordinates, such as ethnographic features and historical origins, could not themselves determine a space in which the twenty stimulus categories would be located in a way that reproduces to some degree of accuracy the configuration of stimulus categories in the space derived from the perception of social distance among those categories.

An answer to the question may be sought through an analysis by means of canonical correlations. Initially each stimulus category was scored on its geographical location by rough coordinates based on the latitude and longitude, then, in order to test a few salient ethnographic and historical characteristics, each stimulus categor⸱⸱ was scored on the presence or absence of cattle-keeping, matriliny, and a tradition of having originated by conquest. These geographical and ethnographical coordinates then were assumed to order the stimulus tribes in some way which we wish to compare with the ordering in the three-dimensional perceived distance space. A canonical correlation in fact measures the coincidence of the points in these two spaces under the condition that the two spaces are so aligned to each other as to achieve as close as possible a fit. (See Hope 1968: 86–100.) The first canonical correlation was 0.978 with a chi square value of 99.06 (15 degrees of freedom), indicating a highly significant relationship. The second canonical correlation was 0.974 with a chi square of 50.56 (8 degrees of freedom), also indicating a highly significant relationship. The third canonical correlation was insignificant.

The five predictor variables are least satisfactory in respect of the second dimension of the space of perceived distances. Only 7.9 per cent of the variance of the first dimension of the space of perceived distances is not accounted for by the five variables; 42.7 per cent of the second dimension is not so accounted for, while 33.3 per cent of the third dimension is not accounted for.

There seems to be little doubt that the simple geographical location of the stimulus groups accounted for most of the perceived distance among the stimulus groups. If only the latitude and longitude are correlated with the three dimensions of the perceived distance space then the two canonical correlations become 0.963 and 0.904 with chi squares of 73.49 (with 6 d.f) and 28.9 (with 2 d.f) respectively. If the three ethnographic variables alone are correlated with the three dimensions of the perceived distance space, then canonical correlations become 0.716 (chi square = 7.43 with 4 d.f) and 0.211 (chi square =

0.75 with 1 d.f). Only the first of these is significant. The effect of the ethnographic variables may be gauged from the fact that the amount of variance of the first dimension of the space of perceived distances not explained by geographic location alone was 12.6 per cent, as against 7.9 per cent when the ethnographic variables were included, 64.3 per cent of the second dimension (as against 42.7 per cent), and 48.4 per cent of the third dimension (as against 33.3 per cent). The ethnographic variables therefore seemed to be associated mainly with the second and to some extent with the third dimension, while the geographic variables seemed to be associated mainly with the first.

The multiple correlation of the values of each stimulus category on each of the three dimensions with the latitude of the stimulus group was in fact 0.938, and with the longitude 0.954. An examination of the standardized regression coefficients showed that the second and third dimensions were about equally related to latitude but in different directions.[13] On the other hand, the first dimension was closely related to longitude.[14] By using the appropriate regression weight as applied to the values of each stimulus category in each of the three dimensions of the perceived distance space, we are able to calculate what the latitude and longitude of each stimulus group would be if predicted from where the stimulus groups were located in the perceived distance space. Map 6.2 sets out the actual geographical location of the stimulus groups as against where they should be in the light of our knowledge of their location in the perceived distance space.

Map 6.2 confirms the point made in connection with the relationship of the clustering stimulus categories in perceived 'distance' space to their clustering in respect of geographic and ethnographic characteristics, that is, the clustering in terms of perceived 'distance' tends on the whole to be tighter than actual geographic clustering; the stimulus categories are seen to be closer than they are physically. But an additional trend shows itself in this map. The concentration of the stimulus categories seems to be related to the province with which they are associated. The most striking illustration is in connection with

[13] Beta of latitude on first dimension = −.212, second dimension = −.597, and third dimension = .691.

[14] Beta of longitude on first dimension = .915, second .244, and on third .116.

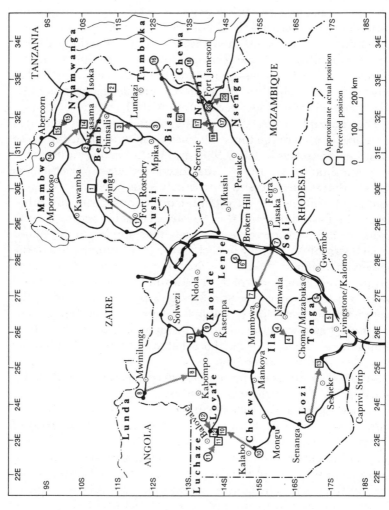

6.2. Actual Position of Stimulus Groups against Position Predicted from Perceived Distance

Ila/Tonga/Lenje/Soli cluster. The locations of the Ila and Tonga as predicted from their positions on the dimensions of the perceived distance space are more central in the Southern Province than they are geographically. The locations of the other two elements in the cluster, the Lenje and the Soli, are seen to be more central in Central Province than they are geographically. The same point can be made about the Lunda and the Kaonde, the Bemba/Busa/Aushi/Nyamwanga/Mambwe cluster, and the Ngoni/Nsenga/Chewa/Tumbuka cluster. The only exception is in respect of the Lozi, who are perceived to be located nearer to the Southern Province than to Barotseland.

It appears from this analysis than at least two related factors influence the perception of these respondents' social distance amongst the stimulus categories. In the first instance a factor associated with the physical location of the stimulus category exercised a major influence in the perception of social distance. But the physical location itself was conditioned by the respondents' own perceptions of these locations in terms of the division of the territories into provinces.[15]

Secondly, the reputation associated with the stimulus category—that they had been warlike people in the past—and certain ethnographic characteristics—that they were cattle-owning people in particular—had a secondary influence on the perception of social distance among the categories.

Social and Personal Factors Affecting the Perception of Ethnicity

It is obvious that sensitivities to ethnicity as an aspect of general social circumstances could well be the consequence of, or at least influenced by, the personal characteristics of the respondents who completed the questionnaire as well as by their attitudes to ethnicity *per se*. The questionnaire was designed to collect some information on these topics, although in the nature of things the data which could be collected was limited. Respondents were asked to provide information on simple background characteristics such as their ethnic origin, age, educational level, gender,

---

[15] The data presented here provides the evidence called for by Levine and Campbell (1972: 38) in respect of my earlier statements linking social distance and geographical distance.

religious affiliation, father's occupation, and length of residence in town.

There were two different aspects of the reactions to ethnicity which could be adduced from the responses to the 'ethnic distance' questionnaire. The first related to the extent to which a respondent reflected a general or overall distance or closeness to all ethnic groups other than his or her own. It was possible for a respondent to react to the items in the ethnic distance question-naire in a way that suggested that the respondent reflected either close or distant relationships equally to *all* other ethnic groups. Those who reflected great social distance could be thought of as equally 'stand-offish' to all ethnic groups, while those who reflected small distance could be thought of as equally 'open-hearted' or generally convivial to all ethnic groups. This component would be reflected in the mean ethnic distance score over the twenty stimulus groups used in the questionnaire.

In contrast, there may have been different reactions to different ethnic groups, in which case the differential reactions to ethnic groups would be construed as indicating ethnic sen-sitivity or 'ethnocentricity'. This component in turn would be reflected in the variance of the ethnic distance scores over all twenty ethnic groups used in the questionnaire.

The effects of the personal characteristics itemized in the questionnaire and of the ethnic origins of the respondents were tested using multivariate regression techniques. The results, however, for both the 'ethnic distance' and 'ethnocentricity' measures were nugatory.

Directly Perceived Aspects of Ethnic Distance

More direct information about the way in which the respondents reacted to the relationship between people of different ethnic groups was available from their responses to an open-ended question in the questionnaire. All respondents were asked if they thought that 'tribalism' was important in the behaviour of Africans to one another, and also asked their reasons for com-menting in the way they did. The question was deliberately worded in a very general form so as to elicit as many different aspects of ethnicity as possible. Naturally respondents inter-preted the question in different ways. Many respondents seem to have taken the word 'important' to refer to the wider social context in the sense of 'important for good relationships among people', as in the response: 'Not important and in fact unnecessary and undesirable because at this time in the progress of we Africans, we are all nearly the same in our standard of living irrespective of our tribe, and tribal discrimination will only lead to a failure in our desire of nationalism which ought to be and is our main aspect.'

Before some quantitative assessment could be attempted it was necessary to categorize the open-ended responses in some way. This is a notoriously difficult task. Miss Janet Longton devised a set of categories for coding the responses. Firstly she separated two aspects of the responses, the orientation of the respondent towards 'tribalism' on the one hand, and the 'reasons' for aspects of 'tribalism' which the respondents referred to in their responses on the other. The orientation could either be opposed to 'tribalism' or 'tolerant towards' 'tribalism'. Each of these orientations may have been supported by reasons which were subjective in the sense that they reflected the personal view of the respondent, as in the comment of one respondent who wrote: 'Tribalism is rubbish. It brings hatred and even unnecessary street quarrels. It impedes progress and disunites the African race. It brings exaggerated self-importance and pride into certain major tribes. Two are better than one. Away with tribalism.' In all 100 of the 325 respondents, 30.8 per cent could be classified as falling into this category.

There were only four respondents who reflected opposition to tribalism and advanced impersonal reasons for this, such as, for example, hostility to intermarriage.

The largest category (125 or 38.5 per cent) were those respondents who accepted 'tribalism' as an existential fact of life and advanced personal reasons as to why this should be so, as for example a Henga respondent who wrote: 'It is differences in habits and customs varying from tribe to tribe that makes tribalism important. Some tribes are warlike: people like the Ngoni, Ila and Tonga who are not easy to get on with.'

The largest remaining category (37 or 11.4 per cent) were those respondents who recognized the significance of 'tribalism' in the social behaviour at the time when the study was made and advanced reasons which were not coloured by personal feelings as the basis for their opinion, as for example the respondent who wrote: 'Yes [tribalism is important]. Differences in customs, habits and general ways of living and historical background made strong bonds of tribalism. Until these vanish tribalism will remain responsible for behaviour of Africans to each other.'

Together these three categories accounted for the majority of responses (80.7 per cent). Only 24 (7.4 per cent) answered the open-ended question negatively, that is maintained that they thought that 'tribalism' was unimportant in social relationships, as with one respondent who replied: 'No [tribalism is not important]. I feel strongly, though I am Ngoni that tribalism be done away with and let tribes have regard even for those much lower than themselves if their country is to advance. Before I was educated I had a very low opinion of the Lovale, Luunda and all accentric (*sic*) tribes of the part. But though I have it it isn't so strong: I wouldn't mind them being brought near me though definitely they would suffer an inferiority complex. Tribalism isn't important to me these days but confess that some 5 or 6 years back I should have shown a dislike and disregard for many of the tribes on this paper.' In spite of the fact that this respondent stated that he thought that 'tribalism' was not important it was nevertheless clear that he thought it was and that it should not be. Several of the respondents other than the one just quoted argued that education had done much to reduce the intensity of ethnic feeling.

The reasons that the respondents advanced for the existence of 'tribalism' or why it should not exist provide additional insight into the attitudes towards ethnicity. The categories of coding were as follows:

1. Arguments based on culture customs, language, and the way of life which differed among peoples of varying ethnic background and therefore justified to some extent their distinctiveness.
2. Arguments based on the desirability of unity among Africans, particularly in relation to gaining independence from colonial rule.
3. Arguments based on ethical and moral (sometimes Christian) principles usually decrying 'tribalism'.
4. Arguments based on the disappearance of 'tribalism' under

modern industrial circumstances or among educated or enlightened people.

5. Arguments based on the assumed or presumed superiority or inferiority of different groups.
6. Arguments based on the appreciation of traditional culture and the desirability of maintaining revered customs.
7. Arguments based on the supposed habits or cleanliness of other groups.
8. Arguments based on the solidarity and co-operation of people from the same ethnic group.
9. Arguments based on a variety of considerations such as employment situations, influence of kinship, marriage, etc. Many of these were vague and they were frequently advanced with one of the other arguments. As a whole this category is not of much analytical value.

Respondents sometimes raised several arguments in their comments so that the total number of arguments (380) exceeded the total number of respondents. Table 6.4 sets out the frequency in the categories listed.

The ambivalence in attitude towards ethnicity is illustrated in this listing of perceived aspects of 'tribalism'. About half the respondents saw 'tribalism' as a real element in the lives of Africans, basing their conclusion on an appreciation of cultural

Table 6.4 *Aspects Advanced by Respondents as being the Basis of 'Tribalism' or the Reason why it should not exist*

Customs, language, way of life as a basis of distinction	116
The need to rise above tribalism for social, economic, and political progress	61
General moral and ethical arguments against tribalism	54
Recognition that social status considerations override tribalism in modern industrial society	42
Assumed 'natural' inferiority or superiority of peoples	24
Appreciation of traditional culture and the desirability of retaining customs	19
Habit and food preferences and 'cleanliness' as factors conducive to distinction	10
Solidarity and mutual support of people from the same tribe	8
Miscellaneous others and vague unspecific replies	34
No answer	12
Total	380

differences, upon observation of how ethnic allegiances united people in specific circumstances, on the supposed superiority and inferiority of ethnic groups, or on the desirability of retaining traditional culture. The other half decried the existence of 'tribalism' by seeing it as a divisive force in the African struggle for independence or more generally in social and economic welfare, or raising ethical and moral reasons as to why it was undesirable. A sizeable minority perceived 'tribalism' as a factor in the social relationship of uneducated and rural people only.

The particular aspects emphasized may have been influenced by the social backgrounds of the respondents concerned. As with the analysis of the effect of background characteristics on the orientation of respondents towards 'tribalism', the influence of the set of personal characteristics on which aspect of ethnicity they mentioned as its basis was assessed by multiple quantal regression.

Background factors did not seem to have any influence on the choice of general moral and ethical arguments against 'tribalism'. The largest effect, other factors being held constant, was that those who were better educated than the average were more likely to emphasize these aspects, but the effect was small.

Those whose fathers held domestic, agricultural, and unskilled occupations tended to emphasize the deleterious effects of 'tribalism' on unity and progress when the effect of the other factors was held constant. Those whose religious backgrounds were in the Free Churches or Independent Churches and those who had lived longer than average in towns also tended to emphasize this aspect of 'tribalism', but the effects in both cases were once again small.

The justification of 'tribalism' on the grounds of customs, way of life, and language was mostly emphasized by those whose educational level was lower than the average, the effect of other factors being held constant and having relatively small influence. Those who were better educated than the average tended to stress the way in which 'tribalism' tends to disappear among those who are well educated, though the effect once again was small. Those whose religious backgrounds were in the Free Churches and Independent Churches also tended to emphasize this aspect of tribalism, as did those who had spent a relatively short period in town. Those who had been in town for a relatively long time and those who were relatively well educated tended to emphasize the natural inferiority or superiority of people, though the effect was not marked.[16]

In general it seems that education played the most important part in determining which aspects of tribalism were likely to be selected as being 'important'. The more highly educated respondents, not unexpectedly, perceived 'tribalism' to be particularly characteristic of rural and uneducated people, and on the whole tended to play down the importance of customs, language, and ways of life as an aspect of 'tribalism'. However, they did tend to perceive this assumed superiority and inferiority of 'tribes' as providing a basis of social relationships among these 'tribes'.

The tendency of respondents who had fathers in relatively low status occupations to stress the deleterious effects of tribal loyalties on political and social unity would be consistent with an emerging populist unity in Northern Rhodesia some ten years before independence was finally achieved. Similarly, the tendency of those who had lived in town for longer than the average to perceive the assumed inferiority or superiority of tribes in their relationships to one another may well be a reflection of the heightened visibility of ethnic differences in towns.

Cues and Characteristics

Ethnicity and regionalism are frequently used analytically to explain social behaviour. But unlike 'structural' variables which exercise direct but implicit effects, variables involving social perception such as ethnicity and regionalism involve by definition the meanings to and understandings of the actors. As such their essentially protean quality should be clearly recognized. Perception implies that an actor imbues certain identifiable characteristics of persons or phenomena with meanings and that these characteristics therefore indirectly provide a rationale for behaviour. Meanings of this sort presumably lay behind the way in which the respondents in this study reacted to the social

[16] The effects of background factors on the selection of other aspects were not analysed because the numbers involved were too small.

distance items used in the questionnaire. The meanings with which identities are infused are social in the first instance, in that they are not idiosyncratic but common at least to certain collectivities of persons, but meanings which are social imply more than that they are simply shared by sets of persons. The epithet 'social' has the additional connotation that the people concerned exchange and communicate the meaning to one another. It is unlikely, for example, that respondents whose fathers were skilled or white-collar workers shared meanings in this sense: father's occupation is a structural variable, which does not depend upon commonly shared meanings stemming directly from the occupation of the father unless we go on to argue that those in these particular occupations are a 'status group' who are conscious of their position and include it as part of the 'collective representations' of their 'class' location. On the other hand the stereotypes about specific ethnic categories which appeared to be widely expressed suggest that some meanings were indeed 'shared' in the sense of being expressed and communicated among people who had some common identity.

These shared meanings need not be based on an accurate appreciation of cultural features which an anthropologist may use to distinguish one ethnic group from another. To the average townsman the fact that the Mambwe royal family is patrilineal and the people cattle-keeping, while the Bemba royal family is matrilineal and the people cultivators, is less important than the fact that they both come from the Northern Province, an identity which is frequently represented by the category 'Bemba'. From this point of view the distinction between regionalism and ethnicity is more apparent than real. The particular indicators which an actor uses to identify another person are probably neither ethnic nor regional but are 'categorical' indicators in which both ethnic and regional characteristics are invested with overlapping meaning. Within larger regional zones it is probable that local areas or more specific ethnographic identities may have come into play to differentiate persons and supply the basis of the orientations of the actors.

Social perception thus provides a set of categories which individuals may call upon to structure relationships with other persons with whom they come into contact. They provide, as it were, a way of organizing cues and indicators that constitute an orientation for behaviour towards others. But the existence of the 'collective representations' does not imply that they shape behaviour mechanically and deterministically. There appear to be at least five different ways in which social perceptions may vary.

Firstly, there may be personal attributes such as gender, education, father's occupation, and degree of contact with urban conditions which provide the basis of identities and hence the conditions in which meanings may be transmitted and exchanged. If the effect of the attribute is indirect the actors are almost certainly unaware that they share the same perception with the others who have the same social background. The effect of occupying a position within a social system, such as being a woman rather than a man, having been educated more than the average, or having lived in towns for years implies common restraints or opportunities which are likely to lead to their sharers interpreting cues and characteristics in similar ways, but *social* perceptions are not involved. In so far as the set of respondents used in this study is concerned, background variables which were assumed to be 'structural' did not seem to have had an appreciable influence on the way in which respondents perceived ethnic and regional cues and characteristics.

Secondly, the regional and ethnic background of respondents seems to have had a clear association with the way in which regional and ethnic characteristics were viewed. It is probably that people brought up with an awareness of specific regional or ethnic identities may be particularly aware of them when they are thrown together with others from contrasting backgrounds, such as in a national school where this study was conducted, or more generally in towns. But the cues and characteristics selected by people from one region may not be the same as those selected to be indicators of ethnic or regional identities by another set.

This raises, then, the problem of the boundaries of the set of persons who share perceptions. There appear to be several different levels of differentiation involved. Some ethnic and regional peoples seem to have acquired distinct identities held by a large number of respondents, that of the Chokwe/Lovale/Luchaze cluster, for example, or the historically based reputations of the Bemba or Ngoni. But many peoples were vaguely identified and tended to be sunk in the identities of other more well-known peoples. For them specific identities were confined to a much more local context.

Thirdly, the same cues and characteristics may be viewed differently when related to specifically defined categories. An illustration of this type of variability is provided by the way in which the social distance items appeared to have been given quite different meanings by respondents with particular ethnic backgrounds when related to particular stimulus categories. Presumably the same procedure operates for all cues and characteristics. A simple example of this is the different evaluations of foodstuffs, upon which a number of respondents commented. Curdled milk, to one set of respondents, was seen to be a delicacy, while to another from a different region it was proof of the uncouth dietary habits of some other people. The distance items used in this analysis were adapted from a well-known instrument: clearly there are many other aspects of perceptions of identities which could be identified and examined outside the restricted framework of social distance as elements of social perceptions *per se*.

Fourthly, of course, there is the obvious variability in social perceptions which flows from historical events. The data used in this study were collected at a time when the colonial system was at its zenith and the struggle for independence was just beginning. This wider context of the study should not be overlooked: the frank comments of the respondents reflected it in a striking way. 'Tribalism' as a divisive factor in the struggle for independence, a point to which many of the respondents in their comments drew attention, became a matter of ideological import. There is no doubt, therefore, that social perceptions of ethnicity and regionalism have changed a good deal and that whatever perceptions there are today they probably have different connotations for social action than they had in 1954. The interest in the data, however, is less in what they tell about the specific ethnic and regional perceptions of the particular respondents than in what they tell us about the variability and nature of social perception as a common human reaction.

Finally there is the variability in social perceptions that flows not from the social and ethnic background of the actors alone but from the location of these background factors in specific social contexts. To appreciate the way in which social perceptions of regional and ethnic identities are emphasized or ignored in specific social situations, observational rather than formal techniques of data collection would be called for, since an essential element in understanding the social action would be an appreciation of how the actors had defined the situation. Clearly the formal procedures through which the data analysed here have been collected would not be appropriate for that sort of study, since it would then be generated in a specific test situation. The connection between social perception on the one hand and the behaviour of people in different contexts on the other, where these social perceptions are potentially relevant but not necessarily mobilized, remains in my opinion a largely uncharted field.

Perception and Behaviour: Co-residence in Single Quarters

It was with the object in view of providing empirical evidence of the relationship between what may be construed to be 'behavioural' manifestations of ethnicity on the one hand and its cognitive expression on the other that two analyses were conducted some years after the initial studies of social distance had been conducted. Circumstances provided conditions in which the 'distances' perceived to exist among the original stimulus groups could be compared with those derived from two different situations in which the consequences of the *actions* of individuals rather than their perceptions alone provided the basis of estimating the 'distances' separating the twenty stimulus groups.

The first of these relates to the extent to which unmarried men belonging to the twenty stimulus groups in the towns of Northern Rhodesia at about the same time that the social distance study was conducted tended to share 'single' accommodation with members of different ethnic groups in the set.

The tendency for single quarters or hostel accommodation to be occupied by men from the same area of origin has been reported for Southern African towns before. Reader (1961: 131–2), reporting on his study in East London, South Africa, states that 'Red' or 'traditionalist' landlords as against 'School' or 'modern' tended to select tenants on specific ethnic and regional criteria, and concludes that: 'There are definite groups of houses in the location, definite streets, definite neighbourhoods, where the lodgers tend all to have come from the same rural locality.' (1961: 131.) Mayer confirms this when he describes the living arrangements of the *amakaya*, the home-people among the Red migrants to East London. Out of thirty-three new migrants of Red extraction to town, thirteen had gone to kin and twenty to home-people (Mayer 1961: 101). In effect all had chosen to live initially not only with co-ethnics but also with people from the same restricted rural locality.

Data presented by Wilson and Mafeje (1963: chap. 3) once again confirms this for Xhosa migrants living in Cape Town. The focus of interest was on the 'home-boy' group, a set of migrants from the same region who met regularly for convivial purposes and who also provided support for their members in town. Some members of the 'home-boy' group also shared accommodation. Wilson and Mafeje describe the way in which the members of a cluster of 'home-boys' from a particular rural origin often displayed the motor-vehicle registration letters of that district over the door to their room, the point being that under the system of motor-vehicle registration in force at that time each district was identified by a sequence of letters. Even if the origin was not openly displayed, they report that common knowledge in the residential area was sufficient for rooms to be associated with particular districts of origin. Consequently, they report, 'Outsiders will know where the men—or some of them—from a given magisterial district live, and they, in turn, will know where the men from a particular village or village section are to be found.' (Wilson and Mafeje 1963: 50.)

A more recent report from the gold-mining area of Witwatersrand in South Africa—a locality notorious for its reliance on unmarried male migrant labour and one in which, not surprisingly, inter-ethnic violence has been endemic—confirms that under these circumstances people from the same area of origin tend to live together (McNamara 1980). McNamara's study also concentrated upon the 'home-boy' phenomenon, particularly in recreational situations: co-residence was only one facet of the home-boy phenomenon. Nevertheless he summarizes his observation in respect of residence in the following way:

Sixteen to twenty residents are accommodated in each hostel room. These rooms are ethnically homogeneous in content, but the rooms inhabited by each ethnic group or language group are scattered throughout the hostel so that one group does not dominate any particular block of rooms, mainly for strategic security reasons. (p. 307.)

In these studies from South Africa the emphasis is much more on the regional than on the ethnic origin of the single men living in hostel accommodation. This contrasts with the data from Northern Rhodesia, but the reason is that the language and cultural groups in South Africa are so large that some basis of internal differentiation must be sought within them, and for this purpose the regionally based administrative unit, or at a lower level the villages or sub-districts, form a natural unit.

The ethnographic situation in South Central Africa, as we have seen, was in marked contrast to this. The population from which the inhabitants of the towns were drawn was made up of a large number of relatively small groups drawn originally from very different major Bantu divisions. The larger divisions were differentiated into subgroups which, although they obviously shared a number of general cultural features, were different from one another in dialect and custom, had been politically independent from their similar neighbours prior to British rule, and were identified as different ethnic groups. This differentiation carried over into the colonial period, resulting in the very complex and varied 'ethnic' mix of the towns of Northern Rhodesia.

But this diversity provided that opportunity both for the examination of the gradations of difference in the perceptions of ethnic distance and for the comparison of the findings from the attitudinal study with the manifestation of ethnic choice in behaviour.[17] The rationale for this procedure was based on the fact that at the time when I was conducting the social surveys in the line-of-rail towns of Northern Rhodesia, housing for Africans was almost entirely under the control either of employers, such as the mining companies or large industrial enterprises, or the local authorities, who in a sense were meeting the legal requirement to house employees collectively on behalf

[17] The material that follows was first presented in Mitchell 1974*b*.

of many smaller employers. Most of the housing was occupied by married couples, but, as noted in chap. 2 above, no less than 47.2 per cent of the adult males in the line-of-rail towns were unmarried, that is had never married, were divorced, were widowed, or had left their wives in the rural areas. These men were normally accommodated in 'single quarters', rooms occupied by several men, frequently under hostel or barrack conditions.

Normally housing was allocated by administrative fiat. People entitled to housing were allocated accommodation where vacancies occurred in the housing stock, so that there was little freedom for individuals to exercise any choice in the matter. Basically the same procedure was adopted in respect of 'single quarters', but since it was of little administrative concern whether individual A lived in room X or in room Y, provided both rooms were fully occupied, it was possible for individuals to change their residences when an opportunity arose. The tendency, then, was for unmarried men to seek convivial room-mates. More often than not this implied seeking the company of men of the same ethnic and regional origin. Hence in due course some homogeneity of membership of single quarters became established.[18]

A total of 891 dwelling units occupied by two or more unmarried men was encountered in the survey. The number of occupants ranged from two to thirteen, with a mean of just over three with a standard deviation of 1.42. In the course of the survey more than one hundred separately identifiable ethnic groups were recorded, but naturally the unmarried men were not drawn from all of them. Since we wanted to compare the co-residence of members of different ethnic groups with the perceived 'distance' between them as derived from the 'social distance' study, the analysis had to be restricted to an examination of the co-residence of men drawn from the twenty ethnic groups included in that study.

A measure was devised which would vary from zero if members of some ethnic group were found distributed exclu-

---

[18] The ethnic homogeneity of single quarters was probably enhanced by the fact that some migrants travelled in groups and presented themselves for employment together. It is very likely that a group of migrants recruited at the same time could find accommodation in the same room.

sively in association with their own ethnic group, to 1.0 when there was no association at all between the two groups.[19] Values between 1.0 and zero would reflect the extent to which different ethnic groups tended to co-reside in single quarters.

The object was, of course, to assess empirically the differences between the cognitive appreciation of ethnic distance on the one hand and the behavioural on the other, as measured by the extent to which different ethnic groups tended to co-reside when they were able to exercise some choice in accommodation. The broad overall agreement between the pattern of ethnic distance as reflected in the two sets of data may be expressed by comparing the location of each ethnic group in a multi-dimensional space in which the distances among the different groups may be reproduced. By using 'smallest space analysis' a set of coordinates defining the location of each group in a three-dimensional 'cognitive' space could be determined (cf. Table 6.3). A similar set of coordinates in three dimensions may be derived for the co-residence data. The substantial agreement between these two sets of coordinates as measured by the first canonical correlation was in fact 0.78.

This in itself is a useful corrective to the widely held contention that cognitive and behavioural phenomena refer to two entirely different orders of reality and are therefore likely to bear little relationship to each other. But the interest in the analysis resides perhaps more in the detail of the patterning of clusters than in the overall similarity.

For this we turn to the device used earlier for displaying the pattern in the cognitive 'distance' material, that is to a

[19] The procedure is described in detail in Mitchell 1974*b*: 11. Basically it proceeds by aggregating the product of the number of occupants in single quarters drawn from each of the twenty ethnic groups used in the cognitive study. This produces a 20 × 20 symmetric matrix of sums of cross-products of numbers from the different ethnic groups in the dwelling units. The diagonal of the matrix contains the sum of squares of numbers in ethnic groups. The values in the matrix are then standardized by dividing the values in all cells by the square roots of the row and column diagonal cells relating to the cell in question. This value was then subtracted from 1.0. By this procedure the diagonal cells would be divided by the product of their own square roots, that is they would become equal to 1.0, which when subtracted from unity leads to zero. If two ethnic groups appeared only in association with each other and with no other group then the distance in the off-diagonal cell under the standardization procedure would also be zero. If one group never appeared in association with another the value in the off-diagonal cell would be zero and the distance therefore the maximum of 1.0. Values between 0.0 and 1.0 would reflect the extent of share accommodation.

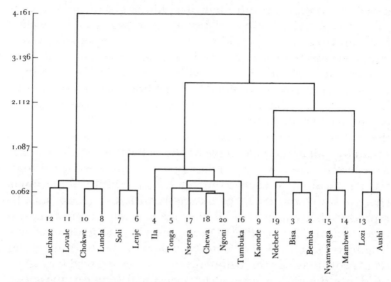

Figure 6.4. Ethnic Groups in Single Quarters: Ward's Clustering Method

dendrogram showing the hierarchical linkage of ethnic groups clustered on the basis of the measure of ethnic co-residence we have used. This dendrogram is set out in Figure 6.4. The general clustering of ethnic groups derived from the analysis of co-residence data may now be compared with that of the cognitive data in Figure 6.3.

In general the overall agreement in the pattern of clustering of ethnic groups in the two diagrams is reasonably close, although there are, of course, some variations. The cognitive data showed the Northern ethnic groups as being linked more closely to the Eastern, and both being more closely linked to the Southern before being linked to the Western. The co-residence data reflects that the Eastern group was linked more closely to the Southern group before they were both linked to the Northern group. In both sets the Western groups were linked most loosely to the rest.

The internal structure of the clusters differs in detail in the two analyses. The most striking difference is that in the co-residence material the outlying group, the Ndebele, was linked most closely with the Bemba and Bisa, whereas in the cognitive data they were linked distantly to both the Northern and the Eastern clusters as wholes before being linked to the Southern group. Secondly the Lozi, who were clustered in the cognitive material with the Southern group to which geographically and ethnographically they were closer, were linked to the Aushi in the co-residence data. I have speculated about the possible reasons for the inclusion of the Ndebele with the Bemba/Bisa cluster in the co-residence data (Mitchell 1974b: 14–15), the main point being that this may have arisen out of the instability of the measure of distance used when only small numbers were involved.[20]

In terms of co-residence, the Ila/Tonga/Soli cluster was linked to the Eastern cluster before they were linked to the ethnographically similar Lenje and Kaonde. This is almost certainly due to the concentration of people from the Eastern Province in Lusaka, in which town there were also relatively large numbers of the Ila/Tonga/Soli people.

The result of this analysis is that the structuring of the perceived distance among the twenty selected ethnic categories, derived as it was from data collected in a decontextualized 'group test' situation, revealed a pattern in which the operation of fairly clear-cut principles of cultural similarity and regional proximity could be postulated. When these general cognitive perceptions were tested against actual behaviour in the specific context of co-residence in single quarters, there was broad overall agreement, but there were nevertheless discrepancies. Where these occurred, they seem to have arisen out of the specific demographic circumstances in the towns in which the co-residence existed. In other words, social perception was apparently influenced by the social setting or context in which it was located.

Perception and Behaviour: Ethnic Intermarriage

The coincidence of the pattern of cognitive social distances with that arising from co-residence patterns was paralleled in an intriguing way by data on the intermarriage of ethnic groups in the Northern Rhodesia line-of-rail towns. Details of the ethnic groups of all spouses or cohabitants, both current and former,

___

[20] At present I have no explanation why the Lozi would be so closely resident with the ethnographically dissimilar Aushi.

and of the place of 'marriage' were recorded in the urban social survey conducted between 1950 and 1955. No attempt was made to establish the formal validity of the union: from the point of view of social distance the fact that a couple had decided to live together constituted prima-facie evidence of social closeness.

For the purposes of the analysis that follows the ethnic groups of 'husbands' and 'wives' were cross-tabulated for all marriages contracted in the line-of-rail towns. A total of 2,923 such 'marriages' were recorded, of which 43 per cent were among the twenty ethnic groups used in the social distance study. A procedure derived from 'block modelling' in social network analysis was adapted to recover the pattern of ethnic intermarriage from this cross-tabulation.[21] This procedure seeks to establish 'blocks' of ethnic groups on the basis of the similarities in the patterns of ethnic intermarriage. Initially the similarities between *pairs* of ethnic groups are estimated by product–moment correlations of both rows and columns of the table of intermarriage frequencies. The rationale for doing this is to look simultaneously at the choice of 'husbands' by 'wives' and the choice of 'wives' by 'husbands' for the same *pair* of ethnic groups. If two ethnic groups 'marry' proportionately into the same ethnic groups then the correlation so derived will be positive and high. In this sense the pair of ethnic groups can be considered to be 'structurally similar'. This structural similarity may then be taken as an index of the social distance separating the two groups, a high positive correlation indicating closeness and a high negative correlation indicating distance. The complete set of correlations among all pairs of ethnic groups may be taken as summarizing the pattern of social distance as reflected in intermarriage frequencies.

Two second-stage procedures were used to abstract the pattern from the correlation matrix. In the first a block modelling procedure was used to partition the matrix successively into blocks which were 'structurally equivalent' internally, as against other blocks in the set at the same level of partitioning. This result is the dendrogram which is set out in Figure 6.5.

This dendrogram may now be compared with that in Figure

---

[21] The procedure used was CONCOR, described initially in Breiger, Boorman, and Arabie 1975, and subsequently in Arabie, Boorman, and Levitt 1978 and Light and Mullins 1979.

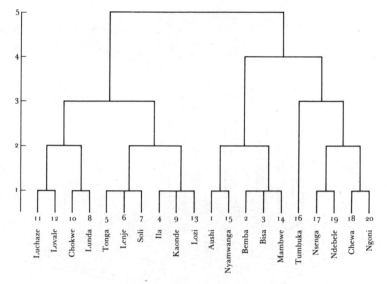

Figure 6.5. Arrangement of Intermarrying Ethnic Groups by CONCOR Procedures

6.2, in which the cognitive social distances are mirrored. It is obvious that essentially the same basic structure has been recovered, in spite of the fact that the types of data and the analytical procedures used to derive the patterns were entirely different. The division into the same broad clusters of Northern, Eastern, Southern, and Western peoples and the same clustering of the Northern with the Eastern as against the Western with the Southern peoples emerges. At the lowest level of partitioning, as with the co-residence data, the coincidence is weakened as the individual pairs are linked differently in the cognitive as against the intermarriage data.

In order to obtain a direct measure of the coincidence of the two structures the second type of analysis was undertaken. This involved a multi-dimensional scaling analysis of the original matrix of correlation coefficients so as to represent, as before, the twenty ethnic groups in a three-dimensional space.[22] The result is set out in Figure 6.6.

The overall similarity of the configuration of ethnic groups

[22] The MINISSA option of the Edinburgh MDS(X) suite as noted in note 11 was used. A coefficient of alienation of 0.16 showed a considerably poorer fit than for the cognitive data.

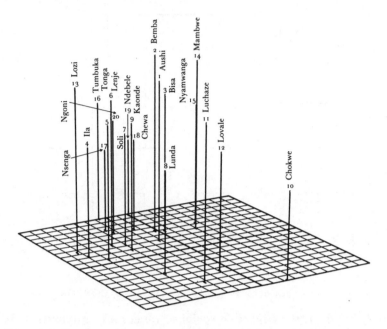

Figure 6.6. Representation of Intermarrying Ethnic Groups in three-dimensional Space

is clear, determined now from the extent to which intermarriage among them take place as compared with the configuration derived from the cognitive distance material as set out in Figure 6.3. It is interesting that once again the cognitive material shows the same simplification of the pattern as was revealed in the analysis of the actual geographical locations of the ethnic groups. Once again this is most clearly demonstrated by the placement of the Lovale/Chokwe/Luchaze cluster. Whereas in the arrangement derived from the cognitive material these three groups were perceived to be almost coincident in space, the intermarriage data shows that, in the context of that aspect of behaviour, while they are still relatively close to one another they are nevertheless clearly separated from one another. In other words these three groups were perceived to be much more like one another than they were in conjugal choice.

A direct measurement of the concordance of the two pat-

terns, therefore, may be determined by using the first canonical correlation between the three-dimensional coordinates
which define the configurations for both sets of material. This
turns out to be 0.946, which reflects a very high agreement
between the pattern of cognitive ethnic distances with that of
the behavioural data as expressed in the frequencies of intermarriage among the twenty ethnic groups used in the cognitive
study.

Structural and Cognitive Ethnicity

These comparisons of ethnic origin, both as an element in
social perception and as an element in social behaviour among
urban Africans in Northern Rhodesia, were made specifically to
test the commonly held assumption that the two orders of
phenomena are in effect independent of one another. The
overall agreement in the two studies suggests that the meanings
people attribute to ethnic identities are not entirely independent
of the social actions they may take.

Harries–Jones (1975: 71–3) has suggested that what is taken
to be ethnicity may in fact be merely the operation of local ties in
urban situations and not strictly ethnicity at all. His point refers
to a phenomenon identified in the vernacular by Philip Mayer
(1961) as *amakaya* and in Harries–Jones's work as *bakumwesu*,
literally in both languages, Xhosa and Bemba, 'those from
home'. We noted that Wilson and Mafeje (1963) had made considerable use of this idea in their analysis of social relationships
in a residential area in Cape Town, as had McNamara (1980) in
his study of gold-mining locations. Pendleton (1975: 15) reports
home-mate groups for migrants in South West Africa.

The existence of 'home-mate' sets, as Harries–Jones translates *bakumwesu*, does not in itself nullify the notion of ethnicity
in urban situations. I would argue that we are dealing with phenomena at different levels of abstraction. In an earlier publication I suggested that even the notion of 'home-mates' could refer
to different kinds of sociological entity. Discussion the notion of
home-mates and extending the points made by Harries–Jones
and Wilson and Mafeje, I argued (Mitchell 1970a: 94) that the
term 'home-mates' could refer to:

1. People who knew one another in the rural areas before they came to town and whose links to one another in town are now reinforced through their common links to rural kinsfolk and friends.

2. People who knew one another in the rural areas before coming to town and who continue to associate in town but whose links with one another through rural links are tenuous. Groups of town dwellers who were born in rural areas but who have grown up in town would fall into this category of home-mate set.

3. People who did not know one another in rural areas before coming to town and whose contacts in the rural areas do not know one another but who form an association in town on the basis of their common origin. This implies that the number of people who are potentially members of home-mate sets on this basis is large, but only some do actually establish contact and develop more than fleeting linkages with one another.

The 'Red home-boy sets' described by Philip Mayer (1961: 94, 100 ff.) are examples of the first type of home-mates, people whose social relationships in town were merely an extension of those in rural areas of origin. The home-boy cliques described by Wilson and Mafeje appeared to be examples of all three types of home-sets, people who knew one another before coming to town and whose kinsfolk were in contact, people who knew one another before coming to town but pursued an existence in town unconnected with their links to the rural areas, and people from more distant areas like Basutoland (now Lesotho), Bechuanaland (now Botswana), or Zululand (now Kwazulu) who established ties in town for mutual support but whose links between contacts in rural areas were obviously disparate. The home-mates that Harries–Jones describes appear to have been people from the same local area or origin who came to know one another in town through sharing a common origin but whose links were otherwise tenuous.

As far as social action is concerned these three types of home-mates imply different consequences for their members. The bond linking members of these different sets was presumably strongest when the ties among home-mates were reinforced by the links among their rural contacts. By the same token the links were presumably weakest when the ties among home-mates arose out of adventitious contacts in town in which the common element was merely their coming from the same rural area of origin. To the extent that urban ties were built up on a basis of existing rural links and were reinforced by them so the bonds among home-mates would be stronger.

The thinking behind my differentiation of home-mate types derives, of course, from social networks. The three types of home-mate groups can be arranged in terms of the increasing multiplexity and intensity of links of the members and therefore, by implication, by the extent to which both town and country are involved in social control. The type of home-mate set represented different degrees of social cohesion, and the distinction was well brought out by Wilson and Mafeje, who distinguish between the close-knit organized cliques of home-boys sharing barrack-type accommodation who were involved in multiplex relationships and which they describe as 'corporate groups', and the sparse network of friends of townsfolk involved in single-stranded relationships (1963: 54–5).

The important feature about these locality-based groups is that they were based on personal relationships and as such contrasted with what I have called categorical relationships (Mitchell 1973: 20). This appears to be the critical distinction between the two sets of phenomena. Home-mate groups may exist within a framework of ethnicity with no radical contradiction. Harries–Jones himself acknowledges the persistence of ethnic stereotypes in Zambia after independence but argues that recognition of local ties was a more important feature than ethnic background (1975: 72). The point is of course that the two phenomena can coexist but are evoked in different circumstances, ethnicity as a categorical relationship in public places and home-mate allegiance as part of the network of individual actors. It is quite possible thus for the *Kalela* dancers to be drawn from a restricted rural area of origin and to be linked to one another by personal ties, sharing common beliefs and values, while at the same time being categorized and related to by outsiders as Bisa.

There is a third way in which ethnicity may emerge in the interpretation of urban social relationships: that is as an abstract analytical category postulated by an observer to order and structure empirical data. Ethnicity here is a relational property of the data which emerges in the process of analysis: it is an abstract postulate of the analyst which provides a general understanding or explanation of the behaviour of the actors and through which, therefore, the patterns in the empirical data may be interpreted. The regularities in the ethnic mix of single quarters in the towns of Northern Rhodesia, for example, could be interpreted as a reflection of an ordered set of ethnic groups each concerned to maintain certain interests, in this case access to housing linked with the support expected from co-ethnics where ethnic groups were poised in hostile and competitive relationships to one another. An approach of this kind is structural and operates with ethnic groups postulated as abstract analytical entities. In analyses of this kind the regularities in the behaviour of categories of people are interpreted in the light of the analyst's identification of the people concerned as members of ethnic groups, and of the command and control of the groups over the disposition of scarce resources. While the actors' own interpretation of their actions is likely to have played some part in the process of analysis, a presentation at the structural level is typically concerned to describe the relational properties of the ethnic groups in general terms, in which the action and perceptions of the individuals are necessarily submerged.

The distinction between ethnicity as a feature of the actors' construction of the springs of social action as against ethnicity as the analyst's construction of their actions on the basis of some interest shared among all those actors construed as members of some ethnic group is related to, but not identical with what Ronald Cohen calls 'the unit problem' (1978: 381 ff.). This is the question of whether ethnic units should be isolated on the basis of what he calls 'social-cultural categories and analysis' or on the loyalties and ascriptions 'made by a people about themselves'. In fact, however, we need also to distinguish between cultural as against behavioural data, so that ethnicity may refer to four different phenomenological entities. On the one hand we have the actors' perceptions of both cultural phenomena and of the behaviour of people attributed to their ethnic identities. These are constructions of reality of the common-sense level and as such constitute the starting-point of any analysis of ethnic phenomena. An analyst starting with the actors' perceptions of both cultural and behavioural phenomena and making use of theoretical notions will have absorbed these phenomena into abstract and general analytical entities, that is the ethnic group or ethnicity. The ethnic group is a set of actors displaying some set of cultural diacritica in contradistinction to some other group, the diacritica themselves being attributed to the cultural milieu in which the actors have been raised. Ethnicity is thus the distinctive pattern of behaviour and beliefs displayed by a set of actors defined as members of some ethnic group (Mitchell 1974*b*: 15–28).

From this perspective, of course, there is no real opposition between cognitive and structural formulations of ethnicity: they deal with different aspects of the same objective phenomenon and arise out of the different interests of analysts. Some, like Magubane (1969: 535–40), argue that concern with ethnicity diverts attention from its root cause, which is the class basis of colonial society. The analysis should be directed, he contends, to that phenomenon instead. Gutkind, taking a somewhat less draconian stance, argues that 'we must reject the view that "tribalism" is at the core of social organization of African towns', and that we should concentrate on 'those features of the urban social systems which cut across ethnicity while at the same time our model must allow for an analysis of its importance when the evidence demands it'. (1974: 137).

Other analysts operating with a structural approach, like Abner Cohen for example, argue that the 'definition of ethnicity as cognition of identity obscures, even nullifies, the conception of differences in degree of ethnicity', and prefer instead to analyse ethnicity in terms of interconnections with economic and political relationships (1974: xv) as Cohen in fact did in his analysis of the control of the cattle and kola nut trade by the Hausa in Ibadan, Nigeria (1969).

The difficulty with structural approaches to ethnicity, however, is that ethnic boundaries frequently coincide with structural divisions which may have a more direct bearing on the issue in question. If this happens a nexus between ethnicity and some theoretical characteristic like political behaviour may be deduced when in fact the real connection may be based on, say, social class. Van Velsen's early (1964) analysis of two Rhodesian African political parties illustrates this. Political commentators commonly linked membership of the Zimbabwe African

Peoples Union with the Ndebele peoples, since Joshua Nkomo, the leader, was of Ndebele extraction. Membership to the Zimbabwe African National Union, on the other hand, was largely attributed to the 'Shona' peoples, since its leadership was largely drawn from them. In fact, as van Velsen points out, the membership of both parties was very mixed but they represented economic interests of rather different types. ZAPU seemed to relate more to the interests of the African working classes, while ZANU seemed to appeal more to the intellectuals.

In analyses of this kind it is important to distinguish social justifications for behaviour on the one hand from necessary connections on the other. Political opposition, as with ZAPU and ZANU, are frequently attributed to ethnic alignments. In fact political oppositions based on socio-economic differences may instead be *phrased* in ethnic terms and so provide the basis upon which social actions may be justified. A challenger may, for example, accuse an opponent of favouring people from the opponent's ethnic group and by so doing mobilize the support of those from other ethnic groups. The point is that ethnicity is a public phenomenon, immediately recognizable, and so becomes an issue amenable to manipulation of this sort.

But although ethnic identity is commonly assumed to arise as it were from descent or parentage, in fact popular merging of political and ethnic categories may serve to confuse the issue. I described an instructive instance of this (Mitchell 1970a: 98; 1974b; 30). Kapferer reports[23] that he was present on an occasion when a respected political leader was being discussed. Although a staunch supporter of independence and an influential member of the ruling party, he nevertheless came from a part of the country which was in general opposed to the ruling party. The ethnic group associated with that part of the country and from which in fact the person concerned came was widely taken to be opposed to the ruling party and hence to the ethnic group with which the leader of the ruling party was associated. However, those discussing the person in question, all of whom came from the ethnic group popularly associated with the government, exculpated the person in question, saying that all his behaviour demonstrated that he was not really a person from

[23] Personal communication.

his own ethnic group but operationally one from their own group. In other words the contradiction between the party and the ethnic group was resolved in terms of the basic assumptions, in effect, by reclassifying the person into the appropriate ethnic group.

The implication is that a social characteristic commonly assumed to be fixed from birth and hence 'ascribed' proves at the interactional level to be variable. This is because whether or not the participants in some social action are going to treat the cultural origin of some of their members as significant turns on the way in which they define the situation. In other words ethnicity (and regionalism, with which I associate ethnicity) is not a pervasive element in social relationships but one which emerges in particular social situations. The analytical regularity in the study of ethnicity resides not in its explicit manifestation so much as in the types of social situation in which it is invoked or not invoked.[24] The sociological analysis of ethnicity, therefore, becomes rooted not in the meanings attributed to ethnic cues so much as in the alignments and interests of the actors in specified situations in which cues and signs *take on* meanings and are used to define the stances that the actors adopt to one another in that interaction.

The regularity in structural ethnicity arises out of the consistency with which attributes that the analyst feels entitled to identify as reflecting ethnic interests are associated with attributes taken to denote some other sphere of life. Epstein, for example, argues that certain ethnic groups in Northern Rhodesia which enjoyed a widespread reputation of a military past were able to use this reputation in commanding prestigious jobs in the towns. He develops the rationale for this proposition from an assessment of the views of various people from different ethnic groups in a number of different occupational statuses, but to confirm its *structural* significance he uses the findings from the social survey of the line-of-rail town to demonstrate the distribution of members of these ethnic groups as against others in different occupational categories (after discounting the

---

[24] I used the situational approach to ethnicity initially in *The Kalela Dance* (1956a), but expanded and developed the idea considerably, especially in Mitchell 1970a and in 1974b. Other writers making use of the approach have been Epstein 1958, Paden 1970, and more recently R. Cohen 1978.

predominance of foreign groups in the more prestigious occupations) (1978: 132–5).

The epistemologically different modes of analysis discussed here, therefore, exist in their own rights independently from one another. They cannot directly contradict one another. Yet at the same time our insights and understandings are extended if we are able to juxtapose the findings from structural analyses of manifestations of ethnicity against those based on cognitive data, since it is by this procedure that *apparent* contradictions may be resolved.

7

COMPARATIVE URBANISM
EARLY AMERICAN AND RECENT
AFRICAN CITIES

The implication of the argument thus far has been that in the analysis of any social situation there are at least two different orders of data to be taken into account. The first relates to the way in which the actors see the situation. We are dealing here with the actors' perceptions of features of social situations to which they are able to attribute meanings that have implications for their behaviour in these situations. The second relates to the abstract structural or morphological characteristics of the settings which derive from the theoretical perspectives adopted by the analyst and which represent regularities which are meaningful in terms of the propositions contained within that theoretical framework. These structural characteristics, by their very nature, are intelligible only in terms of the logical structure of the theory to which they relate, so that the average actor is unlikely to be aware of them in the same terms as the analyst. The perceptions of the actors constitute part of the basic data from which the analyst constructs theoretical formulations so that in general the perceptions may be part of the structural characteristics though not necessarily coincident with them.

In the analysis of social situations the analyst must conduct a dialogue between these two different aspects of reality. The situation as a whole is part of some larger structural context and in a sense is constituted by it. At the same time the actors seek to interpret the situation in terms of their own perceptions. The meanings which they are able to attribute to the actions of others involved in the situation or to symbols displayed in the situation constitute their social perceptions. There is no real opposition between these two different perspectives of the social situation; the distinction lies rather in the emphasis that the analyst puts on the two aspects of social action for the purposes in hand.

To develop theoretically sound general views about urbanism, however, we need consciously to keep the two different levels of abstraction of perception and structure intellectually separate. In order to be able to appreciate the regularities in behaviour that may arise in urbanism we need to separate both the city from the social order and the perception from the situations. Recourse to comparison is obviously an aid in achieving this. In principle what is being achieved in comparative analysis is that the manifestation of certain regular relationships among selected theoretically significant features in the two instances is being demonstrated by showing how the operation of contextual variations enhances or suppresses the expected pattern. Comparative analysis makes a virtue out of *not* letting 'other things be equal'.

While this may be formally true, in practice contextual variations may so complicate the picture that there is an expedient advantage in balancing as many of the significant contextual parameters as is feasible. Obviously there is no exact mathematical way in which contextual parameters can be equalized, but one step in this direction may be taken if, by historical accident, we can find situations which are roughly similar in a number of parameters that we judge to be significant in terms of our theoretical understanding of the situation and where we have sufficient information of the perceptions and behaviour of the actors to enable us to make comparisons.

Industrialization and City Growth

These conditions were loosely approximated, but by no means fully met, in certain American cities at the period of their rapid growth between c. 1890 and c. 1920 and in certain African cities undergoing similar changes some fifty years later. The two periods during which I seek to compare selected aspects of social relationships among migrants have been chosen deliberately because they represent, in some aspects at least, similar phases of economic growth. Chicago, for example, during the period 1860 to 1910 was growing, as we shall see, at a rate similar to that of many African towns between 1930 and 1960. It is true that the periods, separated as they are by at least fifty years, represent different technological eras, and this may influence the social relationships among migrants in several different ways. For example, improved transportation may have enabled families to accompany migrants with greater ease. It is true also that the sort of economic expansion which occasioned the growth of African cities also took place in a different era in the sense that not only are different skills called for under new technological processes, but the whole climate of management and organization of labour is different, even on such a simple level as the growth of trade unions or the development of industrial safety legislation. The market, similarly, had changed over the time separating the two periods, with the development of large-scale mergers and international cartels. The two periods are also separated by the changes in general administrative procedures and the legislative frameworks within which the migrants were moving. These general differences are real and are part of the settings in which the aspects of behaviour we wish to examine are located. But within these somewhat different frameworks it is possible to isolate certain general processes which are sufficiently basic and fundamental to override the differences due to the contextual framework and to establish circumstances that are so similar from the point of view of the behaviour of the migrants that we are justified as treating the different periods, for this purpose, as comparable. The logic of the procedure, then, is to postulate necessary connections between circumstances and behavioural patterns, the two being not trivially connected, and to seek the manifestations of this postulated relationship in empirical data relating to the two periods. In doing this we shall of necessity be asking questions of the material collected and recorded between, say, 1915 and 1935 from the vantage-point of a much more developed theoretical system. We will examine the past with the wisdom of hindsight, with the consequence that a full demonstration of our postulated connections will not always be possible because the relevant data are not always available. The history of developments in social relationships amongst migrants in American towns, by the same token, may provide some lead to the understanding of social processes amongst migrants to African towns, and vice versa.

Table 7.1 *Rate of Growth of Chicago 1860-1930*

1860-1870	112,172	298,977	10.30
1870-1880	298,977	503,185	5.34
1880-1890	503,185	1,099,850	8.13
1890-1900	1,099,850	1,698,575	4.44
1900-1910	1,698,575	2,185,583	2.55
1910-1920	2,185,283	2,701,705	2.14
1920-1930	2,701,705	3,376,438	2.23

Source: US Census Reports.

Rates of City Growth

After the Civil War in America there was a period of very rapid economic expansion, much of which, especially towards the end of the nineteenth century, was concerned with the establishment of industrial enterprises in cities. This expansion continued almost without abatement until the economic recession after the First World War. The position is well illustrated by the expansion of Chicago from 1860 onwards. The population of Chicago at census dates and the geometric rates of growth during those periods were as in Table 7.1. These rates of expansion, especially in the earlier years, may be compared with those of some African towns, as shown in Table 7.2.

There is little significance in the numerical size of these rates of increase themselves;[1] the significance emerges only when they are compared with the natural rates of increase of the popula-

Table 7.2 *Rates of Growth of Specified African Towns 1921-1962*

Dakar	1921-1963	5.65
Accra	1936-1960	9.53
Lagos	1936-1962	6.51
Abidjan	1937-1960	11.02
Freetown	1921-1960	2.13
Five Southern Rhodesian Towns	1931-1961	5.95

Sources: Little (1965: 18) for West African towns.
Southern Rhodesian towns from Table 2.3.

[1] The relationship is not simple since in many African towns the mobility of the population between town and country is so high and so related to the life cycle that it is almost impossible to adduce behavioural characteristics from geographic residence. It would not be reasonable to argue that people at present in town are 'townsfolk' in their behaviour since it is likely that many of them will be 'rural' folk within a short period of time. This was discussed in chap. 4.

tions in the country as a whole. Whether the natural rate of increase in the towns differs from that in the countryside in Africa has not yet been decided. If the age structure of the urban population and the usually better medical and hygienic circumstances of the towns are taken into account then it seems likely that the rate of natural increase of the populations in the towns may be slightly higher than that in the rural areas. But rates of natural increase as a whole are not likely to be greater than say 3 per cent per annum. The implication of this is that the urban populations are growing at a rate much faster than their natural rates of increase, so we must conclude that a certain part of the increase is due to the inflow of migrants from smaller towns, or, more likely, from the rural areas (see chap. 3). Empirical evidence from many of the towns in Africa shows that the majority of present-day town residents have in fact been born in the rural areas and that they migrated to town in search of employment or other economic opportunities in early adulthood.

The basic processes attracting migrants to South Central African towns and to Chicago were sufficiently similar to generate similar demographic, economic, and social contexts, within which the inhabitants of these towns had perforce to solve their problems of day to day living. The apparent attractiveness for young males of occupation opportunities in towns expanding rapidly under the impetus of capital investment compared unfavourably with their social and economic status in peasant societies in Southern Italy (for example) or South Central African rural areas. There was thus a selective movement from rural areas to towns of young males in search of unskilled work in both North America and South Central Africa, although at different times of history.

The effect of this basic migratory process on three different aspects of the structure of urban populations may be noted. The first is the demographic composition of towns, the second is the economic conditions of the migrants, and third is the social differentiation of the population. Each of these three domains, which do not of course exhaust the totality, constitutes a context in which the migrants were forced to find a way of living.

The Demographic Context

Since the demand was essentially for manual workers in both American and African cities—and for relatively unskilled workers at that—it is easy to see that the population in these cities would be drawn disproportionately from the young adult age-range. Not only did the kind of labour opportunities favour physically fit young people, but also, since migration was involved, those who were most likely to move into cities were those who were least encumbered by commitments in their places of origin.

The age and sex structures of the African populations of towns in Zambia and to a lesser extent those in South Africa show a characteristic shape in which there is a high preponderance of adults between the ages of, say, twenty and thirty-five and a corresponding paucity of people over the age of, say, forty-five and between the ages of about ten and twenty. In addition there tend to be rather more males than females in the young adult age-groups due to the greater tendency of young men than women to migrate to the cities in the earlier stages of the expansion[2] (Reader 1961: 44).

Much the same sort of situation existed in Chicago at the end of the nineteenth century just after the peak of its growth. Figure 7.1 shows the age and sex structure of Chicago in 1890 at the end of a decade of spectacular growth, as compared with the total population of the United States in the same year. This diagram illustrates a selection of young adults into the population similar to that in the South Central African towns, but the disproportion in age distribution and sex ratios is not as extreme. There were 99.7 males per 100 females in the ages of 15 to 30 in Chicago in 1890, and 121 per 100 females in the towns of Northern Rhodesia in the 1950s. In Chicago there seem also to have been proportionately more people over the age of forty-five than in the Northern Rhodesian towns. The disproportion in both ages and sex is not unnaturally greater among the migrants: census figures for the foreign-born population are not available for 1890, but in 1910 there were

[2] Age and sex diagrams for towns in Northern Rhodesia are represented in Figure 3.2. For East London by Reader (1961: 44). The structure for East Bank locations is very similar to those for Northern Rhodesian towns.

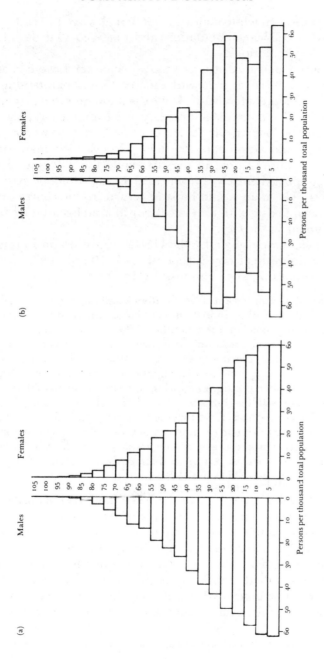

Figure 7.1. (*a* and *b*) Age and Sex Structures: USA Total Population 1890, Chicago 1890

122 foreign-born white males per 100 females aged 15 to 30 (102 in the whole Chicago population) and 144 aged 30 to 34 (116 in the whole population).

In South Central Africa, as we saw in chapter 3, women often remained in the rural areas with their children, maintaining the rural production of foodstuffs while the men migrated to town to seek work. The more distant the city was from the local place of origin the less likely it was, at least initially, that the women and children would accompany the men.[3] Instead the man would work for a limited time in the city while the wife and family would support themselves from rural agricultural and pastoral activities. The man would hope to return in due course to the rural areas, taking with him in cash or in kind his produce from employment in the city.

The description given by the US Commission on Immigration of immigrants from Europe in 1907–10 reflected a similar general situation. The Commission reported:

Like most of the immigrants from Southern and Eastern Europe, those who entered the leading industries were largely single men or married men unaccompanied by their families. There is, of course, in prac- tically all industrial communities a large number of families of the various races, but the majority of the employees are men without families here, whose standard of living is so far below that of the Native American or older immigrant workman that it is impossible for the latter to successfully compete with them. They usually live in cooperative groups and crowd together. Consequently they are able to save a great part of their earnings, much of which is sent or carried abroad. Moreover there is a strong tendency on the part of these unaccompanied men to return to their native countries after a few years of labour here. (Handlin 1959: 55–6.)

It is possible, however, that there is a fundamental difference between the age and sex structures of African and American cities at comparable stages of expansion. The disparity between the age and sex structures of American cities and those of the rural areas tended to be corrected subsequently as immigrants either brought their families to the city with them or left and did not return. The index of dissimilarity of age structures between Chicago and the total population of the United States fell

---

[3] See discussion of this point and illustrative statistics in chap. 3.

steadily from 9.0 in 1890 to 3.3 in 1960.[4] In Britain the corresponding index of towns of 100,000 in 1960 was 1.2. The age
and sex structure of Chicago has not quite equalled that of the
total population of the United States to the extent that this has
happened in Great Britain. For Northern Rhodesia the index in
1960 was 18.4, and for Southern Rhodesian towns 27.2.

In Africa, the persistence of labour circulation meant that the
disparity between rural and urban age and sex structures tended
to endure, because people migrated into towns and out of them
again at specific stages of the life cycle. Thus in East London, for
example, even after 100 years of its existence, there was still a
disparity between its age and sex structure and that of its surrounding rural hinterland.[5] The reason for this probably lay in
the enforced involvement of Africans in continuing rural and
social economic systems to which they hoped eventually to
return in their old age.

The disparity in age and sex structure between cities on the
one hand and rural areas on the other is a manifestation of the
economic, political, and social organization in the society as a
whole. It also constitutes the setting for institutional arrangements through which both country-dwellers and townspeople
must of necessity order their social existence. The most obvious
domains affected by these settings would be those of marriage
and domestic arrangements in both town and rural areas.[6] But
the conditions leading to these imbalances have other wide-
ranging effects, one of which is the disparity in living standards
between the established minority on the one hand and the dis-
possessed majority on the other.

Economic Conditions

The basis of the rapid growth of towns of the sort we are
considering was, at root, capitalistic industrial and commercial
enterprise. The level of technological development with which
the industry or the commercial activities were connected would

---

[4] Measured by half the sum of absolute differences of percentages in age and sex
categories.

[5] The matter is discussed more fully in chap. 3.

[6] The changes in marriage arrangements flowing from industrialization were
discussed by Richards (1940) and Wilson (1941–2). Aspects of marriage in towns are discussed in Mitchell 1957.

clearly affect the sort of skills which were in demand at the time. At the peak of expansion of Chicago at the end of the nineteenth century many of the tasks now performed by machinery were then performed by hand. The industrial enterprises of the time therefore called for many unskilled workers. The peak period of expansion of the South African and Northern Rhodesian towns, however, occurred several decades later when considerable advancement in technology had been made. But here the low wages customarily paid to African workers made it profitable for entrepreneurs to continue to employ workers to perform tasks which if higher wages prevailed might have been done by machinery.[7]

The demand for labour, hence, in both America in the closing years of the nineteenth century, and in East London and the Copperbelt, as far as Africans were concerned, was for unskilled manual labour. This demand itself was a reflection of the supply since the general background of the workers, all of rural or peasant origin, prepared them for no other occupations. The rudimentary skills they could offer fitted them for few tasks other than those of general unskilled labouring. Some were, of course, able to set themselves up as traders and to become wealthy, but by far the majority were confined to unskilled occupations.

Poverty and Overcrowding

It seems inevitable, if there is a large-scale influx into the cities of people who are competing for jobs at the lower ranges of the wage scale, that overcrowding, poverty, and depressed living conditions are likely to ensue. Nearly all scholars who have been concerned with urban conditions among Africans have drawn attention to the poverty, overcrowding, and dismal living conditions which people have suffered. Epstein, comparing William Foote Whyte's description of the Boston slum in which he worked with conditions in African towns, writes: 'We may note how closely Whyte's description of social conditions in Cornerville parallels many of the available accounts of African urban life: poverty, inadequate housing, and general conditions of squalor are the almost universal features of African life in the

---

[7] For a detailed discussion of the flow of labour to the copper mines see Baldwin 1966: chap. 4, Berger 1974, and Ohadike 1969.

towns.' (1958: 225–6; see also Hellman 1949: 268). Reader describes living conditions in East London in 1957 and in general talks of the squalor and overcrowded conditions under which the migrants lived. He showed that 78 per cent of the African population lived in 'wood and iron shacks' or other types of inadequate housing (1961: Table I: 150), and that under the conditions of exploitative renting of accommodation 'there can only be dangerous overcrowding and a noxious multiplicity of unhygienic and utterly inadequate room-units' (p. 105). Municipal control seemed to be firmer on the Copperbelt, where nearly all the housing was provided by the municipalities or the mining companies. But even here there was a tendency for people to use all available space for accommodation, so that buildings originally intended as kitchens, for example, tended to become extra rooms, frequently housing a second married couple. Particularly in single quarters overcrowding tended to become acute, for here it was not uncommon to find as many as ten and eleven men living in a single barrack-type room.

Incomes too were meagre, both in East London and the Copperbelt. In the survey he conducted, Reader found that the median income of the males he interviewed was 58 shillings per week or about £150 per year (1961: 65). This sum can be appreciated only against a poverty datum line or some similar basis of comparison. It is in fact about a quarter or a third of the median income of Whites, and this provides a rough indication of the relative poverty of African town-dwellers in East London. Similar circumstances prevailed in South Central Africa. Gray (1960: 209 ff.), having summarized the evidence concerning the poverty of urban Africans in Southern and Northern Rhodesia between 1940 and 1945, pointed out how several commissions of inquiry following urban disorders drew attention to the inability of most Africans with families to meet the costs of living in towns with the wages they were paid. Fifteen years later, Bettison made an estimate of the poverty datum line in Salisbury and concluded that 65 per cent of Africans with families were in fact living below what he calls the reduced-standard poverty datum line. He later extended his enquiries to Northern Rhodesia and came to a similar conclusion there, that in fact 80 per cent of the Africans with families had incomes below the poverty datum line (Bettison 1960).

The condition of African migrants in a South African town, admittedly under extreme conditions, are described by Hellman:

The yard has a narrow entrance. Flanking the entrance inside the yard stand two cement garbage bins which serve all the residents. The occupants are served by 6 latrines, 3 for men and 3 for women, but they are usually in such a bad state of repair and so neglected that the children shun them, as is simply testified by the condition of the alleyways inside the yard and of the pavements surrounding it. There is a washing room adjoining the lavatories, which consists of four corrugated iron walls, a cement floor and two water-taps one or the other of which is never in working order . . . The 15 outer rooms and 14 of the inner rooms are built of brick and have cement floors . . ., the remainder of the rooms being rickety constructions of corrugated iron and thin, wooden planks. The brick rooms vary in size from 10 by 11 feet to 11 by 12 feet. The . . . partitioning walls, about 10 feet in height, do not reach the roof which, at its apex is about 15 feet high. The other rooms vary in size from 8 by 11 feet to 11 feet square, with a height of 8 to 10 feet. The flooring boards are, in the majority of these seventy-eight rooms, rotten. The doors of the rooms are badly fitted and have no proper locks, being fastened from the outside by a padlock and from the inside by a bent nail or rough contraption of wire. Each room is fitted with two windows but as one window often gives access to an adjoining room, it is usually covered with a plate of tin. Cross-ventilation is not possible in the 63 rooms which are built back to back. In summer the rooms are unbearably hot and in winter the cold winds which enter through the gaps and holes in the walls necessitate the constant burning of large coal braziers, introducing an element of danger and rendering the atmosphere extremely unhealthy. Very few of the roofs are rainproof, many of the window-panes are broken, but as the breaking of windows of the vacant rooms is a favourite diversion of the children of Rooiyard, the owner cannot be entirely blamed. The level of the floor is, in a number of rooms, below the level of the yard and in wet weather the rainwater flows into the rooms carrying with it the debris from the yard. The discomfort of the occupants under these miserable conditions requires very little emphasis. Altogether the rooms are in a state of shocking neglect. The owner does not endeavour to keep them in good repair, and the tenants, as is only natural, show an apathetic indifference to the condition of their rooms. Complaints, they have learnt by experience, are futile. The beer-drinks and dances which take place in the rooms are not conducive to keeping them in good order. If flooring boards give way under the strain of particularly vigorous—or drunken—dancing the tenants simply shrug their shoulders and repair the damage as best they can, often merely covering the hole in the floor with a piece of sacking. (Hellman 1948: 3.)

In the 105 rooms described no less than 376 inhabitants were accommodated, giving density of room occupancy of 3.58 persons (p. 11).

Gray (1960: 253) describes housing conditions in Bulawayo in these terms:

A municipal count taken in 1949 showed that on an average 4.9 persons shared each room in the Old Location. Five young adult males sharing a room of eleven feet by ten feet with a small kitchen built off in the rear is not an unduly alarming figure, but almost half the people were living in rooms containing more than five people. And the count did not of course reveal the full extent of illegal occupation nor the proportion of women and children in these rooms. A sample survey of seventy rooms taken later showed an average of just under one woman per room, and one of the worst cases encountered was of a room that contained five men, two women, and two adolescent girls. Individuals living under these conditions might well be expected to renounce their traditional code of behaviour and even lose all sense of cohesion and human dignity.

In a footnote Gray comments: 'One evening in 1956 I saw some of the worst of these rooms in the Old Location. Ten or twelve men, women and children lived together in one room whose walls were patterned by live and dead cockroaches. The dignity of the inhabitants was in extraordinary contrast to the environment.'

Circumstances such as these could have been echoed in any of the rapidly growing industrial cities of the United States towards the end of the nineteenth century. The spirit is caught by a description of a New York slum in 1853 by John Commons of the New York Association for the Improvement of the Conditions of the Poor. He wrote:

In Oliver Street, Fourth Ward, for example, rear dwelling, 6 feet by 30, two stories and garret, three rooms on each of the first and second floors, and four in the attic—in all, ten small apartments, which contain *fourteen families*. The entrance is through a narrow dirty alley and the yard and appendages of the filthies [*sic*] . . . In Cherry Street, a tenement house on two lots, extending back from the street about 150 feet, five stories above the basement, so arranged as to contain 120 families, or more than 500 persons . . . (Quoted by Strauss, 1961: 96. Original italics.)

The basic conditions are similar and the circumstances are similar too: it is one in which a large mass of underprivileged people fleeing from depressed economic circumstances in rural areas find themselves caught in an urban poverty out of which there appears to be no further escape.

With migrants tending to occupy the lower rungs of the occupational ladder, economic, social, and political power rested in the hands of an élite whose language, customs, and ways of life in general were dissimilar from those of the immigrants. In American cities the division was between the Anglo-Saxon Protestant élite on whose capital investment the rapidly expanding industrial and commercial concerns had been established and the hordes of migrants from Europe, particularly from Eastern and Southern Europe, and later from the Southern and Mid-Western states of the United States. In colonial Africa the élites were a racial minority of European Protestant origin, representing the colonial rulers, and the representatives of the commercial and industrial interests of colonial and settler powers.

Similar social circumstances have led to a similar course of events in industrial relations. Epstein (1958: 115 ff.) describes how on the Copperbelt there were difficulties in the organization of the mineworkers' union amongst a predominantly immigrant and ethnically diverse labour force. He argues that their lack of involvement in the industrialized life, particularly amongst the Nyakyusa tribesman, who were overwhelmingly 'target workers'—that is people whose aim it was to earn a specific sum of money or purchase a particular item and then to return immediately to their home villages—led to difficulties in incorporating them into the union. Some forty years earlier similar processes were being reported in Pennsylvania. The Immigration Commission in America which sat between 1907 and 1910 reported:

Another characteristic of the new immigrants contributed to the situation in Pennsylvania. This was the impossibility of successfully organizing them into labour unions. Several attempts at organization were made, but the constant influx of immigrants to prevailing conditions which seemed unusually favourable contributed to the failure to organize . . . A similar situation has prevailed in the other great industries.

The Immigration Commissioner's interpretation of this fact was in terms of the expectations of the migrants. An interpretation which emerges from the Copperbelt study might be that in both these situations the migrants concerned were only minimally committed to the social and economic order in which they were involved. The subsequent history of Puerto Rican immigrants to New York shows that they rapidly became members of trade unions, but that their attitude to both the unions and the larger society in which they were living was one essentially of hostility and of a feeling of exclusion (Lewis 1968: 218).

Social Differentiation

When cities attract their population from hinterlands as far afield as those of Chicago in the last decades of the nineteenth century, or the Copperbelt in the 1950s and, to a lesser extent, East London in the 1950s, the implication is that the population of the city is likely to be composed of people from differing areas of origin, and the more extensive the hinterlands the more likely it is that they will differ in language and way of life. This is partly the basis of the heterogeneity which Wirth distinguished as one of the characteristics of the urban social scene. We know from historical evidence that the migrants to Chicago came from a wide variety of cultural backgrounds. Most, in the earlier stages, were from Europe, but later they came from the Middle West and later still from the South of the United States. In Africa the same general conditions existed. On the Copperbelt the population enumerated in a set of social surveys was found to have been drawn from over one hundred different linguistic and tribal groups, these groups being drawn from very different Bantu-speaking groups. In general the numbers from many of these ethnic groups were small: nearly half of the distinct groups each enumerated comprised less than 0.5 per cent of the adult males in the Copperbelt towns of Ndola, Lunashya, Kitwe, Mufulira, and Chingola. Only a small proportion of the groups enumerated (7.4 per cent) each had more than 5 per cent of the adult males in it. In each town, therefore, there tended to be small numbers of numerically dominant ethnic categories and a large number of other categories with only a few representatives of each in the town. Southall and Gutkind (1957: 27, 107, Tables 1 and 2) report a similar diversity of people in Kampala, for in a population of 2,154 persons in Kisenyi they enumerated no less than 40 ethnic groups, and in a population of 1,339 in Mulago a total of 31[8] (cf. Little 1965: chaps. 1 and 2).

From the point of view of comparative urbanism, however, the sheer diversity of ethnic origins is irrelevant. The relevant question is: given the strangeness and unfamiliarity of the majority of what the average migrant in a town encounters, and given that there are a relatively small number of persons whose cultural and social backgrounds are similar to those of the migrants, in what way does this set of circumstances influence the pattern of social relationships that the migrant builds up around himself in the town?

It is unlikely that a migrant ever moves to a specific city without at least some prior link in that city. The reason why the migrant moves to the city in general is more than likely a straightforward matter of economics. But why he should move to city A as against city B is likely to be a matter of the sort of person he knows in that city or the associations which he has. This point has been made on the basis of empirical information with respect to African cities, though similar evidence from American cities is not so easily available.[9] The implication of this is that there is likely to be a kinsman or at least a person from a local area that a migrant is able to contact on first arrival and with whom he is able to stay until he finds his feet in the city. The existence of a certain number of people of a specified origin in a section of the city is likely in turn to lead to the development of services to meet the specific demands of this group, such as the kosher shops and German delicatessen shops that characterize the ethnic ghettos in American cities. Hence the appearance of the ecological phenomenon of ethnic segregation in larger cities.

[8] A similar ethnic diversity seems to characterize West African cities. For the example of Kano see Paden 1970: 253 ff.

[9] Some evidence is available from European studies. Braun (1970: 73), for example, quotes evidence which shows that Italian migrants to Switzerland always have in mind a specific friend or kinsman before they leave. Some evidence of a similar position with regard to migrants to the United States is presented in Macdonald and Macdonald (1964).

This phenomenon has long been recognized as one of the marked features of the ecology of American cities. The position in the African cities with which we are concerned is a little less clear. This is because in these cities the basis of housing is in the first instance racial, in that by law and regulation in South Africa, Southern Rhodesia, and in Northern Rhodesia (that is, before Independence) the different racial groups were compelled by regulation to live in specific areas of the town. Hence the division of the town into what were known as 'locations' for African residents, and 'European areas' for Whites. Asians and Eurafricans were similarly confined to 'second class residential areas'. In addition to this the provision of housing or Africans on the Copperbelt and to a less extent in East London was the responsibility of the local governments or, in the case of mine-workers, the mining company. Allocation of housing was there-fore a matter of bureaucratic procedure, so that the possibility of the natural collocation of ethnic groups was counteracted. Where free choice of housing was possible, however, similar patterns emerged, such as in the so-called unauthorized housing in Lusaka or in Ndola.[10]

Here similar processes are operating, and although the constraints on personal choice interfere with the development of ethnic ghettos in African cities with which we are concerned, clearly the same general forces are in operation.[11] The development of the geographical concentrations of people from the same area of origin—the physical ghettos—is not the real concern, for this merely reflects the underlying social relation-ships and perceptions of the people involved. Our real concern is with the social and psychological ghettos into which people were relegated or alternatively into which they withdrew for protection.

Ethnic Association

It is a relatively small step from the existence of a set of ties and

[10] Richards makes this point (1963: 47). She describes what she calls an attempt to reproduce a tribal village in Ndola where a matriarch of a small settlement of Ngoni told her proudly: 'This is the country of the Ngoni here, where everything is done right.' The time period would be between 1931 and 1933.

[11] The concentration of people from the same general ethnic groups in single quarters manifests this tendency far more closely. This was discussed in chap. 6.

obligations among a number of people thrown together because of their sharing at least a common language and place of origin to the organization of a formal association through which the interests of these people may be furthered.

The ethnic mutual aid society is a well-known phenomenon in African cities, and their organization, structure, and the ends they serve for their members have been well documented by Little (1957, 1959, 1965, 1966. See also Banton 1957, 1965). Summarizing his view on these associations, Little writes:

The main *raison d'être* of such associations is that of fostering an interest in tribal songs, history, language and local beliefs, thus maintaining a person's attachment to his native town or village and to his lineage there. In addition, however, these organizations provide schemes for mutual aid, including monetary assistance to sick or bereaved members. Some of them also seek to improve the social amenities of their home towns by building bridges, repairing roads, and by raising money for the education of young people. (1966: 9.)

An example given by Little is that of the Fanti Union described by Busia. In this union all Cape Coast people resident in the town were eligible for membership, and there were in fact 300 members on the roll. Its aims were to bring people of the Cape Coast in the town together, to give members financial assistance when necessary, and to maintain an interest in the welfare of the Cape Coast in general. Members paid a 'foundation fee' of ten shillings and sixpence on admission, and a monthly contribution of ninepence. The Union met once a fortnight and all its affairs were conducted in Fanti. The meeting opened with a hymn and a prayer and closed with a benediction. When a member died the bereaved family received from the society a funeral benefit of seven pounds four shillings. When a member's wife, husband, father or mother died the member was given two pounds two shillings. A sick member received a sick benefit of five shillings. An additional aim of the society was to award scholarships to Cape Coast children, but in fact there have been insufficient funds to start this scheme (1965: 28).

This description could be compared with an association among Italians described by the Commission on the Problem of Immigration to Massachusetts in 1914. It reported:

Among the Italians the societies were not united, for whatever the object of a society its membership is usually drawn from those who come from one town or province in Italy. The result is a great number of associations. In Springfield, for example, where the Italian population according to the Census of 1910 is 2,915 there are twelve societies. One society has recently celebrated its twenty-fifth anniversary with great enthusiasm. It reports 400 members, a fund of $3,500 and a record of having paid out, in sick benefits and to destitute families, about $15,000. It is described in its report as a society that 'unites and gives us strength and will make us more acceptable in the eyes of the American people; that will guide us in all vicissitudes and trouble of life; that will give us work when we are idle; that will succour us with money when we are sick; that will help our families and accompany us with dignified ceremony when we die'. (Handlin 1959: 85.)

Interestingly, voluntary associations of this sort do not appear to have played such an important role in the cities with which we are concerned here as in America or other parts of Africa, especially West Africa. Burial unions of the sort described existed in East London, but it is not clear from Mayer's account how important they were in mediating relationships among migrants in town. Mayer describes them in terms of 'unions consisting mainly of country-rooted men who want to ensure even if they die in town they can be properly buried, which means buried at home in the country' (Mayer 1961: 81), but gives no details of the membership and operation of these unions. With regard to the Copperbelt, it is interesting that there have been few successful burial societies. Several were in fact founded, but they soon disappeared. The reason for this was possibly that so many of the services which burial societies were organized to supply were in fact supplied by mining authorities and the municipalities in the way of funeral expenses, or were met by the operation of informal friendship networks in the form of monetary contributions to the bereaved family.[12]

To understand the nature of the social relationships amongst migrants in towns, however, we need to appreciate these relationships in the framework of the wider urban and national scene within which they operated. The migrants, by reason of their lack of economic skills, the occupations they were prevailed upon to follow, and their general newcomer status in the

---

[12] Cf. Epstein's comment: 'Where coffins are provided by the local authorities (as they once were on the Copperbelt), there is clearly less need for a burial society.' (1967: 293.)

community, tended to occupy the lower-ranking positions of the social structure. This was true of America, as it is true of Africans in the industrial towns of East London and the Copperbelt. The position of migrants of this sort, Poles in Chicago in fact, is well described by Lopata:

Those who migrated during the period of sizeable movement were primarily peasants from the rural, non-industrial areas of Poland. Upon arrival in the United States, however, they settled mainly in urban, industrialized centres. Since they lacked the knowledge and skills which could be utilized there, they obtained only the lowest paying positions within its economic structure. They lacked the economic resources to command any but the lowest rental housing located in areas of the city which were considered undesirable by the economically more successful dominant groups. The lack of education and of familiarity with urban and industrialized life had the further effect of creating a wide social gap between the peasant migrant and the dominant segments of society. On the part of the peasants, it resulted in bewilderment and confusion about the strange and often hostile and deprecatory world in which they found themselves.

In addition both they and the dominant group were affected by the differences in culture. The Polish language is very different from English; and Polish culture at the time of the migration was primarily feudal, patriarchal, Catholic and characterized by Gemeinschaft relations, especially in the more isolated rural areas. The peasant came from the strata of Polish society in which strong kinship ties and ingroup control were accompanied by a more or less unified, single pattern of behaviour resistant to change. This made the learning of a new culture more difficult for the peasant than for the more cosmopolitan middle and upper class migrant. Although lacking biological traits which would make for visible hereditary differentiation from the dominant American society, his culturally acquired characteristics prevented the first generation from easily assimilating into American society and helped create a physical stereotype of Pole.

All these factors combined with family and even village migration resulted in a tendency of the Poles to desire, or to be forced into living in close physical proximity to each other. Gradually the need for services and activities not available for satisfying the wants peculiar to the Poles led to the growth of a service industry and a multiplicity of voluntary associations among them. Thus a real community arose in the ecologically distinct settlement of Poles in America. By the year 1919 it was possible for a person to live, work, shop, go to church, send the children to school, and spend leisure time within the confines of such a community, never needing to speak English or come into primary contact with members of the dominant group.

Purposeful assimilation is undertaken only when there is a desire for membership in the dominant society and knowledge of the means by which this can be gained; and it can be gained only with the help of the dominant society. The presence and functioning of a community which satisfactorily meets all the needs of its residents is a deterrent to both the desire and acquiring of knowledge necessary to join the dominant society. In the case of the Polish immigrant the desire for immediate acculturation was comparatively weak. Also because of the development of Polish nationalism identification with American society was relatively low in its development. (1964: 204–5.)

Here in general terms is a picture of the relationships between African migrants to colonial cities and the European administrators, businessmen, and professional industrialists who maintained control over the political, economic, and social circumstances of the urban Africans. It is true that the presence of what Lopata described as 'biological traits which would make for visible hereditary differentiation', in other words racial differentiation, in the African cities with which we are concerned, simplified the picture by providing an immediate symbol by which the 'dominant' members of the social order could be recognized and therefore providing an insuperable barrier against Africans 'joining the dominant society', as Lopata puts it. And in this distinction lies the difference in the use of their ethnic identity by later citizens of Polish extraction to further their particular interests on the one hand and the growth of militant nationalist movements on the part of urban Africans in Africa on the other.

Processes of Categorization and Incapsulation

In both American and African cities the immigrants moved into social and economic positions which were subservient to those occupied by ethnically (and in Africa racially) distinct members of the host society. In America the enterprise upon which the cities had been established or were expanding so rapidly during the period we are considering was that of White Anglo-Saxon Protestants. The behaviour of these people represented to the migrants 'the American way of life', and assimilation in the cultural sense meant the eschewing of traditional patterns of behaviour in favour of those characteristic of the dominant group in the society. The resistance of the ethnic groups to assimilation, expressed by adhering to their own customs, by isolating themselves from contact with the dominant groups, and by forming voluntary associations in which their ethnic origins were emphasized, was manifested in similar ways among African migrants into towns. At the same time the children born to the original migrants to the towns both in America and in Africa were faced with different pressures. For American migrants these were seen in terms of Americanization, that is the adoption of the American way of life. This was incorporated in the ideal of the 'melting-pot' notion, which was a popular ideology among those in dominant positions at the turn of the century. In this ideology the Anglo-Saxons were presumed to represent a reference group to whose way of life the migrants were assumed to aspire. In colonial Africa much the same process took place. Here the 'civilized way of life' of the Europeans became the ideal to which the rulers assumed Africans would aspire in towns.

But we need to distinguish between ideology and reality. While the ideology may have been a 'melting-pot' theory of Americanization, some migrants may have rejected it and indeed did. Furthermore, an ideological notion such as that of the 'melting-pot' theory is posed in general terms, so that the assumption is that migrants will change their modes of behaviour to resemble those which the reference groups are per-ceived to exhibit in all aspects of activity. Similarly in Africa many Europeans of goodwill such as missionaries and welfare workers and well-disposed administrators encouraged Africans to adopt what they considered to be 'civilized' ways of behaving, and expected behaviour in general to be guided by the notions of 'civilized' behaviour.

There were two ways in which this 'general' notion of the adoption of reference-group behaviour did not take account of facts. First, there were certain classes of migrants who were resistant to the pressures of adopting European ways of beha-viour, and, secondly, the same person may at different times have addressed himself to norms deriving from the European way of life in some circumstances and to norms deriving from an indigenous African way of life in others.

One of the most striking examples of the way in which migrants to town achieve an identity by rejecting the way of life of the dominant members of the urban society is provided by Philip Mayer's description of what he calls the 'incapsulation' of Red migrants in East London, South Africa. In the rural areas surrounding East London, a division in the local Xhosa society developed on the basis of the extent to which they adopted Christianity and therefore the educational and other attributes of the White man's way of life. Those who remained aloof from Christian influence were known as 'Red' people because of their traditional custom of smearing themselves with red clay at the time of initiation. Those who turned Christian, on the other hand, and who, therefore, had been to school, were called School people. Both Red and School people, because of the dire economic circumstances of the reserves, had to seek employment in the towns, but their reactions to town life were strikingly dissimilar. While in general the School migrants tended to adopt 'town ways' relatively quickly and easily, the Red migrants orientated themselves to their rural homes and isolated themselves from participation in activities which were not based on the value premises of Red culture.

Although they may have had to don 'European'-type clothing while at work, and to follow the clock and the traffic light while going about their work activities, whenever they withdrew from these situations they desisted from making use of the ornaments and accoutrements of the European way of life or adopting behaviour in conformity with it. They were, as Mayer puts it, 'in town but not of it': they were, in fact, incapsulated in the town spending their free time together and relating their behaviour to what they considered to be true Xhosa ways of life, espccially as represented in the rural areas from which they came.

There was, of course, considerable pressure among Red migrants in town not to associate with people who followed a different way of life. Cliques of Red men gathered together to drink and to talk whenever they had free time to spare, and not to do as the School people did, go to cinemas, play sports such as tennis and soccer, or attend religious gatherings. The content of their talk was consistently in terms of the values and norms of Red society, and those who were likely to deviate from the appropriate ways of behaviour were subjected to considerable pressure. The younger men in particular were subjected to admonishments if they started associating with women from the town, for these were considered to be of weak moral character and avaricious to boot.

But it was not only that the moral dangers were feared. Mayer points out that:

town girls are supposed to be avoided by Red men on the specific ground that they constitute a threat to incapsulation. They despise Red ways and have no regard for the country home: thus a man who does not want to get seduced into *ukurumsha* or *ukutshipa* had better have nothing to do with them . . . whether the avoidance of town girls is spontaneous, on grounds of disparity, or distaste, or whether it is forced, on grounds of incapsulated morality, it constitutes one of the most important bulwarks of the Red migrant community.[13] (1961: 123.)

Mayer describes, as we have seen above, an organization of men of approximately the same age and from the same rural district of origin, the *amakaya* who constituted the mechanism of the process of incapsulation of Red migrants. This intense face to face clique maintained close control over the activities of its members. Mayer describes its functions thus:

The values of home and family are exalted by the community-in-exile; home visiting is encouraged; the formation of new social ties in town, with non-Reds, is not only rendered unnecessary but represented as a danger. Kinship obligations, always morally pre-eminent, remain directed towards the country. Parents, wives, and children belong at the kraal, and as the incapsulated migrant will not consider marriage with a town girl, the formation of kinship links with urban families is ruled out. Personal relations with friends and sweethearts are kept, if not within the *amakaya* at least within the Red section. The incapsulated migrant refrains from voluntary association with the School and town-bred people who confront him on every side. He refrains from town-type entertainments, creating instead the nearest possible replica of Red rural entertainment that is possible in town, with the help of his own Red friends from home. (1961: 124–5.)

[13] Mayer (1961: 6–7) describes the word *ukurumsha* as indicating a turncoat in the 'cultural' sense, that is in adopting 'town ways' in preference to one's own ethnic or rustic Xhosa ways. The word *ukutshipa*, derived from the English word 'cheap', is a derogatory word meaning to abscond and is applied to one who cuts himself off from the home community, or to one who is lost completely, as by death.

Several comments made by writers working within the framework of the Chicago sociology school suggest that much the same sort of isolation and incapsulation took place amongst migrants to the United States in the early years of the twentieth century. Consider for example the observations of C. Siu concerning the isolation of Chinese migrants to the United States. He writes:

In essence of such isolation he can best be characterised as a sojourner, a type of stranger who clings to the cultural heritage of his own ethnic group in spite of many years of residing in the community which is foreign to him . . . the social world of the Chinese laundryman, his mind and his life organization is oriented toward homeland ties and ethnic group solidarity and therefore produces a low degree of assimilation to the society of his sojourn. (1964: 442.)

The surface similarity of the social situation of the Chinese migrant in the United States and certain types of African migrant in African cities is clear. But it may be argued that the racial differentiation of the Chinese migrant was a crucial factor in his isolation. It would be difficult to deny this, but my argument would be that the racial characteristics exacerbate a condition which is inherent in the social situation of any migrant to rapidly growing cities.

The rejection of migrants and their retreat into their cultural citadels is a more general process. The perceptive Robert Ezra Park noted this many years ago. He wrote:

It is not among the socialists, anarchists, and radicals, however loud their denunciation of American capitalism, that one finds the least understanding and most positive blind hatred of America. It is rather in these isolated colonies of provincials, who have not become settlers, like the German religious sects, but who like the Italians are maintaining a provincial life in the midst of our cities.

These little communities, composed almost entirely of people of the same village, live entirely upon the news and the gossip of the home community. Every letter to any member of the community is news for the whole community. Nothing goes on in the home village that is not known sooner or later in the American colony of that village. Everyone reckons upon eventually returning home, if for nothing more than a visit. If any member of the colony in America marries outside the community or announces finally that he does not intend to return he is regarded as lost. (1955: 161–2.)

Park supports his observations from a study made by Cusumano of a Sicilian colony in New York. They are migrants from the Cinisi area in Sicily. Cusumano writes:

Most of the Cinisari in the Sixty-Ninth Street group intend to return to Sicily. The town of Cinisi is forever in their minds: 'I wonder if I can get back in time for the next crop'—I hope I can get back in time for the fiesta'—'I hope I can reach Cinisi in time to get a full stomach of Indian figs' etc. They receive mail keeping them informed as to the most minute details and about all the gossip that goes on in Cinisi; in addition they keep the home town informed as to what is going on here. They write home of people here who have transgressed some custom: 'So-and-so is married to an American girl. The American girls are libertines. The boy is very disobedient.' 'So-and-so who failed to succeed at College at Palermo, is here. He has married a stranger'—that is an Italian of another town. In this way they blacken a man's name in Cinisi, so that a bad reputation awaits him on his return.

The reputation given them in Cinisi by report from here means much to them, because they expect to return. Whole families have the date fixed. Those who express openly their intention of remaining here are the young Americanized men.[14]

The similarity between Cusumano's description of Sicilians in New York in the first decade of the twentieth century and Red Xhosa tribesmen in East London in the middle of the same century, in spite of the vastly different cultural backgrounds and social settings of the two groups, is striking. Here is the same negative evaluation of city life and the culture of the dominant ethnic group that stands behind it. Here is the same close-knit set of personal relationships in which the behaviour of members of a common rural home community is gossiped about, here is the same expressed wish to return to the home area although in many cases this may never happen. There is the same abhorrence of the loss of the member, in particular by marriage, and the view that women outside the immediate group are immoral and dangerous because they can entice the young men away from their group of attachment. There is no mention here of the economic support sent back by these Sicilians, but we know from other reports that this was an important element in the relationship between the incapsulated European migrants in

---

[14] The original is a document entitled 'A study of the Colony of Cinisi in New York' by Gaspare Cusumano, quoted by Park and Miller (1921: 150).

American cities and their kinsfolk and dependants in their places of origin.

The types of incapsulation described by Mayer for the Red Xhosa in East London or by Cusumano of the Sicilians in New York are probably extreme cases. Their value is that they illustrate processes which are probably general in all situations where migrants with different linguistic and social backgrounds move into cities where the economic, administrative, and social framework has been erected by people with radically different linguistic and social backgrounds.

How far the type of incapsulation that Mayer describes is common in Africa is difficult to estimate. The description of the Zabrama in Accra which Little quotes from Rouch certainly has much in common with Mayer's:

> High rentals and housing shortages force the migrants to share a small room between three, five or ten and obviously these roommates are always people of the same origin—from the same district if not the same village. The room thus becomes—to use Rouch's graphic expression—'a little regional cell' where one takes one's meals in common and where in the evening after work one talks endlessly of one's country. (1965: 25.)

Similar circumstances prevailed amongst certain types of migrant on the Copperbelt in the 1950s. Here the Nyakyusa migrants in particular tended to herd together in single quarters to the exclusion of men from other groups, and to isolate themselves from the predominantly Bemba culture of the Copperbelt.[15] The point, however, is that some process of establishing identity and support of migrants in the strange environment of the cities into which they moved seems always to have operated. Our task is to explain this general tendency of establishing an identity and creating support in the first place and then to elaborate this explanation to show why certain types of migrants adopt the extreme types of isolation as shown by the Sicilians and Xhosa. To do this we need to examine the wider context within which the migrants are finding a way of life.

One consideration is that manifest differences in culture and language are likely to be appraised in different ways by different categories of person and in different social situations. It is

---

[15] See brief description in chap. 6.

unlikely that to be a 'Pole' or an 'Italian' meant the same thing in all American cities or to all people in any one American city at the beginning of the twentieth century. The relevant point is that the ethnic categories exist as diacritical notions in the minds of persons involved in social relationships and as such become the indicators of appropriate behaviour towards people bearing these labels. The process was exemplified clearly in relationships among people of different ethnic origin on the Copperbelt in the 1950s. The Copperbelt African population, as we noted earlier, was made up of a large number of different 'ethnic' groups. People in these groups, though they may have spoken languages almost identical with those spoken by neighbouring groups and although they may have followed customs almost indistinguishable from those of their neighbours, nevertheless saw themselves as separate people. But the range of variation was wide, so that variation between one 'ethnic group' and another may have been very small, but between others there may have been considerable linguistic, cultural, and social differences. Small differences between people, however significant they may have been for the persons concerned, were often imperceptible to outsiders. The tendency was for relatively small differences to be ignored when relationships with markedly dissimilar people were involved. The net result is that the considerable diversity and complexity of peoples on the Copperbelt tended to be reduced and simplified to a relatively small number of major categorizations in handling relationships with relative strangers in the city context.[16] People, for example, who had no historical claims to be involved in institutionalized joking relationships in town nevertheless became so involved when each placed the other into a category which involved this joking.[17] This tendency was reflected also in the responses of secondary-school boys to questions bearing on social distance. The analysis showed, as we have seen, that 'ethnic' groups tended to be bunched together in categories and that sometimes relatively dissimilar tribes were adjudged in a similar way because they were associated with some other tribes whose identity was clear and known to the respondent.[18]

[16] The problem is discussed more fully in chap. 6.
[17] This is described in Mitchell 1956a: 29 ff.
[18] The procedure of this piece of fieldwork and an analysis of the results are set out in chap. 6.

At this point it must be emphasized that ethnicity emerges as a significant category in social relationships in response to a specific social situation. There is nothing inherent in characteristics of customs, beliefs, and languages which make them socially significant. I have argued elsewhere that a migrant is usually unaware of the peculiarity of the specific sets of beliefs, customs, and language he has until he is thrown into juxtaposition with others whose customs, beliefs, and languages are dissimilar, and these differences become the basis of determining in what way people should react to one another. Park and Miller in 1921 had noted this phenomenon in respect to European migrants to America. After discussing the limited social horizons of peasants in Europe they go on to say: 'We have records showing that members of other immigrant groups realize first in America that they are members of a nationality: "I never realized I was an Albanian until my brother came from America in 1909. He belonged to an Albanian society over there." '[19] In our argument ethnic identity is a characteristic of the set of social relationships in which a person becomes involved, and the implications of the limited social horizons about which Park and Miller wrote are that in the social situation in Europe ethnic distinctiveness had no significance for the peasants. It was only when they came to America that ethnic identity became the basis of ordering social relationships in certain situations.

It follows from this that even in America the significance of ethnic identity itself would not be constant: it would vary from situation to situation. For two Sicilians to recognize that they are fellow Sicilians, or better still, fellow Cinisari, would mean that they shared a good deal of common background and had similar concepts of what was right and wrong, polite and impolite, acceptable and unacceptable to refer to. The level of reference, as it were, is the common participation in a set of social relationships based on their membership of some identified small-scale society. But for an Anglo-Saxon American to recognize a fellow citizen as a Sicilian implies a very different matter. Here the context of interaction is the wider political and economic relationships in which these categories are involved, drawing partly

---

[19] Park and Miller (1921: 145–6). The quotation is from an unpublished life history of Menas Laukas recorded by Winifred Rauschenbusch.

from the current relationships, partly from past historical associations. The meaning with which the relationship is now suffused is occasioned by the perceptions of the actors concerned, not their individual idiosyncratic perceptions but those arising out of commonly accepted meanings, what Durkheim called collective representations.

It is interesting that Park described this process explicitly when discussing the position of the immigrant press in the United States. He writes:

Now, the first effect of city life is to destroy the provincialism of the immigrants and to intensify his sense of racial and national solidarity. This explains why the Jewish people, although they use three distinct foreign languages, German, Yiddish, and Landino, have attained in the United States a degree of solidarity and community organization more efficient than they have attained anywhere else since the Dispersion.

What is true for the Jews is likewise true, though to a lesser degree, of the other urban peoples. Italian immigrants, from all the provinces, with their historical and dialectic differences, brought together in our great cities, have developed a national feeling and sense of solidarity that did not exist in Italy. The national Italian society, which figures so largely in the Italian press on patriotic occasions turns out on analysis to be composed of smaller units which every little colony forms among its members as soon as it is established in his country. These societies are in their turn merely formal organizations of the spontaneous neighbourliness of the Italian village.

This effect of city life is visible in the urban press, where both news columns and editorials create and maintain an active interest in the politics, national and international, of the home country. The larger metropolitan papers, with their wide circulation, are bound to address themselves neither to Bavarians nor to Westphalians, not to Saxons but to Germans; not to Genoese, Neapolitans, Abuzzesi, or Girgentesi but simply to Italians. In this way, residence in our cities has broken down to the local and provincial loyalties, with which the immigrants arrived, and substituted a less intense but wider international loyalty in its place. (Park 1955: 157.)

In the light of what we have learnt about African immigrants in industrializing cities in Africa, we might argue that Park is here describing the process of categorization, in which the internal differences among migrants are submerged in a national context. However, in line with the findings from

African towns we would argue that the dissolution of the provincial links to which he refers is almost certainly situationally defined in the sense that in the context of, say, local relationships of Italians to Italians or Germans to Germans the differences which were insignificant in the national context were likely to reappear. The significance of the differences only emerges where they are relevant. It was not that a wider national loyalty was substituted in the place of the narrower loyalties, but that the narrower loyalties were temporarily suspended while issues on a national scale were raised.

The argument, then, is that under the circumstances where people are being drawn into population concentrations from wide hinterlands such that social backgrounds of the migrants are almost certainly widely disparate, then the very visibility of the ethnicity of the migrants will become a factor in the way in which social relationships in these relatively transient and anonymous situations are mediated. Striking similarities in the reactions of European migrants to American cities at the beginning of the twentieth century and those of African migrants to towns in some parts of Africa in the 1950s lend support to this proposition.

As in all comparative analysis, however, the comparison is being made at a fairly high level of abstraction and under the fairly restricted circumstances of a specified phase of industrial growth. We should at the same time be aware of certain differences in the American and African contexts which may affect the issue substantially, particularly if the analysis were to be extended to subsume the subsequent developments in the phenomena under discussion.

The first of these is distance. European migrants to American cities came from distances which were much greater than those travelled by the average African migrant to an African city. European migrants initially had to cross the Atlantic Ocean and then to make a considerable journey to places where economic opportunities presented themselves. African migrants on the other hand were attracted from local areas varying from a few kilometres distant to several thousand kilometres. In East London about half the adult male population came from within 80 km. of the town and nearly all from within 300 km. (Reader 1961: Table 7, 154). On the Copperbelt half the adult males came from more than 500 km. away, but nearly all from within 1500 km. But distance alone is not significant. The important factor is the ease of communication between the migrants and their kinfolk and friends they have left behind. From this point of view there may not have been much to choose between the ship voyage of migrants across the Atlantic at the end of the nineteenth century and the long and sometimes hazardous journeys African migrants made by foot, bus, and train to their places of work. There seems to be no direct way in which the significance of the differences in distances may be assessed as a factor in the system of social relationships migrants built up in towns in America or Africa. The important common feature was the relative isolation of the migrants from those they had left behind them.

A second difference which probably influenced the pattern of social relationships to a greater degree is the fact that in Africa racial differences have played a significant role in the position of migrants in towns. The migrants we have been considering were African migrants to towns established and dominated by settlers and colonists of a different race. Here skin colour signified the social position of the migrant in a way which he could not escape: under a colonial system in Southern Africa there was no way of his doing so.

It is significant, however, that the problems which so fascinated the Chicago sociologists in the 1920s and 1930s seem now to have lost their force. This appears to have happened particularly after the deliberate restriction of immigration by the United States Federal Government during the late 1920s. The children of the migrants were themselves able to participate in American institutions and to lose their ethnic identity for many purposes in everyday affairs. At the same time the problems which have arisen out of the physical identifiability of migrants, as in the cases of Negroes and Puerto Ricans, have become more obvious. In Africa much the same process was going on. Where former colonial territories have become independent, the divisions in towns between the ethnic groups which were formerly obscured by the distinction against the dominant Europeans have now become patent and serve to provide the rationale for the division, for the present at least, of the populations in the towns. In those parts of Africa where the European minority still maintains economic, political, and social dominance, the division between the races still constitutes a salient factor in the structure of social relationships in towns.

A third feature which may substantially influence the position of migrants in American towns as against those in African towns is the difference in the political significance of notions such as 'Americanization', 'Westernization', and 'Europeanization'. At the outset it should be made clear that we are here concerned with folk-notions of cultural change and not those of academic sociologists and anthropologists.[20] A feature of both American and African cities was the notion that migrants from rural areas or from ethnically dissimilar countries should adopt the way of life appropriate to the cities, which by implication was the way of life of those in the economically, politically, and socially dominant positions. But the point of view of those in power in Africa seems to have been diametrically opposed to the one held by those in America. In America the notion of 'Americanization' apparently became popular during the First World War when American Germans were subjected to odium by patriotic Americans. The pressure on immigrant groups then to declare their loyalty to America was acute. The implicit logic in this demand was that it was their different ethnic backgrounds which separated the immigrant groups from the dominant Anglo-Saxons. Becoming American, therefore, in the sense of adopting American customs, language, values, and concepts, demonstrated the identification of the immigrants with their country of adoption. From the immigrant's point of view becoming Americanized pulled down the barrier restricting them from access to important social and political positions. The pressures from the dominant host community were ostensibly towards the adoption of American ways of living.

In Central and Southern Africa, however, there was a strong feeling among Europeans, and also among some Africans, that Westernization was a destructive process, a process which was erosive of traditional modes of life which in themselves were meritorious and praiseworthy. From the point of view of the dominant European group the reason for this attitude was undoubtedly the challenge which the 'modernized' Africans

[20] The sociological and anthropological concepts are discussed in chap. 3.

presented to them in the political, economic, and social fields, for a 'civilized' or 'Westernized' African was much better equipped to compete with them in all these fields. From the African point of view it represented a division of their political ranks, a dilution of the nationalist drive towards achieving a place for African values and customs in the social scheme.

Park made the interesting point that the ambition of the immigrants to gain recognition in America, 'to represent' the national name 'well in America', as Agaton Giller says, was one of the first characteristic manifestations of national consciousness, and that it was because he had been unable to gain recognition in America as an individual that he sought it as a member of a nationality. One reason immigrants lived in a colony was that they could not get out, and one reason they established nationalist societies which sought among other things to 'represent the old country well' in America was that in this way they could participate in American life. If the immigrant chose to remain a hyphenated American, it was frequently because only through an organization of his own language group could he get status and recognition in the larger American world outside. As a leader in an immigrant community he and the community were enabled to participate in American life in ways which they could not as individuals, unacquainted as they were with the language and customs of the country (1955: 158–9). Park was in effect arguing here that ethnicity as expressed through association was not a fundamental attribute of the migrants but rather that it was the product of a social order in which they occupied a particular location, a location which led them to utilize their ethnic distinctiveness to further their ends in that order.[21] This is in line with the way in which some of us have argued about what has been called 'tribalism' in African cities. The similarity in the reaction of migrants, then, we could argue, arose out of the similarity of the social circumstances in the two instances.

Looking upon ethnicity as a reaction to a social order rather than as an attribute of the persons involved allows us to ask questions about the process of assimilation in America and presumably also in Africa. Gordon (1964) has drawn the distinction between cultural assimilation on the one hand and structural

---

[21] The reference is to Park and Miller 1921: 288.

assimilation on the other. Cultural assimilation refers to the process whereby people adopt the beliefs, customs, attitudes, and orientations of some other group, whereas structural assimilation refers to the involvement of the migrant group in social relationships with the host group. It is quite clear that cultural assimilation does not imply structural assimilation, for it is abundantly clear that however much the way of life of an African resembled that of the Europeans in colonial Africa this did not mean that he would be accepted into close personal social relationships with them. This presumably was the case in America: it is implicit in the statement that Park made. Structural assimilation would mean that the migrant groups would have equal access to positions of influence and power as the Anglo-Saxon élite. Clearly this did not occur very easily. Instead we find that people who were identified in ethnic terms began to use their ethnic identity to compete for power within the larger social order. Thus the Polish voluntary associations that Lopata described in Chicago eventually became pressure groups putting forward their own representatives for political office and using those who succeeded as a means of improving their position within the social order as a whole.

There are certain similarities, therefore, in ethnicity in African and American cities. The similarities lie in the way which migrants drawn into a city in which there is a relatively well-established economic and administrative system and where the earlier entrepreneurs have already established themselves in residential areas and in industrial, commercial, and political office fall back upon their manifest cultural distinctiveness and utilize this distinctiveness in their relationships with both their fellow countrymen and the outsiders with whom they come into daily contact. The similarity in the two sets of phenomena arose not out of ethnicity as a basic circumstance of human existence, but rather out of the general set of social circumstances that have arisen at different times and at different places in history.

8

COMPARISON AND ANALYSIS:
FORMULATIONS OF CITY LIFE

The purpose of comparative analysis is to make apparent the connections between events which otherwise we may take as unrelated. In the 'case study' approach to comparative analysis, which I advocate, the analyst, by choosing stategically informative instances, should be able to show why expected behaviour in similar circumstances is different or why actual behaviour in apparently different circumstances is similar. The art of comparative analysis is that of locating social behaviour in similar or different settings and situations so as to demonstrate logical connections.

The theoretical notions which are the medium through which these logical connections may be established arise out of the interaction between current modes of thought and the particular set of empirical data with which the analyst is confronted. The similarities in the descriptions of urban conditions in America during its phase of industrial expansion and those in Africa in a comparable phase are a reflection of this interaction.

It is, I argue, no accident that there were two related concepts which ran through the work of the sociologists at Chicago in the inter-war years that are of direct relevance to studies of towns in Africa. The first of these is the incorporation of the notion of 'culture' into the analyses of urban behaviour and the second is the concern with the notion of disorganization.

It seems reasonably certain that Chicago sociologists were familiar with the idea of culture, since foremost amongst their number had been W. I. Thomas, whose *Source Book for Social Origins*, published in 1909, was a collection of data on the material culture and social institutions of primitive peoples. He followed this in 1927 with *Primitive Behaviour*, in which he used the concept of culture quite explicitly. Thomas seems to have had a direct influence on Park's thinking. Thomas had recruited

Park for the University of Chicago in 1913, and it is reported that they remained close friends for the rest of their lives. The problem of the adjustment of migrants to host communities was one in which Thomas has become involved in his study *The Polish Peasant*. The influence of Thomas' thinking is evident in *Old World Traits Transplanted* (Park and Miller 1921). Certainly, however, Park made good use of the material presented in that work and quoted extensively from it in his later essays. In Park's writings there are frequent references to the writings of Clark Wissler, W. H. R. Rivers, and later to Malinowski. Throughout his writings he made extensive use of the notion of culture, and this is shown in the titles of many of his essays, such as 'Culture and Civilization', 'The Problem of Cultural Differences', 'Cultures and Cultural Trends', and 'Personality and Cultural Conflict and the Marginal Man'. In due course the problems of the adjustment of migrants to life in the towns through the processes of culture change and culture conflict became for Park the essence of the nature of the city. Cities thus became centres of social change through the agencies of social contact. He writes:

Modern life is characteristically urban, but modern cities are notoriously the products of the steamship, the locomotive, and the automobile. Modern life is, by the same token, the product of the telegraph, the telephone and the newspaper, particularly since communication has, in the long run, the same social consequences as locomotion. Both tend to break up what Bagehot calls 'the cake of custom', to release the individual from the routine of tradition, and to stimulate him to undertake new enterprises.' (1950: 11.)

For Park then the human consequences of living in cities were that controls, intellectual and moral, on the individual were weakened and that this allowed new ideas, new values, and new ways of behaving to come into being and develop. The city, therefore, was the focal point of social change. The very forces which engendered change were necessarily the forces which led to the breakdown of stability in values, social relationships and the pattern of social behaviour. The city, therefore, was also the focal point of 'disorganization'. Burgess and Bogue describe this approach thus:

Burgeoning American cities were filled with migrants who had been released from old established customs and definitions in their home communities, and who were relocated in a context where a new social organization and forms of social control had not yet been firmly established. The city was regarded as a type of human community where social organization was literally inadequate and incomplete, and hence where disorganization was common. Social problems could be regarded as side effects of social changes, and something that would tend to disappear as social organization, accommodation and assimilation progressed. This approach holds that in the urban setting many cultures are brought into contact with each other, with the result that old and established customs and definitions cease to command adherence and exercise social control. Persons become familiar with two or more value systems and feel loyalty or moral obligation to no one system. The result is comparative normlessness and ego-centred and highly diverse behaviour. (1964: 488.)

It is interesting that many of those who had set out initially to study towns in the Central and Southern part of Africa should have seen problems in much the same way. They were concerned with a large number of people, most of whom had formerly lived in a traditional order in rural areas, who were now gathered from many diverse regions in the dense settlements of expanding industrial towns. There was little in the traditional backgrounds of these migrants to which they could have turned as the basis of ordering their relationships with authorities, employers, fellow migrants, and the numerous contingencies that impinge upon a town dweller in the course of the ordinary day. In these circumstances the problem could be posed in terms of the migrants learning new ways of behaviour or simply as acculturation. 'Urbanization', therefore, in this approach was an aspect of 'culture change', and since the way of life particularly relevant to urban living was that of the Europeans who had established the towns, urbanization was in many ways synonymous with Westernization, and, at the same time, since it meant abjuring traditional modes of behaviour, it was also consistent with 'detribalization'. Not surprisingly, administrators and politicians in particular formulated the problems of urbanization of Africans in these terms, but in addition many anthropologists and sociologists in the inter-war years, such as Krige, Hellman, and Hunter, conceptualized the problems in much the same way. These scholars working in Africa were well into the mainstream of thought at the time.

Many had studied under Malinowski, who was working then on his notions of culture change, a consequence of which he considered to be social and personal disorganization in towns. He wrote, for example, in a book devoted to the problem of culture change:

But the complete extinction of really effective authority, of an orderly way of carrying out the business of procreation, of safeguarding property and maintaining law and order or producing food and other necessities for society, would result in complete anarchy and disorganization. In fact, there are sections of detribalized Africa where something like such a state as this already exists in some respects.

In a footnote he instances 'the floating population of the Copperbelt and in the lowest Black proletariat of Native townships and locations' (1945: 33). Later he compares the situation of a family living in a tribal reserve with that of one living in an urban location. He writes: 'The detribalized household has been accustomed to a much higher standard of living, essentially inherent in the fact that it is a partly Europeanized family, with the needs of education, clothing, hygiene and cleanliness' (1945: 159). Here the association of detribalization with acculturation is clearly implied. It is the substitution of one culture for the other.

Thus in this argument the processes of urbanization, detribalization, and Europeanization (or Westernization) are closely connected. When Africans come to live in towns they are confronted with circumstances in which traditional ways of life are no longer appropriate, since the major patterns of social behaviour in the towns are based on activities connected with Western economic, political, and administrative processes. Detribalization in its positive aspect refers to Westernization, in the sense that traditional modes of belief, behaviour, and of evaluation are replaced by 'Western' modes.

The interpretation of the social behaviour of migrants in towns in terms of these general processes, however adequate it may have seemed at the time, has since come to be recognized as inadequate in at least two ways. Firstly, the sort of behaviour which might have been anticipated from an understanding of these processes rarely occurred. Secondly, there were instances of behaviour which did occur, but which were difficult to interpret in terms of the general processes assumed to lie behind them. These discrepancies arose not from faulty observations, for it is in their own descriptions of the behaviour of migrants that the inconsistencies are to be seen. They stemmed rather from the set of assumptions the earlier writers made about the nature of social phenomena.

There were at least two basic types of assumption which writers in the 1920s and 1930s made about the epistemological status of the concepts they were using which unwittingly led them to overlook important aspects of the behaviour of migrants in towns, assumptions which still occasionally appear in the writings of sociologists and anthropologists. For convenience we might label these 'psychologistic' and 'ethnologistic' assumptions.

The task before the analyst was that of providing an interpretation of the patterns of behaviour of migrants from rural areas or small towns who had moved into industrial towns which were expanding at a rate which far outstripped the capacity of the urban population to replace itself naturally. Furthermore, the problem was not that of providing a complete explanation of the behaviour of the migrants, but merely those aspects of behaviour which could be taken as orientated to other people, in other words *social* behaviour. From the outset, therefore, a problem of circumscription is involved: the problem is circumscribed by accepting only some aspects of behaviour as representing the phenomena to be explained. The restriction of the behaviour to the 'social' implies that the relationships of the migrants to one another and to various 'outsiders' are an essential part of the process of circumscription.

I mean by 'psychologistic assumptions' that analysts, in the way they describe and explain the behaviour of migrants in town, appear to assume implicitly that these behaviour patterns have their origin essentially in the psychic organization of individuals: they are part of the habit structure of individuals. It would be captious to argue that they are not. The difficulty arises when it is assumed that these patterns are not affected by social relationships in which people happen to be involved and that these relationships are not likely to change abruptly at times. To caricature the argument one might say that those who make psychologistic assumptions explain social behaviour as if it were part of the neural structure of individuals who react in a simple stimulus–response way to situations which confront them. Ethnologistic assumptions are of the same type, except that those who are trying to explain the behaviour of migrants in the towns and who make these assumptions argue as if the ways of behaving, of believing, and of evaluating have an existence in their own right, almost independently, as it were, of the actual set of social relationships in which the migrants are involved. By this argument migrants behave in accordance with their 'cultures', and these cultures are capable of being described systematically by the observer almost as a set of rules which determine the behaviour of migrants in whatever circumstances they find themselves.

Psychologistic Assumptions

Both these assumptions refer to the way in which the concept of 'culture' is related to behaviour and turn essentially on the way in which the notion of a 'culture' is initially arrived at. How psychologistic assumptions operated to obscure certain insights into the behaviour of migrants in town may be illustrated by the way in which Park moved from the notion of culture to the behaviour of individuals. Park defined culture as 'those habits in individuals which have become customary, conventionalized and accepted in the community' (1950: 3). Note that Park sees 'culture' as being rooted primarily in 'habits in individuals', and he relates these to the social environment through restricting these habits to those which have become socially accepted. It is possible that we may read too much into what Park implied by 'habits', and that he merely meant by this word 'regular ways of behaving'. Whatever the intention, however, the issue is that from a sociological point of view it shifts the focus of analysis away from social relationships toward the individual, and this is where the difficulties in making psychologistic assumptions arise in analysing social behaviour. Later Park distinguishes between 'culture' on the one hand and 'civilization' on the other, culture being the sort of order existing in a society that has a cult or a religion. It 'preserves morals and enables the group to act collectively. Most of our institutions enable us in our society to act with unanimity in times of danger . . . They serve to maintain the integrity of the system.' Civilization, on the other hand, refers to a wider territorial system. He says, therefore: 'if we could use the word *culture* to refer to a society that has a moral order and civilization to refer to the order that applies to a territorial group we could bring out the important distinction more clearly' (1950: 16).

The distinction Park makes between 'culture' and 'civilization' is not the point at issue here. What I want to draw from these definitions is rather that Park and those who followed his way of thinking used the word 'culture' to refer essentially to the normative order of social relationships. The moral or normative aspect of behaviour they thought of essentially as being incorporated in the personality, or, perhaps better, the character structure of individuals. In this sense assimilation to American culture, or Americanization, as it came to be known, was conceived of as the process whereby individuals adopted the habits and modes of behaviour that were in accord with the norms of American society.

Much the same sort of approach characterized studies of 'detribalization' in African towns. Traditional norms of behaviour or in other words 'tribal culture' relate to the individual and therefore lead to the expectation that an individual facing the social circumstances that arise in towns should react to them in terms of the norms previously internalized. The disorganized behaviour which is taken to be characteristic of the 'detribalized' migrant in this formation is due either to the fact that the individual internalized no norms which are appropriate to the circumstances in which he finds himself, or that the norms he has internalized are inappropriate, so that this leads to conflict and frustration and ultimately to anti-social behaviour.

The psychologistic assumptions underlying the relationship between culture on the one hand and behaviour on the other are perhaps most clearly brought out in the writings concerning 'the marginal man'. It is in these writings too that the concordance between the approach of the Chicago sociologists and the Africanists studying towns is most apparent. Park expresses the assumptions explicitly in discussing the notion of the marginal man, for in this context he writes: 'It is in the mind of the marginal man that the moral turmoil which new cultural contacts occasion, manifests itself in the most obvious forms. It is in the mind of the marginal man—where changes and fusions of culture are going on—that we can study the processes of civilization and of progress' (1950: 365). Or, referring specifically to social disorganization, he writes: 'Cultural conflicts when they do not provoke mass movement are likely to manifest themselves in family disorganization, in delinquency, and in functional derangement of the individual psyche' (1950: 369). We are again in difficulties when trying to decide to what extent Park uses a word like 'mind' in a technical and highly specific way, or what he meant exactly when he said that cultural conflicts are likely to *manifest* themselves in derangements of the individual psyche. If he uses the word *mind* here as a general word for the sets of perceptions of individuals, then there could be no objection to the statement. Or if by 'manifesting' he means that psychological derangements are more common under circumstances where the individual perceives himself to be in a state of conflict, then similarly there could be little objection to the use of the word. But the implication of these interpretations is that they are treated sociologically as a derivative of the *social* circumstances in which the individual finds himself. Our attention should then be directed to the social circumstances and not to the psychological states. This is not to deny the validity of the study of the psychological states of individuals who are conscious of conflicting demands based on different evaluations of normal expectations upon them. It is merely that in studies of that sort the 'culture' would need to be taken as given or assumed in the Devons and Gluckman sense, that is as part of the context of the analysis of the psychological states of individuals, and would be treated as primitive data while the main attention was devoted to the form of the differing expectations to which an individual is subjected.

The mode of thinking which flows from psychologistic assumptions of this sort emerges particularly clearly when problems of what is called 'culture conflict' are discussed. Park writes:

Cultural conflict seems to be an incident of cultural assimilation and the result is that those persons who are, so to speak, in transit become the melting pot or melting pots in which the cultural processes take place. This is the case in a peculiar sense of the so-called marginal man, i.e. the individual who finds himself on the margins of two cultures and not fully or permanently accommodated to either. (1950: 370.)

Note here that the persons are 'in transit' and that the individuals are the 'melting pots', where the plural form is highly significant. It is true that Park here was writing deliberately about the relationship between personality on the one hand and the conflicts and uncertainty with which individuals are confronted under changing circumstances on the other. But the problem before us is to understand the changing forms themselves as sociological phenomena, an analysis which can proceed independently of the consequences of these changes on the emotions, perceptions, and reactions of the individuals who are involved in them.

The difficulty with making psychologistic assumptions in anthropological or sociological analyses is that unless they are explicitly acknowledged and recognized by those who are making them they may lead to fallacies of misplaced concreteness. I mean by this that the regularities we perceive in the process of anthropological or sociological observation and analysis are abstractions made from the behaviour of individuals. To assume that these abstractions necessarily relate to a basis of behaviour which was not germane to the original observation attributes a concreteness to the regularities which is not an essential part of them. The anthropologist notes, for example, that whenever a man meets his mother-in-law in a rural area he politely steps aside to allow her to pass. At this level of observation all that he is entitled to do is establish the regularity of the behaviour as part of a social situation. To make further assumptions about the way this behaviour is incorporated into the personalities of the actors would entail going beyond the limits of this kind of observation.

Some untoward consequences of making psychologistic assumptions are manifested when observers studying the behaviour of African migrants in towns attribute norms and patterns of behaviour of the migrants to their individual characters rather than to their behaving within an appropriate institutional context. 'Individuals behaving within an institutional context' is a different order of abstraction from that of individuals alone, and the error comes when the behaviour is assumed to be fixed in *any* social situation. It is to this assumption that I drew attention when I distinguished between processual and situational change.[1] (Mitchell 1966b: 44). The notion of an institution, after all, is an abstraction from the actual behaviour of people who are taken to be interacting in terms of that institution. The norms and patterns of expectation of the behaviour are characteristic of the relationships among the members of the institution and not of the members themselves, so that if for some reason the institutional context should change, we would tautologously expect the behaviour to change as well.

Ethnologistic Assumptions

Analyses involving ethnologistic assumptions are similar to those involving psychologistic assumptions in two respects. Firstly these analyses tend, as do those involving psychologistic assumptions, to attribute undue concreteness to the notion of 'culture'. Secondly like the analyses which involve psychologistic assumptions they tend to state the regularities of social behaviour as generalizations without sufficient attention to the interactional contexts in which they appear, and therefore they tend to obscure the salience of social contexts.

Analysts who make ethnologistic assumptions are prone to reify the abstract notion of 'culture' as a causative factor in social behaviour. Meyer Fortes drew attention to this point as early as 1938, when he castigated those who spoke in terms of 'culture contact', and pointed out that in fact it was the persons themselves who were coming into contact and not their cultures (1938: 11). Writing in this way was common in the 1930s during the period when Malinowski was developing his schema for analysing changes in cultures using his 'three column approach'. The methodological weaknesses of this approach have been adequately exposed by Gluckman's analysis (1949), and it is not my intention to cover the same ground here. All that I wish to emphasize is that one of the pitfalls in this procedure is that each cultural state in Malinowski's schema is looked upon as an entity on its own—the culture that results from the contact

---

[1] Processual change is the change in institutions or patterns of behaviour over time. Situational change is the change in behaviour of an actor moving from one situation to another.

of European and Africans as in towns, for example is, in Malinowski's own terminology, a *tertium quid*. The abstractions thus are treated as if they were substantive realities and are attributed with the qualities of substantive realities in the analytical schema of the analyst who makes this type of assumption. We find, for example, Hellman writing in the late 1930s: 'The available evidence suggests however that, despite the extent to which cultural absorption is undoubtedly taking place, native culture is not being submerged by European culture.' (1937: 433.)

The same difficulty crops up in analyses made by the Chicago sociologists concerning social change in relation to migrants. This is particularly well illustrated by the way in which Stonequist writes of the marginal man. Referring particularly to what he calls 'Europeanized Africans', Stonequist writes:

migration of natives to new work centers and the loss of land in some areas is likely to detribalize and individualize the native African. Tribal public opinion weakens as does the authority of the chiefs and elders. Missionary education has also had important effects in loosening the ties of African societies without always integrating the convert to a Western group; and the role of the missionary is contradicted in practice by the effect of economic exploitation. Thus the sequence may be one where detribalization breaks down traditional ideas and introduces some of the western. (1964: 332–3.)

The basic argument in this passage seems to be that certain general processes are going on—individualization and detribalization—which are presumably manifested in the behaviour of particular migrants in particular social actions in particular towns. But the interactional contexts in which these phenomena are manifested are not specified. Instead Stonequist writes of the processes as if they were substantive phenomena. So he writes 'detribalization breaks down traditional ideas and introduces some of the Western'.

Inexplicit psychologistic and ethnologistic assumptions were of course a feature of a stage in the development of sociological thought. At the time when the studies in Chicago were being made and when Malinowski and his students were making studies of social change in Africa, the notion of culture was a new tool in the analyst's hands. The advantages of analysing social phenomena in terms of the concept of culture as against current alternatives must have been considerable at that time. Equally, social psychology had only recently established itself as an academic discipline and the study of social behaviour as manifested in individual behaviour was only then in its beginnings. This does not mean that I imply that similar assumptions are not made implicitly today: they sometimes are. The point is that the sophistication in the use of these concepts had to wait until their novelty had worn off.

It is interesting, however, that towards the end of the 1930s several scholars began to re-examine the implicit assumptions which were being made in current sociological analysis, and that out of these criticisms have developed several approaches which avoid some of the defects of the older and introduce new demands of their own.

Situational Analysis

One of these approaches is situational analysis, which throws the weight of the analysis on to the interactional context rather than the backgrounds of the individuals involved or the 'cultures' in terms of which they are interacting. The starting point was W. I. Thomas's notion of the definition of the situation. The importance of this idea was that it located the reality of norms and customs in the perceptions of the actors in a social situation. Thomas's famous dictum that 'If men define situations as real, they are real in their consequences' implied shifting the emphasis from phenomena to the subjective perceptions of actors. In a sociological framework this meant that the way in which an actor perceived the actions of people with whom he was involved determined the way in which he would act in response. In fact, however, Thomas himself still thought of social situations as learning situations, that is as sets of circumstances in which individuals learn to behave in certain ways. He writes: 'It appears that the particular behaviour patterns and the total personality are overwhelmingly conditioned by the types of situations and trains of experience encountered by the individual in the course of his life.' (1966: 154). He defines the situations as 'the configuration of the factors conditioning the behaviour reaction'. His view of the role of the social situation is perhaps most clearly shown by the following passage:

The situations which the individual encounters, into which he is forced, or which he creates, disclose the character of his adaptive strivings, positive or negative, progressive or regressive, his claims, attainments, renunciations, and compromise. For the human personality also the most important content of situations is the attitudes and values of other persons with which his own come into conflict and cooperation, and I have thus in mind the study of types of situation which reveal the role of attitudes and values in the process of behavior adaptation. (1966: 155.)

It is true that Thomas is here concerned not with the social situation *per se*, but rather with the effect of the social situation on personality problems, particularly on juvenile delinquency, which he then goes on to analyse. But the implication is nevertheless that behaviour is construed as a fixed attribute of the individual rather than, as we shall argue, a reaction to the meaning which an actor reads into the social cues which are presented to him in a situation. The implication of this change in emphasis is that the same individual is likely to react quite differently to the same objective situation if that individual perceives a different set of meanings in it.

The notion of situational selection was used by Evans-Pritchard, as I pointed out in his analysis of Azande witchcraft in 1937 (see chap. 1). In the course of this study Evans-Pritchard argued that Azande, when consulting oracles, were likely to select from a variety of possible constructions of actions one that suited their purpose at the time. Thus from one seance to another the behaviour may have appeared to have lacked consistency and regularity, but when seen in the context of the circumstances that the individual saw himself to be in at each seance the rationality and logic in the behaviour became immediately apparent. Gluckman applied and developed this basic idea in a paper dealing with an entirely different topic in 1940 (Gluckman 1958). In this paper he sets out an analysis of the behaviour of a variety of social personalities during the formal opening of a bridge in Zululand. The behaviour of the people present at this ceremony, Gluckman shows, can be related directly to the positions these people hold in the social structure of the local community and in the nation as a whole on the one hand, and to the way in which these individuals perceive the situation on the other. Thus while the Native Commissioner behaves, in so far as Gluckman's observations are concerned, mainly in terms of his official role, the Zulu chief whom Gluckman was accompanying to the opening adopts different patterns of behaviour as he encounters people in different roles during the day. This is strikingly illustrated when he encounters a policeman who is at the same time a member of the royal clan. The chief's behaviour vacillates between paying respect to the royal Zulu clan and treating the policeman as a representative of the White-dominated government. The behaviour of the chief here, if one makes the assumptions that his attitudes are a fixed part of his personality or that they are simply an attribute of the culture of the Zulu in general or of Zulu chiefs in particular, is inconsistent. But Gluckman's analysis shows clearly that the inconsistency has its origins in the structure of social relationships as a whole in which the chief is involved. Through understanding the structure of social relationships as a whole we can understand the behaviour of the chief as a rational reaction to a social situation.

The advantages of using an approach of this kind can be shown by referring to a contradiction which Park, with his usual acuteness and perspicacity, described in the behaviour of Chinese immigrants to the United States. Park noted that the behaviour of Chinese immigrants was likely to change during different phases of their life:

Children do not inherit the cultural complexes of their parents, and when children of immigrants grow up in the country of their adoption they inevitably take over all the accents, the inflection, the local cultural idioms of the native population. This is true of the Chinese of America, even though they are reared—as most of them are—in a ghetto. Most of the native sons among the Chinese in California are outrageously American in their manners and in their sentiments. It is only in later life, if at all, that they revert to the ancestral traditions and achieve a secondary racial loyalty. (1950: 26–7.)

Clearly there is an inconsistency here if one adopts the point of view either that the attitudes and behaviour patterns of the Chinese immigrants are part and parcel of their psychological make-up, or the view that the attitudes and behaviour patterns are part of the culture of the immigrants in America. Park does not seem to have been aware of the significance of this contradiction, since although he comments on this problem he does not return to explain it or to explore it any further.

Using an approach developed from the notions of situational selection and situational analysis, and drawing from experience of analysing similar sorts of phenomena among migrants in African towns, we may attempt to refine the analysis of the behaviour of the Chinese immigrants to their American experiences by relating it to different life phases in the following way: the behaviour of Chinese persons in the United States as a whole was a function in the first instance of their position in the overall social structure. The high-ranking status positions in the overall social structure were pre-empted initially by persons of white skin colour, typically Anglo-Saxon Protestants. Initially young Chinese persons evaluated themselves against young White Americans in their peer groups and adopted the behaviour characteristics and ways of behaving which resembled these. Their identification at this stage of their careers therefore was with their White American peers. They sought prestige and status in terms of these criteria and became, as Park put it, 'outrageously American'. In time, however, the frustrations arising from the lack of access to highly prestigious positions in the social order and in particular their exclusion from association on an equal basis with White Americans led some of them to seek prestige in terms of a set of evaluative criteria which the White Americans did not and in fact could not possess. They now sought an identity which reinforced their ethnic distinctiveness and reverted, as Parks put it, 'to the ancestral traditions and achieve[d] a secondary racial loyalty'.

A formulation in these terms enables us to understand both why native sons of Chinese immigrants were so 'outrageously American' and also possibly why the same Chinese immigrants in later life adopted what Park calls 'ancestral traditions'. Furthermore, treating the cultural characteristics of the Chinese immigrants as diacritical elements in their relationships with non-Chinese, that is as elements which served to signify their identities, we are able to understand that the 'ancestral traditions' did not need in fact to represent traditional Chinese customs accurately, but merely to serve to advertise that the person practising these customs was marking himself off from the non-Chinese. It is sufficient that the customs should be *seen* to be Chinese: they did not need necessarily to be ethnographically accurate. The question now raised is what were the circumstances in the lives of those who 'reverted', in Park's words. Are we able to specify what sort of factors operated to lead some Chinese immigrants in later life to 'revert to ancestral traditions', while others do not'? Our theoretical orientation, thus, leads us on to new empirical enquiries.

This is an application of the thinking used by Gluckman in his analysis of the formal opening of the bridge in Zululand. By adopting an approach that accepts that there may be several different and sometimes contradictory norms against which an actor may measure his behaviour in different situations, we avoid the difficulties that flow from making either psychologistic or ethnologistic assumptions. The Polish immigrant, we may argue, would not be a Pole in every social situation in which he was involved throughout the day. He may be a machine operator abiding by the work-restricting norms of his job and siding in this matter with fellow workman of different ethnic origin at one point of time; at lunch-time he may associate with other Poles and enjoy Polish food with them, thus cutting himself off from his fellow workers of different ethnic origins; to his peasant mother and father he may nevertheless appear to be 'outrageously American', however 'outrageously Polish' he may appear to his non-Polish workmates. He may co-operate with other Poles from the urban district in which he lives to safeguard his rights against what he considers to be political exploitation and use a Polish ethnic association to do so, emphasizing his Polish origin in the process, but a Negro neighbour may categorize him together with Anglo-Saxon Whites as but another white oppressor. In terms of situational analysis we would expect that a Polish immigrant would not be a Polish immigrant in all contexts through which he moves in his daily life. His Polish origins at times would be submerged by wider loyalties or would not appear to be relevant, but at other times would become the major element in his interaction in different ways with some other person who was, or was not, Polish. The immigrant status, in other words, is an emergent property of the relationship between persons and not of the individual himself.

We could thus interpret in a sociological framework the secondary loyalty of the son of the Chinese immigrant in terms of the position of that person in the whole status system of the city without referring to the internalized norms that the American-Chinese acquired as a child.

The situational approach also helps us to appreciate two points which have appeared in the studies of Americanization in the United States. The first arises in connection with the way in which children of immigrants related their behaviour in domestic situations, for example, particularly to the norms of the Anglo-Saxon Americans rather than to those which their parents had expected they would, that is, those of the ethnic group from which they had originated. Wirth perceptively noted that: 'The term "Americanization" as Park and Miller point out is not used popularly among immigrants as we use it. They call a badly demoralized boy "completely Americanized".' (Wirth 1964*b*: 235.)[2] Clearly reference to the norms associated with Anglo-Saxon Americans did not have the same cachet in all social situations. These norms appear to have had a positive value for the children of immigrant parents in the peer group, while in a domestic situation they had a negative value. One would expect that the children of foreign-born parents would avoid embarassment by behaving in terms of different sets of norms in different situations and would be faced with conflict only if and when they found themselves in a position where they had to appeal simultaneously to contradictory norms in order to justify their behaviour.

The other situation refers to the position of German Americans in the First World War or of Japanese Americans in the Second World War. Prior to these national crises the putative dual loyalty of these categories presented no public problem. Their German or Japanese ethnic background became significant only in some situations: it did not provide the basis of a total categorization such as skin colour does in Southern Africa or in some parts of the United States. But during the crisis such indeterminacy could not be tolerated, and Americans of German origin in the First World War, and those of Japanese origin in the Second, were called upon to shed one of their

[2] The reference is to Park and Miller 1921: 288.

conflicting statuses in favour of the other. In sociological terms we are dealing with a process of categorization called forth by the national crisis in which the identity of the person had to be resolved so that the norms in terms of which social relationships should be had with them could be specified.

The pressure to resolve equivocal statuses in crisis situations is a common feature of social relationships. The implication of this is, however, that equivocal identities and categorizations may coexist in social relationships among a set of persons without giving rise to conflict. It is only when some crisis arises in which the equivocality of the statuses gives rise to uncertainty in social relationships that some public demand for clarification arises. The classic example from the Copperbelt studies is that of the position of Tribal Representatives in their relationship with the management of the copper-mining companies on the one hand and the African Mineworkers Trade Union on the other (Epstein 1958). African workers, grouped according to their tribal origins in the copper-mines since the early 1930s, had elected one of their number to represent their interests to management. At this time there were no African trade unions, and for many years the Tribal Representatives served as an adequate channel of communication between workers and management. Crises between the African workers and management, however, arose periodically as time went on. There were riots leading to Commissions of Enquiry in 1935 and 1940. It is significant that during these riots the Tribal Representatives were rejected by the African workers as their representatives to the mine managements. At these times of crisis the disaffected workers apparently identified the Tribal Representatives with the management and sought other means to make their demands known to the management. The intermediary or 'intercalary' role of the Tribal Representatives called for a resolution in terms of the sharply divided allegiances at the time of crisis.

Much the same argument could be applied to the position of the African chiefs whose traditional role located them firmly within the 'tribal' social systems but whose administrative role aligned them with the colonial governments. While there were no open oppositions between the two categories the chiefs could maintain their dual role without too much difficulty. But as

alignments polarized with the growth of the African independence movement, the chiefs were required to declare their
stands. Some elected to emphasize their official role with the
colonial governments, others their role as leaders of an indigenous African population in opposition to the government, but
few could maintain their dual status (Watson 1958).

The position of national minorities whose parent countries
were at war with the United States appears to have been identical, and we can perhaps interpret the behaviour of patriotic
Americans at this time as an expression of solidarity during a
crisis in which those who might align themselves wholeheartedly
with the war effort had to be identified.

Disorganization: Primary Contacts and Networks

We have been considering thus far the general or macroscopic
features of the relationships of members of ethnic categories to
one another and to members of dominant ethnic categories
during a time when, owing to rapid economic growth, large
numbers of migrants were thrown together in expanding towns
and cities. The processes manifested here are phrased in terms of
the abstract qualities of ethnic membership and the identities of
people as representatives of these categories.

The behaviour of these same migrants, however, when
examined at the personal level has attracted the attention of
social analysts both in Africa and America because of its discrepancy with the behaviour evinced by these same migrants in
their rural homes prior to their departure. This is implicit in the
analysis, as was common in the 1930s, of the behaviour of
Africans in towns in terms of 'detribalization'. In America, the
caustic comment has been made that the Chicago sociologists
were in fact all imbued with the myth of Arcadia and implicitly
used an idealized rural community as the comparative base
point against which to assess the behaviour of migrants in
towns.[3]

In the Chicago school much of the thinking on this topic seems
to have stemmed from Thomas's work on the Polish migrants to
America. The personal disorganization of migrants in America

---

[3] See for example Stein's (1960: 15–16) comments on the Chicago sociologists.

and particularly in American cities in this formulation was related to the breakdown of the primary relations in these circumstances. The argument is summarized clearly in this passage from *The Polish Peasant*:

But it must be further realized that an individual who, like the peasant, has been brought up as a member of a permanent and coherent primary-group and accustomed to rely for all regulation of conduct upon habit and the immediate suggestions and reactions of his social milieu is much more helpless when his milieu fails to give him stimuli sufficiently continuous, varied and coercive for socially normal action than an individual who, like a city intellectual, has been accustomed to be satisfied with such superficial social stimulations as can be obtained from mere acquaintances or business contacts, has been trained to foresee and to be influenced by distant and indirect social consequences of his behaviour, knows how to regulate his conduct consciously in accordance with general abstract schemes and supplements any insufficiency of present social influences by personal ideals which society has helped him to develop in the past . . . In order to recognize his [the Polish peasant's] life on a new basis he needs a primary group as strong and coherent as the one he left in the old country. The Polish-American society gives him a few new schemes of life, but not enough to cover all of his activities. A certain lowering of his moral level is thus inevitable. Though it does not always lead to active demoralization, to anti-social behaviour, it manifests itself at least in what we may call passive demoralization, a partial or a general weakening of social interests, a growing narrowness or shallowness of the individual's social life. (Thomas and Znaniecki 1958: vol. ii, 1649–50.)

The relationship between primary contacts and 'demoralization' was stated more baldly by Park and Miller. They wrote:

If the face-to-face organization which made the immigrant moral at home is suddenly dissolved in this country, we have the general situation presented in the documents on demoralization [earlier in the book]. We saw there that men removed from the restraining influence of an organized community, tend to follow their immediate impulses and behave in monstrous ways. Ethnologists have shown that when the uncivilized races come into contact with the products of our civilization they appropriate the vices and the ornaments, the whisky and beads, and leave the more substantial values. The same tendency appears among immigrants, especially the children. (1921: 288.)

Park, in somewhat more sophisticated theoretical terms,

reflected precisely the same point of view. He wrote, with Burgess:

the ultimate effect upon the individual as he becomes accommodated to secondary society was to find a substitute for his primary responses in the artificial environment of the city. The detachment of the person from intimate, direct and spontaneous contacts with social reality is in large measure responsible for the intricate maze of problems of urban life. (1923: 287.)

Very much the same sort of observation was made about the behaviour of African migrants to towns. It was argued that the isolation of the migrants from the immediate village community, in particular from their kinsmen, meant that they were no longer subject to the sanctions and controls of these kinsmen and lapsed into criminal and immoral behaviour. In a sense the lack of primary relationships of this sort was interposed as a variable linking urbanization on the one hand with 'detribalization' on the other.

The distinction between 'primary' relations on the one hand and 'secondary' on the other, and the relative balance between them in rural and urban social environments, was later to become a crucial element in the formulation of urbanism by Louis Wirth. Wirth's seminal essay on 'Urbanism as a Way of Life' was published in 1938 and in a way may be taken as a synthesis of the major propositions which had been developed by the Chicago sociologists over the previous quarter of a century (Wirth 1964*a*).

In this essay Wirth defined the city as a 'relatively large dense, and permanent settlement of socially heterogeneous individuals'. Correlated with the social composition of cities there were, he argued, certain sociological concomitants. These were the weakening of kinship bonds, family life, and neighbourliness and the emergence of impersonality, superficiality, anonymity, and transitoriness in personal relationships. In line with the formulation of the origins of social disorganization postulated by Thomas, therefore, social disorganization was a natural consequence of urbanization. In these circumstances personal relationships became what he called segmental and selective and were secondary rather than primary.

The crucial distinction between city life and rural life for Wirth and indeed for the other Chicago sociologists of his time was precisely in the quality of personal relationships in which they were involved. The distinction they made was based upon Cooley's earlier distinction between primary and secondary contacts. As applied to social behaviour in cities Wirth interpreted with implications of the statement that the city was characterized by secondary rather than primary contacts in this way:

Characteristically, urbanites meet one another in highly segmental roles. They are, to be sure, dependent upon more people for the satisfactions of their life-needs than are rural people and thus are associated with a greater number of organized groups, but they are less dependent upon particular persons, and their dependence upon others is confined to highly fractionalized aspects of the other's round of activity. . . . The contacts of the city may indeed be face to face, but they are nevertheless impersonal, superficial, transitory, and segmental. The reserve, the indifference, and the blasé outlook which urbanites manifest in their relationships may thus be regarded as devices for immunizing themselves against the personal claims and expectations of others. (1964*a*: 71.)

This is an extension of the point which Park and Burgess made in their discussion between primary and secondary contacts:

In primary association individuals are in contact with each other at practically all points of their lives. In the village 'everyone knows everything about everyone else'. Canons of conduct are absolute, social control is omnipotent, the status of the family and the individual fixed. In secondary association individuals are in contact with each other at one or two points in their lives. In the city, the individual becomes anonymous; at best he is generally known in only one or two aspects of life. (1923: 285.)

Now it is quite clear that Park, Wirth, and the other urban sociologists at Chicago were not oblivious to the fact that individuals, even in cities, were involved in primary as well as secondary contacts. Several of the studies made under the direction and stimulus of Park and his colleagues, such as for example *The Jack Roller*, concentrated particularly upon the personal relationships of individuals in town. Wirth himself in his analysis of the ghetto has written:

While the Jew's contacts with the outside world were categorical and abstract, within his own community he was at home. Here he could relax from etiquette and formalism. His contacts with his fellow Jews were warm, intimate and free. Especially was this true of his family life, within the inner circle of which he received that appreciation and sympathetic understanding which the larger world could not offer. (1964c: 88.)

Throughout the essay on 'Urbanism as a Way of Life' the implication of what Wirth is saying is that primary relationships undoubtedly exist but that they constitute a proportionately less important part of an urbanite's total set of social relationships than they do of a person who lives in a rural society.[4]

Equally it is clear that the Chicago sociologists were not unaware that there was considerable organization as well as personal disorganization among the migrants to the city. They had collected a good deal of information about the operation of voluntary associations that operated among migrants and were aware of studies, such as that by Cusumano among the Sicilians in New York, which emphasized the intense personal relationships that existed among the migrants, all of whom lived in close proximity to one another in a particular part of New York. But the two views of social relationships among migrants to cities seemed to be held concurrently without, it appears, an explicit realization of the contradiction between them.

How then did this apparent inconsistency persist among a group of scholars whose analytical ability and acuity of observation were surely unsurpassed at this time? My own interpretation is that they were trapped in psychologistic and ethnologistic assumptions which prevented them from realizing that the phenomenological context of interaction for a migrant, or for that matter for any city dweller, could vary from one situation to another while going about daily affairs in the city. It was not that the city-dweller was overwhelmed, as it were, by impersonal, superficial, transitory, and segmental relationships in day to day contacts. It was rather than superficial contacts obtained with some persons and intimate relations with others, impersonal with some, personal with others. This seems to me to be contained in Wirth's statements about the way in which the number of contacts that a person must make in a densely settled

---

[4] Good summaries, bibliographies, and criticisms of this essay are provided by Morris (1968), Gans (1962), and Fischer (1972).

large population agglomeration produces what he called 'segmentalization' of human relationships:

This is not to say that the urban inhabitants have fewer acquaintances than rural inhabitants, for the reverse may be true: it means rather that in relation to the number of people whom they see and with whom they rub elbows in the course of daily life, they know a smaller proportion, and of these they have less intensive knowledge. (1964a: 71.)

Wirth seemed here not to be saying that no primary relationships existed but rather that in the nature of things the town-dweller was less involved in them than a village-dweller.

From the perspective of situational analysis urban people may be thought of as moving through a series of different social situations during the course of their daily activities. The type of behaviour they engage in these different situations becomes intelligible in terms of the way both the actors and the analyst construe them. The townsperson moves from a family situation in which norms of behaviour are defined by the status of that person in the household. On the way to a place of work or on a shopping trip the norms of behaviour in public prevail. At the workplace the townsperson takes on a new status and the behaviour appropriate to that status so defined. As the actor moves through recreational situations, situations of religious observance, and so on, similar shared understandings of appropriate behaviour prevail. Some of these relationships will be primary while others will be secondary, and rules for appropriate behaviour in them will exist as part of the stock of social perceptions with which urban people operate.

Social Networks and Social Situations

Adopting a situational approach enables us to shift our attention away from the general quality of the type of relationships in which townspeople are involved to the pattern of the actual social links in which they are involved. The notion through which this may be achieved is that of the social network, the formal analytical principles of which have only recently become available. The initial impetus for studies of this kind came from Barnes's dissatisfaction with attempting to interpret everyday behaviour in terms of large-scale structural notions. This had led him to introduce the notion of 'social network' to reconcile day to day behaviour in a Norwegian island parish with the class system (1954). Subsequently Bott introduced the concept of the 'immediate social environment' in order to explain behaviour which until then she had been trying to explain in terms of structural variables such as social class or neighbourhood composition. She realized that in fact the families whose conjugal role segregation she was trying to explain lived in what she called an *immediate* social environment which she described as 'their actual external relationships with friends, neighbours, relatives, clubs, shops and so forth' (1971: 56). Similar difficulties with institutional interpretations of behaviour then current in British social anthropology led me and a number of my colleagues to develop the notion of social networks in order to facilitate our understanding of day to day behaviour in towns (Mitchell 1969c).[5]

The basic departure point of the network perspective in the study of urban social behaviour is that people in the classical Wirthian anonymous, fleeting, and multitudinous contexts of urban existence relate initially to a very much smaller set of significant others who constitute for them, in Bott's words, 'an immediate social environment'. These relationships are personal in the sense that the actor is conscious of the people who constitute that social environment. They may be kinsfolk, neighbours, friends, co-workers, fellow worshippers in religious meetings, co-participants in recreational activities, or co-participants in any other of the wide range of activities in which townspeople take part. These relationships may vary, of course, from very specific and superficial relationships, as, say, with a co-worker, to the intense and intimate relationship, say with a kinsperson. In all they constitute the immediate social ambience within which the personal and emotional lives of townspeople are conducted.

These relationships do not constitute the totality of a towns-person's social relationships. There will be some persons with whom the interaction is purely impersonal and solely in terms of a formal role, as, for example, with sales personnel or bureau-

---

[5] Its use has been taken up and extended by a number of scholars, in particular M. Estellie Smith (1976), Lomnitz (1977), Fischer (1977), Wellman (1977).

cratic officials in banks or government offices. These 'structural' relations also constitute an element in the day to day
activities of townspeople but play a less important personal and
emotional role than those in the personal network.

A large number of the contacts a townsperson may have
with others in the city will be even more superficial—merely
with people in the streets, concourses, and other public places
where external characteristics such as gender, class, colour, or
ethnicity index these people socially. These are categorical relationships implying the least personal involvement of all.[6] By
formulating problems of social behaviour in terms of the
characteristics of social networks we are able to appreciate a little
more clearly where some of the difficulties in the formulations of
Park and Wirth and their colleagues lay. Let us return to the
distinction Park and Burgess drew between the characteristics of
hypothetical village life on the one hand and hypothetical city
life on the other. The characteristics of village life were that individuals were in contact with one another at practically 'all points
of their lives'; everyone knew everything about everyone else,
and canons of conduct were absolute, social control omnipotent,
and the status of the family and individuals fixed.

When it comes to analysing social networks there are in fact
several distinct aspects of the ideal-type sets of social relationships in town postulated by Park and Burgess. On the one hand
there is what has come to be called the element of multiplexity in
social relationships. By this we mean that two individuals may
relate to each other in a number of different social contexts. Two
men may be, for example, employer and employee of each
other, members of the same church congregation, members of
the same political party, play golf together at weekends, and so
on. This is presumably what Park and Burgess mean when they
write that 'individuals are in contact with each other at
practically all points of their lives'.

The other component, however, refers to the process
whereby, as Park and Burgess put it, 'canons of conduct are
absolute, social control is omnipotent'. While descriptively this
may be true, the reason is buried in the contention that in the

---

[6] These types of relationship are more fully discussed in Mitchell 1969c: 9–10; 1973:
20, and Hannerz 1980: 149–50.

village 'everyone knows everything about everyone else'. This is achieved through the feature in societies of this sort whereby most individuals are usually linked to most other individuals either directly or at least by very few intermediaries. This characteristic of social networks has been referred to as 'mesh' (Barnes 1969: 61–3), and refers to the extent to which links radiating out from some given starting person through other persons eventually return to that same person. In formal terms this refers to reachability in networks (Mitchell 1969c: 12–16). In close-knit networks the mesh of the network will be small, in loose-knit ones it will be large. The sociological implication of this feature of networks is that information about the behaviour of a specified individual is likely to circulate quickly through the set of people involved and so colour their behaviour towards the person concerned.

Several writers have pointed out that multiplexity is one of the characteristics of relationships in small-scale societies, and at the same time we know that relationships tend to be relatively 'close-knit', that is on average there are relatively few steps in the path that leads out from any person and leads back to that person through other people (Barnes 1954; Gluckman 1962; Frankenberg 1966). But the coexistence of multiplexity and close-knit relationships in small-scale societies does not necessarily imply that there is a direct relationship between them. Both may be the common circumstance of some other necessary feature of small-scale society. Given that the society is small-scale the average individual must be in contact with a relatively small number of other persons. Given also that there is a certain minimum range of activities that constitute the normal life of an individual in these societies, it then seems likely that relationships must necessarily be multiplex, since the individuals will have to co-operate with others in several of the different activities in which they must engage. It is presumably in this limiting sense that Wirth postulates the relationship between what he calls segmental relationships and city life. The fact is, however, that given the notions of the social network it is now possible to pose the question in a form which is amenable to empirical testing.

Philip Mayer in his study of Red and School migrants was one of the first to undertake this task. The intriguing finding that emerged from his study in terms of the formulation of the characteristics of city life put forward by the Chicago sociologists was that he was able to distinguish at least three different categories of town-dweller. The first was made up of townspeople whose sets of personal relations were characteristic of townspeople everywhere. The other two categories were composed of migrants distinguished particularly in terms of their differing cultural backgrounds. One category was composed of those members of the Xhosa people who for generations had resisted becoming converted to Christianity and by extension following European ways of life. The other category was made up of those Xhosa who had at some time in the past become Christians, been to school, and adopted European ways of dress and diet and many European customs. When people of these categories moved to town as migrants they reacted, in general, in different ways to city life. The 'traditionalist' type of migrant, or 'Red' migrant,[7] tended to form close-knit cliques in the town, in which they spent all their leisure time. These cliques exercised a tight social control over their members, ensuring that the traditionalist values to which they subscribed were faithfully adhered to. The relationships linking the members of these cliques to one another were typically multiplex. One of the consequences to the migrant of membership of a clique of this nature was that he was accorded a clear-cut structure of norms and activities while in town and hence to some extent shielded from personal disorganization. The situation seems similar to that of the Jewish ghetto-dweller described by Wirth:

Even when he was far removed from his kin he lived his real inner life in his dreads and hopes with them. He could converse with his own kin in that familiar tongue which the rest of the world could not understand. He was bound by common troubles, by numerous ceremonies and sentiments to his small group that lived its own life oblivious of the world beyond the confines of the ghetto. (1964c: 88.)

Among the other type of Xhosa migrants (called the 'School' migrants because of their involvement in formal western education) the pattern of social relationships was different. Mayer describes them thus:

[7] So called because they traditionally smeared themselves with red clay during tribal initiation ceremonies.

Where people recognize a high proportion of optional or alternative (non-compulsory) institutions, the conditions which automatically make for close-knit networks and multiplex relations are lacking. This applies to the School migrants. Although the School rural community appears to offer little more institutional diversity than the Red rural community, its limits are set more by poverty of resources than by disapproval in principle. For a migrant from an 'undiversified' school community, movement into the more varied society of the East London locations straight away means a demand for choice between the various available alternatives there, which his culture recognizes as all equally proper (e.g. which church, or none; which recreation, or none). In making such choices A diverges from B in one respect, from C in another. Only if two School individuals happen to build up the same synthesis of preferred habits will they find themselves remaining compatible for all purposes of their private lives. More likely each man needs, for his different purposes different individual friends or sets of friends, whose roles in relation to himself become specific and distinct, perhaps even antipathetic (as in the case of church friends). Thus in the case of School migrants the allotment of roles or functions to the various associates is much less combinative, the close-knit type of network much less practicable. (1961: 289.)

Mayer pursued this argument by relating it to the varied styles of life that School migrants exhibited. He wrote:

when one departs from the close-knit pattern of network (as most School migrants do) the possibility of experiencing alternately a number of inconsistent culture influences or pressures is admitted. There is, it is true, no reason in principle why a network of the loose-knit type might not happen to consist of culturally similar individuals, all exercising compatible moral and cultural pressures. . . . But a loose-knit network offers no such *guarantee*. A migrant with a loose-knit network in town may start to apply, when with his clubmates, standards of conduct or etiquette which differ from the standards taught by his church associates, or his girl-friend; more probably still, any or all of these may differ from standards expected at home in the country. We have noticed the significant case of the School migrant who cannot bear his drinking-friends to recognize him if he happens to meet them when he is in the company of his church friends. This is the loose-knit principle carried to extreme: not merely an absence of relations between the component members (with the different standards) but a deliberate policy of preventing such relations. It can be done in town; it could not be done in the face-to-face rural community. (1961: 289. Original italics.)

We are here presented with an account of how the relationships which different types of migrants in an industrial city established in their leisure time were appropriate to the fractionalized or disoriented types of social relationships to which Wirth drew attention. Outside specific leisure time activities the relationships of both Red and School migrants to employers, representatives of law and authority, the administration, shopkeepers, and so on in this racially divided society would be much the same as they might be in the rural areas. Posing questions in this way, however, brings us back to the necessity of specifying the situations in which the activities are located. The immediate social environment of any townsperson is made up of a set of significant others with whom that person may interact as the occasion demands. Which relationships are mobilized at any particular juncture depends on the social situation in which the townsperson happens to be located. Many of the relationships which an actor may consider to constitute his or her set of direct contacts with others would be activated only in specific situations. Otherwise the relationships would remain real but latent.

The approach to the understanding of urban social behaviour through social networks clearly has its foundations in data at a fairly low level of abstraction. I mean by this that the starting-point of the analysis must be the data that the observer is able to assemble about *de facto* social relationships of some arbitrarily chosen townsperson. The actor will relate to a set of other people, many of them in the same town, in terms of a variety of different social contexts. The actor will construe this immediate social environment in terms of sets of expectations and norms that help to define relationships towards these others. There is, for example, a social definition of what minimal rights and duties neighbours owe one another. To be a neighbour implies not only close residential proximity but also social obligations attached to being a neighbour. Kinsfolk are similarly marked off from friends and acquaintances by the special obligations kinsfolk owe one another. The blood link may be a necessary condition for the existence of a kinship link but it is not sufficient: a kinsperson is also one who abides by the behavioural obligations of a kinsperson. The same may be said about co-workers, co-religionists, friends, or any of the other categories of person who constitute the immediate social environment of our arbitrarily chosen townsperson.

Formal network analysis is concerned in general with tracing the links originating from or impinging upon our chosen reference actor. For example, the mesh may be traced, that is the extent to which links originating with our chosen actor can be traced back to that actor, through a finite number of steps, the cycle length. The sociological interest would lie in assessing the impact of this circuit of influence or information on the behaviour of the actor. The extent to which persons to whom our actor is linked are themselves involved in social relationships with one another may also be assessed, by establishing the clustering in the network and assessing what this means for the behaviour of the actor. At a slightly more abstract level, regularities of the set of people linked to an actor by the extent to which they share social characteristics are 'structurally equivalent'.

At this level of enquiry, issues which are germane to classical urbanism appear to rest in particular on three network characteristics.[8] The first of these is mesh, and this feature was the basis of Bott's hypothesis which linked conjugal role segregation with close-knit networks and joint conjugal roles with sparse networks.[9] For example, she found that the couples who shared domestic tasks typically related to outsiders who had little contact with one another (1971). Consequently there was little opportunity for domestic tasks to be divided into those done by the wife and her contacts and those done by the husband and his contacts. Similarly, Philip Mayer's formulation of the differences between Red and School migrants in his study turned upon the effects of mesh in defining appropriate behaviour patterns. It is commonly accepted that urban meshes are larger

[8] The characteristics of social networks are discussed more fully in Mitchell 1969c: 20–4.

[9] The essential network characteristics involved are not always clearly stated. Some investigators have measured 'close-knit' networks by density, but I have shown (Mitchell 1969c: 15–18) that the flow of influence in two networks with precisely the same density may be entirely different. The operative question is really the ease with which social pressures, for example, exerted through the network will in fact impinge upon the target person. A necessary condition for this to take place is a traceable path between the starting-point and the target person, but sufficient conditions are established only when it is demonstrated that the pressures will in fact be communicated by the actors in the chain.

than rural meshes (see Barnes 1954, Frankenberg 1966), but so far there has been very little empirical evidence against which this assumption may be tested. Part of the reason for this is that there appear to be considerable difficulties in arriving at an appropriate measure of the average mesh (Mitchell 1969c: 12).

The second characteristic is multiplexity—the extent to which relationships arising in different circumstances coincide in particular dyadic links. As yet we lack detailed and systematic data on the empirical evidence of multiplexity in urban contexts (but see Cubitt's neglected 1973 paper). One of the intriguing possibilities is the establishment of particularly significant or empirically frequent combinations of different components in dyadic links. What special significance accrues, for example, to a link that combines being a neighbour with a kinsperson? The standard proposition is that links in small-scale society will tend to be multiplex whereas links in urban contexts are likely to be single-stranded, but there is very little hard evidence either to support or refute this point of view.

The last network characteristic which is potentially significant in urban social relationships is that of intensity. I have defined intensity as 'the degree to which individuals are prepared to honour obligations, or feel free to exercise the rights implied in their link to some other person' (1969c: 27). The more intense the relationship, the more demanding the obligations will be, the more certainly they will be met. Intensity should be distinguished from intimacy, which reflects the extent of trust and emotional involvement in a relationship. It is possible that intimate relationships will also be intense in my meaning of the word, but there is no necessary connection.

Using network concepts the proposition developed by Park and Wirth about the secondary nature of urban social relationships could be rephrased in empirically testable form. The postulate would be that typically urban relationships are single-stranded lists of low intensity (and intimacy) in networks of large mesh. In fact a number of urban sociologists such as Whyte (1943) and Gans (1962) have demonstrated that in many urban contexts social relationships are not all of this kind. A recent enquiry has shown that even the quintessential isolate of Chicago, the denizen of skid row, nearly always has an immediate social environment to which he can relate (Cohen and Sokolovsky 1981).

Social Networks and Social Settings

There is, however, a problem, as yet unresolved, about the epistemological status of the notion of the immediate social environment. It is that, as formulated so far, there appears to be a sharp disjunction between the personal network of urban dwellers and the very much more abstract formulation of city life cast in structural terms. The resolution of this problem lies, I think, in the process of abstraction and theoretical construction that proceeds as an analyst moves from interpersonal inter-actions at one level to formulations of regularities in terms of structural concept on the other. The starting-point is that while for ease of analysis the microsociologist starts with some arbi-trary actor and traces social relationships out from that person, in general each of the persons included in the initial network is in fact the central node of yet another network. It does not need much imagination to see that by systematically tracing out all links starting with some arbitrarily chosen person, before long the entire range of social activities in the city could be covered. The city is, in the evocative phrase of Craven and Wellman (1973), a 'network of networks'.

The process of moving from the 'network of networks' to formulations of a general sociological kind about urban life requires the application of two related analytical procedures. The first is the deliberate circumscription of the multiplex and variegated strands linking actors in social relationships.[10] An analyst interested in industrial sociology, for example, will select from the links of actors only those governed by the context of work relationships. The network circumscribed in this way by a single defined context is what Barnes (1969: 57) calls a 'partial network'. It is a second-order abstraction from the original field material. It is at this stage that the second analytical process becomes relevant. The links in a partial network are by

[10] I use variegated to mean a sequence or path of links of different kinds, as for example those used by the candidate for political office, described by A. Mayer (1966), who contracted potential voters through chains of very different content. Multiplex relations apply, of course, to the same link.

themselves merely descriptive: to become sociologically meaningful the more specific content of the links must be related to one another within a framework that postulates some logical nexus among them. The co-worker partial network, for example, must be subsumed into the categories of industrial sociology—management–trade union relations, line-of-authority relationships, etc.

It is through this process of abstraction and analytical synthesis that the link between the setting or large-scale sociological phenomena such as the operation of institutions and the microsociological data in network analysis may be established.[11] (See Mitchell 1973: 29 ff.)

When rephrased in terms of social networks the problems of city life as formulated by the early Chicago sociologists become amenable to direct empirical testing through the combination of both theoretical thinking and procedures of rigorous network analysis. At the same time more general formulations of social processes may be stated by developing the appropriate theoretical incorporation of the material contained in network data into logically connected abstract constructions. The way in which this analytical simplification may be achieved is through separating the abstract and general contexts of social action, that is the setting, from the more concrete and specific contexts, that is the situations.

Settings, Situations, and Analysis

In summary, the strategy which I advocate for the analysis of interpersonal behaviour in towns begins with the premiss that in the study of urban life it is feasible to isolate only a small part for intensive analysis. Given this premiss the analyst must of necessity 'seal off' some part of the social action and examine in detail the set of events so circumscribed if a cogent analysis of urban behaviour is to be achieved. Moreover, as urban social life is always part of some wider social order the process of circumscription must be pitched at several different levels of abstraction.

[11] This is presented in terms of starting from the analyst's appreciation of the actor's assessment of the norms implicit in social relationships. It would presumably be feasible to rephrase these procedures in terms of the properties of network links which emerge from exchange contents of networks.

In this book something of the process and discipline of this research strategy has been described. In the first instance, the African towns with which we have been mainly concerned were all set within colonial social orders of different kinds, so that the characteristics of these orders constituted a general context within which urban social relationships were enacted. The logic of comparative analysis in this procedure consists of showing how in different settings regular sociological processes operate to produce similar or different effects. Within this wider social context it will usually prove expedient to specify more particular settings in which social actions are located. Epstein, for example, in his analysis of the structure of trade unions defined the characteristics of mining towns as against municipal towns in the overall colonial context. An understanding of the structural features of colonial society was necessary to interpret the specific effects of these structural features on the different forms that trade union activities took in each of them.

For the analyst interested in interpreting patterns of interpersonal relationships in towns yet a further stage of specification is necessary. The actors' own interpretations of their behaviour must be included in the analysis. This is achieved by accepting the actors' cognitive definition of the situation as a datum. The analysis then consists of showing the logical connection between these definitions of situations and the wider set of actions in which the actors are involved. A technique for making the patterns manifest in the observational material at the interactional level, I have suggested, is that of network analysis. The starting-point here is the links which the town-dwellers have with one another in different domains of social action. The sets of these links and their interconnections, together with indices of the intensity or strength of the links, may be represented as matrices. As such they are amenable to processing by formal operations based on graph theory or some other mathematical procedure. The extraction of the patterns in the data by these formal operations is, however, merely the first step in analytical interpretation. The latter is achieved when the patterns extracted from the data are logically linked to a set of theoretical propositions in terms of which the analyst has been conducting the enquiry. This in turn involves referring the new insights derived from the formal analysis of the detailed data back to the social situation and then to its setting.

It should be clear from this description of my chosen strategy of enquiry that an analysis of this sort cannot supplant structural analyses of urban life. On the contrary, situational analyses draw upon structural analyses and their insights for specification of the settings. However, situational analyses take into account details and intricacies of interpersonal behaviour with which a structural analysis is not concerned. The two approaches are in fact needed to complement each other.

APPENDIX

Items Used in Questionnaire, and Distribution of Respondents on Items

	SA	A	U	D	SD	Don't know
1. The relatives of a man who has worked all his life in town should not expect him to go back to the rural areas when he is too old to work.	111	155	53	374	682	17
2. Boys who have grown up in rural areas do not know how to behave properly.	62	67	40	270	946	7
3. Because there are no social amenities like cinemas, sports, beer halls, and clubs in rural areas it is better to stay in town where they can be found.	155	290	115	425	381	26
4. Town is a place for working in: as soon as a man has earned the money he wants he should go back to his rural home.	261	291	127	402	300	11
5. Girls should always grow up in rural areas because town customs are bad for them.	356	252	83	377	314	10
6. People from rural areas are more honest than those who have grown up in urban areas.	449	433	131	212	160	7
7. Life in the rural areas cannot interest young people.	242	413	122	355	256	4
8. Life in the rural areas is good because there are always relatives there who can look after you if you are sick or have lost your job.	450	525	102	210	104	1
9. Customs in rural areas are good because young people do not bath together with old people.	364	428	148	259	175	18
10. It is better for old people to live in rural areas than in town.	539	471	123	161	89	9
11. Fear of witchcraft in rural areas stops those who have finished	180	299	133	345	432	3

Items Used in Questionnaire, and Distribution of Respondents on Items — Continued

	SA	A	U	D	SD	Don't know
working from going back to those rural areas.						
12. It is better to live in town because the hospitals and clinics there are better than in rural areas.	367	476	115	260	164	10
13. A man should return to his rural home before he gets too old.	367	504	188	219	107	7
14. Customs in rural areas are not good because even the uneducated people expect to be respected there.	35	54	84	339	872	8
15. Having a child before marriage is not considered to be a bad thing by girls and their parents in towns.	134	154	85	310	698	11
16. A townsman should always help his relatives who live in the rural areas by sending them money and clothes.	811	372	77	82	40	10
17. Most people who work in town would rather buy cattle with their money than a house and land of their own in town.	268	354	224	308	230	8
18. It is all right for a townsman to marry a women of his own clan (*mutupo*).	84	185	152	303	662	6
19. Towns are bad because there women learn to wear short and tight dresses.	239	282	122	405	334	10
20. Parents in towns should send their children to spend school holidays in rural areas so that they may grow up to respect the older people.	745	417	57	112	57	4
21. A man should be expected to look after his wife and children only and not his other relatives.	49	81	58	383	811	10
22. People would rather spend all their lives in town if they had enough money to live on after they have stopped working.	243	430	202	330	173	14

Items Used in Questionnaire, and Distribution of Respondents on Items — Continued

	SA	A	U	D	SD	Don't know
23. Friendship in the towns is based only on money.	440	399	104	274	168	7
24. Tribal life in rural areas is good because there are village headmen there to settle quarrels and troubles according to the customs of the people in the area.	335	503	131	219	193	11
25. A man should not be expected to help many relatives in these modern times.	163	374	102	371	378	4
26. Children who have grown up in rural areas are more polite than the children who have grown up in towns.	562	484	99	143	89	15
27. One of the worst things that happened to people when they moved from their villages into big cities was a loss of respect and politeness for one another.	449	488	135	215	100	5
28. Town life is bad because you starve there when you are out of work.	556	555	98	116	62	5
29. Living in urban areas is bad because it stops good customs, such as worshipping the spirits of dead relatives.	220	255	242	365	302	8
30. Rural customs are better than town customs because only old women attend a woman in childbirth whereas in town nurses who are young women do so.	129	177	224	438	414	10
31. A townsman should marry a town woman if he wants to have a happy married life.	192	256	152	404	381	7
32. The peaceful quiet of the rural areas is better for people than the interesting excitement of the towns.	242	370	247	358	169	6

SA = Strongly Agree; A = Agree; U = Undecided; D = Disagree;
SD = Strongly Disagree

BIBLIOGRAPHY

ABRAMS, P. (1978) 'Towns and Economic Growth: Some Theories and Problems' in Abrams and Wrigley (eds.) *Towns and Society: Essays in Economic History and Historical Sociology*, Cambridge, Cambridge University Press.

ALLPORT, G. (1954) *The Nature of Prejudice*, New York, Anchor Books.

ARABIE, P., BOORMAN, S., and LEVITT, P. (1978) 'Constructing Block Models: How and Why', *Journal of Mathematical Psychology*, vol. 17, 21–63.

ARRIGHI, G. (1967) *The Political Economy of Rhodesia*, The Hague, Mouton.

BALANDIER, G. (1956) 'Urbanism in West and Central Africa: The Scope and Aims of Research' in Forde (ed.) *Social Implications of Industrialization and Urbanization in Africa South of the Sahara*, Tensions and Technology Series, Paris, UNESCO.

BALDWIN, ROBERT E. (1966) *Economic Development and Export Growth: A Study of Northern Rhodesia, 1920–1960*, London, Cambridge University Press.

BANTON, M. (1957) *West African City: A Study of Tribal Life in Freetown*, London, Oxford University Press for International African Institute.

—— (1960) 'Social Distance: A New Appreciation', *The Sociological Review*, vol. 8.

—— (1965) 'Social Alignment and Identity in a West African City' in Kuper (ed.) *Urbanization and Migration in West Africa*, Berkeley, University of California Press, 131–47.

—— (1983) *Racial and Ethnic Competition*, Cambridge, Cambridge University Press.

BARBER, WILLIAM J. (1961) *The Economy of British Central Africa: A Case Study of Economic Development in a Dualistic Society*, London, Oxford University Press.

—— (1967) 'Urbanisation and Economic Growth: The Case of Two White Settler Territories' in Miner (ed.) *The City in Modern Africa*, London, Pall Mall Press, 91–125.

BARNES, J. A. (1954) 'Class and Committes in a Norwegian Island Parish', *Human Relations*, vol. 7.

—— (1969) 'Networks and Political Process' in Mitchell (ed.) *Social Networks in Urban Situations: Analyses of Personal Relationships in Central African Towns*, Manchester, Manchester University Press for Institute for African Studies.

BARTH, F. (ed.) (1969) *Ethnic Groups and Boundaries*, London, Allen and Unwin.

BASCOM, W. (1955) 'Urbanization among the Yoruba', *American Journal of Sociology*, vol. 60.

—— (1959) 'Urbanism as a Traditional African Pattern', *The Sociological Review*, vol. 7 (NS).

—— (1962) 'Some Aspects of Yoruba Urbanism', *American Anthropology*, vol. 64.

—— (1963) 'The Urban African and his World', *Cahiers D' Etudes Africaines*.

BENOIT-SMULLYAN, E. (1944) 'Status, Status Types and Status Inter-relations', *American Sociology Review*, vol. 9.

BERGERS, ELENA L. (1974) *Labour, Race and Colonial Rule: The Copperbelt from 1924 to Independence*, Oxford, Clarendon Press.

BETTISON, DAVID G. (1959) *Numerical Data on African Dwellers of Lusaka, Northern Rhodesia*, Rhodes–Livingstone Communication no. 16, Lusaka, Rhodes–Livingstone Institute.

—— (1960) 'The Poverty Datum Line in Central Africa', *Rhodes–Livingstone Journal*, vol. 27.

BLAU, P. M. (1957) 'Occupational Bias and Mobility', *American Sociological Review*, vol. 22.

BOGARDUS, EMORY S. (1933) 'A Social Distance Scale', *Sociology and Social Research*, vol. 18.

BOSWELL, DAVID M. (1969) 'Personal Crises and the Mobilization of the Social Network' in Mitchell (ed.) *Social Network in Urban Situations*, Manchester, Manchester University Press for Institute of Social Research, Zambia.

—— (1975) 'Kinship, Friendship and the Concept of a Social Network' in Kileff and Pendleton (eds.) *Urban Man in Southern Africa*, Gwelo, Mambo Press.

BOTT, E. (1971) *Family and Social Network* 2nd edition, London, Tavistock Publications.

BOZZOLI, BELINDA (1981) *The Political Nature of a Ideology in South Africa 1890–1933*, London, Routledge.

BRAUN, RUDOLF (1970) *Sozio-kulturelle Probleme der Eingliederung italienischer Arbeitskräfte in der Schweiz*, Erlenback-Zurich and Stuttgart, Eugen Rentsch Verlag.

BREESE, GERALD (ed.) (1969) *The City in Newly Developing Countries: Readings on Urbanism and Urbanization*, Englewood Cliffs, NJ, Prentice–Hall.

BREIGER, R., BOORMAN, S. and ARABIE, P. (1975) 'An Algorithm for Clustering Relational Data with Applications to Social Network Analysis and Comparison with Multi-dimensional Scaling', *Journal of Mathematical Psychology*, vol. 12.

BRIGGS, ASA (1963) *Victorian Cities*, London, Odhams Press.

BROWN, MORGAN C. (1955) 'Occupations as Evaluated by an Urban Negro Sample', *American Sociological Review*, vol. 20.

BURAWOY, MICHAEL (1972) *The Colour of Class on the Copper Mines: From*

African Advancement to Zambianization, Zambian Papers no. 7, Manchester, Manchester University Press for Institute for African Studies.

BURGESS, E. W. and BOGUE, D. J. (eds.) (1964) *Contributions to Urban Sociology*, Chicago, University of Chicago Press.

CAPLOW, THEODORE M. (1954) *The Sociology of Work*, Minneapolis, University of Minnesota Press.

CASTELLS, MANUEL (1976a) 'Is there an urban sociology?' in Pickvance (ed.) *Urban Sociology: Critical Essays*, London, Tavistock Publications.

—— (1976b) 'Theory and Ideology in Urban Sociology' in Pickvance (ed.) *Urban Sociology: Critical Essays*, London, Tavistock Publications, 60–84.

—— (1977) *The Urban Question: A Marxist Approach*, London, Edward Arnold.

—— (1983) *The City and Grassroots: A Cross-Cultural Theory of Urban Social Movements*, London, Edward Arnold.

CLOGG, CLIFFORD C. (1977) *Unrestricted and Restricted Maximum Likelihood Latent Structure Analysis: A Manual for Users*, Pennsylvania, Population Issues Research Office, Pennsylvania State University.

COALE, ANSLEY J. and DEMENY, PAUL (1966) *Regional Model Life Tables and Stable Populations*, Princeton, Princeton University Press.

COHEN, ABNER (1969) *Custom and Politics in Urban Africa*, London, Routledge and Kegan Paul.

—— (1974) 'Introduction: The Lesson of Ethnicity' in Cohen, Abner (ed.) *Urban Ethnicity*, London, Tavistock Publications.

COHEN, CARL I. and SOKOLOVSKY, JAY (1981) 'A Reassessment of the Sociability of Long-term Skid Row Residents: A Social Network Approach', *Social Networks* vol. 3, 93–105.

COHEN, ROBIN (1972) 'Class in Africa: Analytical Problems and Perspectives' in Miliband and Savile (eds.) *The Socialist Register 1972*, London, The Merlin Press.

COHEN, RONALD (1978) 'Ethnicity: Problem and Focus in Anthropology' in Siegel, Beals, and Tyler (eds.) *Annual Review of Anthropology*, Palo Alto, Annual Review Inc.

COHEN, RONALD, and MIDDLETON, JOHN (eds.) (1970) *From Tribe to Nation in Africa: Studies in Incorporation Processes*, Scranton, Chandler.

COLSON, E. (1948) 'Modern Political Organization of the Plateau Tonga', *African Studies*, vol. 7.

CONGALTON, A. A. (1953) 'Social Grading of Occupations in New Zealand', *British Journal of Sociology*, vol. 4.

COULTER, G. W. (1933) 'The Sociological Problem' in Davis (ed.) *Modern Industry and the African*, London, Macmillan.

COXON, ANTHONY P. M. and JONES, CHARLES L. (1978) *The Images of Occupational Prestige*, London, Macmillan.

COXON, ANTHONY P. M. and JONES, CHARLES L. (1979) *Class and Hierarchy: The Social Meaning of Occupations*, London, Macmillan.

CRAVEN, PAUL and WELLMAN, BARRY (1973) 'The Network City', *Sociological Enquiry*, vol. 43.

CUBITT, TESSA (1973) 'Network Density among Urban Families' in Boissevain and Mitchell (eds.) *Network Analysis: Studies in Human Interaction*, The Hague, Mouton.

DAVIES, P. M. and COXON, A. P. M. (1983) *MDS(X) User Manual: The MD(X) Series of Multidimensional Scaling Programs*, Inter-University Research Council Series Report no. 55, Edinburgh, University of London Program Library Unit.

DAVIES, R. (1979) *Capital, The State and the White Wage-Earners in South Africa: A Historical Materialist Analysis*, London, Harvester Press.

DAVIS, A. F. (1952) 'Prestige of Occupations', *British Journal of Sociology*, vol. 3.

DAVIS, KINGSLEY (1969) *World Urbanization: 1950–1970, Vol. I Basic Data for Cities, Countries and Regions*, Population Monograph Series no. 4, Berkeley, Institute of International Studies, University of California.

—— and GOLDEN, HILDA HERTZ (1957) 'Urbanization and the Development of Pre-Industrial Areas' in Hatt and Reiss (eds.) *Cities & Society*, Glencoe, The Free Press.

DERRY, J. (ed.) (1968) *Cobbett's England*, London, The Folio Society.

DEVONS, E. and GLUCKMAN, M. (1964) 'Conclusion: Modes and Consequences of Limiting a Field of Study' in Gluckman (ed.) *Closed Systems and Open Minds: The Limits of Naivety in Social Anthropology*, Edinburgh, Oliver and Boyd.

D'SOUZA, S. (1962) 'Social Grading of Occupations in India', *Sociological Review*, vol. 10.

EAMES, EDWIN and GOODE, JUDITH G. (1977) *Anthropology of the City: An Introduction to Urban Anthropology*, Englewood Cliffs, Prentice-Hall.

ENGELS, FRIEDRICH (1950) *The Condition of the Working Class in England*, London, George Allen and Unwin.

EPSTEIN, A. L. (1953) *The Administration of Justice and the Urban African*, London, HMSO.

—— (1954) *Juridical Techniques and the Judicial Process*, Rhodes–Livingstone Paper no. 23, Manchester, Manchester University Press.

—— (1958) *Politics in an Urban African Community*, Manchester, Manchester University Press for Rhodes–Livingstone Institute.

—— (1961) 'The Network and Urban Social Organization', *Rhodes–Livingstone Journal*, vol. 29.

—— (1964) 'Urban Communities in Africa' in Gluckman (ed.) *Closed Systems and Open Minds: The Limits of Naivety in Social Anthropology*, Edinburgh, Oliver and Boyd.

—— (1967) 'Urbanization and Social Change in Africa', *Current Anthropology*, vol. 8, reprinted in Breese (ed.) 1969.

—— (1969) 'The Network and Urban Social Organization' in Mitchell (ed.) *Social Networks in Urban Situations: Analyses of Personal Relationships in Central African Towns*, Manchester, Manchester University Press for Institute of African Studies, 77–116.

—— (1978) *Ethos and Identity: Three Studies in Ethnicity*, London, Tavistock Publications.

—— (1981) *Urbanization and Kinship: The Domestic Domain on the Copperbelt of Zambia 1950–1956*, London, The Academic Press.

EVANS-PRITCHARD, E. E. (1937) *Magic, Witchcraft & Oracles among the Azande*, London, Oxford University Press.

FISCHER, CLAUDE S. (1972) ' "Urbanism as a way of life:" ' A Review and an agenda', *Sociological Methods and Research*, vol. 1.

—— (1976) *The Urban Experience*, New York, Harcourt Brace Jovanovich.

—— (1977) *Networks and Places: Social Relations in the Urban Setting*, London, The Free Press.

FORTES, MEYER (1938) 'Culture Contact as a Dynamic Process' in Mair (ed.) *Methods of Study of Culture Contact in Africa*, International African Institute, memo. 25.

FOX, RICHARD G. (1972) 'Rationale and Romance in Urban Anthropology', *Urban Anthropology*, vol. 1.

—— (1977) *Urban Anthropology: Cities in their Cultural Settings*, Englewood Cliffs, NJ, Prentice-Hall.

FRANKENBERG, R. (1966) *Communities in Britain: Social Life in Town and Country*, Harmondsworth, Penguin Books.

FRY, JAMES (1975) 'Rural–Urban Terms of Trade; 1960–1973: a Note', *African Social Research*, vol. 19.

GANN, L. H. (1958) *The Birth of a Plural Society: The Development of Northern Rhodesia Under the British South Africa Company 1894–1914*, Manchester, Manchester University Press for Rhodes–Livingstone Institute.

GANS, HERBERT J. (1962) 'Urbanism and Suburbanism as Ways of Life: A Re-evaluation of Definitions' in Rose (ed.) *Human Behaviour and Social Processes*, Boston, Houghton Mifflin.

GARBETT, G. KINGSLEY (1960) *Growth and Change in a Shona Ward*, Occasional Papers from the University College of Rhodesia and Nyasaland, African Studies no. 1.

—— (1970) 'The Analysis of Social Situations', *Man*, vol. 5, 214–17.

—— (1975) 'Circulatory Migration in Rhodesia: Towards a Decision Model' in Parkin (ed.) *Town and Country in Central and Eastern Africa*, London, Oxford University Press for International African Institute.

GERSTL, JOEL E. and COHEN, LOIS K. (1964) 'Dissensus, Situs and Egocentrism in Occupational Ranking', *British Journal of Sociology*, vol. 15.

GLASS, Y. (1960) *The Black Industrial Worker: A Social Psychological Study*, Johannesburg, National Institute for Personnel Research.

GLAZER, NATHAN and MOYNIHAN, DANIEL (eds.) (1975) *Ethnicity: Theory and Experience*, Cambridge, Mass., Harvard University Press.

GLUCKMAN, M. (1949) *Malinowski's Sociological Theories*, Rhodes-Livingstone Paper no. 16, Manchester, Manchester University Press.

—— (1955) *Customs and Conflict in Africa*, Oxford, Basil Blackwell.

—— (1958) *An Analysis of a Social Situation in Modern Zululand*, Rhodes–Livingstone Paper no. 14, Manchester, Manchester University Press. Previously published in *African Studies*, vol. 14, 1940.

—— (1961) 'Anthropological Problems arising from the African Industrial Revolution' in Southall (ed.) *Social Change in Modern Africa*, London, Oxford University Press for International African Institute.

—— (1962) 'Les Rites de Passage' in Gluckman (ed.) *Essays in the Ritual of Social Relations*, London, Cohen and West.

GLUCKMAN, M. MITCHELL, J. C., and BARNES, J. A. (1949) 'The Village Headman in British Central Africa', *Africa*, vol. 19.

GORDON, MILTON M. (1964) *Assimilation in American Life, The Role of Race, Religious and National Origins*, London, Oxford University Press.

GRAY, RICHARD (1960) *The Two Nations: Aspects of the Development of Race Relations in the Rhodesias and Nyasaland*, London, Oxford University Press for Institute of Race Relations.

GREELEY, ANDREW M. (1974) *Ethnicity in the United States: A Preliminary Reconnaissance*. New York, John Riley and Sons.

GREENBERG, S. (1980) *Race and State in Capitalist Development: Comparative Perspectives*, New Haven, Yale University Press.

GUSSMAN, BORIS (1952) *African Life in an Urban Area: A Study of the African Population of Bulawayo*, Bulawayo, Federation of African Welfare Societies of Southern Rhodesia, 2 vols.

GUTKIND, PETER C. W. (1974) *Urban Anthropology: Perspectives on 'Third World' Urbanization and Urbanism*, Assen, The Netherlands, Van Gorcum.

GUTTMANN, LOUIS (1968) 'A General Non-metric Technique for Finding the Smallest Coordinate Space for a Configuration of Points', *Psychometrika*, vol. 33.

HALL, J. and JONES, C. (1950) 'Social Grading of Occupations', *British Journal of Sociology*, vol. 1.

HANDLIN, OSCAR (ed.) (1959) *Immigration as a Factor in American History*, Englewood Cliffs, NJ, Prentice–Hall.

HANNERZ, ULF (1980) *Exploring the City: Inquiries toward an Urban Anthropology*, New York, Columbia University Press.

HARMAN, HARRY H. (1960) *Modern Factor Analysis*, Chicago, Chicago University Press.

HARRIES-JONES, PETER (1969) '"Home-boy" Ties and Political Organization in a Copperbelt Township' in Mitchell (ed.) *Social Networks in Urban Situations*, Manchester, Manchester University Press for Institute of Social Research.

—— (1975) *Freedom and Labour: Mobilization and Political Control on the Zambian Copperbelt*, Oxford, Basil Blackwell.

HARRIS, MARVIN (1969) *The Rise of Anthropological Theory: A History of Theories of Culture*, London, Routledge and Kegan Paul.

—— (1976) 'History and Significance of the Emic/Etic Distinction' in Siegel, Beals, and Tyler (eds.) *Annual Review of Anthropology*, Palo Alto, California, Annual Reviews Inc, 329–50.

HARVEY, DAVID (1973) *Social Justice and the City*, London, Edward Arnold.

HECHTER, MICHAEL (1975) *Internal Colonialism: The Celtic Fringe in British National Development: 1536–1966*, London, Routledge and Kegan Paul.

HELLMAN, ELLEN (1937) 'The Native in the Towns' in Schapena (ed.) *The Bantu-Speaking Tribes of South Africa: An Ethnographic Survey*, Cape Town, Maskew Miller, 405–34.

—— (1948) *Rooiyard: A Sociological Study of an Urban Slum Yard*, Rhodes–Livingstone Paper no. 13, Manchester, Manchester University Press for Rhodes–Livingstone Institute.

—— (1949) 'Urban Areas' in *Handbook of Race Relations in South Africa*, London, Oxford University Press, 229–74.

HICKS, R. E. (1966) 'Occupational Prestige and Its Factors: A Study of Zambian Railway Workers', *African Social Research*, vol. 1.

—— (1967) 'Similarities and Differences in Occupational Prestige Ratings: A Comparative Study of Two Cultural Groups in Zambia', *African Social Research*, vol. 3.

HILL, MOZELL (1953) 'Some Problems of Social Distance in Inter-group Relations' in Sherif, Muzater, and Wilson (eds.) *Group Relations at the Crossroads*, New York, Harper.

HOFSTADER, RICHARD (1955) *The Age of Reform*, New York, Alfred A. Knopf.

HOLLEMAN, J. H. and BIESHEUVEL, S. (1973) *White Mine Workers in Northern Rhodesia 1959-60*, Leiden, Afrika-Studie Centrum.

HOPE, KEITH (1968) *Methods of Multivariate Analysis*, London, University of London Press.

IBBOTSON, P. (1943) *Report on a Survey of Urban African Conditions in Southern Rhodesia 1942/3*, Bulawayo, Federation of African Welfare Societies of Southern Rhodesia.

INKELES, ALEX and ROSSI, PETER H. (1956) 'National Comparisons of Occupational Prestige', *American Journal of Sociology*, vol. 61.

INNES, DUNCAN (1983) *Monopoly Capital and Imperialism in South Africa: Anglo-American and Southern Africa*, London, Heinemann.

JOHNSON, S. C. (1967) 'Hierarchical Clustering Schemes', *Psychometrika*, vol. 32.

KAPFERER, BRUCE (1966) *The Population of a Zambian Municipal Township*, Institute For Social Research Communication no. 1, Lusaka, Institute for Social Research.

—— (1969) 'Norms and the Manipulation of Relationships in a Work Context' in Mitchell (ed.) *Social Networks in Urban Situations*, Manchester, Manchester University Press for Institute of Social Research.

—— (1972) *Strategy and Transaction in an African Factory: African Workers and Indian Management in a Zambian Town*, Manchester, Manchester University Press.

KASHOKI, MUBANGA E. (1975) 'Migration and Language Change, the Interaction of Town and Country', *African Social Research*, vol. 19.

KAY, GEORGE (1967) *A Social Geography of Zambia*, London, University of London Press.

KILEFF, CLIVE (1975) 'Black Suburbanites: An African Elite in Salisbury, Rhodesia' in Kileff and Pendleton (eds.) *Urban Man in Southern Africa*, Gwelo, Mambo Press.

KILEFF, C. and PENDLETON, WADE G. (eds.) (1975) *Urban Man in Southern Africa*, Gwelo, Mambo Press.

KING, ANTHONY D. (1976) *Colonial Urban Development Culture, Social Power and Environment*, London, Routledge and Kegan Paul.

KITCHING, G. N. (1972) 'The Concept of Class in the Study of Africa', *African Review*, vol. 2, 327–50.

KRAPF-ASKARI, EVA (1969) *Yoruba Towns and Cities: An Enquiry into the Nature of Urban Social Phenomena*, Oxford, Clarendon Press.

KRETCH, DAVID and CRUTCHFIELD, RICHARDS S. (1948) *Theory and Problems of Social Psychology*, New York, McGraw-Hill.

LEVINE, R. A. and CAMPBELL, D. T. (1972) *Ethnocentrism: Theories of Conflict, Ethnic Attitudes and Group Behaviour*, New York, Wiley and Sons.

LEWIS, OSCAR (1968) *The Study of Slum Culture: Backgrounds for La Vida*, New York, Random House.

LIGHT, JOHN M. and MULLINS, NICHOLAS C. (1979) 'A Primer on Blockmodeling Procedure' in Holland and Leinhardt (eds.) *Perspectives on Social Network Research*, New York, Academic Press, 85–118.

LINGOES, J. C. (1965) 'An IBM—7090 Program for Guttman–Lingoes Smallest Space Analysis—1', *Behavioural Science*, vol. 10.

LITTLE, K. (1957) 'The Role of Voluntary Associations in West African Urbanization', *American Anthropologist*, vol. 54.

—— (1959) The Organization of Voluntary Associations in West Africa', *Civilization*, vol. 9.

—— (1965) *West African Urbanization: A Study of Voluntary Organizations in Social Change*, Cambridge, Cambridge University Press.

—— (1966) *Some Contemporary Trends in African Urbanization*, Evanston, Northwestern University Press.

LLOYD, PETER (1953) 'Craft Organization in Yoruba Towns', *Africa*, vol. 23.

—— (1959) 'The Yoruba Town Today,' *The Sociological Review*, vol. 7.

LOMNITZ, LARISSA A. (1977) *Networks and Marginality: Life in a Mexican Shanty Town*, London, The Academic Press.

LONG, NORMAN (1968) *Social Change and the Individual: A Study of the Social and Religious Responses to Innovation in a Zambian Rural Community*, Manchester, Manchester University Press for Institute of Social Research.

LOPATA, HELENA ZNANIECKI (1964) 'The Function of Voluntary Associations in an Ethnic Community: "Polonia" in Burgess and Bogue (eds.) *Contributions to Urban Sociology*, Chicago, University of Chicago Press.

MCCULLOCH, MERRAN (1956) *A Social Survey of the African Population of Livingstone*, Rhodes–Livingstone Paper no. 26, Manchester, Manchester University Press for Rhodes–Livingstone Institute.

MACDONALD, J. S. and MACDONALD, L. D. (1964) 'Chain Migration, Ethnic Neighbourhood Formation and Social Networks', *Milbank Memorial Fund Quarterly*, vol. 42.

MCEWAN, P. J. M. (1963) 'The Urban African Population of Southern Rhodesia: A Provisional Analysis', *Civilization*, vol. 13.

MCNAMARA, J. K. (1980) 'Brothers and Workmates: Home Friend Networks in the Social Life in a Gold Mine Hostel' in Mayer (ed.) *Black Villages in an Industrial Society: Anthropological Perspectives on Labour Migration in South Africa*, Cape Town, Oxford University Press.

MAGUBANE, BERNARD (1969) 'Pluralism and Conflict Situations in Africa: a New Look', *African Social Research*, vol. 7.

—— (1971) 'A Critical look at Indices Used in the Study of Social Change in Colonial Africa', *Current Anthropology*, vol. 12.

—— (1976) 'The Evolution of the Class Structure in Africa', in Gutkind and Wallerstein (eds.) *The Political Economy of Contemporary Africa*, London, Sage Publications, 169–197.

—— (1979) *The Political Economy of Race and Class in South Africa*, New York, Monthly Review Press.

MAIMBO, FABIAN J. M. and FRY, JAMES (1971) 'An Investigation into the Change in the Terms of Trade between the Rural and Urban sectors of Zambia', *African Social Research*, vol. 12.

MALINOWSKI, B. (1945) '*Dynamics of Culture Change: An Inquiry into Race Relations in Africa*' In Kaberry (ed.), Yale, Yale University Press.

MAYER, ADRIAN (1966) 'The Significance of Quasi-groups in the Study of Complex Societies' in Banton (ed.) *The Social Anthropology of Complex Societies, ASA Monograph no. 4*, London, Tavistock Publications.

MAYER, PHILIP (1961) *Townsmen or Tribesmen: Conservatism and the Process of Urbanization in a South African City*, Cape Town, Oxford University Press.

—— (1962) 'Migrancy and the Study of Towns', *American Anthropologist*, vol. 64.

—— (1963) 'Some Forms of Religious Organization among Africans in a South African City' in *Urbanization in African Social Change*, Edinburgh, Centre of African Studies.

MITCHELL, J. C. (1949) 'The Political Organization of the Yao in Southern Nyasaland', *African Studies*, vol. 8, 141–59.

—— (1954a) 'The Distribution of African Labour by Area of Origin in the Copper Mines of Northern Rhodesia', *Rhodes–Livingstone Journal*, vol. 14.

—— (1954b) *African Urbanization Ndola and Luanshya*, Rhodes-Livingstone Communication no. 6, Lusaka, Rhodes-Livingstone Institute.

—— (1956a) *The Kalela Dance: Aspects of Social Relationships among Urban Africans in Northern Rhodesia*, Rhodes-Livingstone Paper no. 27, Manchester, Manchester University Press for Rhodes-Livingstone Institute.

—— (1956b) 'The African Middle Classes in British Central Africa' in *The Development of a Middle Class in Tropical and Sub-Tropical Countries*, Brussels, INCIDI.

—— (1957) 'Aspects of African Marriage on the Copperbelt in Northern Rhodesia', *Rhodes–Livingstone Journal*, vol. 22.

—— (1959) 'Labour Migration in Africa South of the Sahara: The Cause of Labour Migration', *Bulletin of the Inter-African Labour Institute*, vol. 6.

—— (1960a) *Tribalism and the Plural Society: An Inaugural Lecture given in the University College of Rhodesia and Nyasaland*, London, Oxford University Press.

—— (1960b) 'The African Peoples' in Brelsford (ed.) *Handbook of the Federation of Rhodesia and Nyasaland*, London, Cassell and Son.

—— (1961) 'Wage Labour and African Population Movements in Central Africa' in Barbour and Prothero (eds.) *Essays on African Population*, London, Routledge and Kegan Paul.

—— (1962) 'Some Aspects of Tribal Social Distance' in Dubb (ed.) *The Multi-Tribal Society: Proceedings of the Sixteenth Conference of the Rhodes–Livingstone Institute*, Lusaka, Rhodes–Livingstone Institute.

——(1964a) 'Occupational Prestige and the Social System: A Problem in Comparative Sociology', *International Journal of Comparative Sociology*, vol. 5.

—— (1964b) 'The Meaning of Misfortune to Urban Africans' in Fortes and Dieterlen (eds.) *African System of Thought*, London, Oxford University Press for International African Institute.

—— (1966a) 'Theoretical Orientations in African Urban Studies' in Banton (ed.) *The Anthropological Study of Complex Societies*, London, Tavistock, 137–68.

—— (1966b) 'Aspects of Occupational Prestige in a Plural Society' in Lloyd (ed.) *Elites in Tropical Africa: Studies Presented at the Sixth International African Institute Seminars at the University of Ibadan Nigeria July 1964*, London, Oxford University Press for International African Institute.

—— (1969a) 'Urbanization, Detribalization, Stabilization and Urban Commitment in Southern Africa' in Mizruchi and Meadows (eds.) *A Reader in Urbanization*, New York, Addison Wesley.

—— (1969b) 'Structural Plurality, Urbanization and Labour Circulation in

Southern Rhodesia' in Jackson (ed.) *Migration*, Cambridge, Cambridge University Press.

—— (1969c) 'The Concept of Use of Social Networks' in Mitchell (ed.) *Social Networks in Urban Situations: Analysis of Personal Relationships in Central African Towns*, Manchester, Manchester University Press for the Institute for African Studies.

—— (1969d) 'African Urban Images: A Quantitative Exploration', *Transactions of the Manchester Statistical Society*, 1968–9.

—— (1970a) 'Tribe and Social Change in South Central Africa', *Journal of Asian and African Studies*, vol. 5.

—— (1970b) 'Contextual Parameters and the Study of Towns', paper presented to the University of Wisconsin/Milwaukee Conference on Urban Anthropology.

—— (1970c) 'Race, Clan and Status in South Central Africa' in Tuden and Plotnicov (eds.) *Social Stratification in Africa*, London, Collier–Macmillan.

—— (1973) 'Networks, Norms and Institutions' in Boissevain and Mitchell (eds.) *Network Analysis: Studies in Human Interaction*, The Hague, Mouton.

—— (1974a) 'Distance, Transportation and Urban Involvement in Zambia' in Southall (ed.) *Urban Anthropology Cross-Cultural Studies of Urbanization*, London, Oxford University Press.

—— (1974b) 'Perceptions of Ethnicity and Ethnic Behaviour: An Empirical Exploration' in Cohen (ed.) *Urban Ethnicity*, ASA Monograph no. 12, London, Tavistock.

—— (1983) 'Case and Situation Analysis', *The Sociological Review*, vol. 31.

MITCHELL, J. C. and EPSTEIN, A. L. (1957) 'Power and Prestige among Urban Africans in Northern Rhodesia', *Proceedings of the Rhodesian Scientific Association*, vol. 43.

—— (1959) 'Occupational Prestige and Social Class among Urban Africans in Northern Rhodesia', *Africa*, vol. 19.

MITCHELL, J. C. and IRVINE, S. H. (1965) 'Social Position and the Grading of Occupations', *Rhodes–Livingstone Journal*, vol. 38.

MOORE, KENNETH (1975) 'The City as Context: Context as Process', *Urban Anthropology*, vol. 4.

MOORE, R. J. B. (1948) *These African Copper Mines*, London, Livingstone Press.

MORRIS, R. N. (1968) *Urban Sociology*, London, George Allen and Unwin.

MOSER, C. A. and HALL, J. R. (1954) 'The Social Grading of Occupations' in Glass (ed.) *Social Mobility in Britain*, London, Routledge and Kegan Paul.

NEWCOMB, CHARLES (1957) 'Graphic Representation of Age & Sex Distributions of Population in the City' in Hatt and Reiss (eds.) *Cities and Society: The Revised Reader in Urban Sociology*, Glencoe, The Free Press.

NIDDRIE, D. (1954) 'The Road to Work: A Survey of the Influence of Transport on Migrant Labour in Central Africa', *Rhodes–Livingstone Journal*, vol. 15.

NORTH, N. N. and HATT, P. K. (1954) 'Jobs and Occupations: a Popular Evaluation' in Bendix and Lipset (eds.) *Class Status and Power*, London, Routledge and Kegan Paul.

OHADIKE, PATRICK O. (1969) *Development of and Factors in the Employment of African Migrants in the Copper Mines of Zambia 1940-66*, Zambian Papers no. 4, Manchester, Manchester University Press for Institute for Social Research.

PADEN, JOHN N. (1970) 'Urban Pluralism, Integration and Adaptation of Communal Identity in Kano, Nigeria' in Cohen and Middleton (eds.) *From Tribe to Nation in Africa: Studies in Incorporation Processes*, Scranton, Chandler.

PARK, ROBERT EZRA (1950) *Race and Culture*, Glencoe, Illinois, The Free Press.

—— (1955) 'Society: Collective Behaviour News & Opinion, Sociology & Modern Society', Hughes *et al.* (eds.) in *Collected Papers of Robert E. Park*, vol. 3, Glencoe, The Free Press.

—— and BURGESS, E. W. (1923) *Introduction to the Science of Society*, Chicago, University of Chicago Press.

PARK, ROBERT E. and MILLER, HERBERT A. (1921) *Old World Traits Transplanted*, Chicago, University of Chicago Society for Social Research.

PARKIN, DAVID (1978) *The Cultural Definition of Political Response: Lineal Destiny among the Luo*, London, Academic Press.

PARPART, JANE (1980) *Labour Strategies in Northern Rhodesia Coppermines, 1926-1936*, African Studies Center Working Papers no. 23, Boston, Boston University African Studies Center.

—— (1982) *Class Consciousness among Zambian Coppermines, 1950-1966*, African Studies Working Papers no. 53, Boston, Boston University African Studies Center.

PENDLETON, WADE C. (1975) 'Introduction' in Kileff and Pendleton (eds.) *Urban Man in Southern Africa*, Gwelo, Mambo Press.

PERRINGS, CHARLES (1980) 'A Moment in the "Proletarianization" of the New Middle Class: Race, Value and Division of Labour in the Copperbelt, 1946-1966', *Journal of Southern African Studies*, vol. 6.

PLEWMAN REPORT (1958) *Report of the Urban African Affairs Commission*, Salisbury, Government Printer.

PLOTNICOV, LEONARD (1967) *Strangers in the City: Urban Man in Jos, Nigeria*, Pittsburg, University of Pittsburg Press.

PONS (1956) 'The Growth of Stanleyville and the Composition of its African Population' in Fforde (ed.) *Social Implication of Industrializations and Urbanization in Africa South of the Sahara*, Tensions and Technology Series, Paris, UNESCO.

POSEL, DEBORAH (1983) 'Rethinking the "Race-Class Debate" in South African Historiography', *Social Dynamics*, vol. 9, 50-65.

POWDERMAKER, HORTENSE (1962) *Coppertown: Changing Africa. The Human Situation on the Rhodesian Copperbelt*, New York, Harper and Row.

READ, MARGARET (1942) Migrant Labour in Africa and its Effects on Tribal Life', *International Labour Review*, vol. 14.

READER, DESMOND (1961) *Black Man's Portion: History Demography and Living Conditions in the Native Locations of East Province, Cape Province*, Cape Town, Oxford University Press for Institute of Social and Economic Research, Rhodes University.

REISS, A. J. Jr. (1961) *Occupations and Social Classes*, Glencoe, Free Press.

RICHARDS, AUDREY T. (1939) *Land, Labour and Diet in Northern Rhodesia: An Economic Study of the Bemba Tribe*, London, Oxford University Press for International African Institute.

—— (1940) *Bemba Marriage and Present Economic Conditions*, Rhodes–Livingstone Paper no. 4, Livingstone, Rhodes–Livingstone Institute.

—— (1963) 'Multi-Tribalism in African Studies Areas' in *Urbanization in African Social Change*, Edinburgh, Centre of African Studies.

ROBINSON, E. A. G. (1933) 'The Economic Problem' in Davis (ed.) *Modern Industry and the African*, London, Macmillan.

ROLLWAGEN, JACK (1972) 'A Comparative Framework for the Investigation of the City-as-Context: A Discussion of the Mexican Case', *Urban Anthropology*, vol. 1.

—— (1975) 'The City as Context: The Puerto Ricans of Rochester, New York', *Urban Anthropology*, vol. 4.

SCHUTZ, ALFRED (1967) 'Common Sense and Scientific Interpretation of Human Action' in Natanson (ed.) *Alfred Schutz: Collected Papers*, vol. 1, The Hague, Martinmus Nijhoff.

SCHWAB, W. B. (1949) 'Social Stratification in Gwelo' in Southall (ed.) *Social Change in Modern Africa*, London, Oxford University Press for International African Institute.

SCOTT, P. (1954a) 'Migrant Labour in Southern Rhodesia', *Geographical Review*, vol. 44, 29–48.

—— (1954b) 'The Role of Northern Rhodesia in African Labour Migration', *Geographical Review*, vol. 44, 432–4.

SIU, PAUL C. P. (1964) 'The Isolation of the Chinese Laundry-man' in Burgess and Bogue (eds.) *Contributions to Urban Sociology*, Chicago, University of Chicago.

SJOBERG, GIDEON(1960) *The Pre-Industrial City: Past and Present*, New York, The Free Press.

SMITH, ESTELLIE M. (1975) 'A Tale of Two Cities: The Reality of Historical Differences', *Urban Anthropology*, vol. 4, 61–72.

—— (1976) 'Question of Urban Analysis', *Urban Anthropology*, vol. 5.

SOUTHALL, A. W. (1961) 'Introductory Summary' in Southall (ed.) *Social Change in Modern Africa*, London, Oxford University Press for International African Institute.

SOUTHALL, A. W. and GUTKIND, P. C. W. (1957) *Townsmen in the Making: Kampala and its Suburbs*, East African Studies no. 9, 2nd imp., Kampala, East African Institue of Social Research.

STEIN, MAURICE R. (1960) *The Eclipse of Community: An Interpretation of American Studies*, Princeton, Princeton University Press.

STONEQUIST, EVERETT V. (1964) 'The Marginal Man: A Study in Personality and Culture Conflict' in Burgess and Bogue (eds.) *Contributions to Urban Sociology*, Chicago, Chicago University Press, 327–45.

STOUFFER, S. A. (1949) 'An Analysis of Conflicting Social Norms', *American Sociological Review*, vol. 14, 707–17.

STRAUSS, ANSELM (1961) *Images of the American City*, New York, The Free Press.

TAFT, RONALD (1953) 'The Social Grading of Occupations in Australia', *British Journal of Sociology*, vol. 4, 181–7.

THOMAS, R. MURRAY (1962) 'Respecting a Structural Position on Occupational Prestige' *American Journal of Sociology*, vol. 67, 561–5.

THOMAS, W. I. (1966) *W. I. Thomas On Social Organization and Social Personality*, ed. M. Janowitz, Heritage of Sociology Series, Chicago, Phoenix Books.

THOMAS, W. I. and ZNANIECKI, F. (1958) *The Polish Peasant in Europe and America*, New York, Dover.

TORGERSON, WARREN S. (1958) *Theory & Method of Scaling*, New York, Wiley and Sons.

TREIMAN, DONALD J. (1977) *Occupational Prestige in Comparative Perspective*, London, Academic Press.

VAN BINSBERGEN, WIM (1979) *Religious Studies in Zambia: Exploratory Studies*, Haarlem, Inde Knipscheer.

VAN ONSELEN, CHARLES (1980) *Chibaro: African Mine Labour in Southern Rhodesia 1900–1933*, London, Pluto Press.

VAN VELSEN, J. (1960) 'Labour Migration as a Positive Factor in the Continuity of Tonga Tribal Society', *Economic Development & Cultural Change*, vol. 8, 265–78.

—— (1964) 'Trends in African Nationalism in Southern Rhodesia', *Kroniek van Africa*, 139–57.

—— (1967) 'The Extended-case Method and Situational Analysis' in Epstein (ed.) *The Craft of Social Anthropology*, London, Tavistock, 129–49.

—— (1975) 'Urban Squatters: Problem on Solution' in Parkin (ed.) *Town and Country in Central and Eastern Africa*, London, Oxford University Press for International African Institute, 294–307.

WALLERSTEIN, IMMANUEL (1974) *The Modern World-System: Capitalist Agriculture and the Origins of the European World Economy in the Nineteenth Century*, London, Academic Press.

—— (1981) *The Modern World System II: Mercantilism, and the Consolidation of the European World Economy 1600–1750*, London, Academic Press.

WATSON, WILLIAM (1958) *Tribal Cohesion in a Money Economy*, Manchester, Manchester University Press for Rhodes–Livingstone Institute.

—— (1959) 'Labour Migration in Africa South of the Sahara: Migrant Labour and Detribalization', *Bulletin of the Inter-African Institute*, vol. 7, 8–32.

WELLMAN, BARRY (1977) *The Community Question: Intimate Ties in East York*, Research Paper no. 90, Toronto, University of Toronto Centre for Urban and Community Studies.

WHYTE, WILLIAM FOOTE (1943) *Street Corner Society*, Chicago, University of Chicago Press.

WILLIAMS, RAYMOND (1976) *The Country and the City*, St Albans, Paladin.

WILSON, GODFREY (1941-2) *An Essay on the Economics of Detribalization in Northern Rhodesia*, Rhodes-Livingstone Papers nos. 5 and 6, Livingstone, Rhodes-Livingstone Institute.

WILSON, MONICA and MAFEJE, ARCHIE (1963) *Langa: A Study of Social Groups in An African Township*, Cape Town, Oxford University Press.

WIRTH, LOUIS (1964a) 'Urbanism as a Way of Life' in Reiss (ed.) *Louis Wirth on Cities and Social Life*, Chicago, University of Chicago Press, 60–83.

—— (1964b) 'Culture Conflict and Misconduct' in Reiss (ed.) *Louis Wirth on Cities and Social Life*, Chicago, University of Chicago Press, 229–43.

—— (1964c) 'The Ghetto' in Reiss (ed.) *Louis Wirth on Cities and Social Life*, Chicago, University of Chicago Press, 84–98.

WOLPE, HAROLD (1975) 'The Theory of Internal Colonialism: the South African Case' in Oxaal, Barnett, and Booth (eds.) *Beyond the Sociology of Development Economy and Society in Latin America and Africa*, London, Routledge and Kegan Paul, 229–52.

YAUKEY, D. (1955) 'A Metric Measurement of Occupational Status', *Sociology and Social Research*, vol. 29, 317–23.

YOUNG, C. E. (1971) 'Rural-Urban Terms of Trade', *African Social Research*, vol. 12, 91–4.

ZNANIECKI, FLORIAN (1934) *The Method of Sociology*, New York, Rinehart.

INDEX